P9-AGL-236

URANOMETRIA 2000.0

Volume II – The Southern Hemisphere to +6°

URANOMETRIA 2000.0

Volume II – The Southern Hemisphere to +6°

Wil Tirion
Barry Rappaport
George Lovi

Published by:

Willmann–Bell, Inc.

P. O. Box 35025
Richmond, Virginia 23235 ☎ (804)
United States of America 320-7016

Publishers and Booksellers

Serving Astronomers Worldwide
Since 1973

Copyright ©1987, 1988 Willmann–Bell, Inc.

All rights reserved. Except for brief passages quoted in a review, no part of this book may be reproduced by any mechanical, photographic, or electronic process, nor may it be stored in any information retrieval system, transmitted, or otherwise copied for public or private use, without the written permission of the publisher. Requests for permission or further information should be addressed to Permissions Department, Willmann–Bell Inc. P.O. Box 35025, Richmond, VA 23235.

First Published October 1988
Reprinted:
June 1989
September 1992

Printed in the United States of America

Library of Congress Cataloging-in-Publication Data

Tirion, Wil
   Uranometria 2000.0.
   Includes Bibliographies.
   Contents: v. 1. The Northern Hemisphere to −6° –
v. 2. The Southern Hemisphere to +6°.
   1. Stars–Atlases. I. Rappaport, Barry, 1960 –
II. Lovi, George. III. Title
QB65.T65 1988   534.8′9   87-14769
ISBN 0-943396-14-X (v. 1)
ISBN 0-943396-15-8 (v. 2)

The front and back endpapers to this volume are full-scale reverse-printed reproductions of the equatorial zones from the hemispheric maps as published by Johann Elert Bode in his Uranographia *of 1801. Bode's atlas was published almost midway between the nearly 400 years separating Bayer's* Uranometria *of 1603 and* URANOMETRIA 2000.0 *and it is generally regarded as representing the pinnacle of oldtime pictorial star atlases. U.S. Naval Observatory, Washington, D.C.*

INTRODUCTION

With the publication of this volume URANOMETRIA 2000.0's coverage of the sky is complete. Those elements of the Introduction to Volume I that facilitate usage are included here so that they may be readily available. See Volume I for additional information about this atlas.

The Data Base

The Revised New General Catalogue of Nonstellar Objects (RNGC) by Sulentic and Tifft formed the machine readable nonstellar data base for URANOMETRIA 2000.0. This catalogue is also available as a book. To augment the RNGC, additional deep sky objects have been plotted by Wil Tirion. Many of these additional nonstellar objects accessible to the observer are listed in the excellent *Sky Catalogue 2000.0, Volume 2: Double Stars, Variable Stars and Nonstellar Objects* by Hirshfeld and Sinnott. To facilitate cross referencing between these two catalogues and this atlas we have generally adhered to the abbreviations used in the catalogues.

The BD, SBD, and CoD star catalogs provided the basic stellar data for this atlas. These works record about 1,100,000 stars, and in some areas of the sky reach magnitude 10 to 11. The BD and SBD had a working limit of magnitude 9.5, but later studies have shown that various systematic errors caused star brightnesses to be underestimated by about one-half magnitude toward the faint end. To achieve a relatively uniform limiting magnitude, all BD and SBD stars brighter than 9.3 were combined with 9.5 magnitude or brighter stars from the CoD. The result was a data base of 332,556 stars.

One major departure from earlier comprehensive atlases is our decision to show stellar magnitudes in whole-magnitude steps (magnitude bins) on the charts; for example, any star that falls between 4.50 and 5.49 is shown as 5th magnitude. This not only makes it easier to differentiate the various magnitudes on the charts by eye (and to compare them with the scale on each chart) but in practice astronomers still speak of 4th magnitude stars, 7th-magnitude stars, and so on. For exact values one should refer to standard catalogues or listings.

URANOMETRIA 2000.0's stellar data base was then augmented to include the 50 nearest stars and the 25 greatest proper motion stars no matter how faint (stars beyond 9.5 have their magnitudes noted). All the stars' positions were then precessed to equinox 2000.0. Analysis of the resulting data has shown the error in precession to epoch 2000.0 is less than the resolution of the charts. Specifically, an error of one second (of time) exists at zone 70°, while at zone 80° the error increases to approximately 30 seconds (time) for precession of 125 years (1875.0 to 2000.0). The overall working resolution of the atlas is estimated to be approximately 1′ at 85°, 30″ at 60°, and 10″ at 10°.

Since many catalogs use epoch 1950.0, we indicate on each chart how its coordinate grid could be shifted to read 1950 positions. Note the thin crosses close to each corner. Near each cross, an intersection of the coordinate grid is slightly darkened. If the grid were moved so the darker intersections fell on the crosses it would show 1950 positions.

In order to correct for stars with large proper motion the data were matched to a Luyten (NLTT) star data base to identify stars with proper motions greater than 0″.2 a year. A final positional and magnitude test was to compare URANOMETRIA 2000.0's data base to that of the *Yale Bright Star Catalogue* (YBS), 4th edition. Where differences were found the YBS data were used.

While the *Durchmusterung* star catalogs have been in use for years and are reliable, a small number of errors and omissions remain. To further reduce these, URANOMETRIA 2000.0's plots were compared to *The True Visual Magnitude Photographic Star Atlas*. When differences existed other atlases and catalogs were consulted to resolve the discrepancy; these are listed in the Reference Section.

Chart Arrangement and Labeling

Table 1 describes the general arrangement of URANOMETRIA 2000.0's charts, which were computer plotted at twice the final size of 1.85 cm = 1° per degree of declination. Stars were drawn as open circles, their relative sizes determined by their visual magnitudes rounded to the nearest whole number. The stars were plotted as open circles so as not to hide fainter companion stars. These circles were then filled by hand and where a bright star could hide a fainter neighbor, a ring of white space was left around the smaller disk. Working with the computer plots, Wil Tirion provided stellar notation based upon the following criteria: Star brightnesses are shown in whole magnitudes by tapered circles from −1 through 9.5. All first magnitude stars and other well known stars are labeled with their proper names (Castor, Polaris, etc.). The brighter stars are labeled first by Flamsteed number, then Bayer letter (if one exists). Double or multiple stars are shown with a line protruding from opposite sides of standard-sized dots. When these stars are separated by less than 1′ they are plotted with a dot size based on integrated magnitude (rounded to whole magnitudes). With separations greater than 1′ the components are plotted independently.

Variable stars are denoted with a concentric circle-and-dot symbol showing approximate maximum (outer) and minimum (inner) circle. For stars whose minimum brightness is below the atlas's 9.5 limit an open circle stands alone. Novae and supernovae whose maxima exceeded 9.5 are indicated as 9.5 magnitude variables with year of outburst preceded by an N or SN.

TABLE 1					
URANOMETRIA 2000.0 CHART ARRANGEMENT					
Declination Range	Number of Charts	Vol. No.	R.A. Range of Chart		
			Main	Overlap	Total
North Pole	2	I	12^h00^m	1^h00^m	13^h00^m
+85° to +72°	12	I	2^h00^m	20^m	2^h20^m
+73° to +60°	20	I	1^h12^m	8^m	1^h20^m
+62° to +49°	24	I	1^h00^m	4^m	1^h04^m
+51° to +38°	30	I	48^m	8^m	56^m
+40° to +27°	36	I	40^m	20^m	56^m
+29° to +16°	45	I	32^m	8^m	40^m
+18° to +05°	45	I	32^m	8^m	40^m
+06° to −06°	45	I, II	32^m	8^m	40^m
−05° to −18°	45	II	32^m	8^m	40^m
−16° to −29°	45	II	32^m	8^m	40^m
−27° to −40°	36	II	40^m	20^m	56^m
−38° to −51°	30	II	48^m	8^m	56^m
−49° to −62°	24	II	1^h00^m	4^m	1^h04^m
−60° to −73°	20	II	1^h12^m	8^m	1^h20^m
−72° to −85°	12	II	2^h00^m	20^m	2^h20^m
South Pole	2	II	12^h00^m	1^h00^m	13^h00^m
Total Charts	473				

The 50 nearest stars are shown with their labels (no matter how faint) as catalogued by Batten in the Royal Astronomical Society of Canada's *1985 Observer's Handbook*. If these stars do not have a Flamsteed number or Bayer letter, their popular name, e.g. Barnard's Star, Ross 154, or catalog number (BD+36°2147) is shown; if fainter than 9.5 magnitude, their magnitude is added: Proxima (11^m1).

The 25 greatest-proper-motion stars as catalogued in *Burnham's Celestial Handbook* have been plotted (no matter how faint). Labeling follows the procedure described for the nearest stars.

Constellation boundaries are those of E. Delporte endorsed, in 1930, by the International Astronomical Union (*Report of Commission 3*). Constellation names are placed near a border for easy identification. The Ecliptic is shown with a dashed line, labeled (once per chart) "Ecliptic," and calibrated each 1° in longitude. The Galactic Equator is shown with a dashed-dotted line, labeled (once per chart) "Galactic Equator," calibrated each 1° in galactic longitude. Also labeled are the North and South Galactic Poles and the North and South Ecliptic Poles. For added convenience, along the margins of each chart are numbers in ovals indicating the chart that covers that adjoining area.

In general, deep sky objects are labeled by NGC number (without prefix) or IC number (with prefix "I") and in the Messier catalogue, by a number preceded by an "M." Deep sky objects may also be labeled by popular names. Objects catalogued only in other works generally are identified by the catalogue or by an abbreviation of the authors' names. The abbreviations used are given in brackets at the end of each listing in the Reference Section. Distinctive symbols are used for 9 types of objects:

1. **Globular Clusters** are shown as a continuous-line open circle with an internal cross. Clusters larger than 5′ are drawn to scale.

2. **Open Clusters** are shown as a dotted open circle. Not included are scattered groups larger than 1°. Objects larger than 5′ but smaller than 1° are drawn to scale.

3. **Planetary Nebulae** are shown as open circles with four protruding lines in 4 selected sizes: Greater than 120″, 120″ to 60″, 60″ to 30″ and less than 30″.

4. **Bright Diffuse Nebulae** (selected) are drawn to scale with a solid outline if larger than 10′. Objects smaller than 10′ are drawn as solid-line square boxes in two sizes (10′ to 5′ and less than 5′).

5. **Dark Nebulae** (selected) are drawn to scale with a dotted line if larger than 10′. Objects smaller than 10′ are drawn as dotted square boxes in two sizes (10′ to 5′ and less than 5′).

6. **Galaxies** are drawn as open ovals, with objects greater than 5′ to scale. Included are members of the Local Group of galaxies not in the RNGC which are designated with their IC or UGC number, or if none, by their popular name (e.g. Sculptor System or UMi Dwarf galaxy).

7. **Radio Sources** are shown as open triangles when the source is invisible or below the chart's limit. Where the visible source is plotted, as in the case of a bright star (e.g. δ Cas) or a galaxy, the special symbol does not appear. In order of preference they are identified by 3C number, 4C number and then PKS without prefix formed by concatenating the hours and minutes of 1950 R.A. with declination truncated to tenths of a degree.

8. **X-ray Sources** are shown with an open-centered "X" when the source is invisible or below the chart's limit. Where the visible source is plotted the special symbol does not appear. Objects are generally labeled by common name (e.g., M82, NGC 1851, LMC X-2 [Large Magellanic Cloud], or γ Cas).

9. **Quasars** (Quasi-stellar objects) are identified by an open circle with a superimposed diagonal line. In order of preference they are labeled: 3C number, 4C number, and then coordinate designation as established in *Sky Catalogue 2000.0, Volume 2,* formed by concatenating the hours and minutes of 1950 R.A. with declination truncated to tenths of a degree.

Acknowledgments

The assistance of Richard Berry, William G. Tifft, Jack W. Sulentic, Stephen J. Edberg, Charles Seitz, Brenda Corbin, Sandra Kitt, Raymond de Visser, C. Bruce Stephenson, Wayne H. Warren, Jr. and Carlos Jaschek has been detailed in Volume I and applies equally to this Volume.

References

STARS

Argelander, F.W.A., Bonner Sternverzeichniss, Sec 1-3. *Astron. Beob. Sternwarte Königl.* Rhein. Friedrich-Wilhelms-Univ. Bonn, Vols. 3, 4, 5. 1859–1862. [BD]

Batten, A.H., "The Nearest Stars," *Observers Handbook 1986,* Toronto, 1986: Royal Astronomical Society of Canada.

Bečvář, A., *Atlas of the Heavens—II: Catalogue 1950.0*, 4th edition, Prague and Cambridge, MA., 1964: Czechoslovak Academy of Sciences.

Bečvář, A., *Atlas Australis 1950.0*, 2nd edition, Prague and Cambridge, MA., 1976: Czechoslovak Academy of Sciences.

Bečvář, A., *Atlas Borealis 1950.0*, 2nd edition, Prague and Cambridge, MA., 1978: Czechoslovak Academy of Sciences.

Bečvář, A., *Atlas Eclipticalis*, 2nd edition, Prague and Cambridge, MA., 1974: Czechoslovak Academy of Sciences.

Delporte, E. *Délimitation Scientifique des Constellations*, Cambridge, 1930: Cambridge University Press.

Hirshfeld, A., R.W. Sinnott, *Sky Catalogue 2000.0, Vol. 1., Stars to Magnitude 8.0*, Cambridge, MA. 1982: Sky Publishing Corp.

Hoffleit, D., *The Bright Star Catalogue,* 4th revised edition, New Haven, CT., 1982: Yale University Observatory. [YBS]

Kholopov, P.N., *General Catalogue of Variable Stars,* 4th edition, Vols 1 and 2, Moscow, 1985: Astronomical Council of the USSR Academy of Sciences.

Kukarkin, B.V., *et al., General Catalogue of Variable Stars,* 3rd edition, Moscow, 1969–70; 1st, 2nd and 3rd Supplements, Moscow, 1971, 1974, 1976: Astronomical Council of the USSR Academy of Sciences.

Kukarkin, B.V., *et al., New Catalogue of Suspected Variable Stars,* Moscow, 1982: Astronomical Council of the USSR Academy of Sciences.

Luyten, W.J., *New Less Than Two Tenths Catalogue,* Minneapolis, MN. 1979, 1980: University of Minnesota. [NLTT]

Papadopoulos, C., *True Visual Magnitude Photographic Star Atlas*, Vol. 1.—Southern Stars, Vol 2.—Equatorial Stars, Oxford, 1979: Pergamon Press Ltd.

Papadopoulos, C., C. Scovil, *True Visual Magnitude Photographic Star Atlas*, Vol. 3.—Northern Stars, Oxford, 1980: Pergamon Press Ltd.

Perrine, C.D., Cordoba Durchmusterung, Part V. *Resultados Obs. Nacional Argentino*, vol. 21, −62° to −90°. 1932. [CoD].

Pickering, E.C., *Scale of the Bonn Durchmusterung*, Harvard College Observatory Annals, **72,** 6, Cambridge, MA, 1913.

Pickering, E.C., *Scale of the Cordoba Durchmusterung*, Harvard College Observatory Annals, **72,** 7, Cambridge, MA, 1913.

Schönfeld, E., Bonner Sternverzeichniss, Sec. 4. *Astron. Beob. Sternwarte Königl.* Rhein. Friedrich-Wilhelms-Univ. Bonn, vol. 8. 1886. [SBD]

Smithsonian Institution, *Smithsonian Astrophysical Observatory Star Catalog* Washington, D.C., 1966, 1971: Smithsonian Institution. [SAO]

Scovil, C.E., *The AAVSO Variable Star Atlas*, Cambridge, MA, 1980: Sky Publishing Corporation.

Thome, J.M., Cordoba Durchmusterung, Parts I-IV. *Resultados Obs. Nacional Argentino*, vol 16, −22° to −32°; vol. 17, −32° to −42°; vol. 18, −42° to −52°; vol. 21, −52° to −62°. 1892–1914. [CoD]

GENERAL STELLAR AND NONSTELLAR OBJECTS

Burnham, Jr., R., *Burnham's Celestial Handbook,* New York, 1978: Dover Publications, Inc.

Hirshfeld, A., R.W. Sinnott, *Sky Catalogue 2000.0, Vol 2., Double Stars, Variable Stars and Nonstellar Objects*, Cambridge, MA, 1985: Sky Publishing Corp.

Neckel, Th., H. Vehrenberg, *Atlas of Galactic Nebulae*, Düsseldorf, vols. 1 and 2, 1985 and 1986: Treugesell-Verlag Dr. Vehrenberg KG.

Sulentic, J.W., and W.G. Tifft, *The Revised New General Catalogue of Nonstellar Astronomical Objects* Tucson, AZ, 1973, 1980: University of Arizona Press.

TABLE 2	
GLOBULAR AND OPEN CLUSTER DESIGNATIONS	
A–Antalova	K–King
Bar–Barkhatova	Lo–Loden
Bas–Basel	Ly–Lynga
Be–Berkley	Mrk–Markarian
Bi–Biurakan	Mel–Melotte
Bl–Blanco	Pi–Pismis
Bo–Bochum	Ro–Roslund
Cr–Collinder	Ru–Ruprecht
Cz–Czernik	Sh–Sher
Do–Dolidze	Ste–Stephenson
DoDz–Dolidze/ Dzimselejsvili	St–Stock
Fei–Feinstein	Tom–Tombaugh
Fr–Frolov	Tr–Trumpler
Haf–Haffner	Up–Upgren
H–Harvard	vdB–van den Bergh–Waterloo
Ho–Hogg	We–Westerlund
Isk–Iskudarian	

GLOBULAR AND OPEN CLUSTERS

Ruprecht, J., B. Baláz, R.E. White, *Catalogue of Star Clusters and Associations,* Supplement 1: Part A (Introduction), Part B1 (New Data for Open Clusters), Part B2 (New Data for Associations, Globular Clusters and Extragalactic Objects, Budapest, 1981: Akadémiai Kiadó. [See Table 2 for author(s) symbol]

van den Bergh, S., and G.L. Hagen, "UBV Photometry of Star Clusters in the Magellanic Clouds," *Astronomical Journal*, **73,** 569, 1968. [vdB-Ha]

BRIGHT NEBULAE

Cederblad, S., "Catalogue of Bright Diffuse Galactic Nebulae," *Meddelanden* fran Lunds Astronomiska Observatorium, Ser. 2, **12,** No. 119, 1946. [Ced]

Gum, C.S., "A Survey of Southern H II Regions," *Memoirs* of the Royal Astronomical Society, **67,** 21, 1955 [Gum]

Lynds, B.T., "Catalogue of Bright Nebulae," *Astrophysical Journal Supplement Series*, **12,** 163, 1965. [LBN]

Minkowski, R., "New Emission Nebulae," *Publications* of the Astronomical Society of the Pacific, **58,** 305, 1946. [Mi]

Rogers, A.W., C.T. Campbell, and J.B. Whiteoak, "A Catalogue of Hα-Emission Regions in the Southern Milky Way," *Monthly Notices* of the Royal Astronomical Society, **121**, 103, 1960. [RCW]

Sharpless, S. "A Catalogue of H II Regions," *Astrophysical Journal Supplement Series*, **4**, 257, 1959. [Sh2]

van den Bergh, S., "A Study of Reflection Nebulae." *Astronomical Journal*, **71**, 990, 1966. [vdB]

van den Bergh, S., and W. Herbst, "Catalogue of Southern Stars Embedded in Nebulosity," *Astronomical Journal*, **80**, 212, 1975. [vdBH]

Planetary Nebulae

Perek, L., and L. Kohoutek, *Catalogue of Galactic Planetary Nebulae,* Prague, 1967: Academia Publishing House of the Czecholosovak Academy of Sciences. [PK]

Dark Nebulae

Barnard, E.E., "Catalogue of 349 Dark Objects in the Sky," *A Photographic Atlas of Selected Regions of the Milky Way* Washington, D.C., 1927: Carnegie Institution. [B]

Bernes, C., "A Catalogue of Bright Nebulosities in Opaque Dust Clouds," *Astronomy and Astrophysics Supplement Series*, **29**, 65, 1977. [Be]

Lynds, B.T., "Catalogue of Dark Nebulae," *Astrophysical Journal Supplement Series,* **7**, 1, 1962. [LDN]

Sandqvist, Aa., "More Southern Dark Dust Clouds," *Astronomy and Astrophysics*, **57**, 467, 1977 [Sa]

Sandqvist, Aa., and K.P. Lindroos, "Interstellar Formaldehyde in Southern Dark Dust Clouds," *Astronomy and Astrophysics* **53**, 179, 1976. [SL]

Galaxies

Abell, G.O. "The Distribution of Rich Clusters of Galaxies," *Astrophysical Journal Supplement Series*, **3**, 211, 1958. [A]

Corwin, Jr. H.G., A. de Vaucouleurs, and G. de Vaucouleurs, *Southern Galaxy Catalogue*, Austin, TX, 1985: University of Texas Monographs in Astronomy No. 4.

de Vaucouleurs, G., A. de Vaucouleurs, and H.G. Corwin, Jr., *Second Reference Catalogue of Bright Galaxies*, Austin, TX, 1976: University of Texas Press. [RC2]

Nilson, P.N., *Uppsala General Catalogue of Galaxies*, Uppsala, 1973: Uppsala Astronomical Observatory. [UGC]

Nilson, P.N., *Catalogue of Selected Non-UGC Galaxies,* Uppsala, 1974: Uppsala Astronomical Observatory. [UGCA]

van den Bergh, S., "Luminosity Classifications of Dwarf Galaxies," *Astronomical Journal*, **71**, 922, 1966. [D or DDO]

Zwicky, F., *Catalogue of Galaxies and Clusters of Galaxies* Pasadena, CA, 1961–68, 6v.: California Institute of Technology. [ZWG]

Radio Sources

Bennett, A.S., "The Revised 3C Catalogue of Radio Sources," *Memoirs* of the Royal Astronomical Society, **68**, 163, 1962. [3C or 3CR]

Boulton, J.G., and A.J. Shimmins, "The Parkes 2700 MHz Survey (fifth Part): Catalogue for the Declination Zone

−35° to −45°," *Australian Journal of Physics*, Astrophysical Supplement, No. 30, 1, 1973. [PKS]

Boulton, J.G., A.J. Shimmins, J.V. Wall, and P.W. Butler, "The Parkes 2700 MHz Survey (Seventh, Eighth, Ninth and Tenth Parts)," *Australian Journal of Physics,* Astrophysical Supplement, No. 34, 1, 1975. [PKS]

Ekers, J.A., "The Parkes Catalogue of Radio Sources," *Australian Journal of Physics,* Astrophysical Suppl., No. 7, 1, 1969. [PKS]

Gower, J.F.R., P.F. Scott, and D. Wills, "A Survey of Radio Sources in the Declination Ranges −07° to 20° and 40° to 80°," *Memoirs* of the Royal Astr. Soc., **71**, 49, 1967. [4C part 2]

Pilkington, J.D.H., and P.F. Scott, "A Survey of Radio Sources Between Declinations 20° and 40°," *Memoirs* of the Royal Astronomical Society, **69**, 183, 1965. [4C, part 1]

Shimmins, A.J., "The Parkes 2700 MHz Survey: Catalogue for 03^h, 1^h, 19^h, and 23^h Zone, Declinations −33° to −75°," *Australian Journal of Physics*, Astrophysical Supplement, No. 21, 1, 1971. [PKS]

Shimmins, A.J., and J.G. Boulton, "The Parkes 2700 MHz Survey (Fourth Part): Catalogue for the South Polar Cap Zone, declination −75° to −90°," *Australian Journal of Physics,* Astrophysical Supplement, No. 26, 1, 1972. [PKS]

Shimmins, A.J., and H. Spinard, and E.O. Smith, "The Parkes 2700 MHz Survey (Sixth Part): Catalogue for the Declination Zone −30° to −35°," *Australian Journal of Physics* Astrophysical Supplement, No. 32, 1, 1974. [PKS]

Wall, J.V., A.J. Shimmins, and J.K. Merkelijn, "The Parkes 2700 MHz Survey: Catalogues for the ±4° Declination Zone and for the Selected Regions," *Australian Journal of Physics,* Astrophysical Supplement, No. 19, 1, 1971. [PKS]

X-ray Sources

Amnuel, P.R., O.H. Guseinov, and Sh. Yu. Rakhamimov, "A Catalog of X-ray Sources," *Astrophysical Journal Supplement Series*, **41**, 327, 1979.

Amnuel, P.R., O.H. Guseinov, and Sh. Yu. Rakhamimov, "Second Catalogue of X-ray Sources," *Astrophysics and Space Science,* **82**, 3, 1982.

Bradt, H.V., R.E. Doxsey, and J.G. Jernigan, "Positions and Identifications of Galactic X-ray Sources, "*Advances in Space Exploration*, **3**, 3, 1979.

Bradt, H.V., and J.E. McClintock, "The Optical Counterparts of Compact galactic X-ray Sources," *Annual Review of Astronomy and Astrophysics* **21**, 13, 1983.

Manchester, R.N., and J.H. Taylor, "Observed and Derived Parameters for 330 Pulsars," *Astronomical Journal*, **86**, 1953, 1981.

Quasi-stellar Objects

Craine, E.R., *A Handbook of Quasi-stellar and BL Lacertae Objects,* Tucson, AZ., 1977: Pachart.

Hewitt, A., and G. Burbidge, "A Revised Optical Catalogue of Quasi-stellar Objects," *Astrophysical Journal Supplement Series*, **43**, 57, 1980; **46**, 113, 1981.

Véron-Cetty, M.-P., and P. Véron, "A Catalogue of Quasars and Active Nuclei," European Southern Observatory *Report*, No. 1, 1984.

URANOMETRIA 2000.0

Volume II – The Southern Hemisphere to +6°

Arrangement of Charts

URANOMETRIA 2000.0's charts are numbered and ordered in an orthodox star-atlas manner: by declination zones working downward from the north to the south pole. Within each zone the charts are numbered by increasing right ascension, or west to east.

These charts have generous overlap areas along their margins for maximum user convenience, as well as numbers in small ovals outside each margin which indicate the particular map that abuts there. Note: because of their overall arrangement, charts on facing pages do *not* necessarily abut along their nearest margins. Refer to the Index Chart at the back of the book to see the overall plan. Also, the listing on page IV in the Introduction provides this information in tabular form.

Finally, for those who wish to read off directly the position of any plotted star or object in URANOMETRIA 2000.0, we provide in the inside back cover pocket two 8 by 10 inch clear acetate overlays with fine grid lines arranged by declination zones.

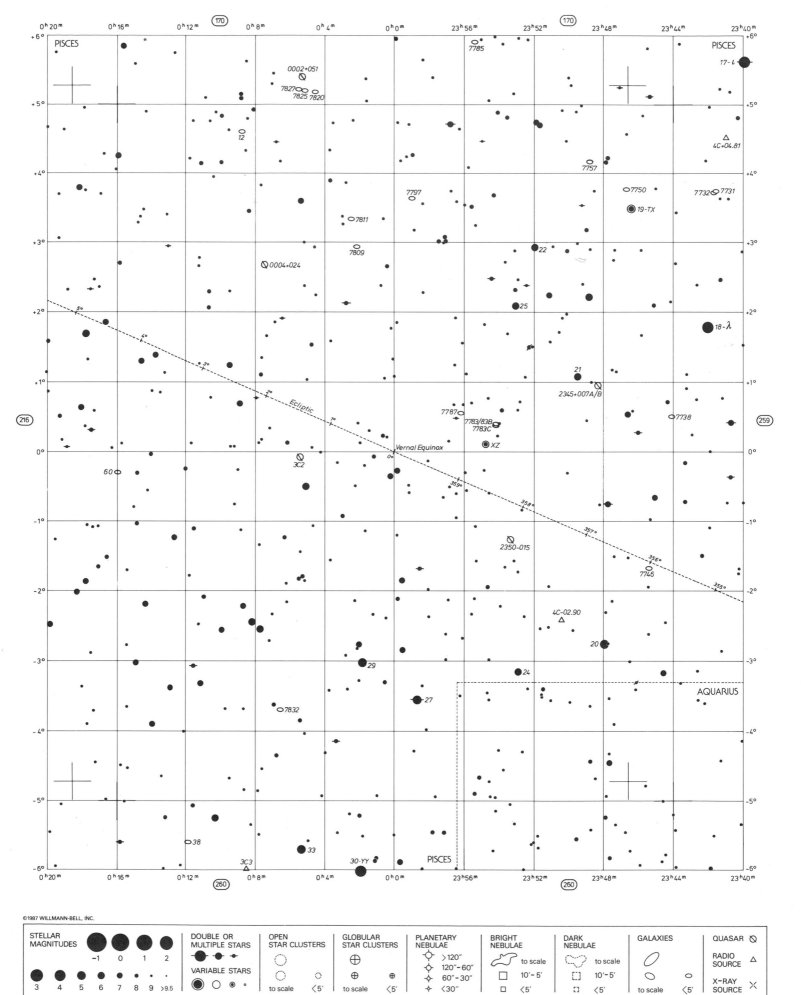

©1987 WILLMANN-BELL, INC.

Barry Rappaport & Wil Tirion

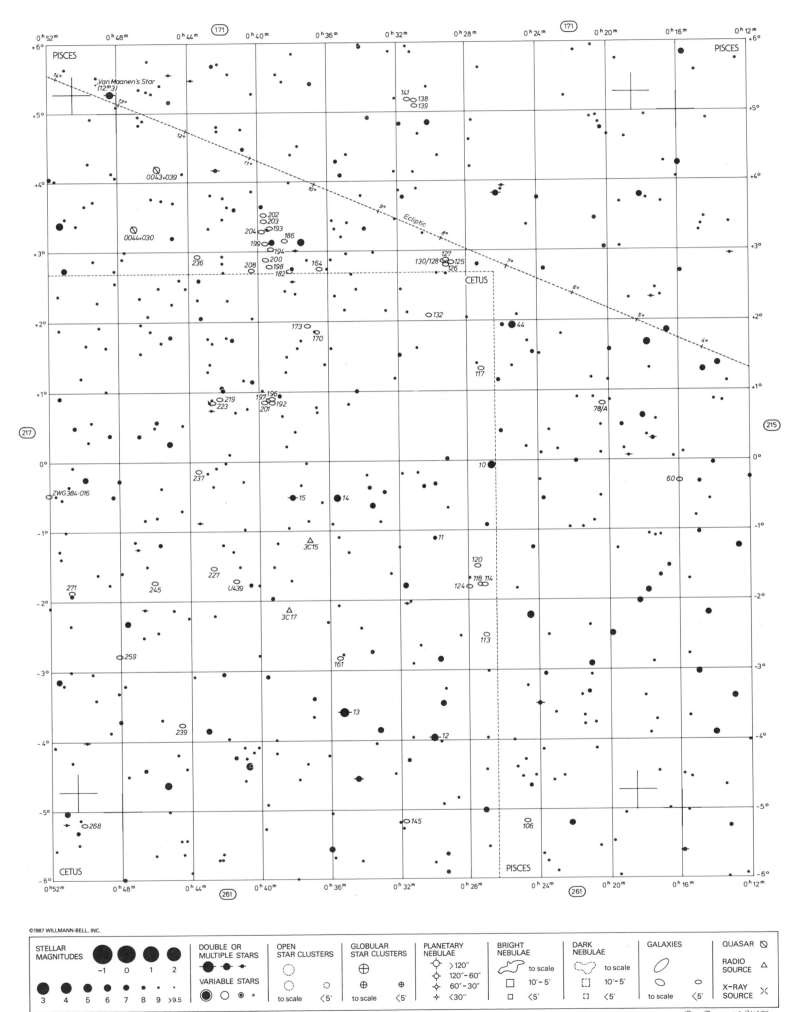

©1987 WILLMANN-BELL, INC.

Barry Rappaport & Wil Tirion

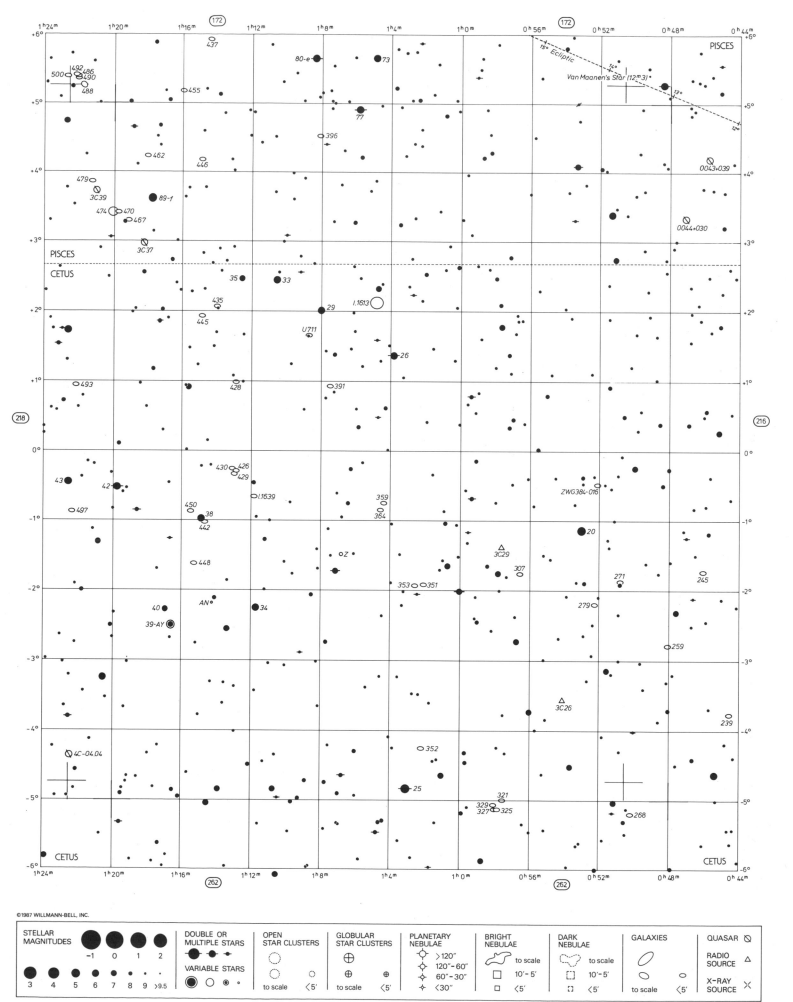

©1987 WILLMANN-BELL, INC.

Barry Rappaport & Wil Tirion

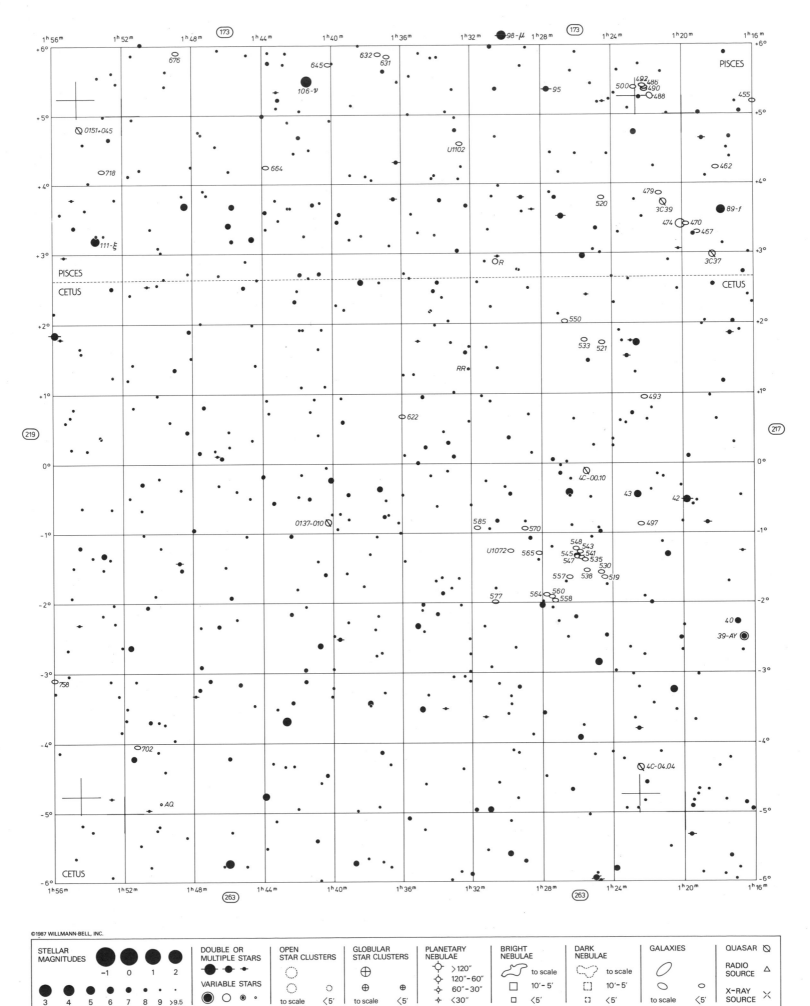

©1987 WILLMANN-BELL, INC.

Barry Rappaport & Wil Tirion

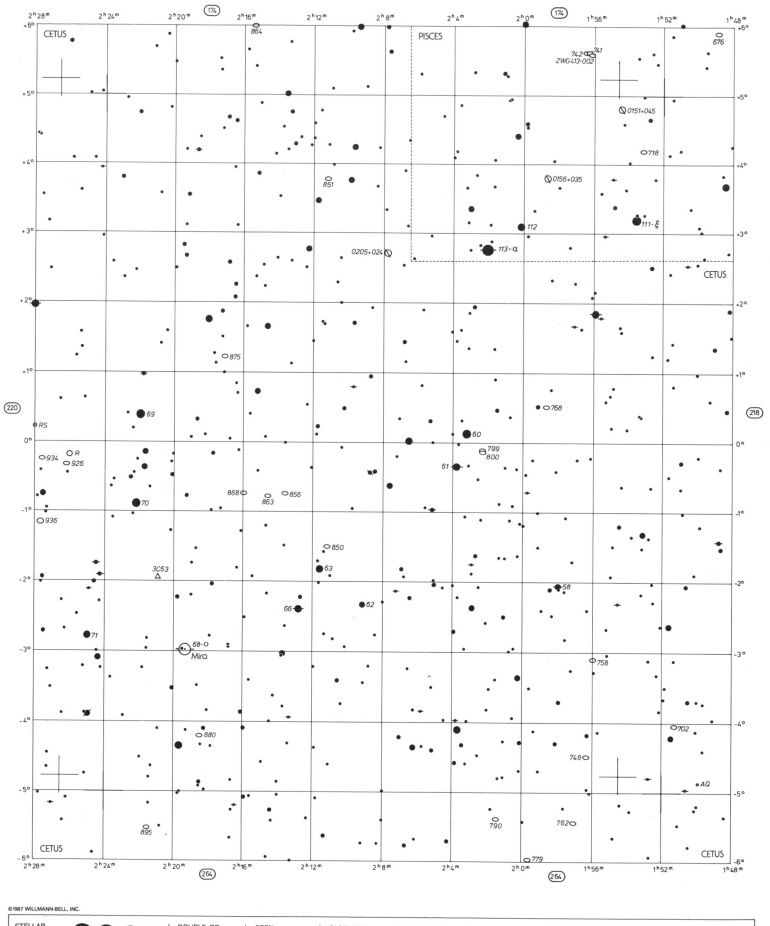

©1987 WILLMANN-BELL, INC.

STELLAR MAGNITUDES	DOUBLE OR MULTIPLE STARS	OPEN STAR CLUSTERS	GLOBULAR STAR CLUSTERS	PLANETARY NEBULAE	BRIGHT NEBULAE	DARK NEBULAE	GALAXIES	QUASAR

Barry Rappaport & Wil Tirion

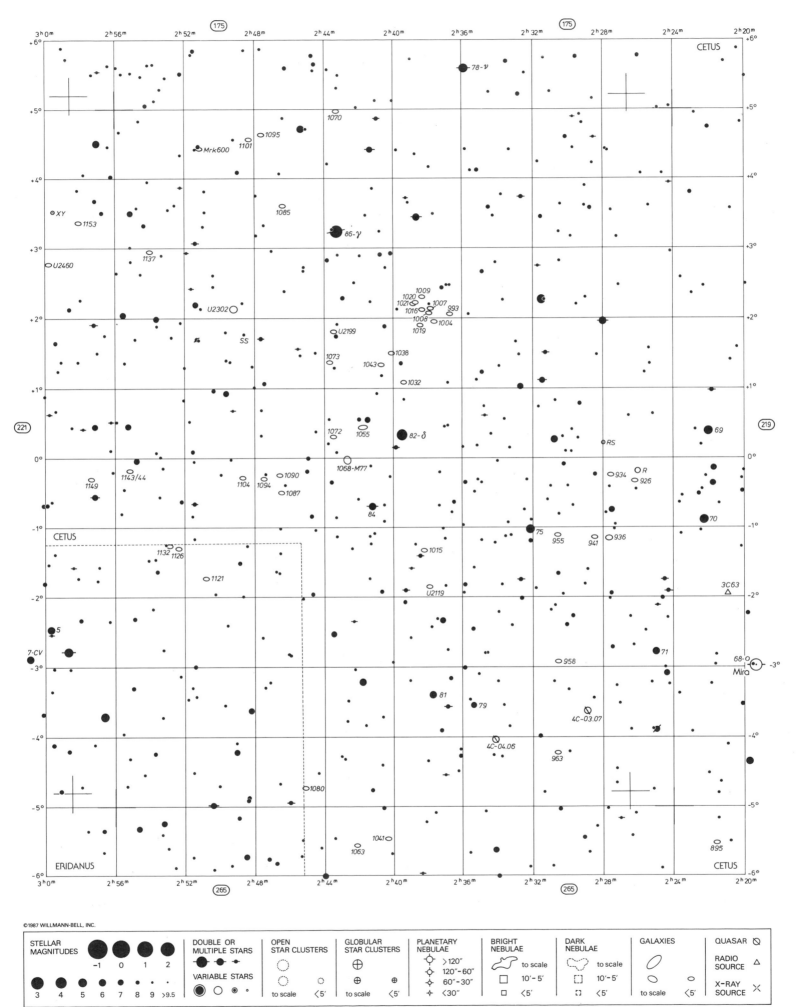

©1987 WILLMANN-BELL, INC.

Barry Rappaport & Wil Tirion

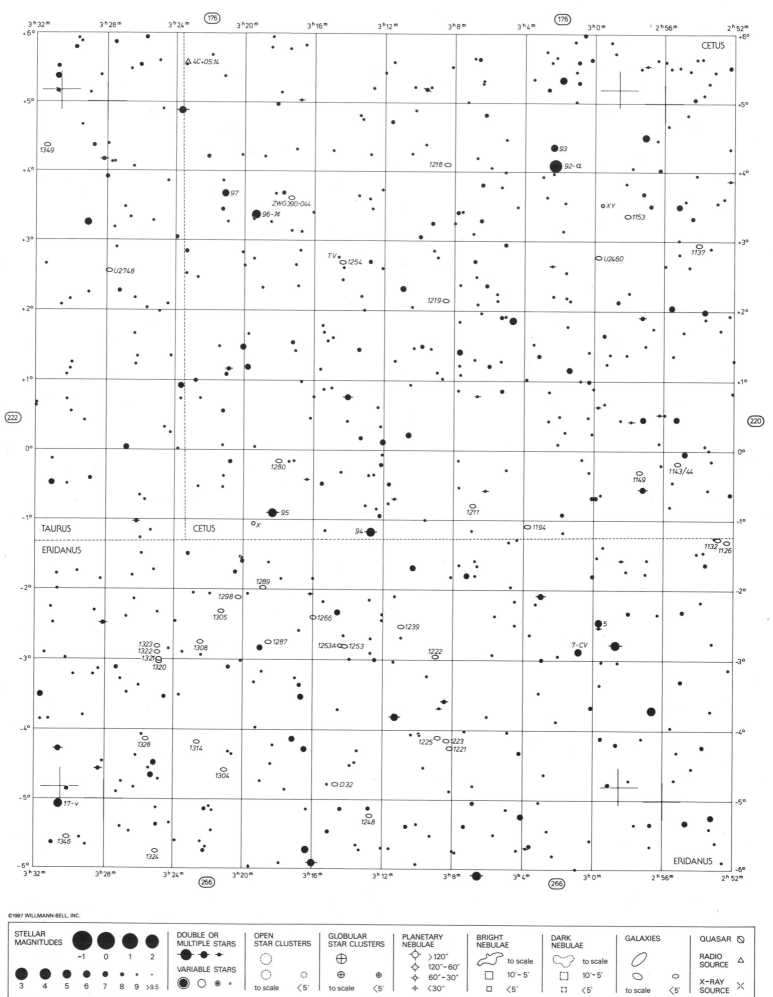

©1987 WILLMANN-BELL, INC.

Barry Rappaport & Wil Tirion

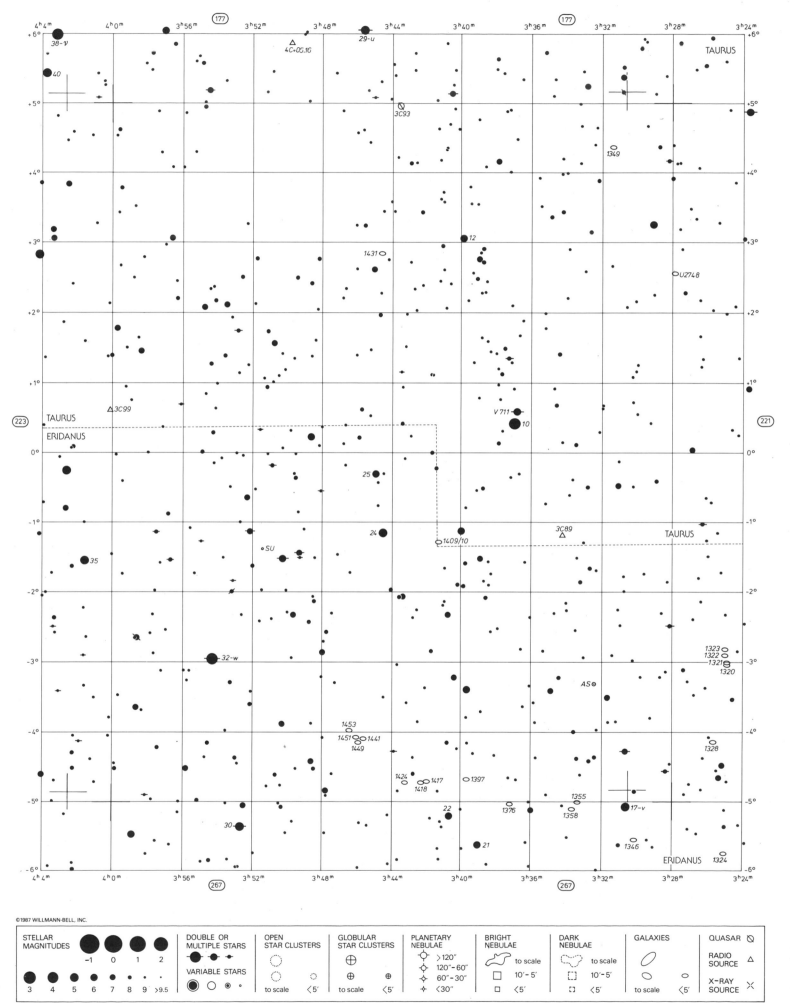

©1987 WILLMANN-BELL, INC.

Barry Rappaport & Wil Tirion

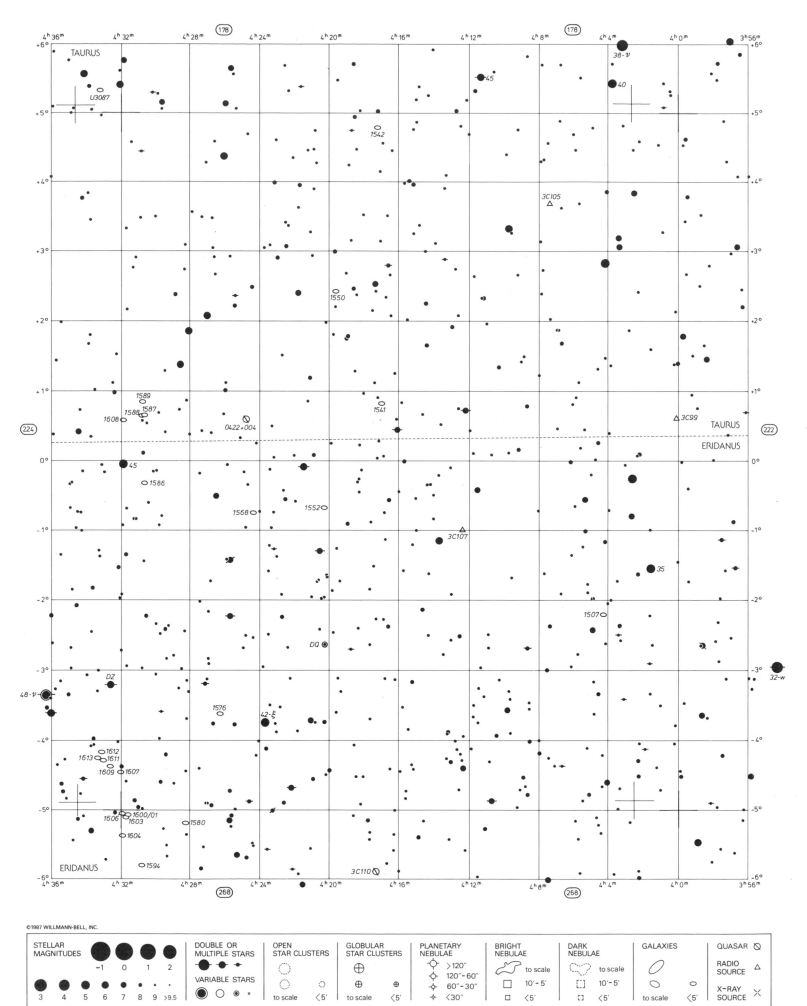

©1987 WILLMANN-BELL, INC.

Barry Rappaport & Wil Tirion

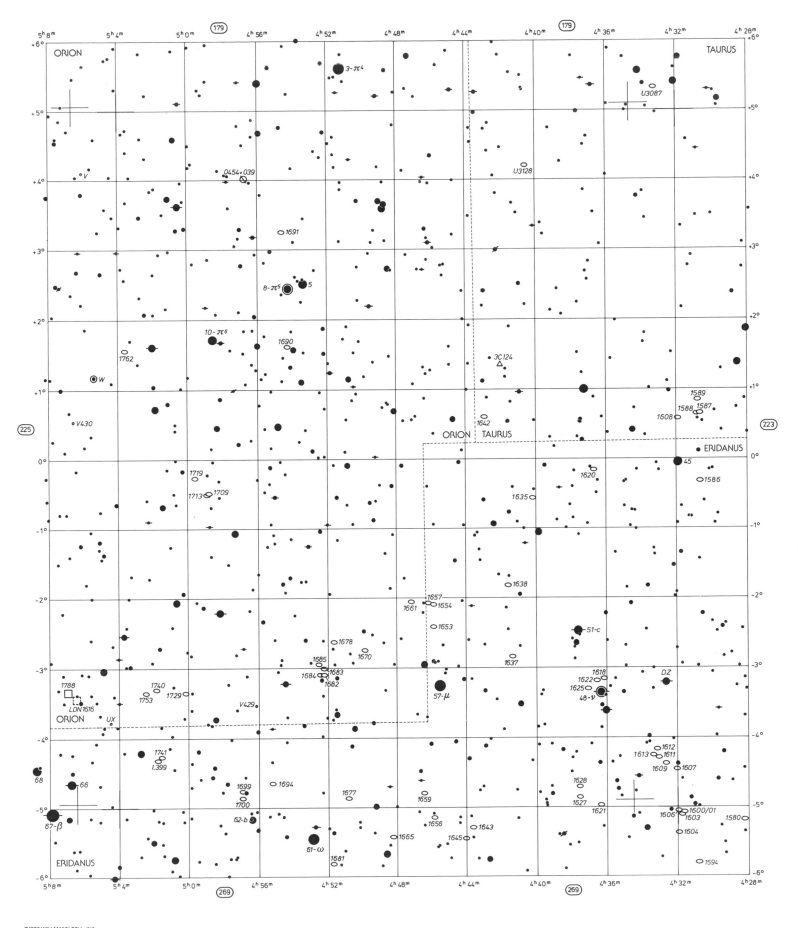

©1987 WILLMANN-BELL, INC.

Barry Rappaport & Wil Tirion

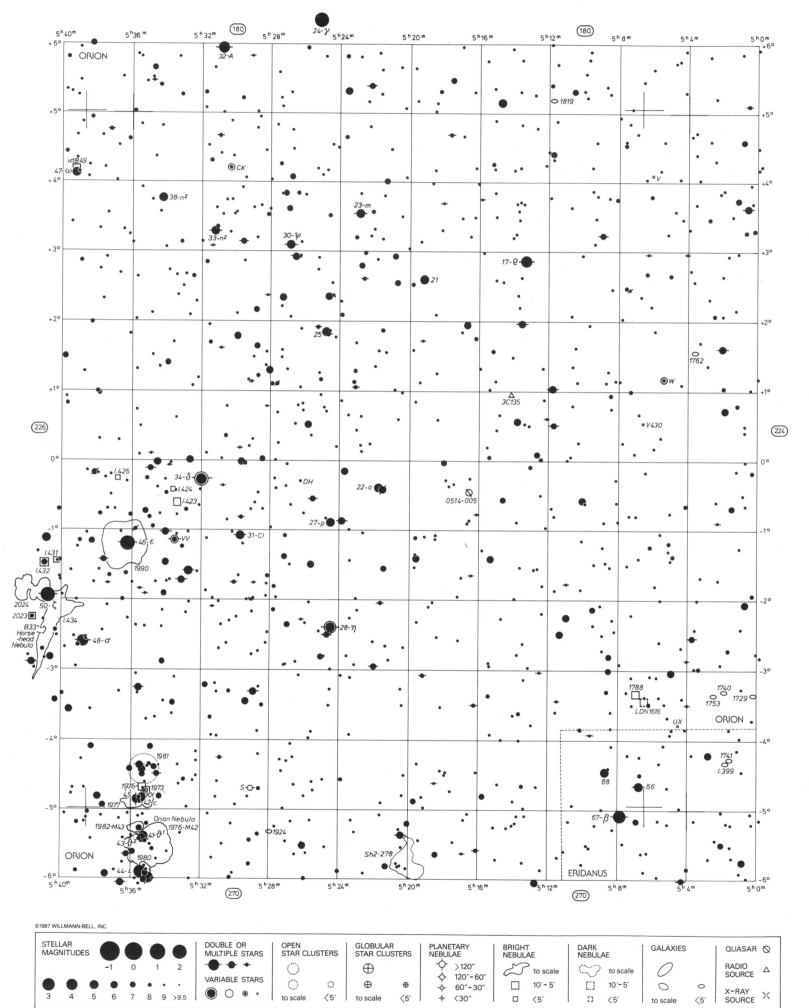

©1987 WILLMANN-BELL, INC.

Barry Rappaport & Wil Tirion

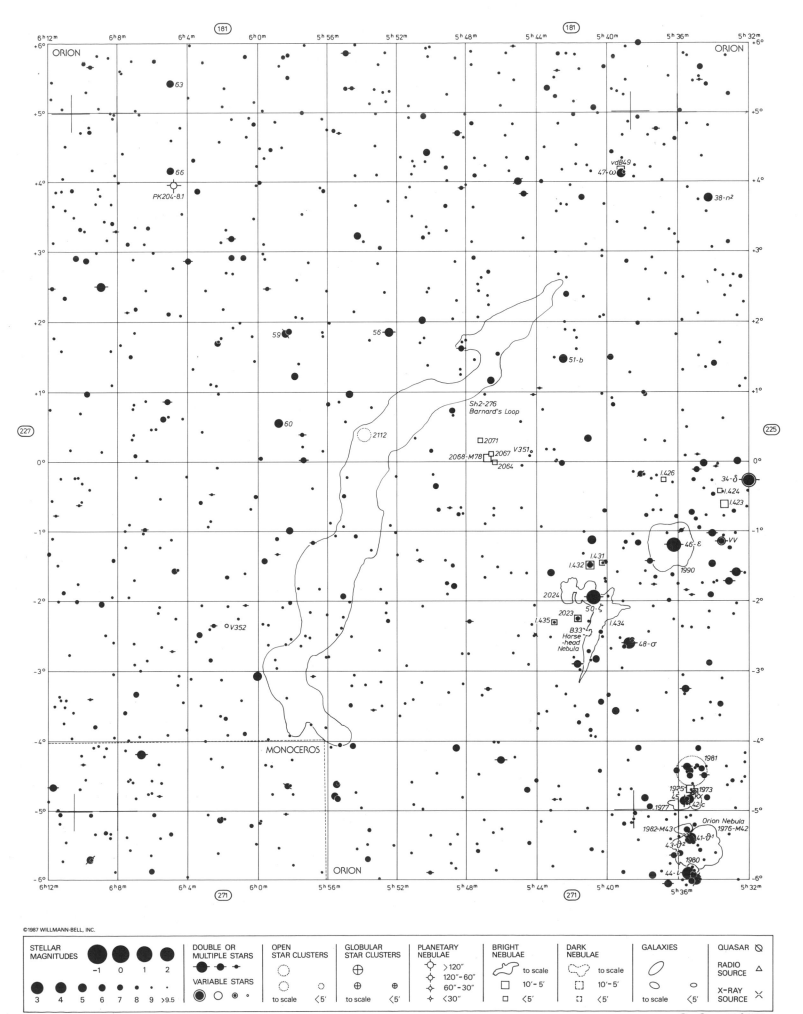

©1987 WILLMANN-BELL, INC.

Barry Rappaport & Wil Tirion

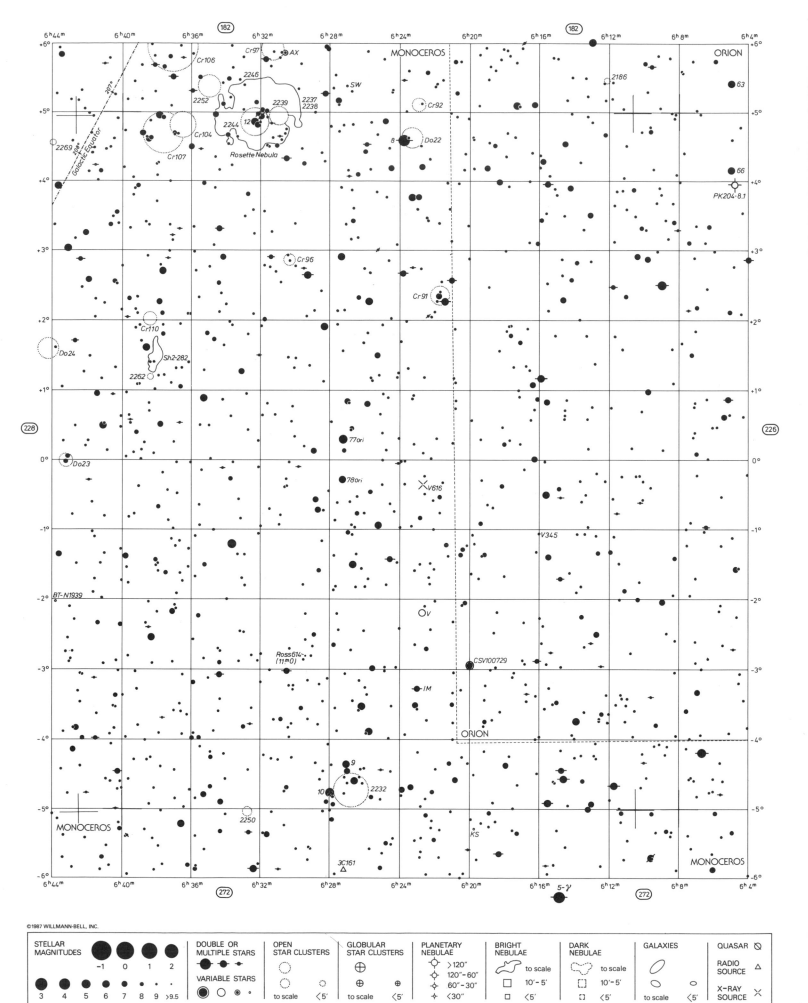

©1987 WILLMANN-BELL, INC.

Barry Rappaport & Wil Tirion

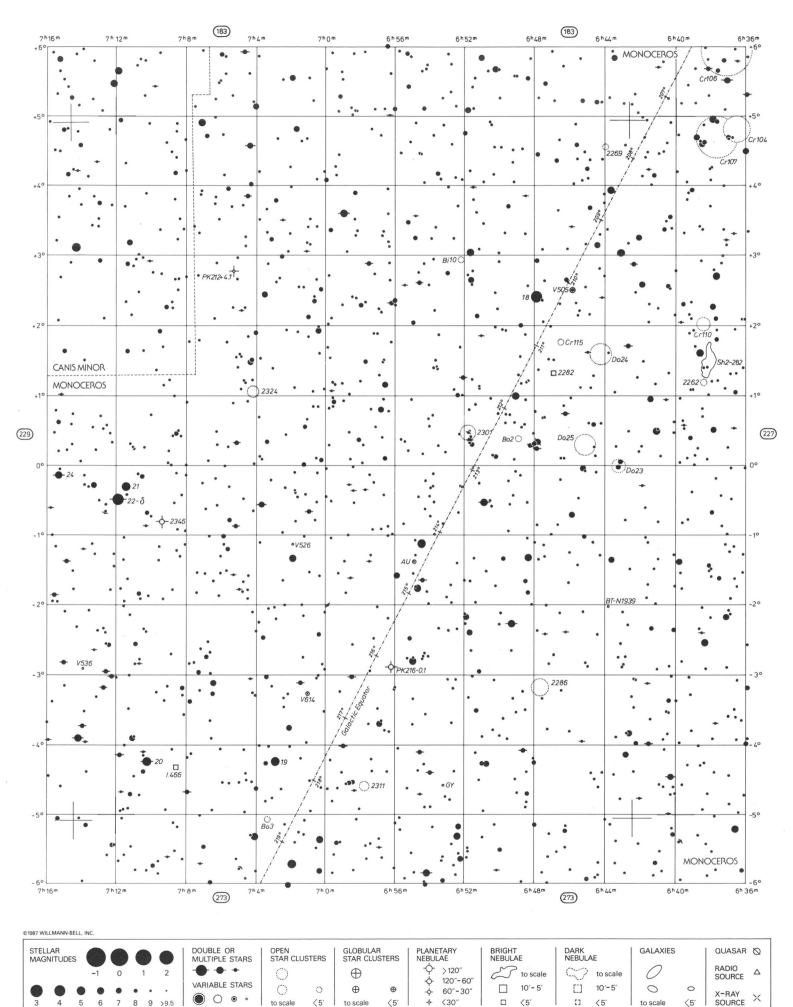

©1987 WILLMANN-BELL, INC.

STELLAR MAGNITUDES

DOUBLE OR MULTIPLE STARS

VARIABLE STARS

OPEN STAR CLUSTERS

to scale   <5'

GLOBULAR STAR CLUSTERS

to scale   <5'

PLANETARY NEBULAE
>120"
120"-60"
60"-30"
<30"

BRIGHT NEBULAE
to scale
10'-5'
<5'

DARK NEBULAE
to scale
10'-5'
<5'

GALAXIES
to scale   <5'

QUASAR

RADIO SOURCE

X-RAY SOURCE

Barry Rappaport & Wil Tirion

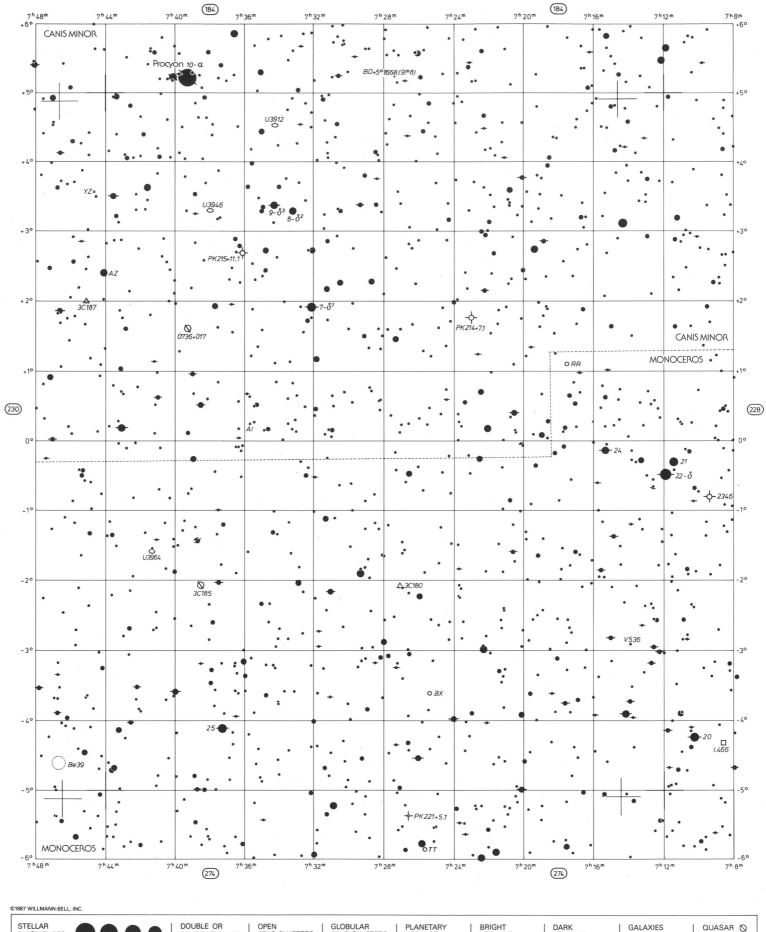

©1987 WILLMANN-BELL, INC.

STELLAR MAGNITUDES					DOUBLE OR MULTIPLE STARS	OPEN STAR CLUSTERS	GLOBULAR STAR CLUSTERS	PLANETARY NEBULAE	BRIGHT NEBULAE	DARK NEBULAE	GALAXIES	QUASAR

Barry Rappaport & Wil Tirion

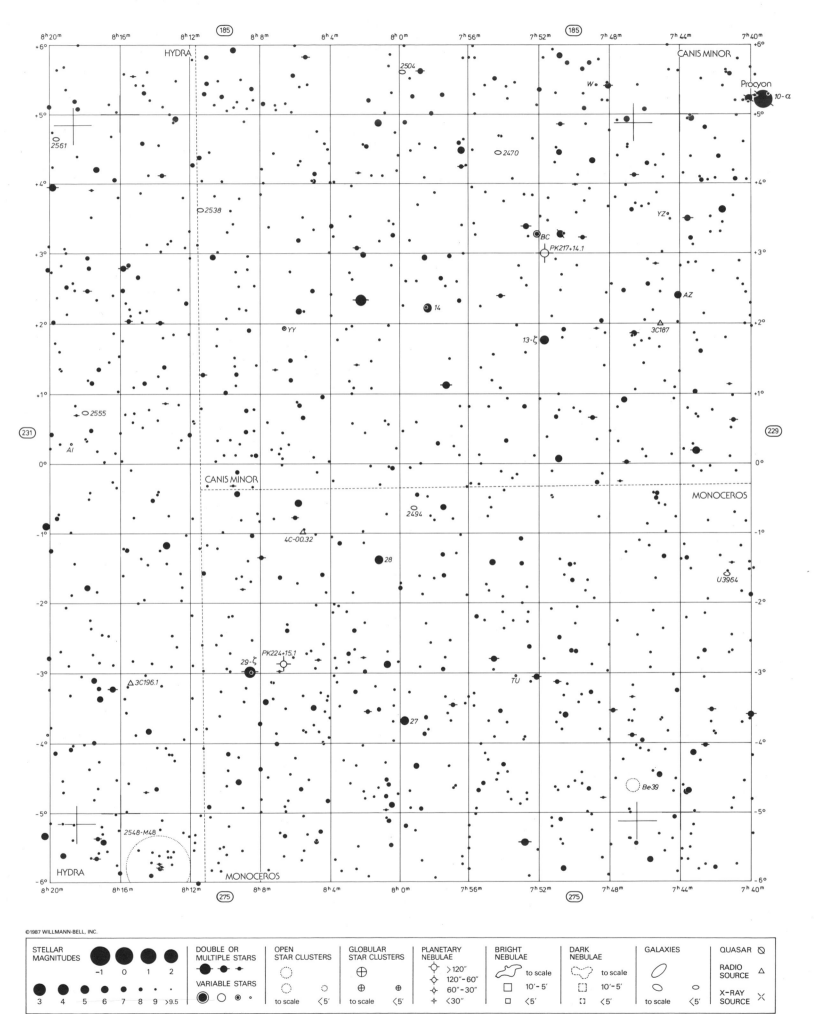

©1987 WILLMANN-BELL, INC.

Barry Rappaport & Wil Tirion

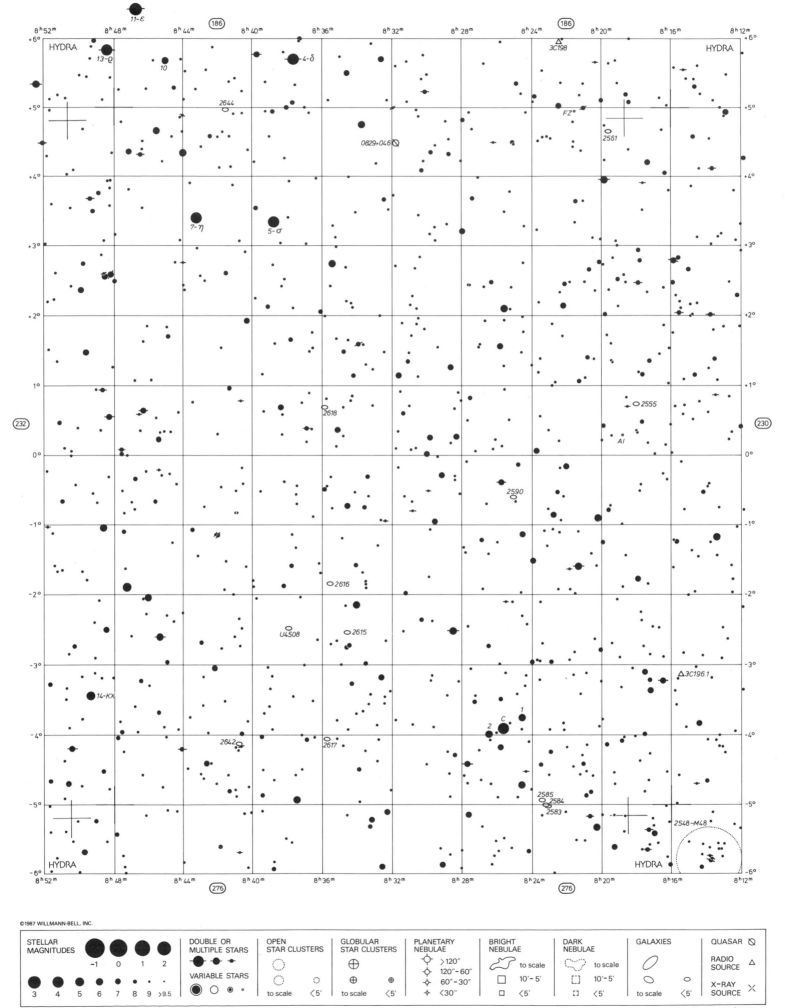

©1987 WILLMANN-BELL, INC.

Barry Rappaport & Wil Tirion

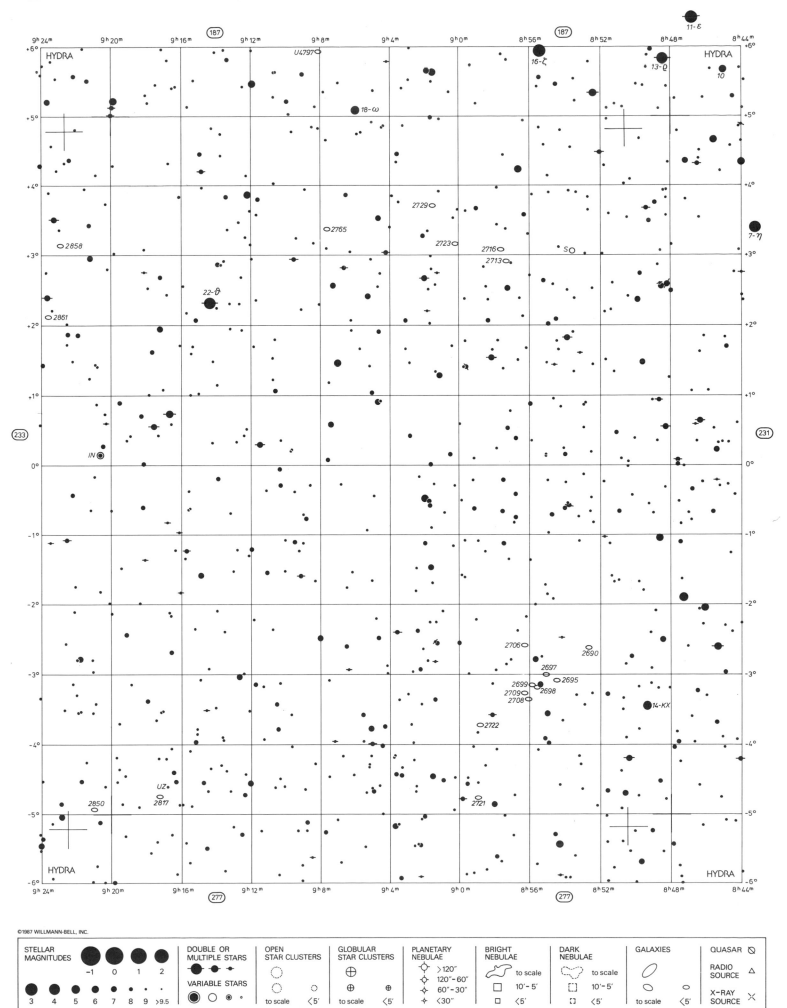

©1987 WILLMANN-BELL, INC.

Barry Rappaport & Wil Tirion

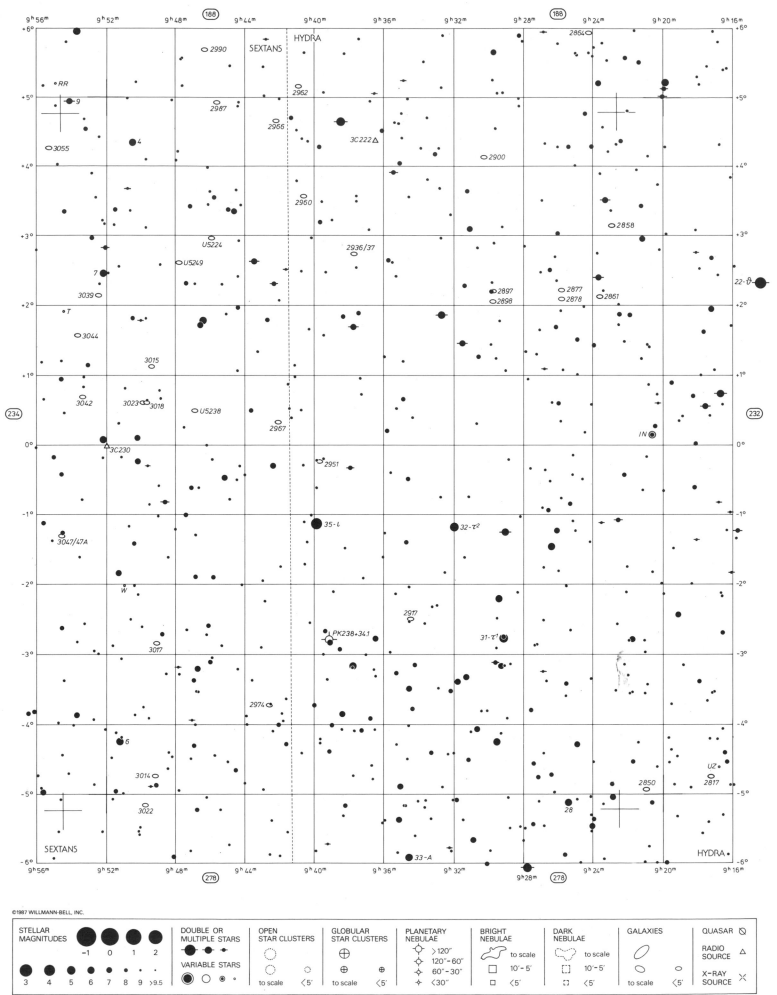

©1987 WILLMANN-BELL, INC.

STELLAR MAGNITUDES				DOUBLE OR MULTIPLE STARS	OPEN STAR CLUSTERS	GLOBULAR STAR CLUSTERS	PLANETARY NEBULAE	BRIGHT NEBULAE	DARK NEBULAE	GALAXIES	QUASAR

Barry Rappaport & Wil Tirion

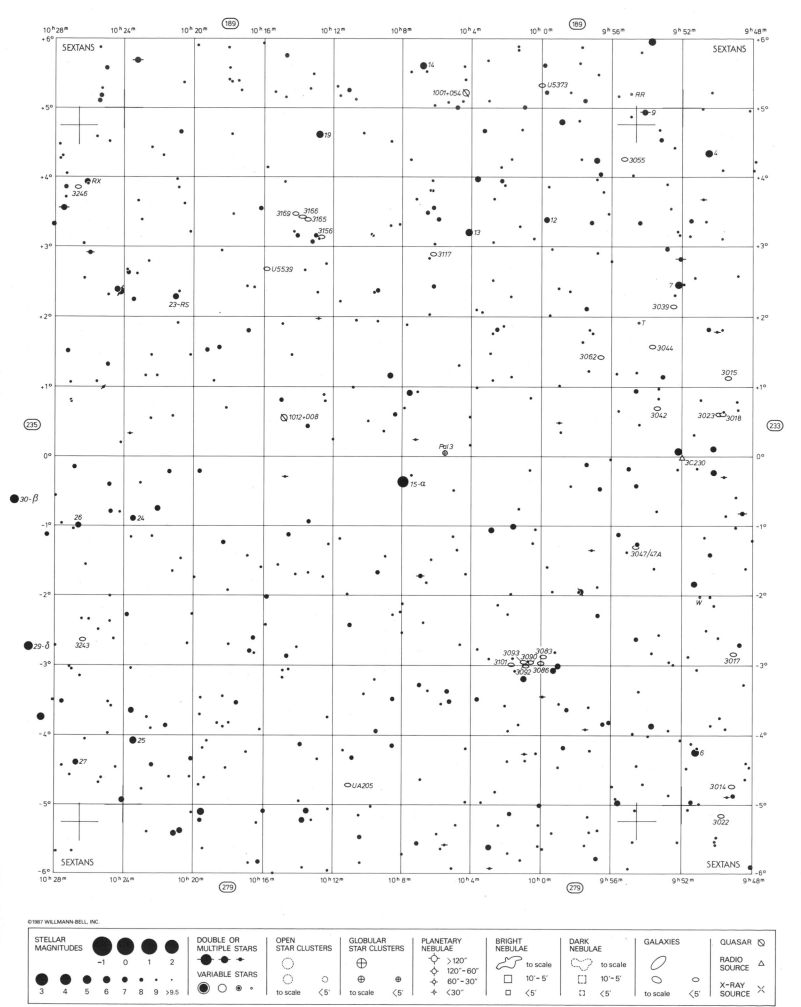

©1987 WILLMANN-BELL, INC.

Barry Rappaport & Wil Tirion

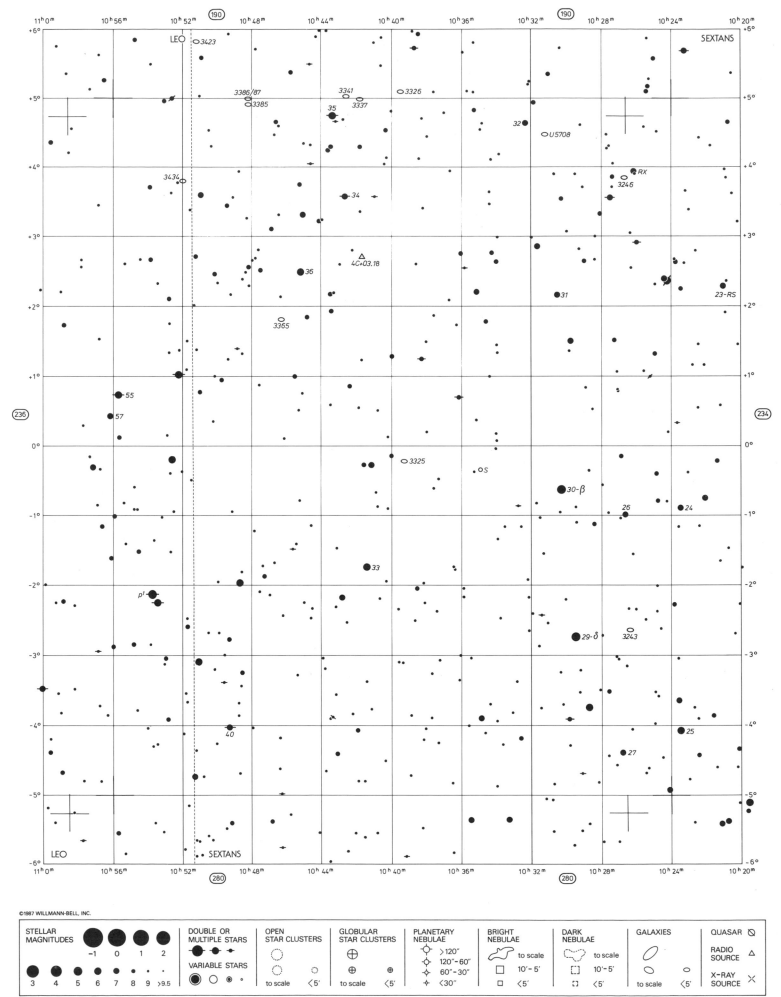

©1987 WILLMANN-BELL, INC.

Barry Rappaport & Wil Tirion

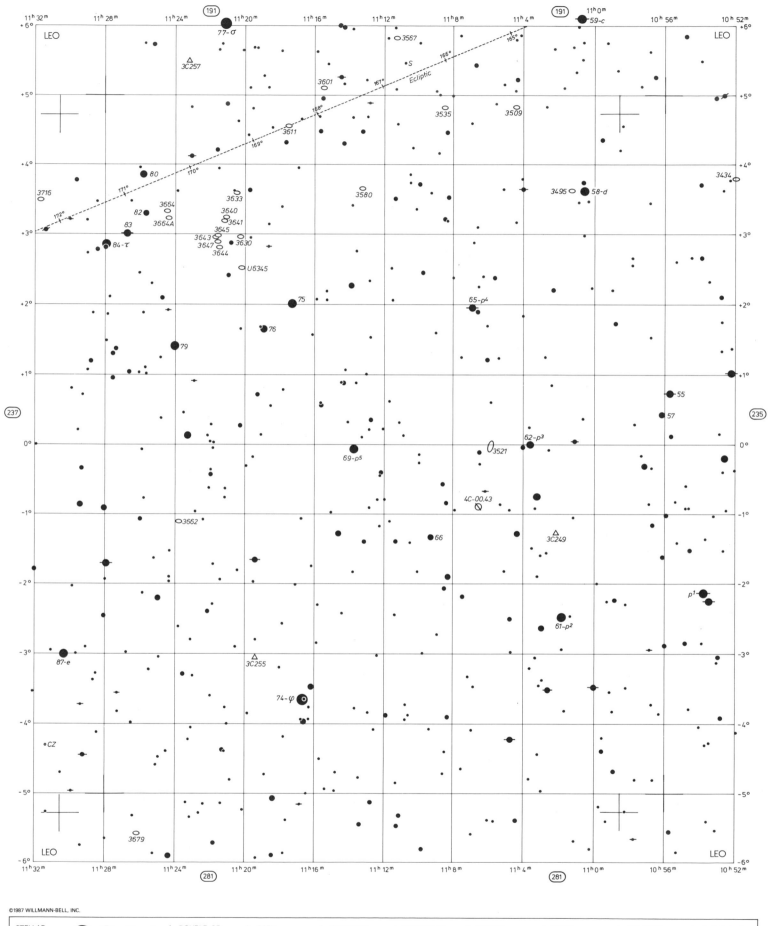

©1987 WILLMANN-BELL, INC.

Barry Rappaport & Wil Tirion

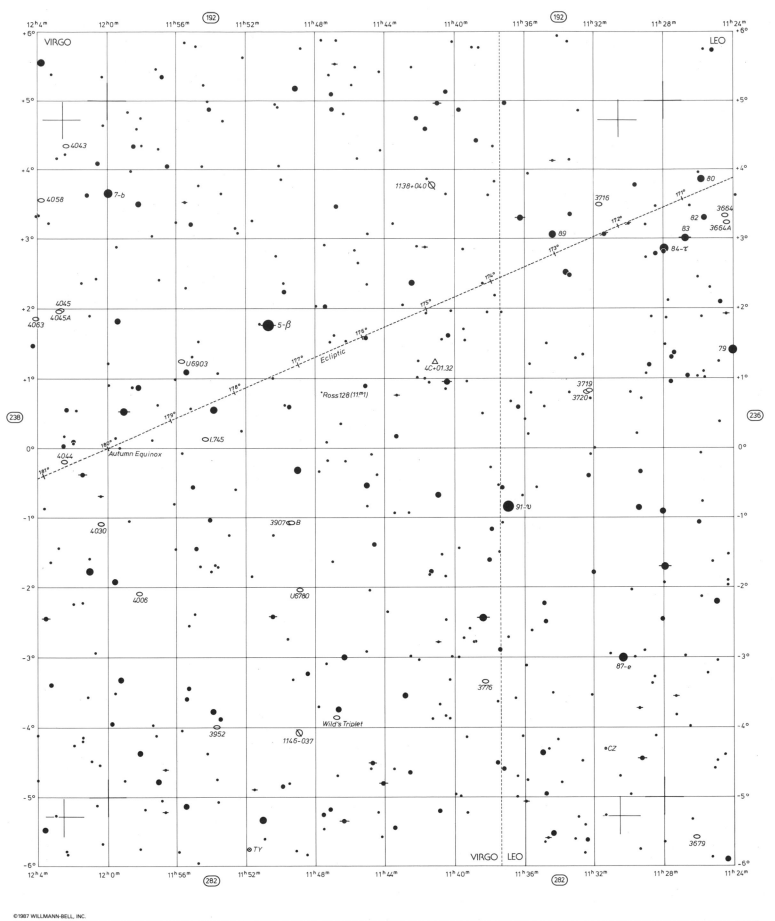

©1987 WILLMANN-BELL, INC.

STELLAR MAGNITUDES	DOUBLE OR MULTIPLE STARS	OPEN STAR CLUSTERS	GLOBULAR STAR CLUSTERS	PLANETARY NEBULAE	BRIGHT NEBULAE	DARK NEBULAE	GALAXIES	QUASAR
-1 0 1 2				>120"	to scale	to scale	to scale	
	VARIABLE STARS	to scale <5'	to scale <5'	120"-60"	10'-5'	10'-5'		RADIO SOURCE
3 4 5 6 7 8 9 >9.5				60"-30" <30"	<5'	<5'	to scale <5'	X-RAY SOURCE

Barry Rappaport & Wil Tirion

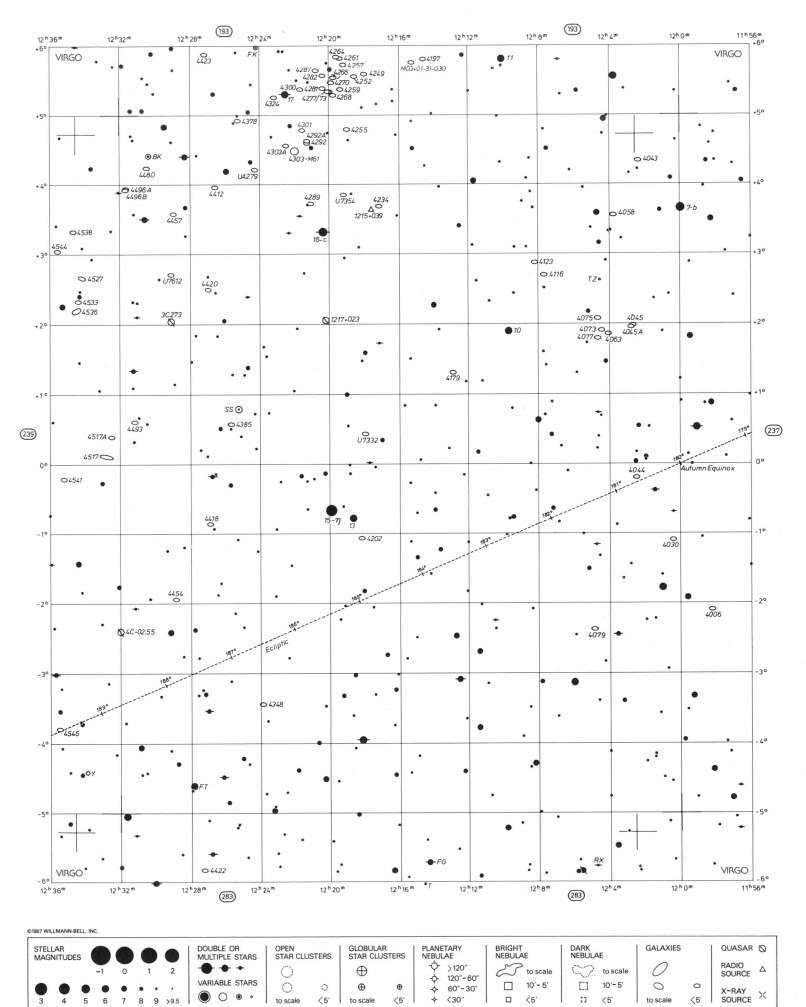

©1987 WILLMANN-BELL, INC.

Barry Rappaport & Will Tirion

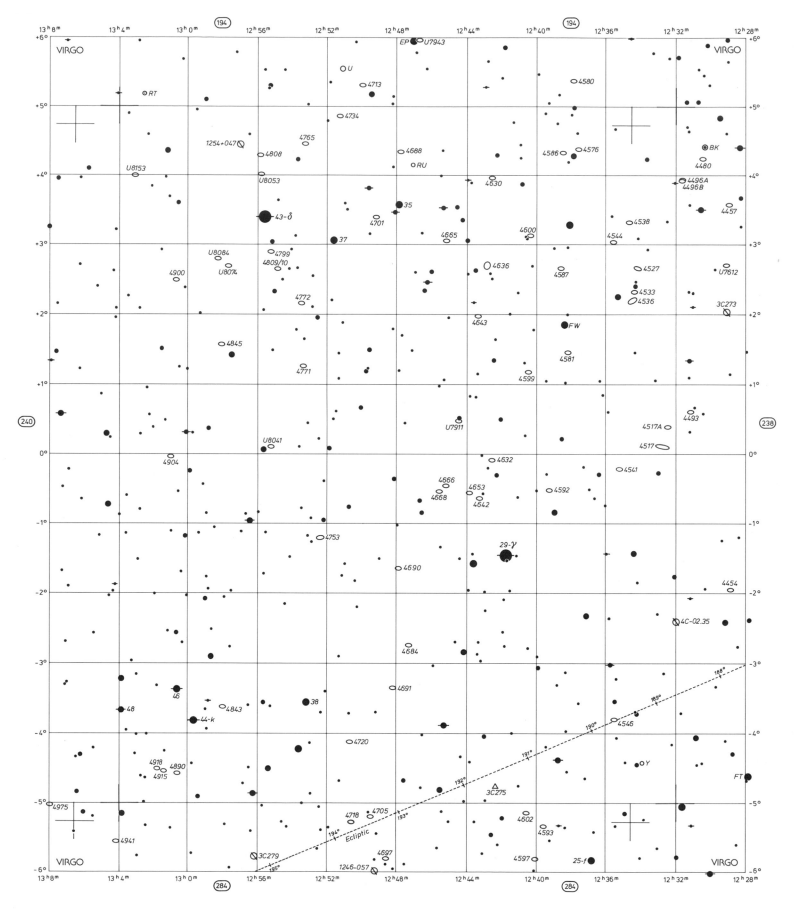

©1987 WILLMANN-BELL, INC.

STELLAR MAGNITUDES		DOUBLE OR MULTIPLE STARS	OPEN STAR CLUSTERS	GLOBULAR STAR CLUSTERS	PLANETARY NEBULAE	BRIGHT NEBULAE	DARK NEBULAE	GALAXIES	QUASAR

Barry Rappaport & Wil Tirion

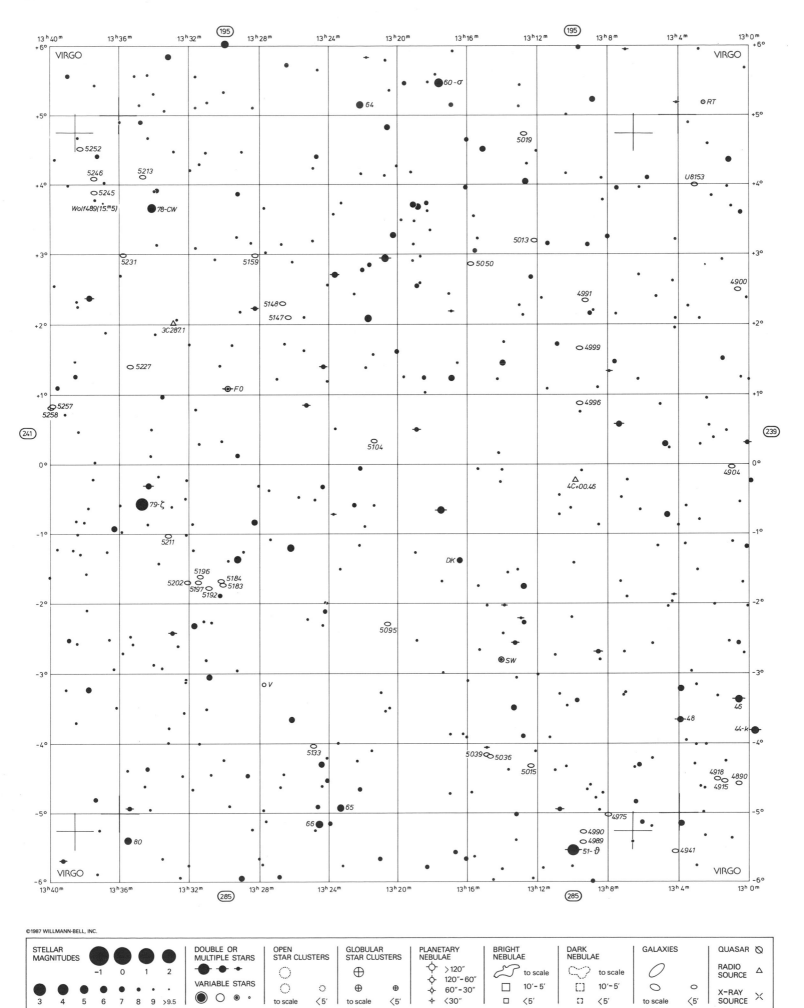

©1987 WILLMANN-BELL, INC.

Barry Rappaport & Wil Tirion

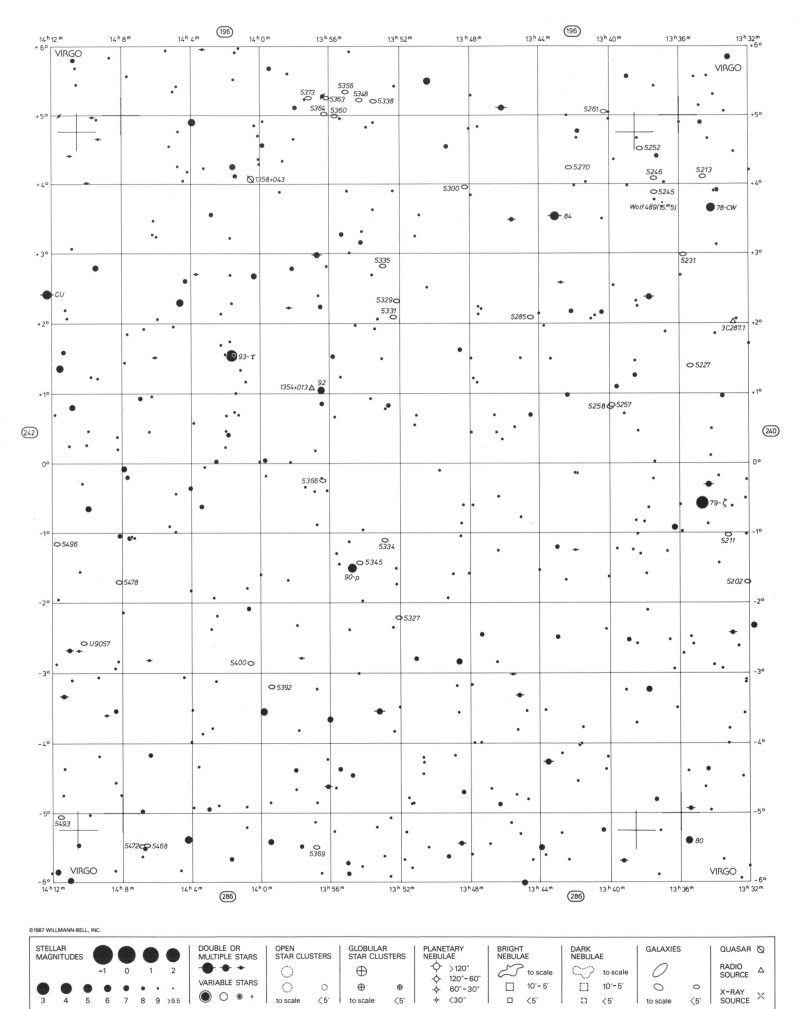

©1987 WILLMANN-BELL, INC.

Barry Rappaport & Wil Tirion

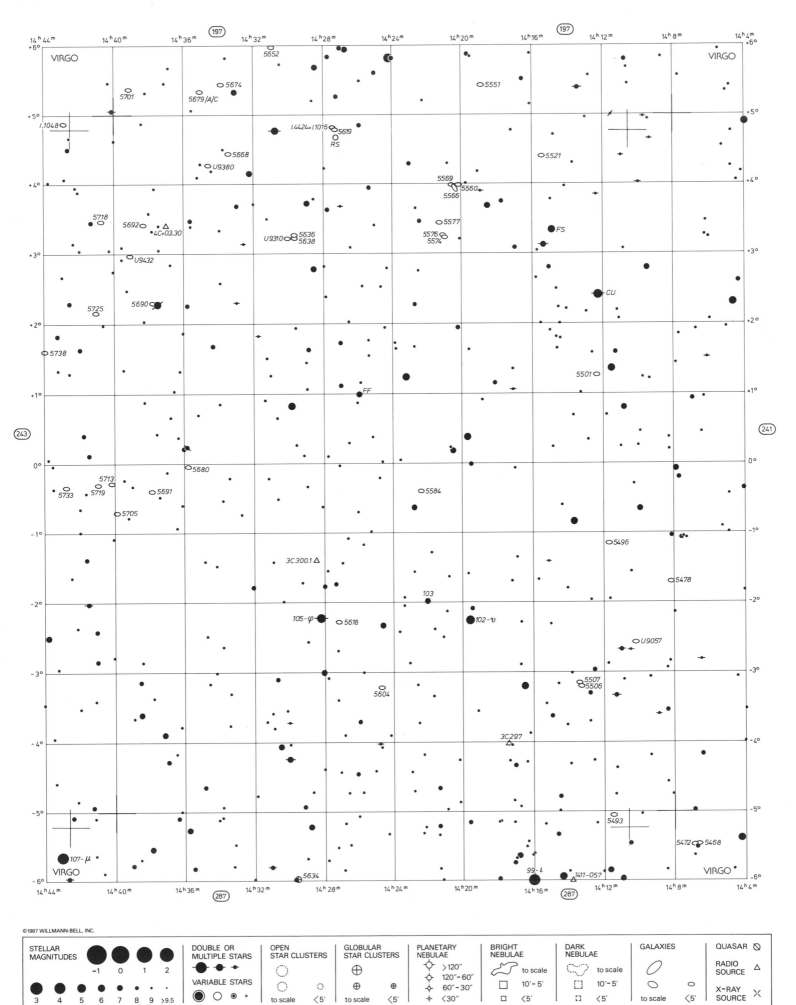

©1987 WILLMANN-BELL, INC.

STELLAR MAGNITUDES		DOUBLE OR MULTIPLE STARS	OPEN STAR CLUSTERS	GLOBULAR STAR CLUSTERS	PLANETARY NEBULAE	BRIGHT NEBULAE	DARK NEBULAE	GALAXIES	QUASAR

Barry Rappaport & Wil Tirion

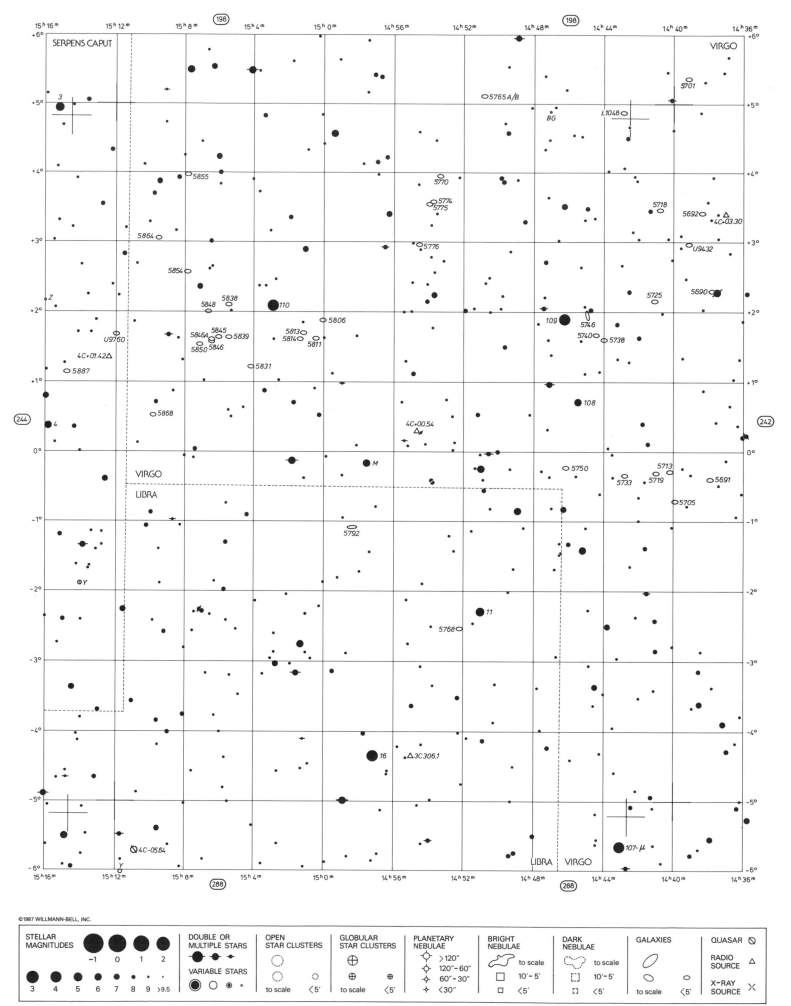

©1987 WILLMANN-BELL, INC.

Barry Rappaport & Wil Tirion

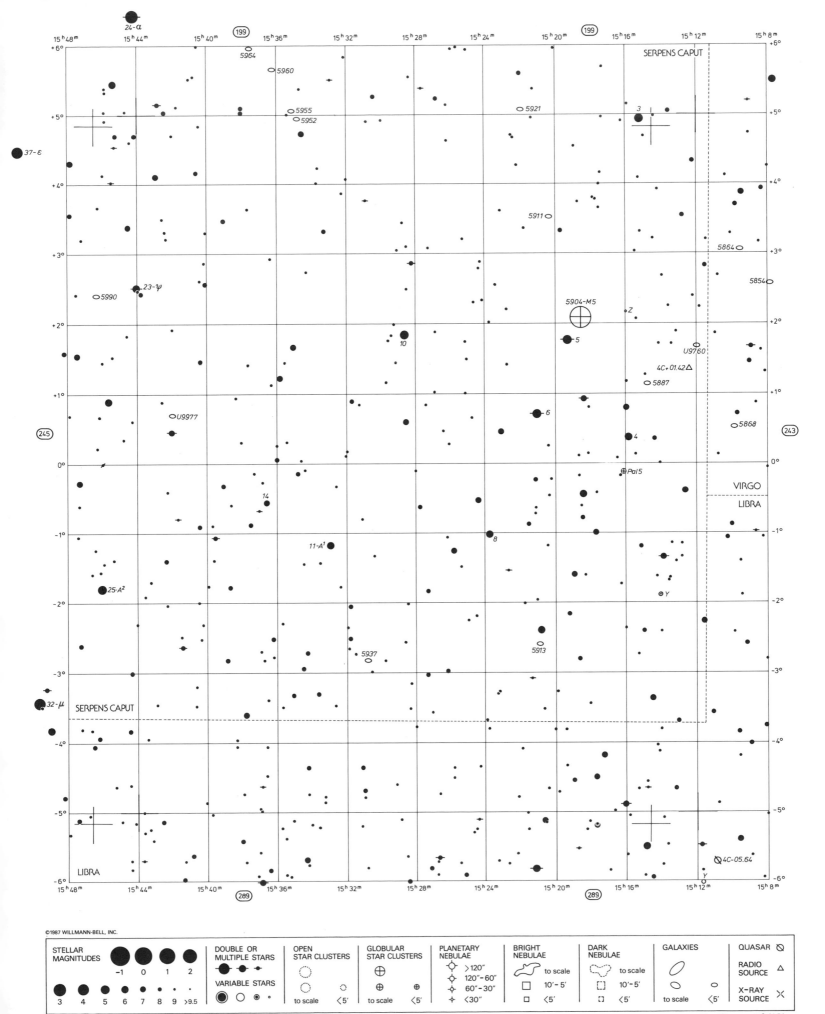

©1987 WILLMANN-BELL, INC.

Barry Rappaport & Wil Tirion

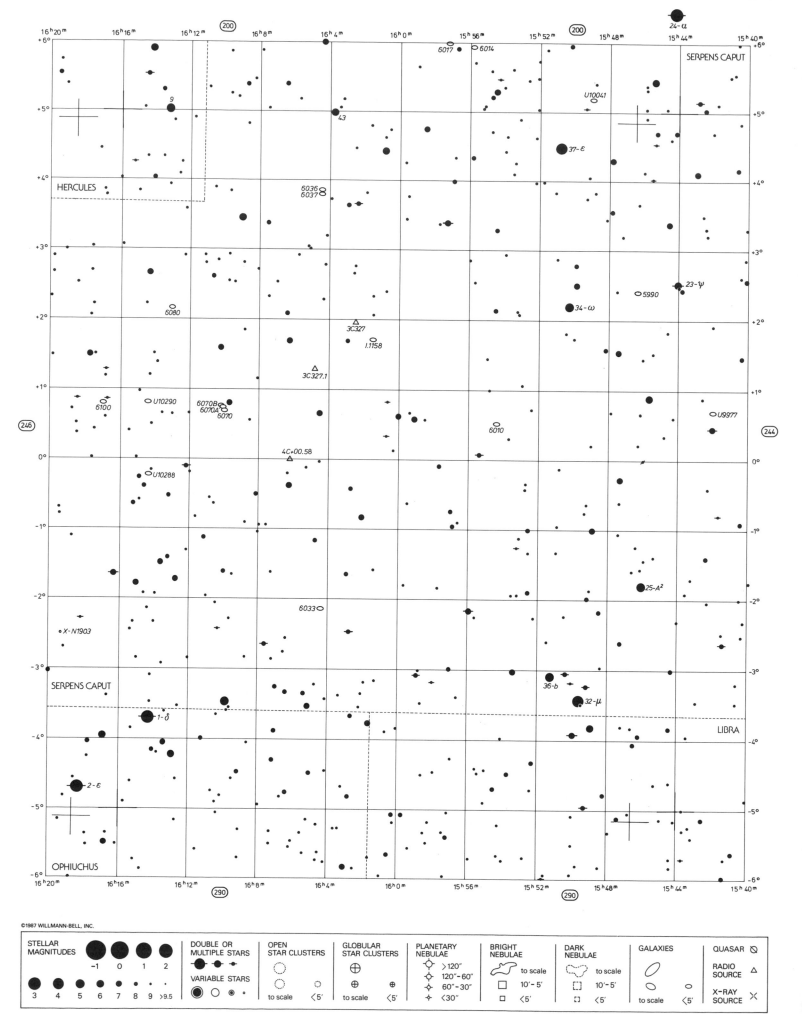

©1987 WILLMANN-BELL, INC.

Barry Rappaport & Wil Tirion

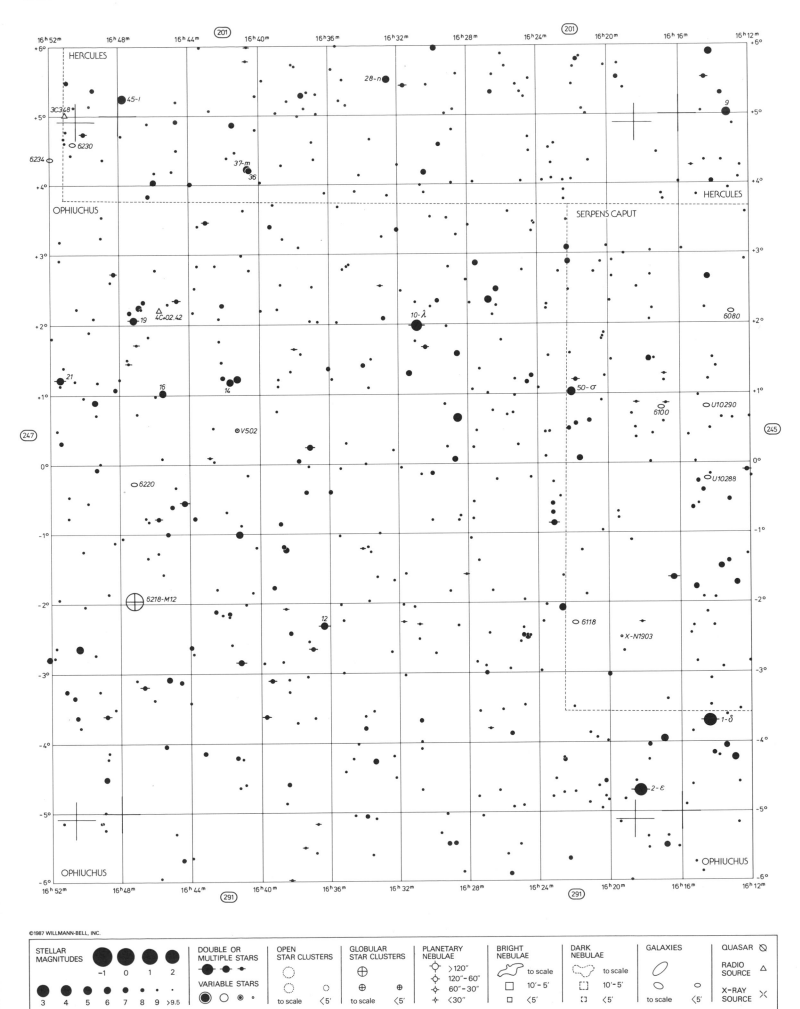

©1987 WILLMANN-BELL, INC.

Barry Rappaport & Wil Tirion

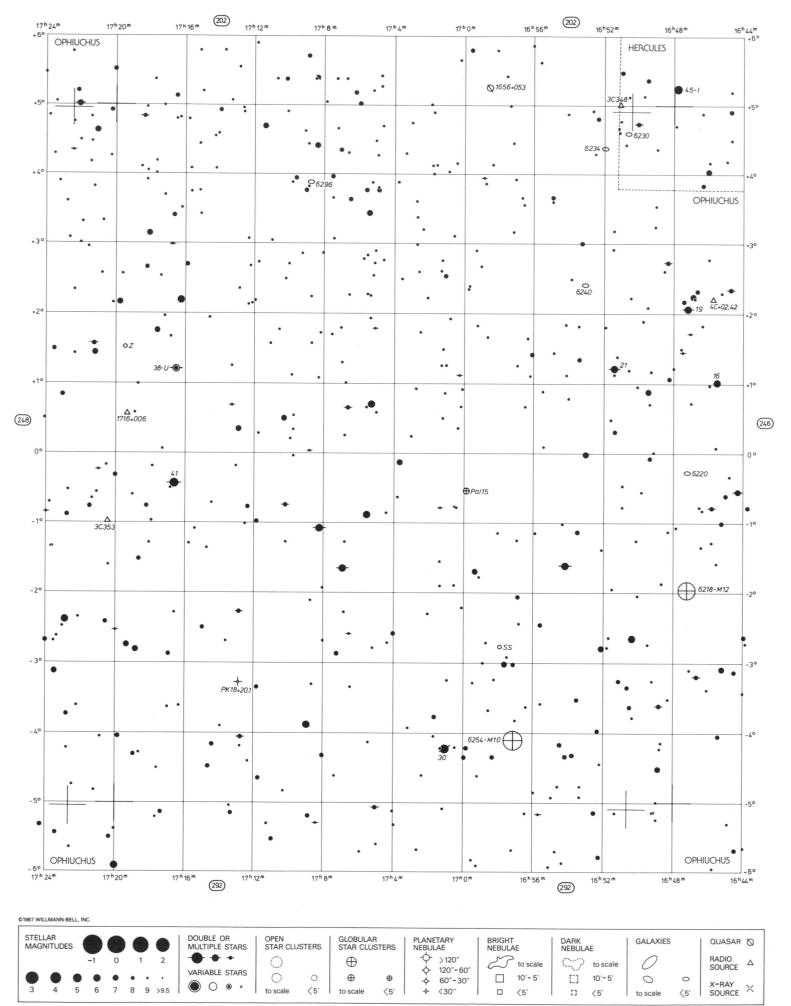

©1987 WILLMANN-BELL, INC.

Barry Rappaport & Wil Tirion

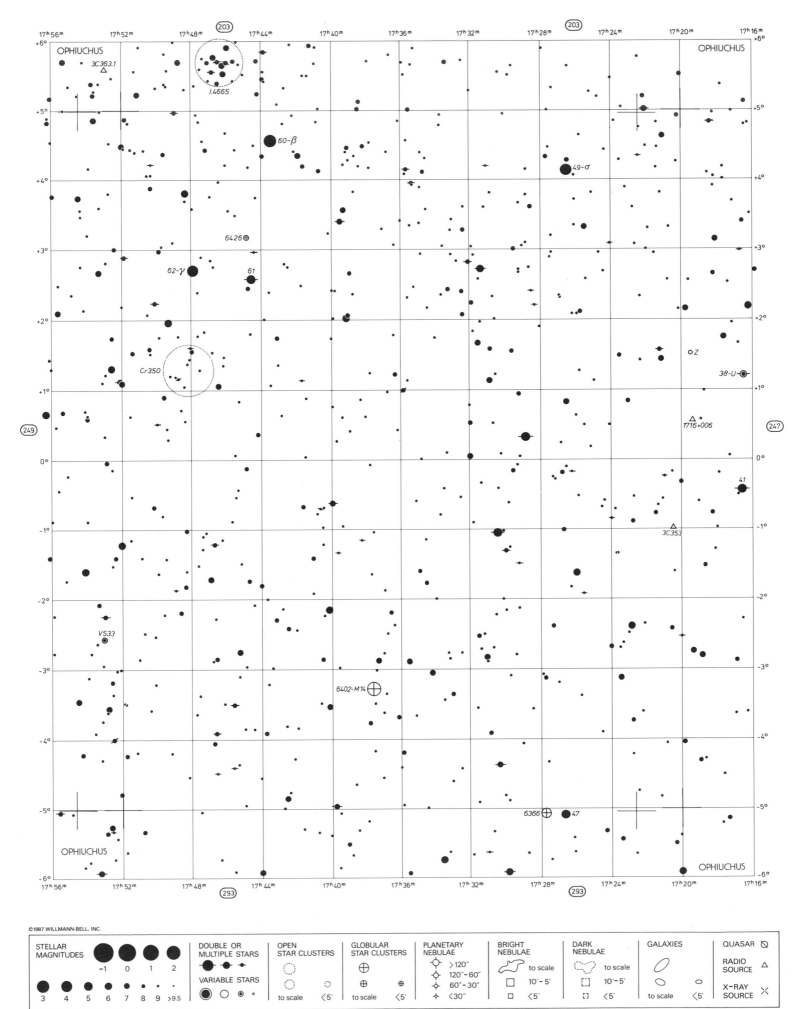

©1987 WILLMANN-BELL, INC.

Barry Rappaport & Wil Tirion

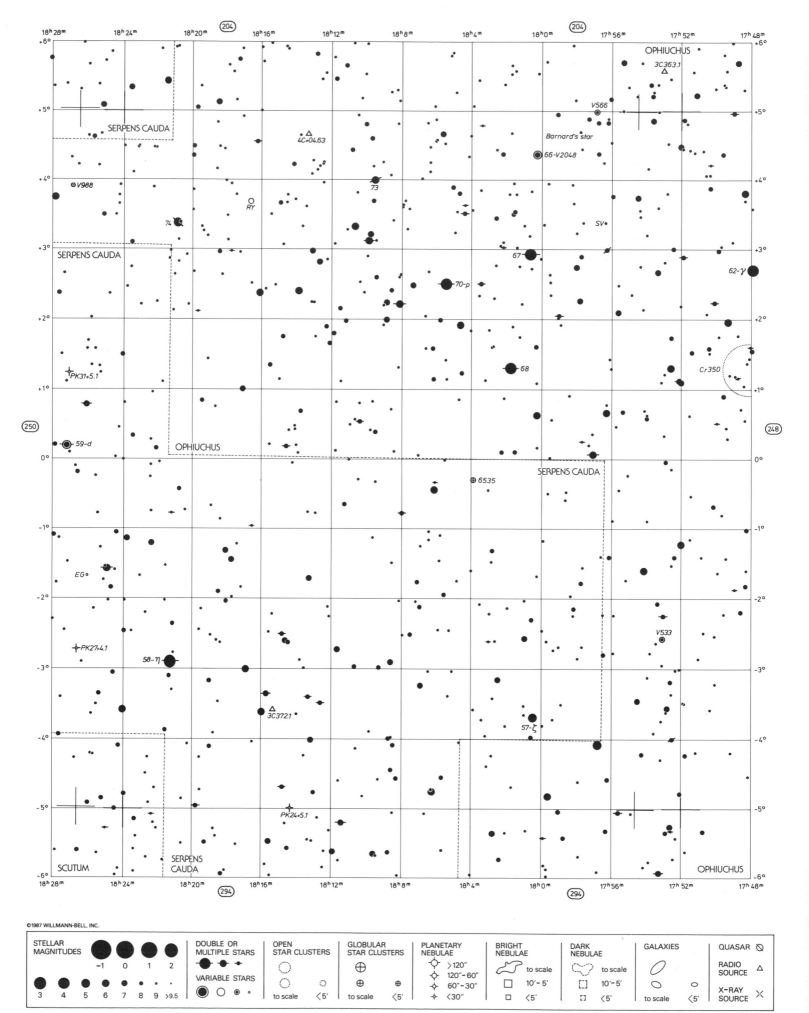

©1987 WILLMANN-BELL, INC.

Barry Rappaport & Wil Tirion

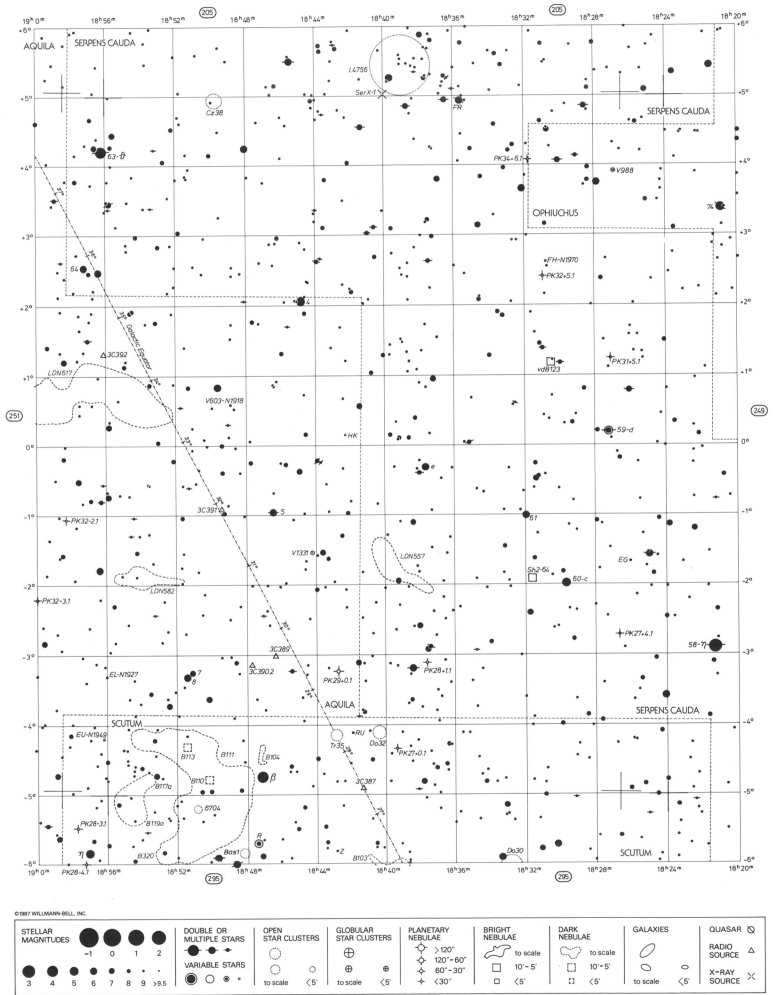

©1987 WILLMANN-BELL, INC.

Barry Rappaport & Wil Tirion

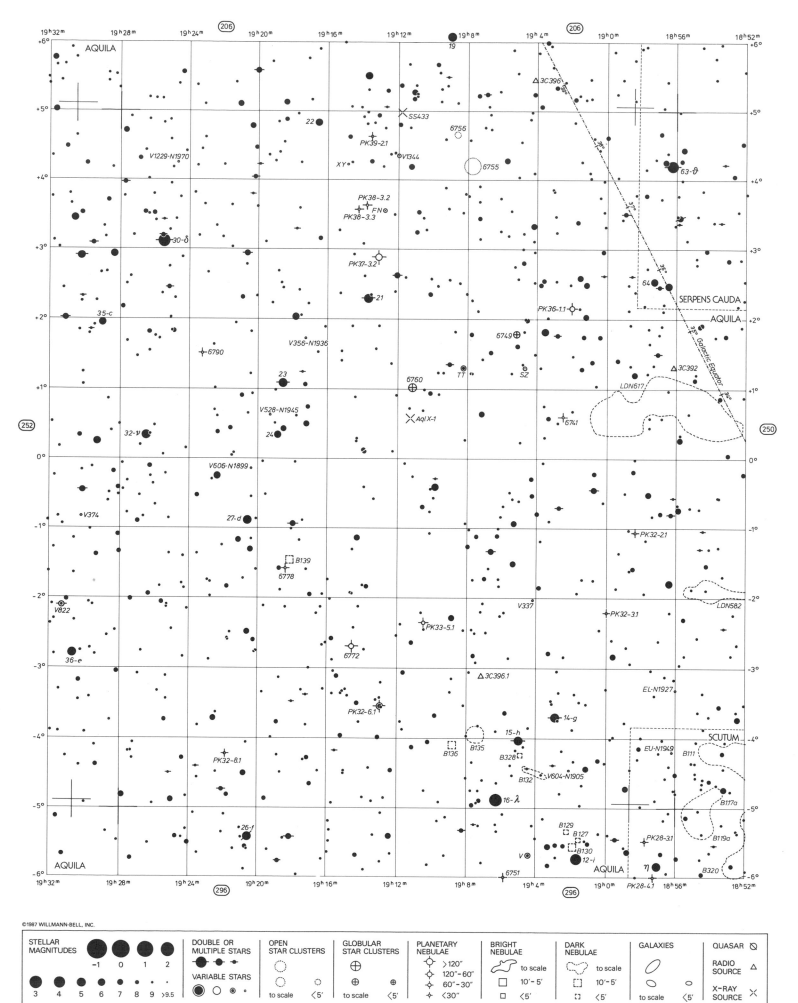

AQUILA

19

3C 396

SS433

22

6756

PK 39-2.1

V1229-N1970

V1344

6755

XY

63-ϑ

PK 38-3.2
FN
PK 38-3.3

30-δ

64

PK 37-3.2

SERPENS CAUDA

21

AQUILA

35-c

PK 36-1.1

6749

6790

3C 392

V356-N1936

6760

TT

SZ

LDN617

23

6741

V528-N1945

Aql X-1

32-v

24

V606-N1899

PK 32-2.1

V374

27-d

B139

6778

V822

V337

PK 32-3.1

LDN582

PK 33-5.1

36-e

6772

3C 396.1

EL-N1927

PK 32-6.1

14-g

15-h

SCUTUM

B136   B135

EU-N1949

B111

PK 32-8.1

B328

V604-N1905

B132

16-λ

B117a

26-f

B129
B127
PK 28-3.1
B119a
v
B130
12-i

AQUILA

η

B320

6751

PK 28-4.1

©1987 WILLMANN-BELL, INC.

STELLAR MAGNITUDES	DOUBLE OR MULTIPLE STARS	OPEN STAR CLUSTERS	GLOBULAR STAR CLUSTERS	PLANETARY NEBULAE	BRIGHT NEBULAE	DARK NEBULAE	GALAXIES	QUASAR
-1 0 1 2				> 120"	to scale	to scale	to scale	RADIO SOURCE
VARIABLE STARS		120"-60"					X-RAY SOURCE
3 4 5 6 7 8 9 >9.5		to scale < 5'	to scale < 5'	60"-30" < 30"	10'-5' < 5'	10'-5' < 5'	to scale < 5'	

Barry Rappaport & Wil Tirion

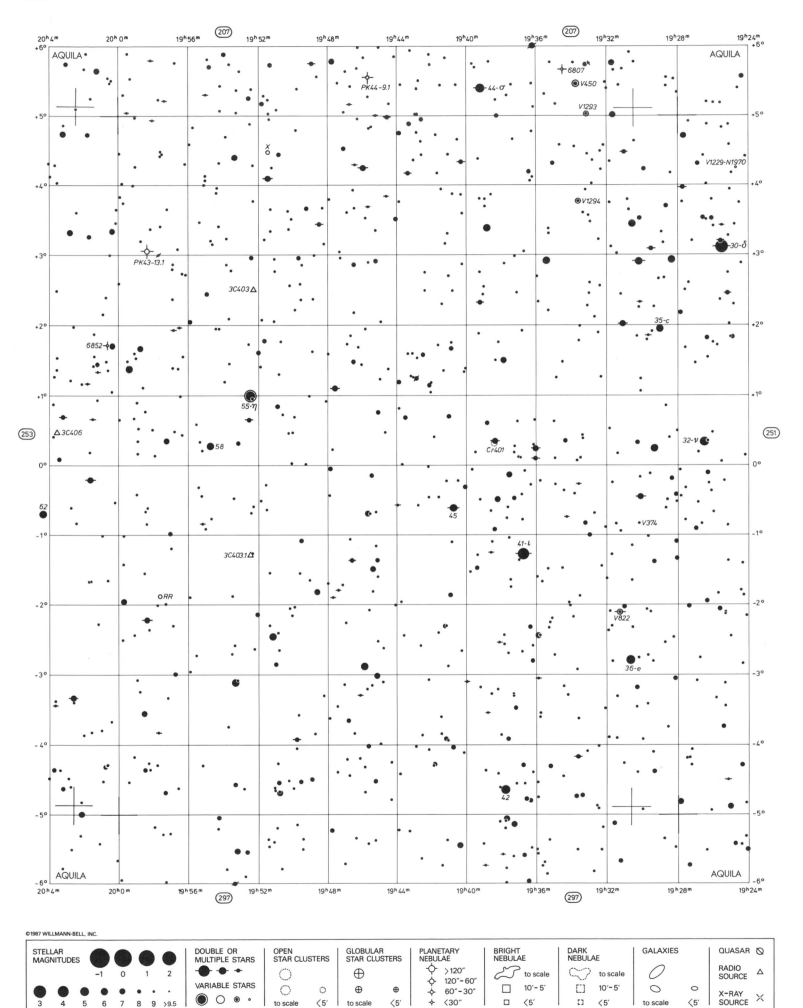

©1987 WILLMANN-BELL, INC.

Barry Rappaport & Wil Tirion

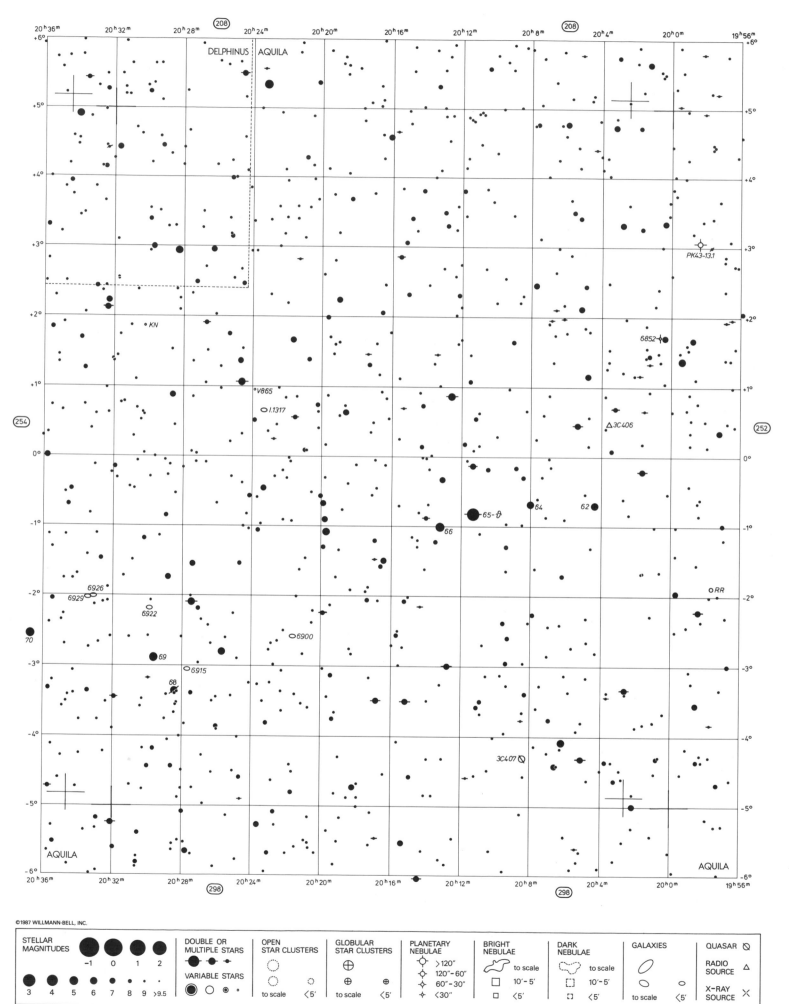

©1987 WILLMANN-BELL, INC.

Barry Rappaport & Wil Tirion

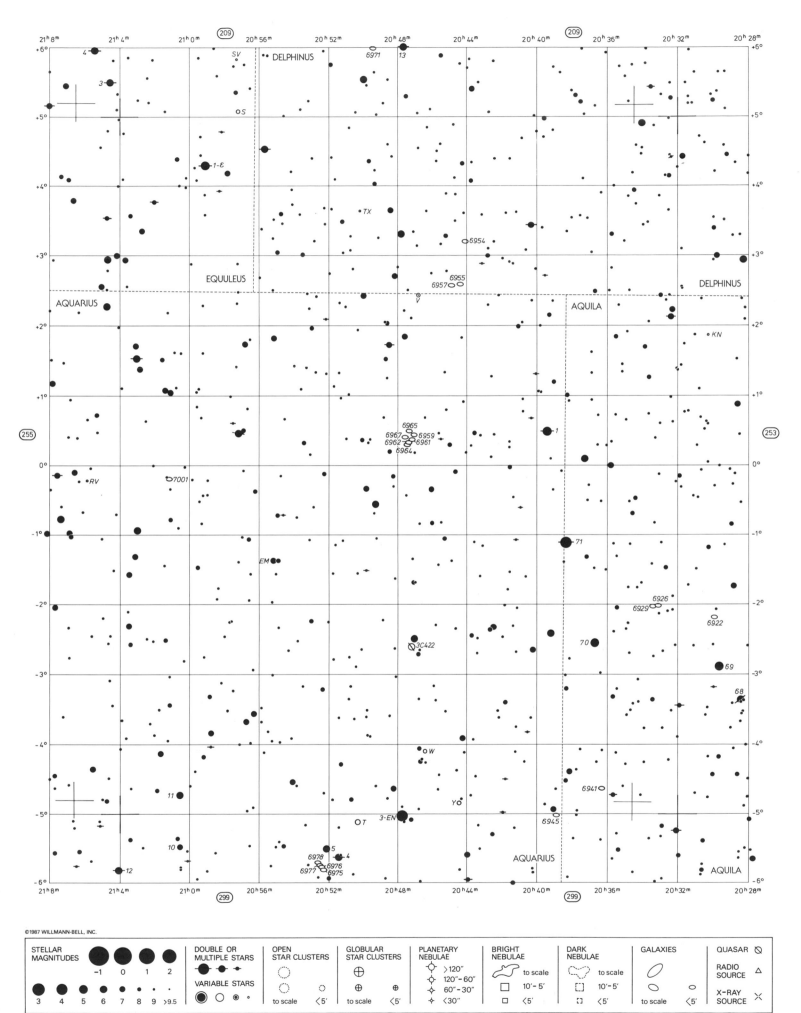

©1987 WILLMANN-BELL, INC.

Barry Rappaport & Wil Tirion

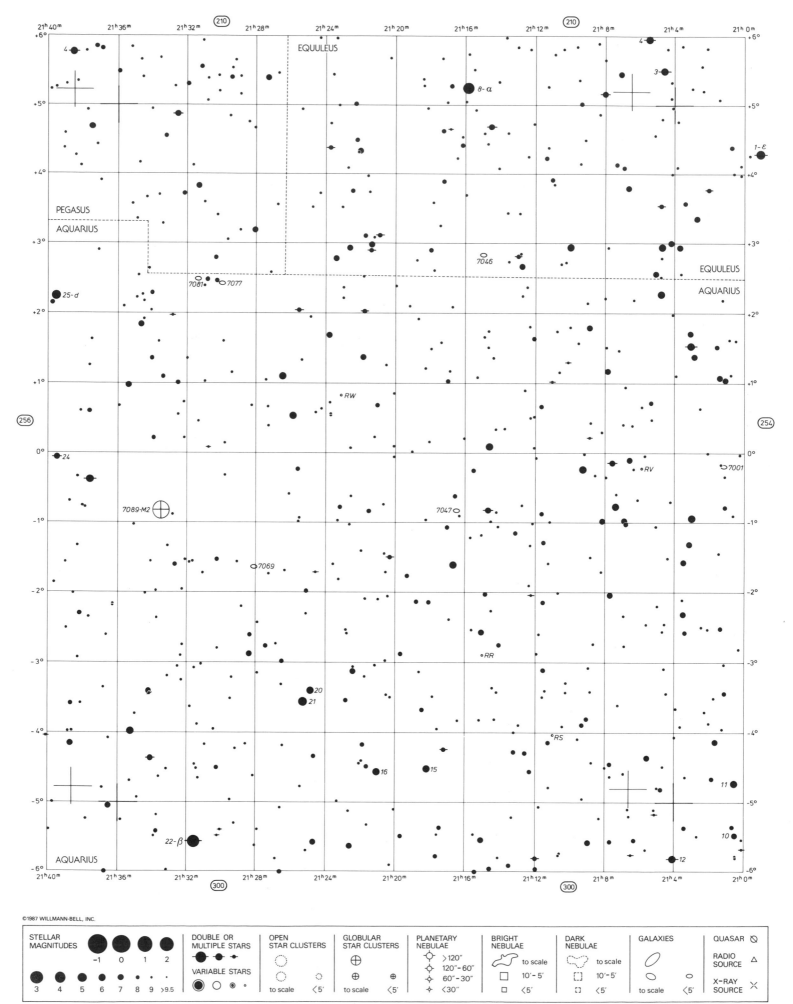

©1987 WILLMANN-BELL, INC.

Barry Rappaport & Wil Tirion

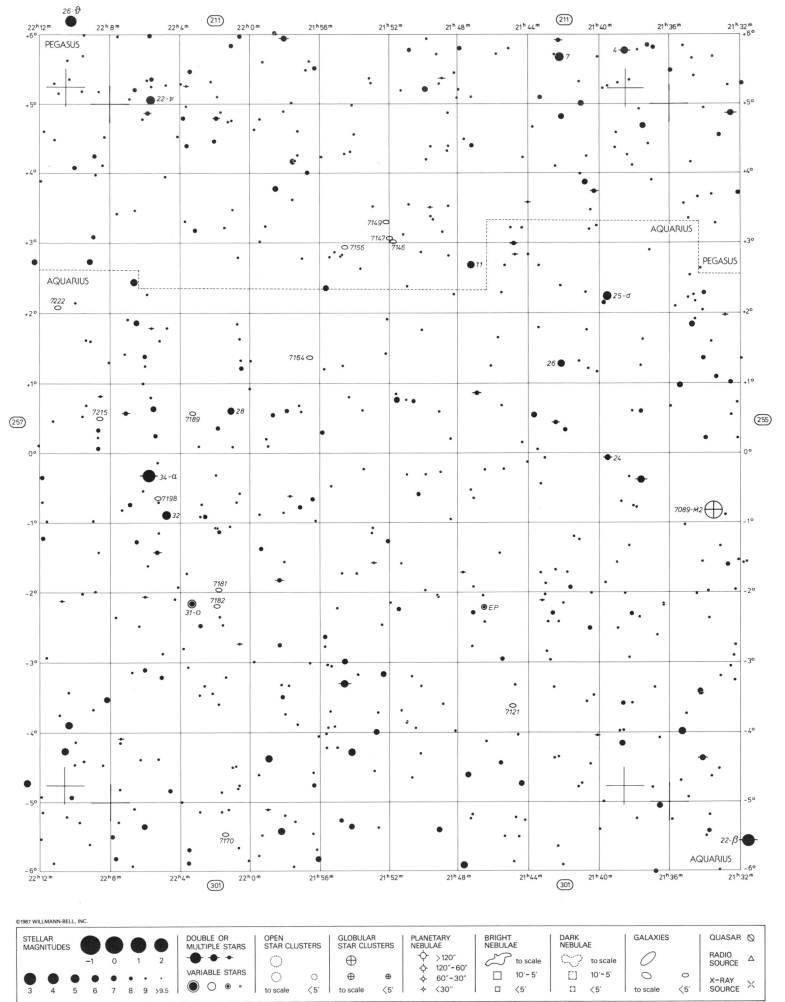

©1987 WILLMANN-BELL, INC.

Barry Rappaport & Wil Tirion

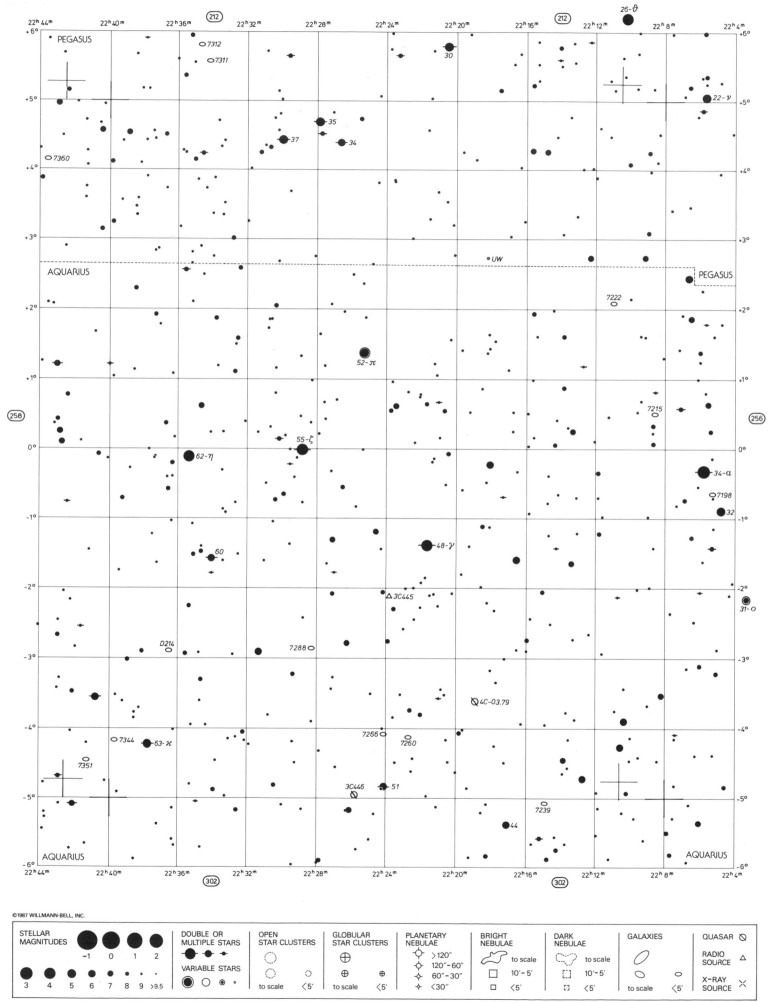

©1987 WILLMANN-BELL, INC.

Barry Rappaport & Wil Tirion

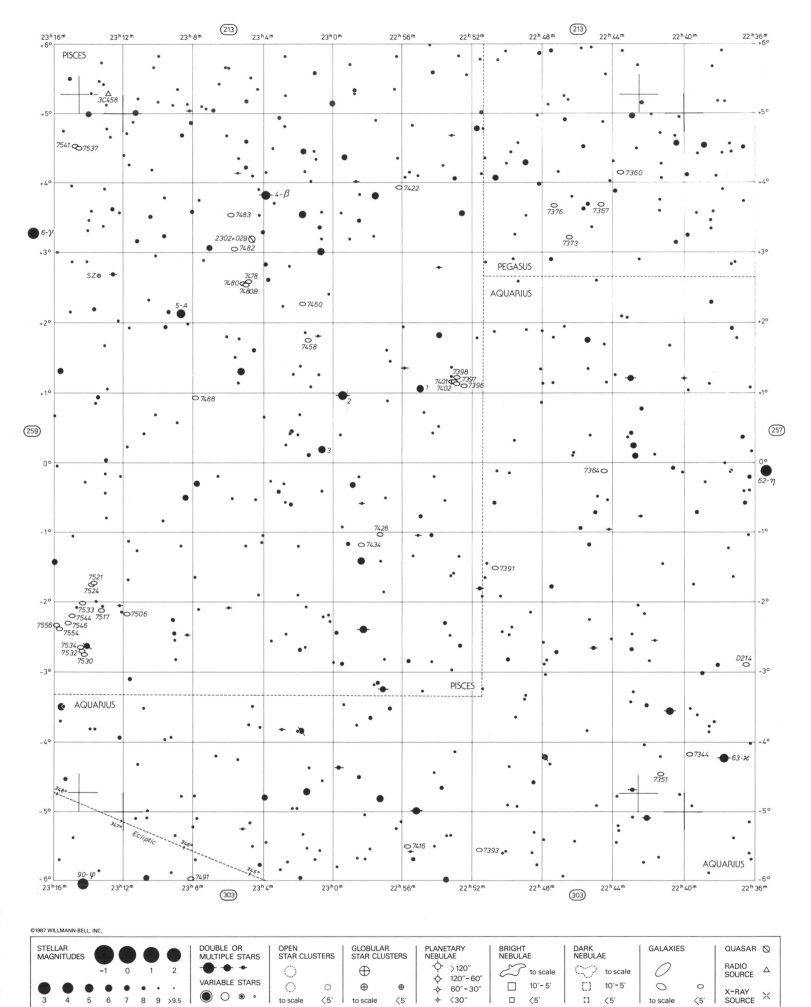

©1987 WILLMANN-BELL, INC.

Barry Rappaport & Wil Tirion

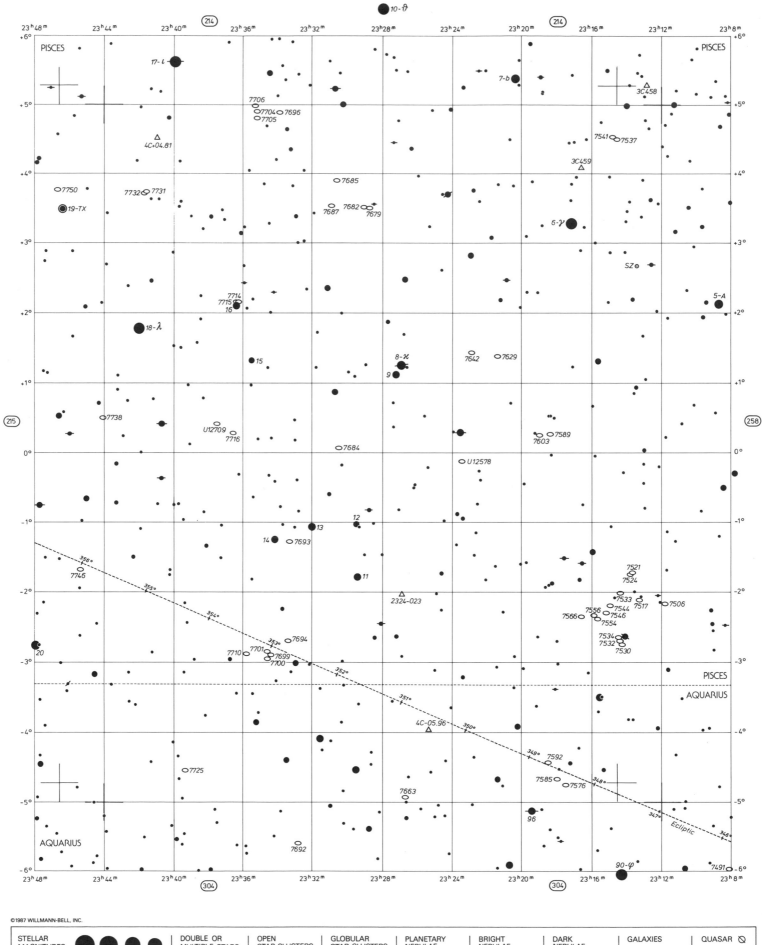

©1987 WILLMANN-BELL, INC.

Barry Rappaport & Wil Tirion

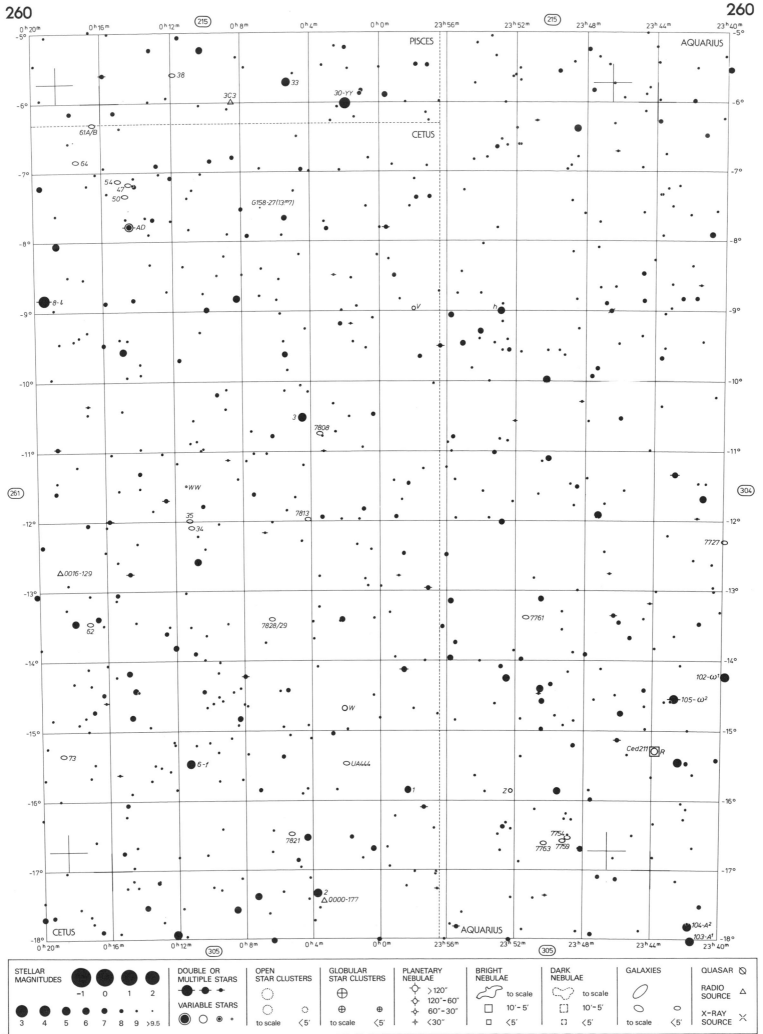

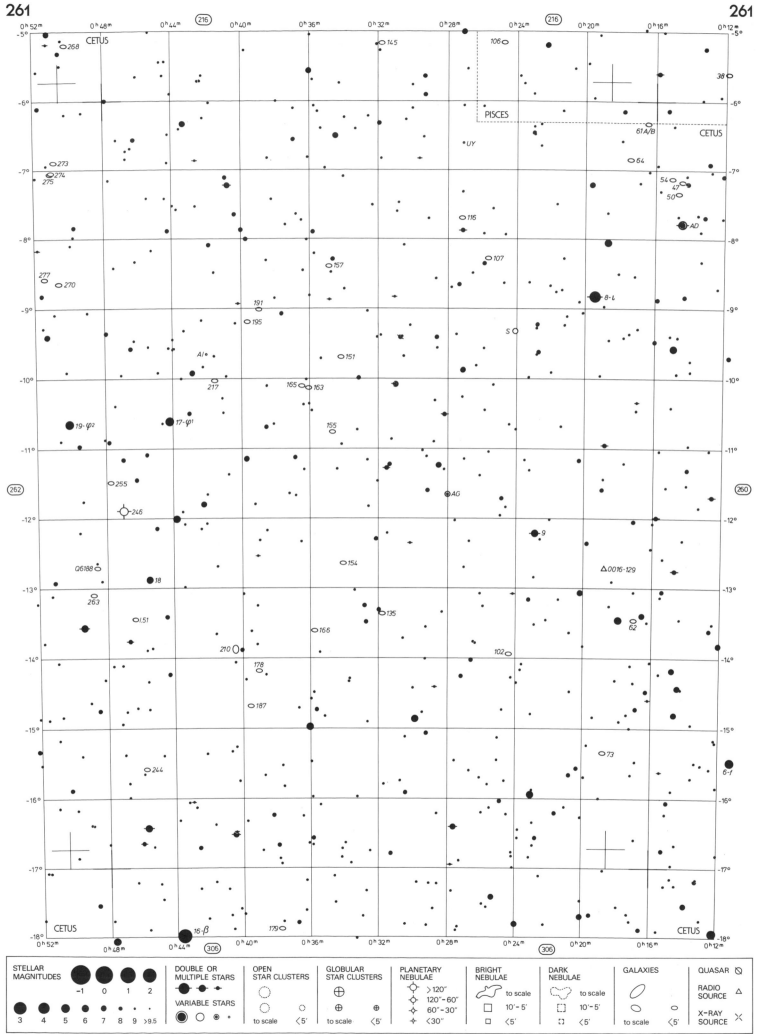

© 1988 WILLMANN-BELL, INC.

Barry Rappaport & Wil Tirion

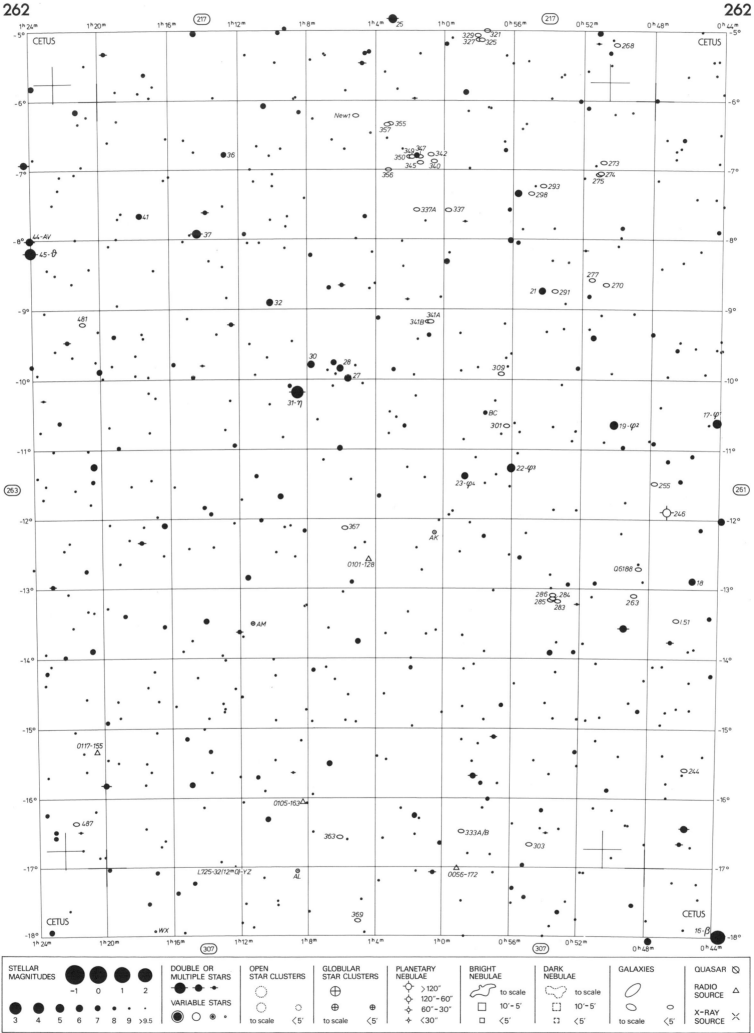

© 1988 WILLMANN-BELL, INC.

Barry Rappaport & Wil Tirion

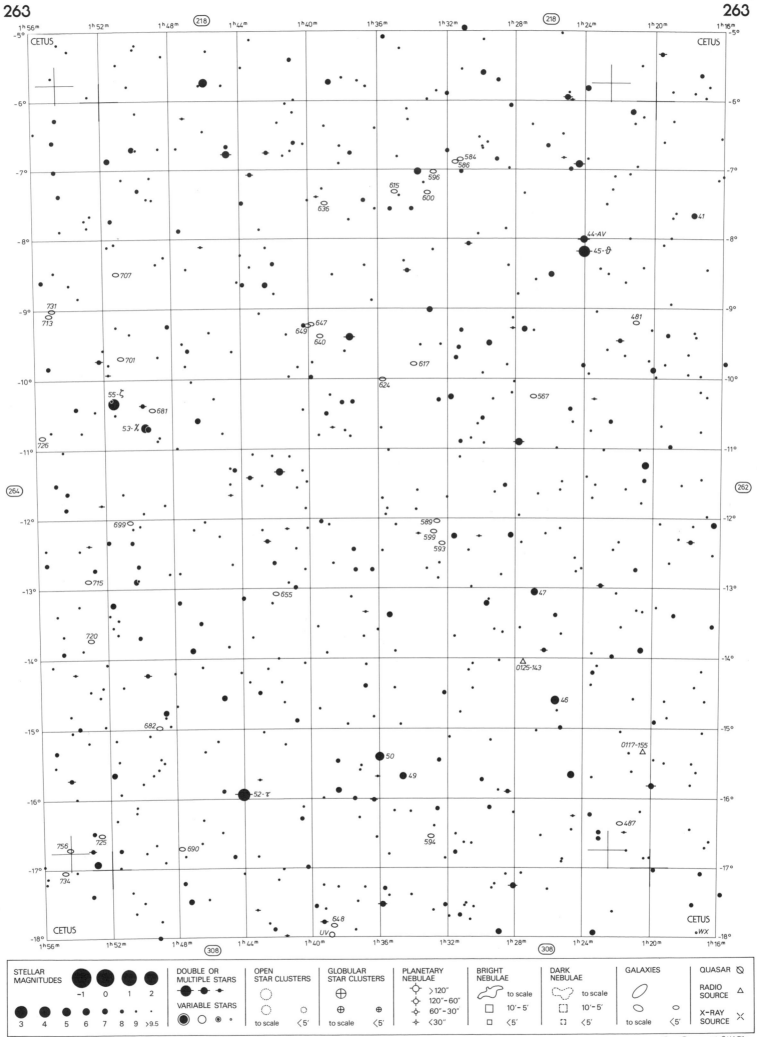

© 1988 WILLMANN-BELL, INC.

Barry Rappaport & Wil Tirion

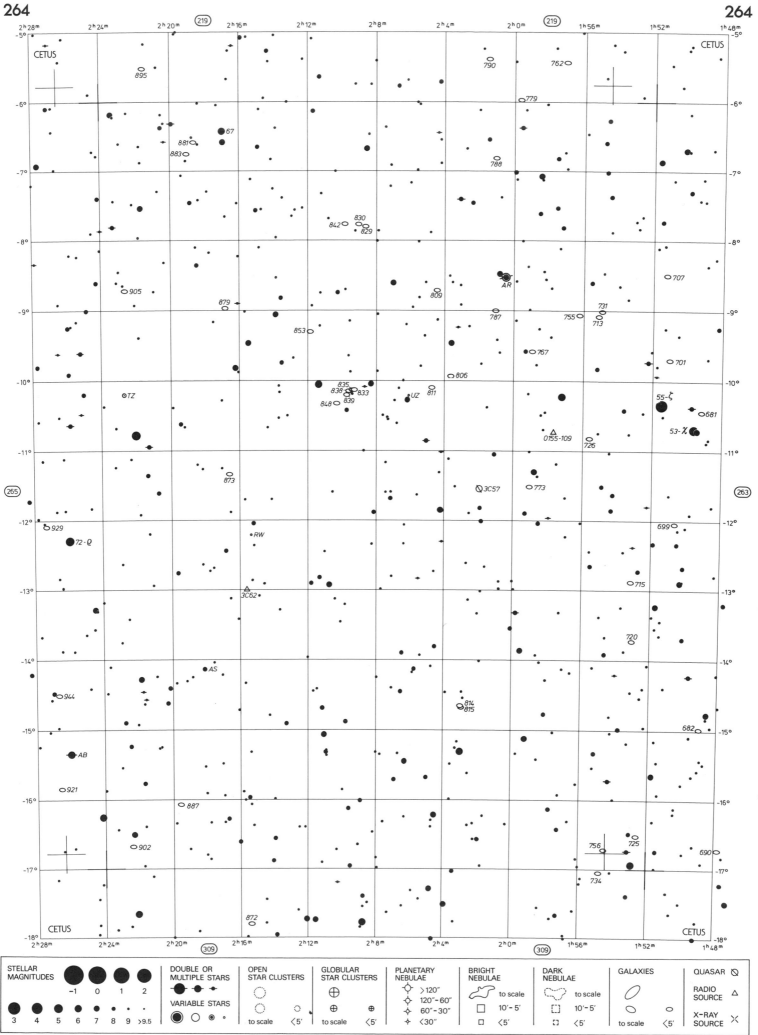

Barry Rappaport & Wil Tirion

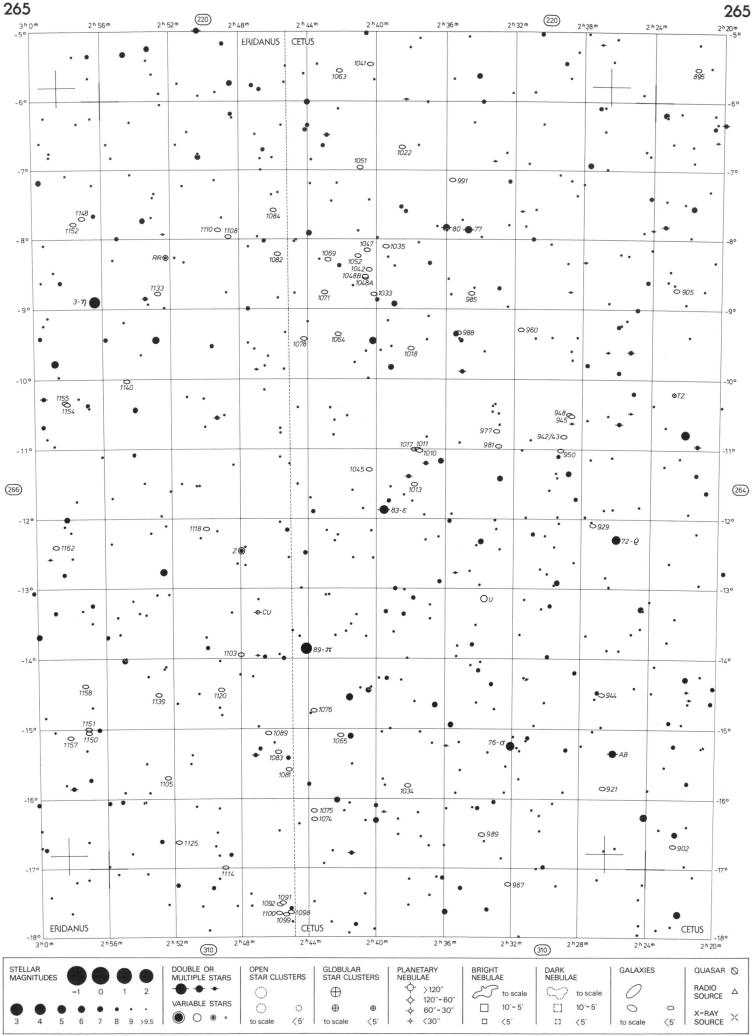

Barry Rappaport & Wil Tirion

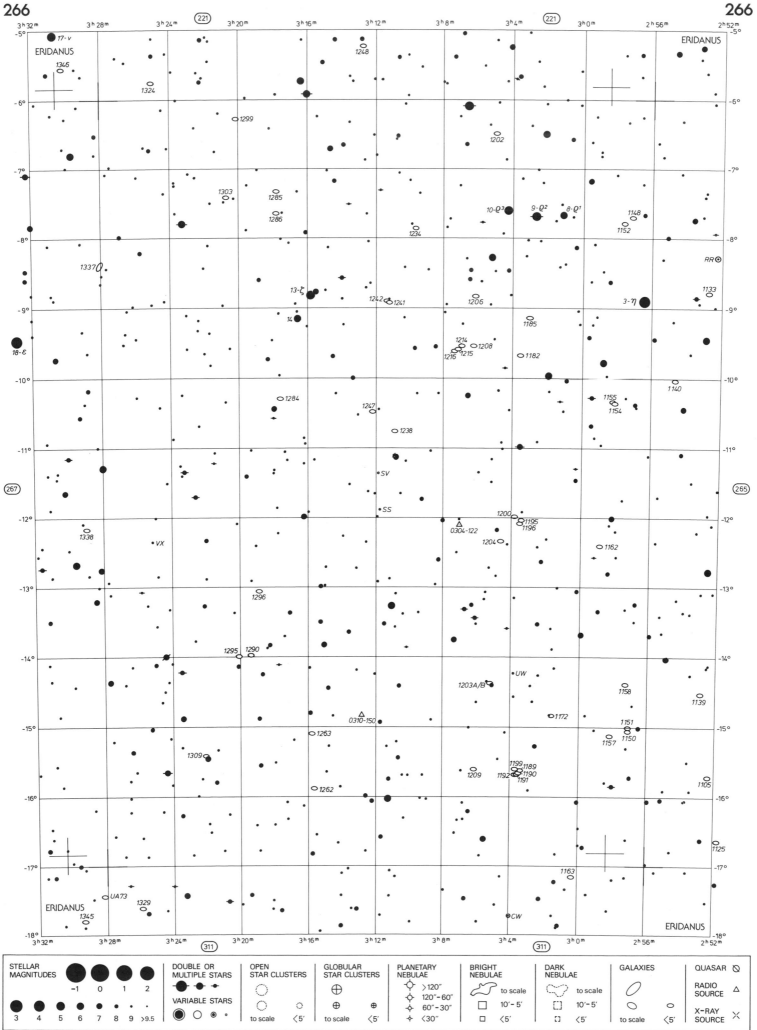

Barry Rappaport & Wil Tirion

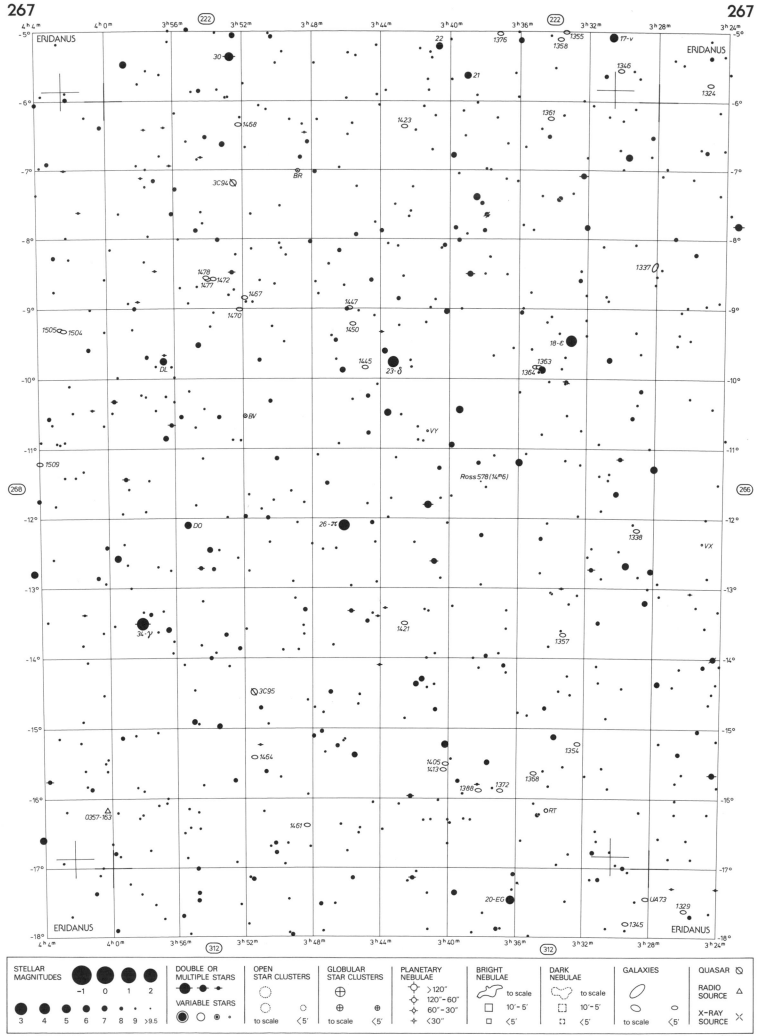

© 1988 WILLMANN-BELL, INC.

Barry Rappaport & Wil Tirion

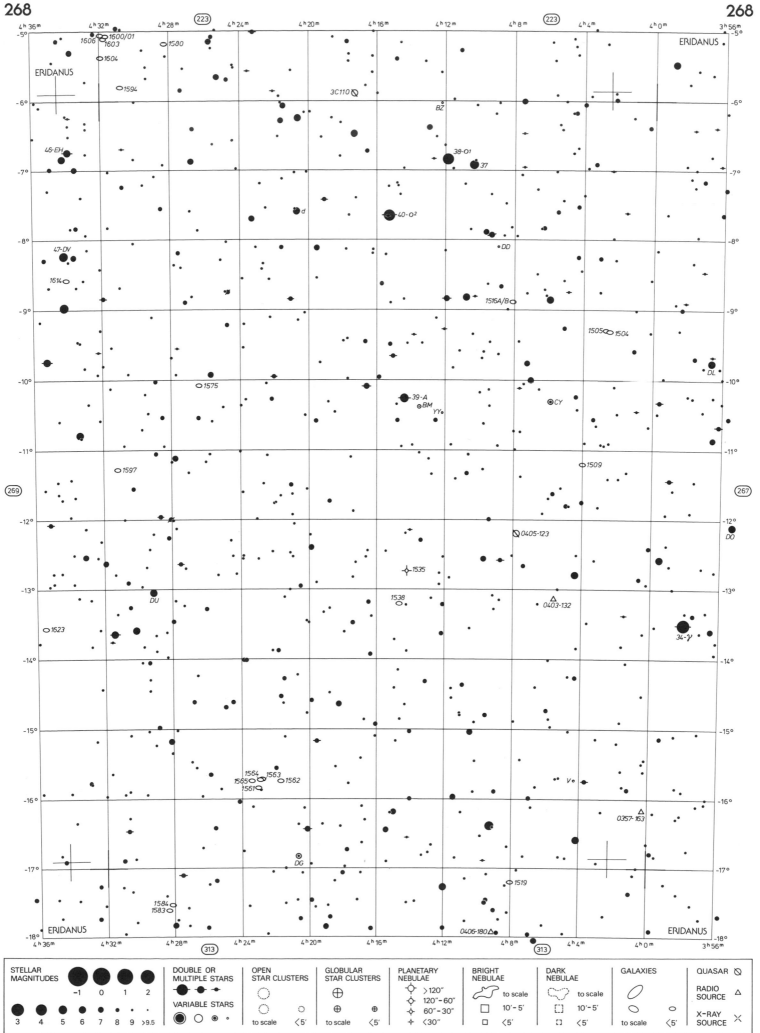

© 1988 WILLMANN-BELL, INC.

Barry Rappaport & Wil Tirion

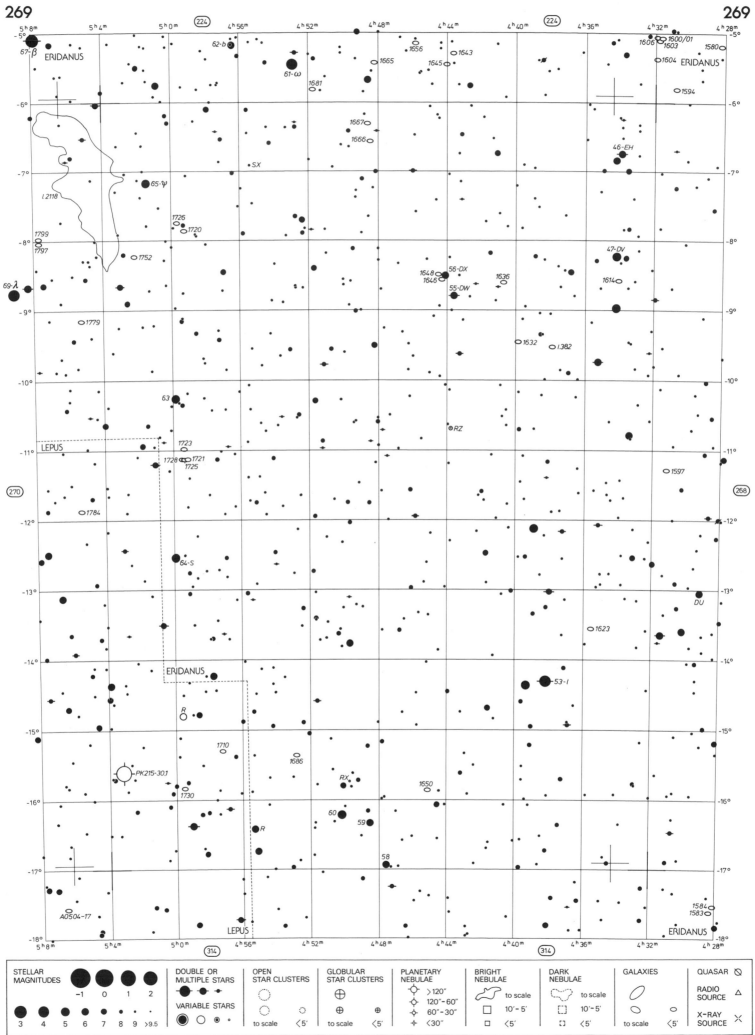

© 1988 WILLMANN-BELL, INC.

Barry Rappaport & Wil Tirion

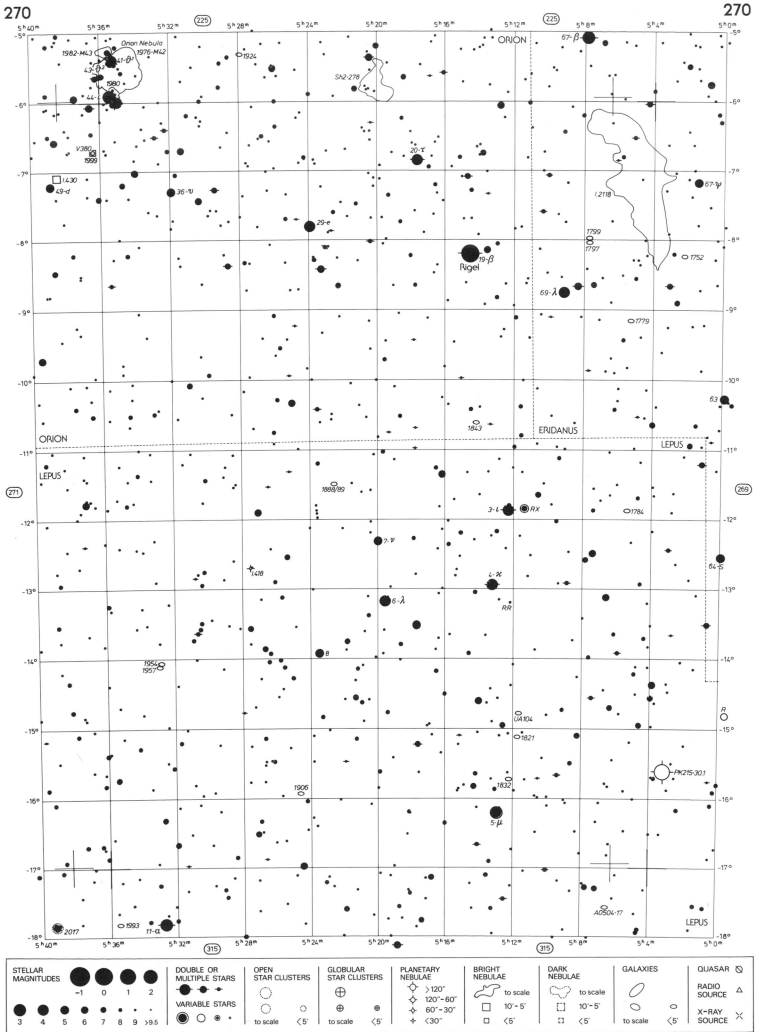

© 1988 WILLMANN-BELL, INC.

Barry Rappaport & Wil Tirion

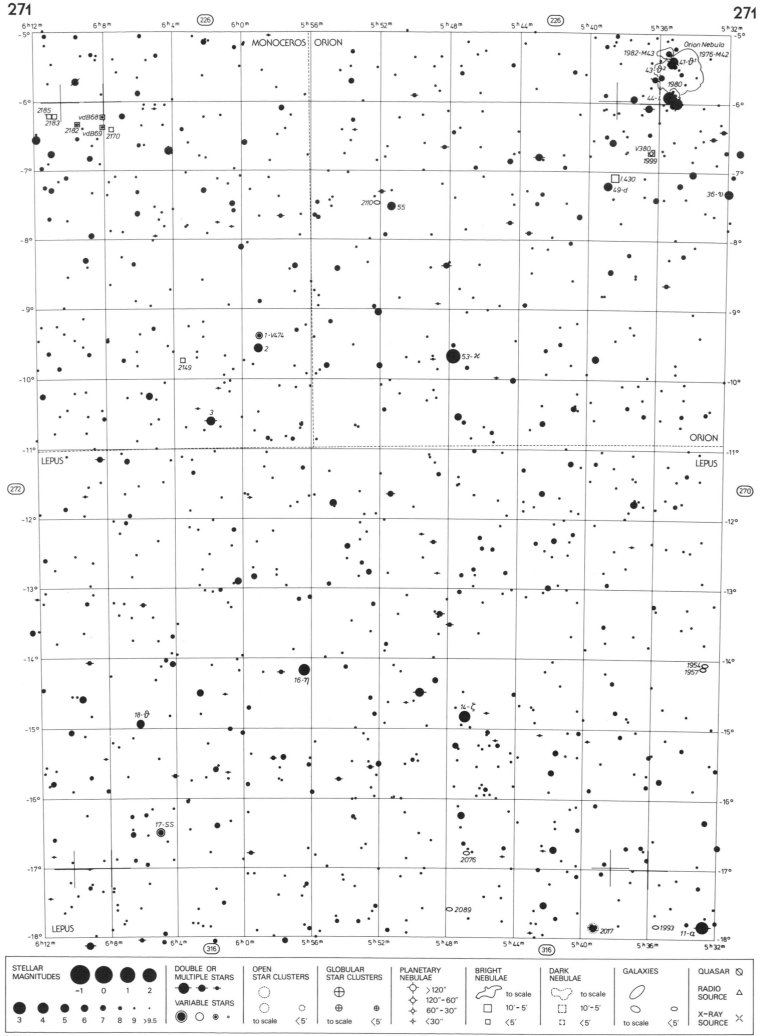

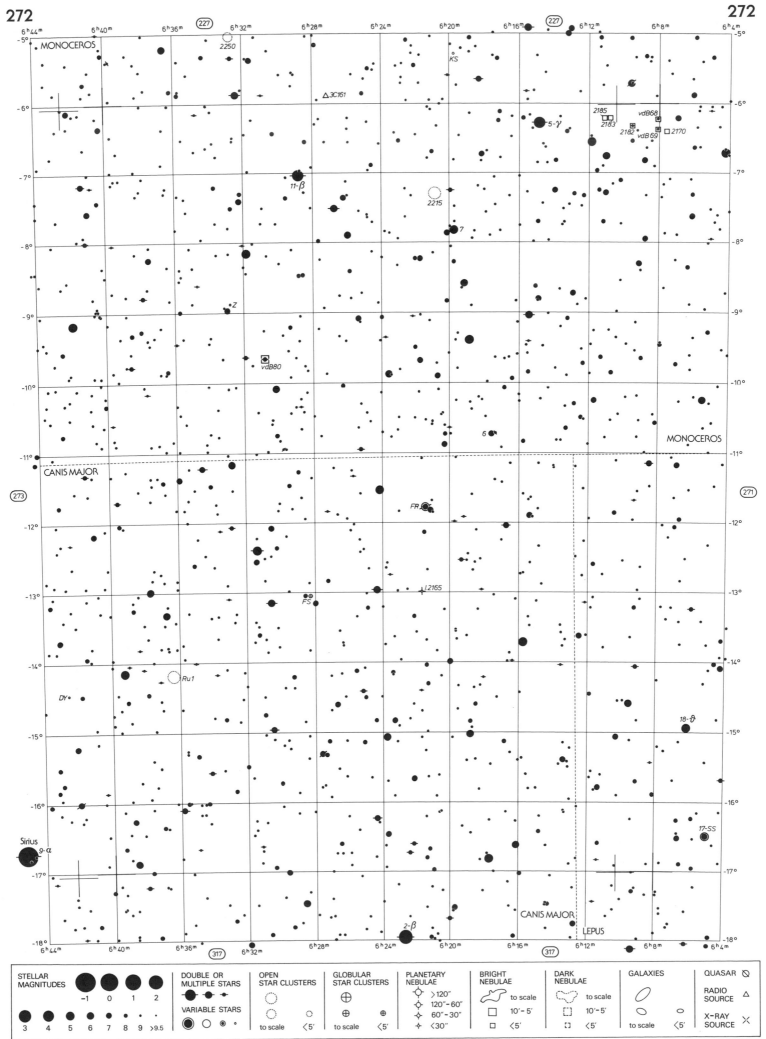

Barry Rappaport & Wil Tirion

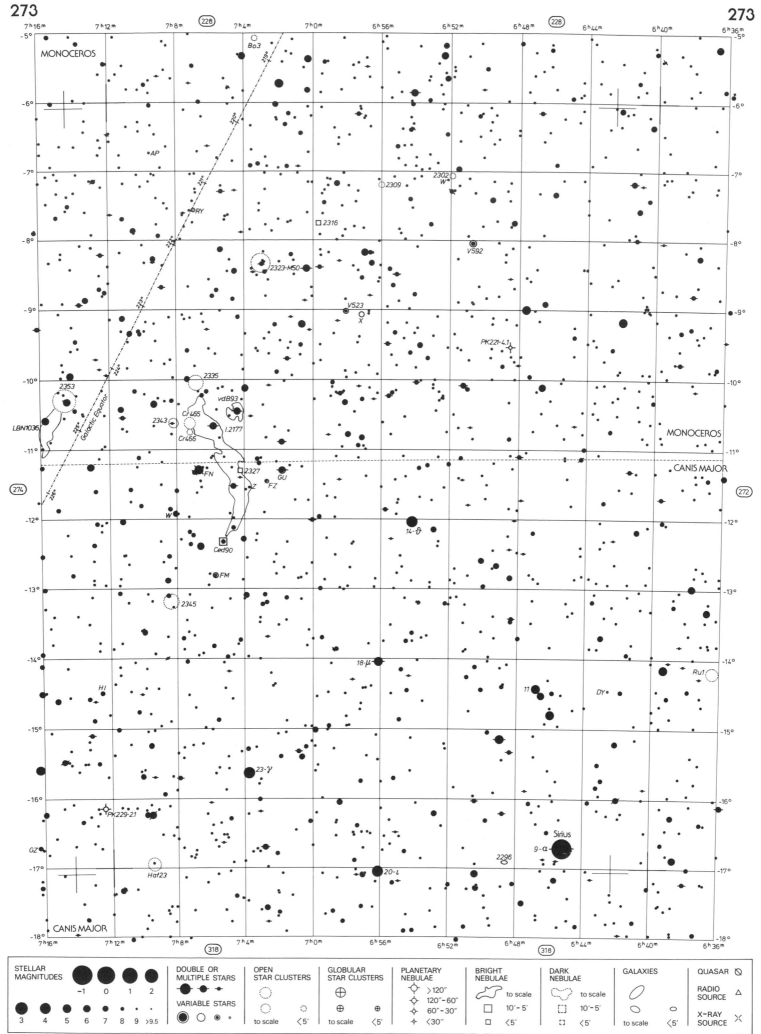

© 1988 WILLMANN-BELL, INC.

Barry Rappaport & Wil Tirion

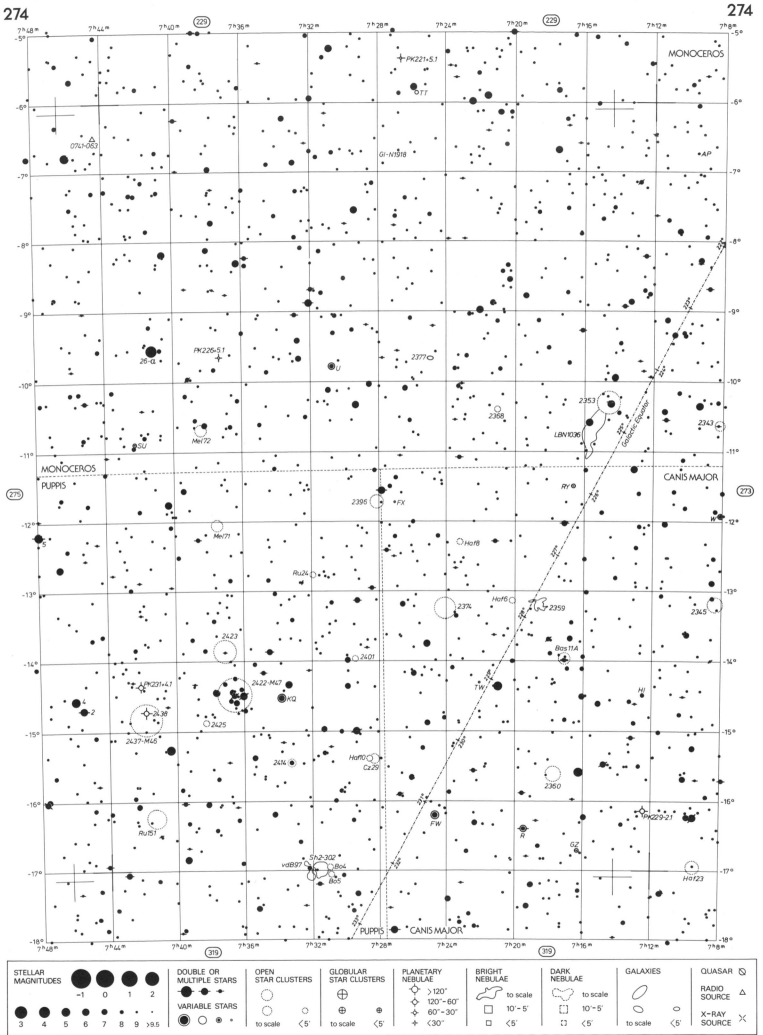

MONOCEROS

PK221+5.1

TT

GI-N1918

AP

0741-063

PK226+5.1

26-α

U

2377

2353

2368

LBN1036

SU

Mel72

2343

MONOCEROS

PUPPIS

RY

CANIS MAJOR

2396 FX

W

5

Mel71

Haf8

Ru24

2374 Haf6 2359

2345

2423

Bas11A

2401

TW

Hl

PK231+4.1

2422-M47

4

2 KQ

2438

2425

2437-M46

2414

Haf10
Cz29

2360

Ru151

FW

R

GZ

PK229-2.1

Sh2-302
vdB97 Bo4
Bo5

Haf23

PUPPIS CANIS MAJOR

© 1988 WILLMANN-BELL, INC.

STELLAR MAGNITUDES				DOUBLE OR MULTIPLE STARS	OPEN STAR CLUSTERS	GLOBULAR STAR CLUSTERS	PLANETARY NEBULAE	BRIGHT NEBULAE	DARK NEBULAE	GALAXIES	QUASAR
-1	0	1	2				>120"	to scale	to scale		RADIO SOURCE
				VARIABLE STARS		⊕	120"-60"	10'-5'	10'-5'		
3 4 5 6 7 8 9 >9.5					to scale <5'	to scale <5'	60"-30" <30"	<5'	<5'	to scale <5'	X-RAY SOURCE

Barry Rappaport & Wil Tirion

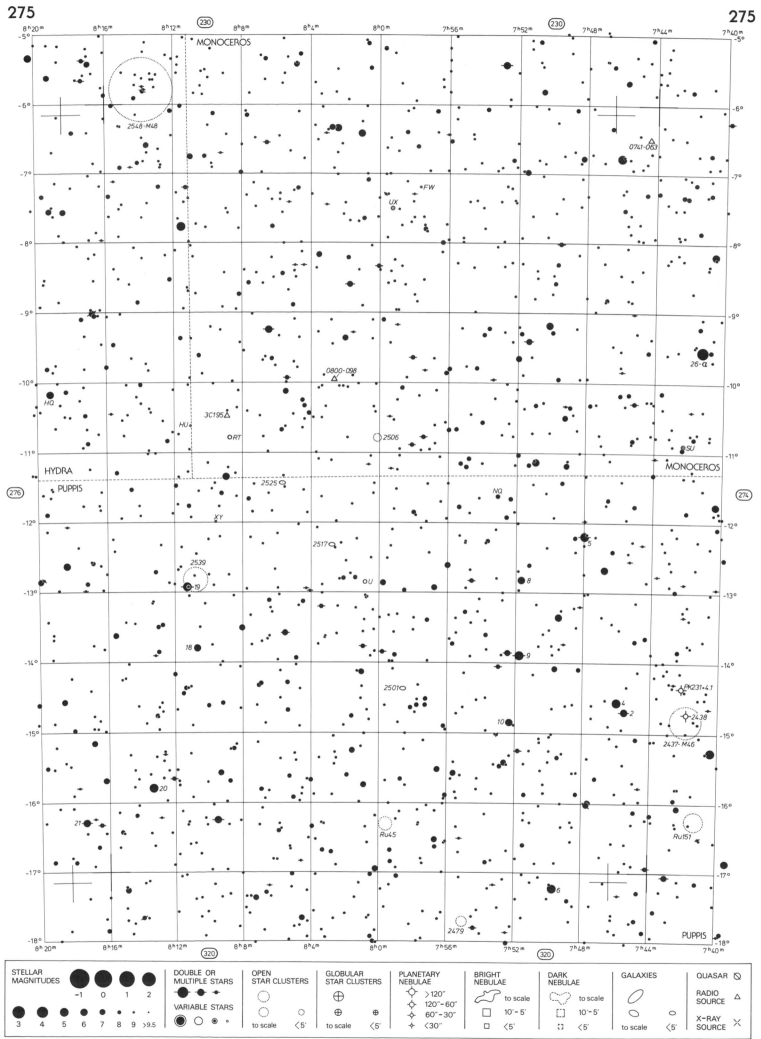

MONOCEROS

2548-M48

0741-063

FW
UX

0800-098

HYDRA

HU
3C195

RT

2506

SU

MONOCEROS

PUPPIS

2525

NQ

XY

2517

5

2539
19

U

8

18

9

2501

PK231+4.1

4
2
2438

10

2437-M46

20

21

6

Ru45

Ru151

2479

PUPPIS

26-α

HQ

© 1988 WILLMANN-BELL, INC.

STELLAR MAGNITUDES					DOUBLE OR MULTIPLE STARS	OPEN STAR CLUSTERS	GLOBULAR STAR CLUSTERS	PLANETARY NEBULAE	BRIGHT NEBULAE	DARK NEBULAE	GALAXIES	QUASAR

-1 0 1 2
3 4 5 6 7 8 9 >9.5

VARIABLE STARS

to scale   <5'

to scale   <5'

>120"
120"-60"
60"-30"
<30"

to scale
10'-5'
<5'

to scale
10'-5'
<5'

to scale
<5'

RADIO SOURCE
X-RAY SOURCE

Barry Rappaport & Wil Tirion

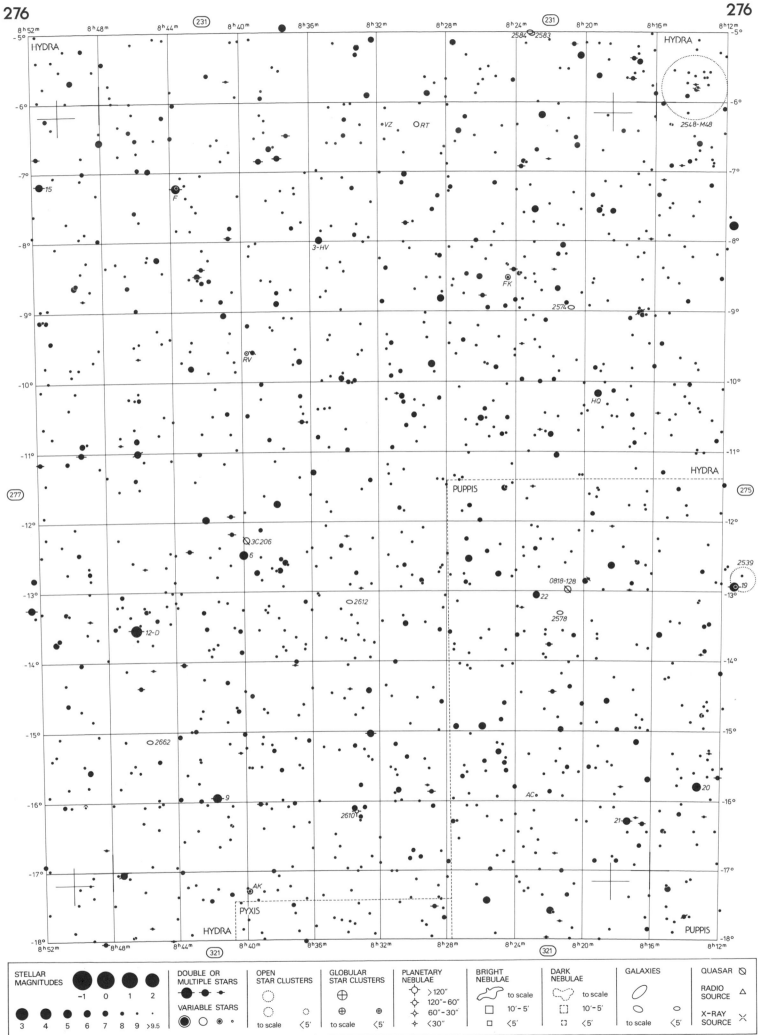

© 1988 WILLMANN-BELL, INC.

Barry Rappaport & Wil Tirion

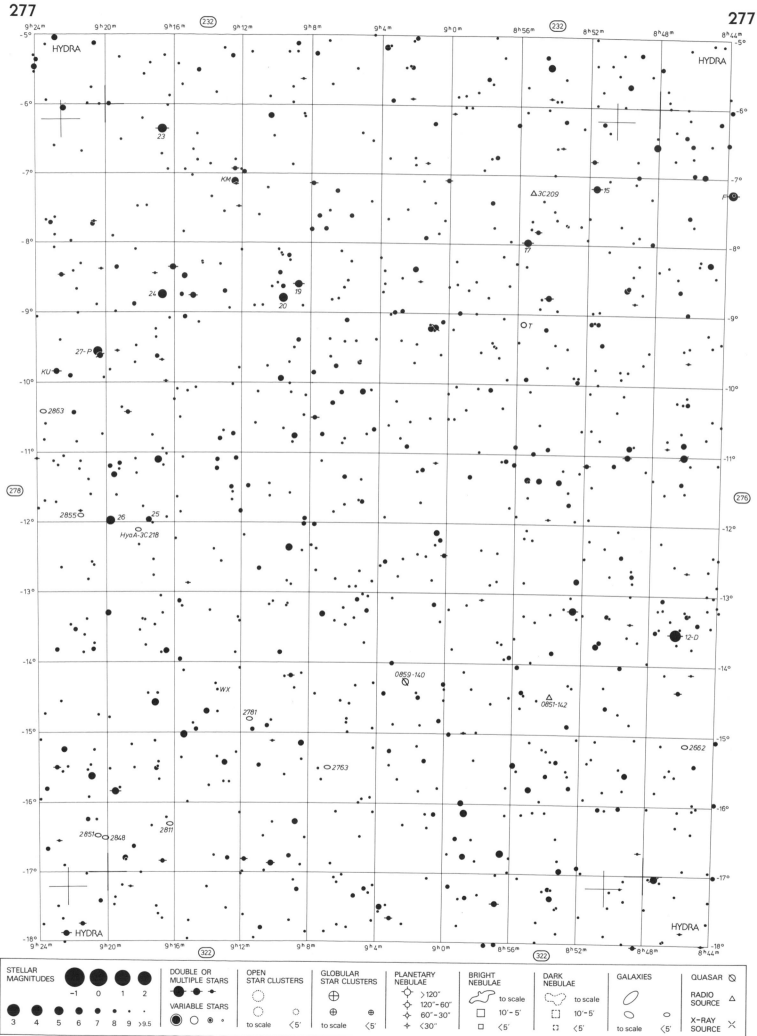

STELLAR MAGNITUDES

−1 0 1 2

3 4 5 6 7 8 9 >9.5

DOUBLE OR MULTIPLE STARS

VARIABLE STARS

OPEN STAR CLUSTERS

to scale   <5'

GLOBULAR STAR CLUSTERS

to scale   <5'

PLANETARY NEBULAE

>120"
120"−60"
60"−30"
<30"

BRIGHT NEBULAE

to scale
10'−5'
<5'

DARK NEBULAE

to scale
10'−5'
<5'

GALAXIES

to scale   <5'

QUASAR

RADIO SOURCE

X−RAY SOURCE

© 1988 WILLMANN-BELL, INC.

Barry Rappaport & Wil Tirion

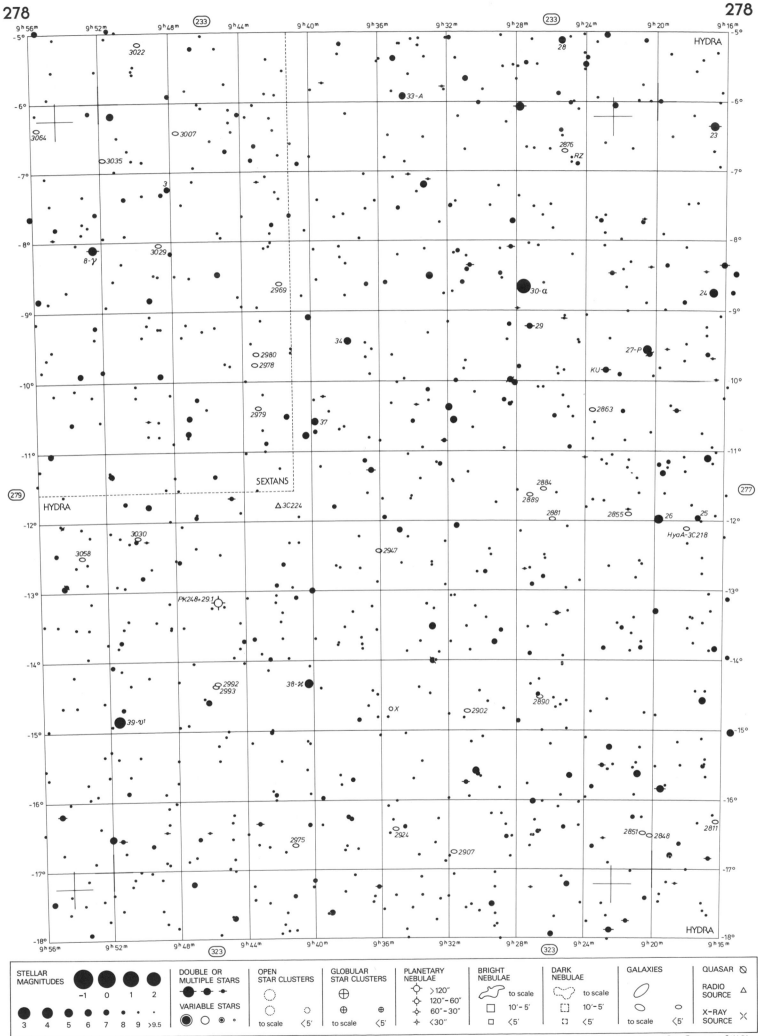

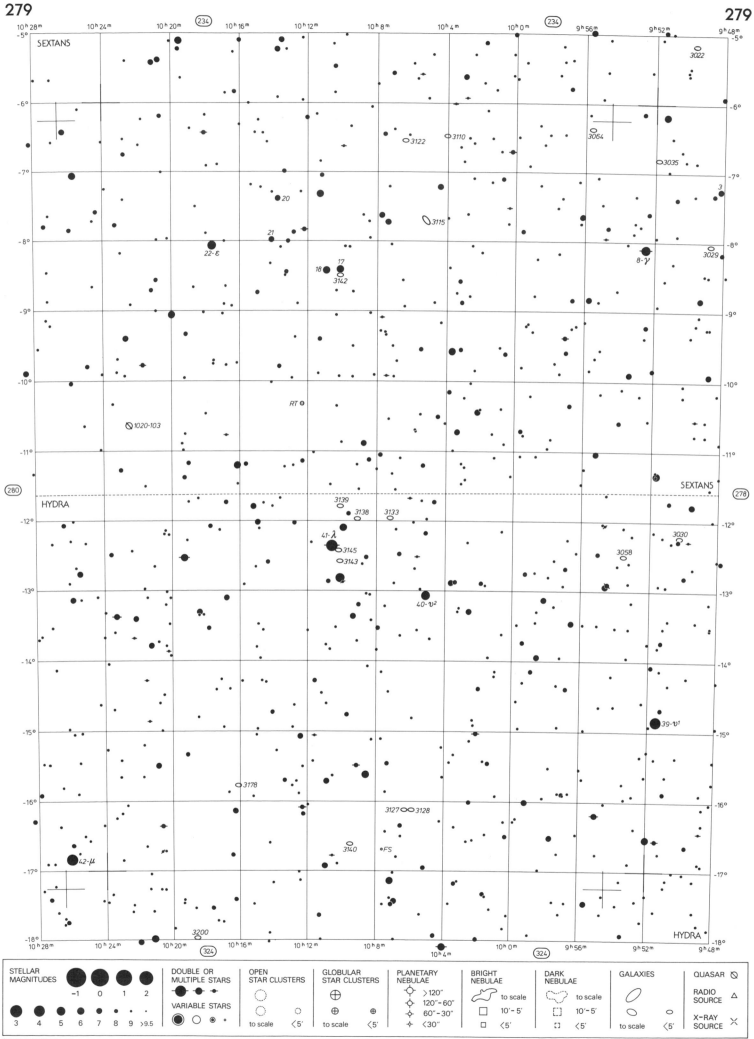

© 1988 WILLMANN-BELL, INC.

Barry Rappaport & Wil Tirion

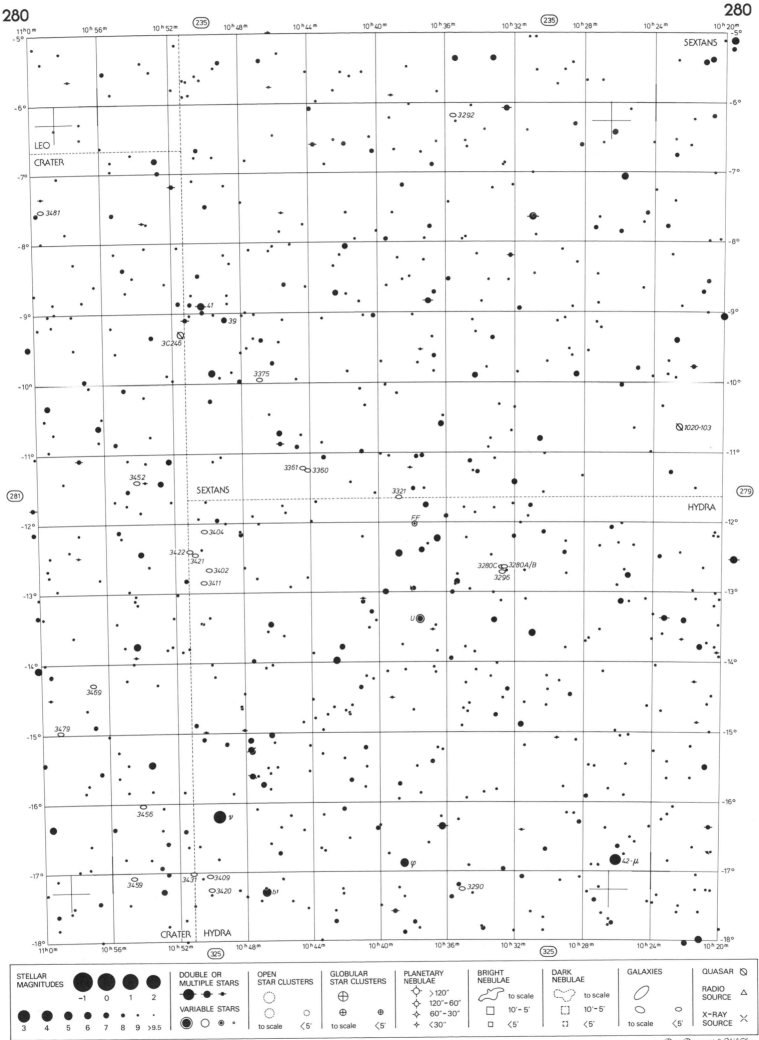

SEXTANS

LEO

CRATER

3481

41

39

3C246

3375

3452

SEXTANS

3361 3360

3321

FF

3404

3422

3421

3402

3411

3469

3479

3456

v

3459

3431

3409

3420

b1

φ

CRATER   HYDRA

3292

1020-103

3280C 3280A/B
3296

U

42-μ

3290

HYDRA

STELLAR MAGNITUDES	DOUBLE OR MULTIPLE STARS	OPEN STAR CLUSTERS	GLOBULAR STAR CLUSTERS	PLANETARY NEBULAE	BRIGHT NEBULAE	DARK NEBULAE	GALAXIES	QUASAR

STELLAR MAGNITUDES -1 0 1 2

3 4 5 6 7 8 9 >9.5

DOUBLE OR MULTIPLE STARS

VARIABLE STARS

OPEN STAR CLUSTERS   to scale   <5'

GLOBULAR STAR CLUSTERS   to scale   <5'

PLANETARY NEBULAE
>120"
120"-60"
60"-30"
<30"

BRIGHT NEBULAE
to scale
10'-5'
<5'

DARK NEBULAE
to scale
10'-5'
<5'

GALAXIES
to scale
<5'

QUASAR

RADIO SOURCE

X-RAY SOURCE

© 1988 WILLMANN-BELL, INC.

Barry Rappaport & Wil Tirion

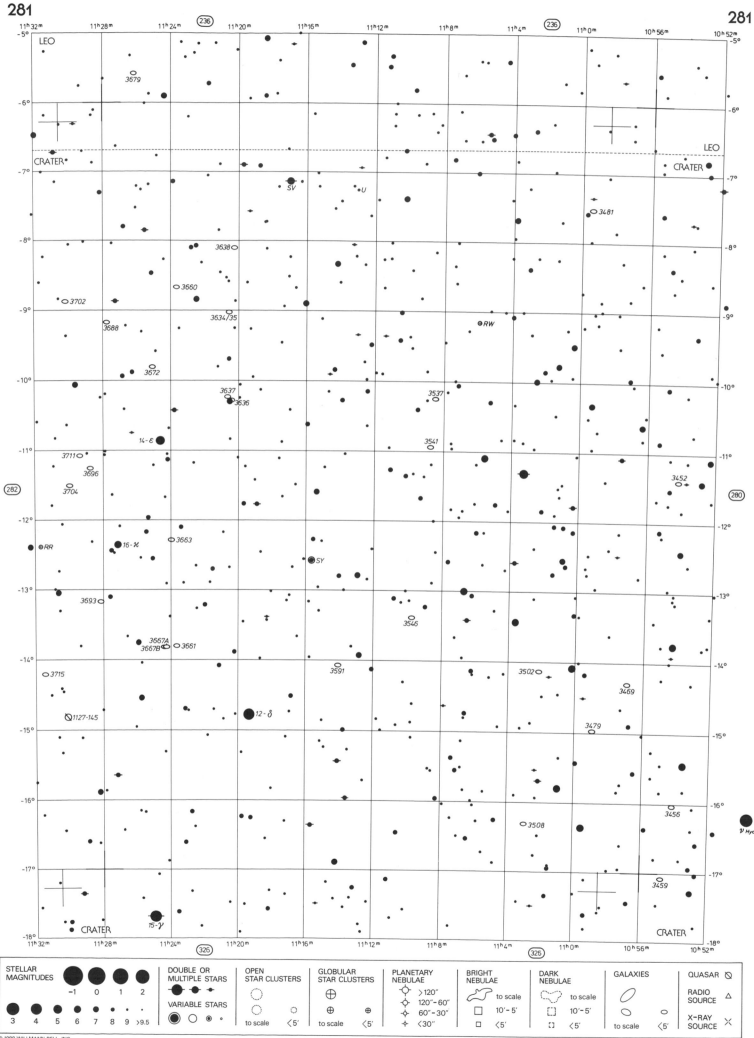

© 1988 WILLMANN-BELL, INC.

Barry Rappaport & Wil Tirion

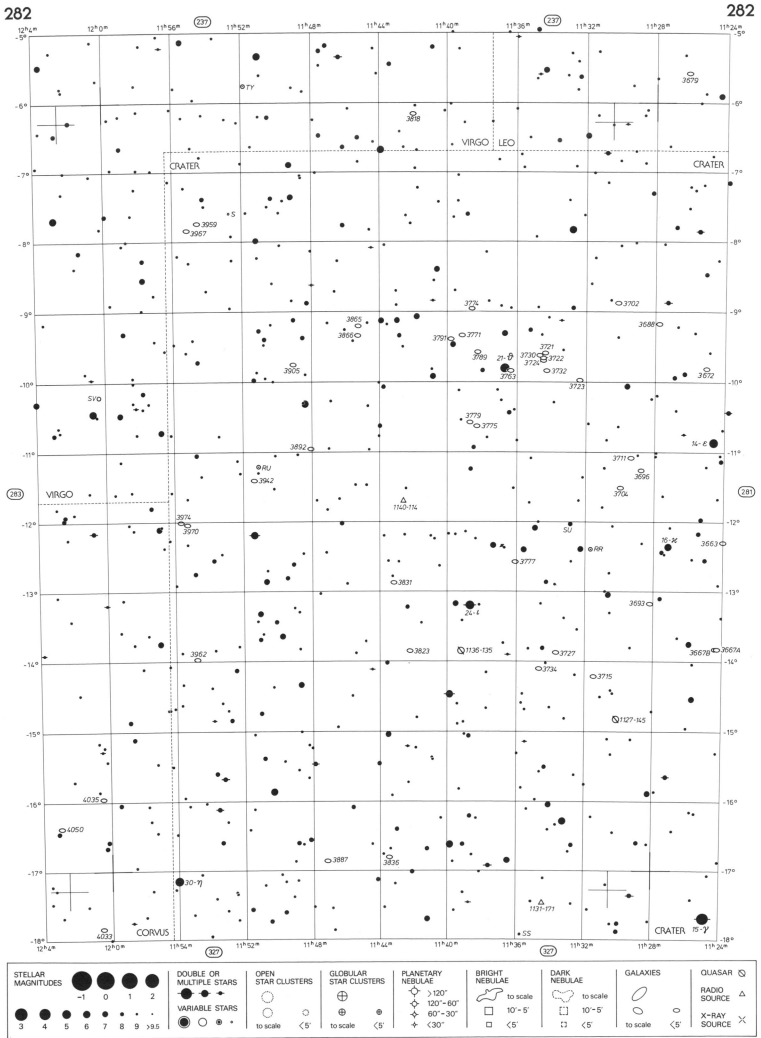

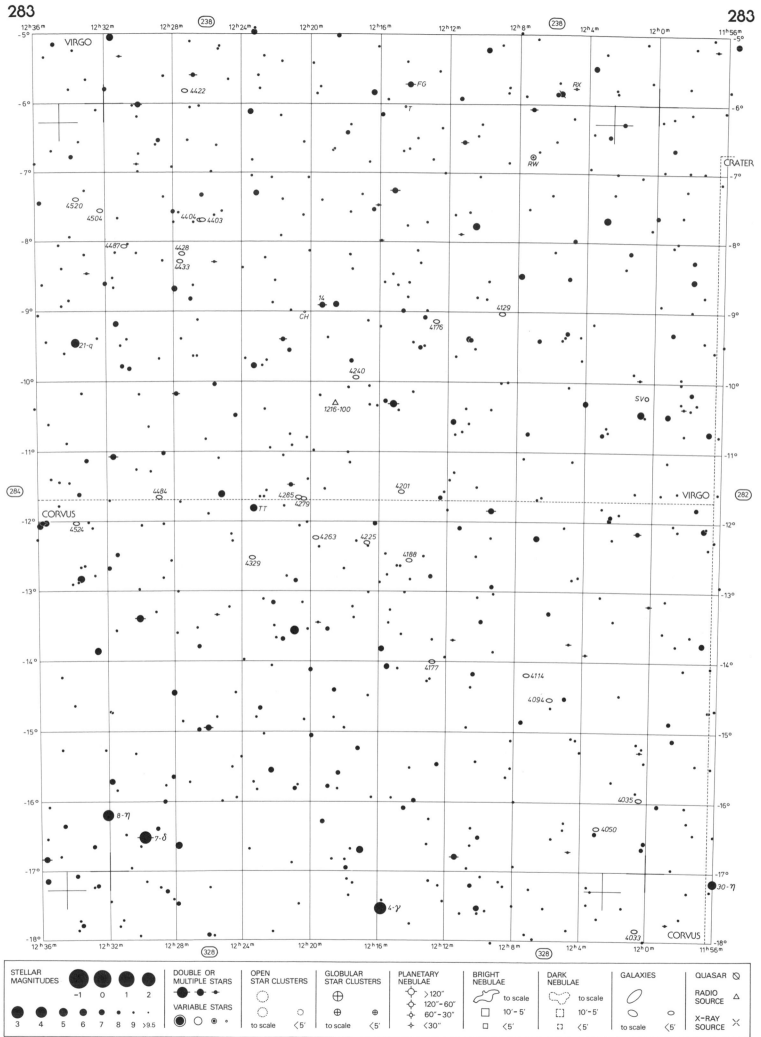

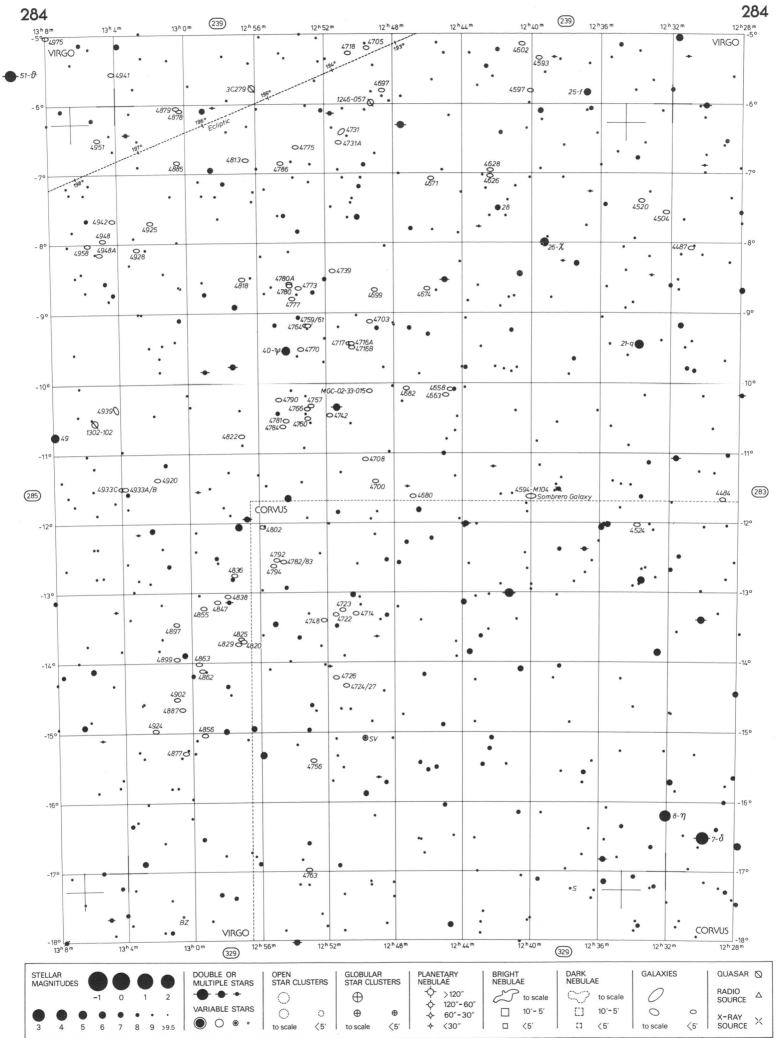

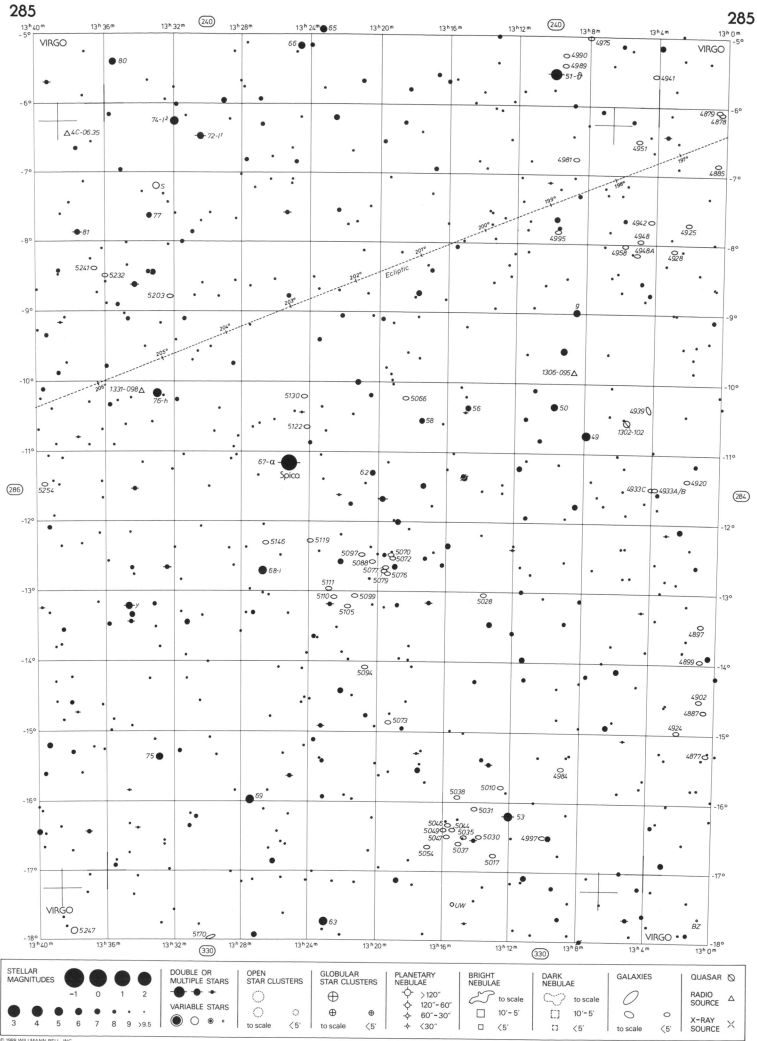

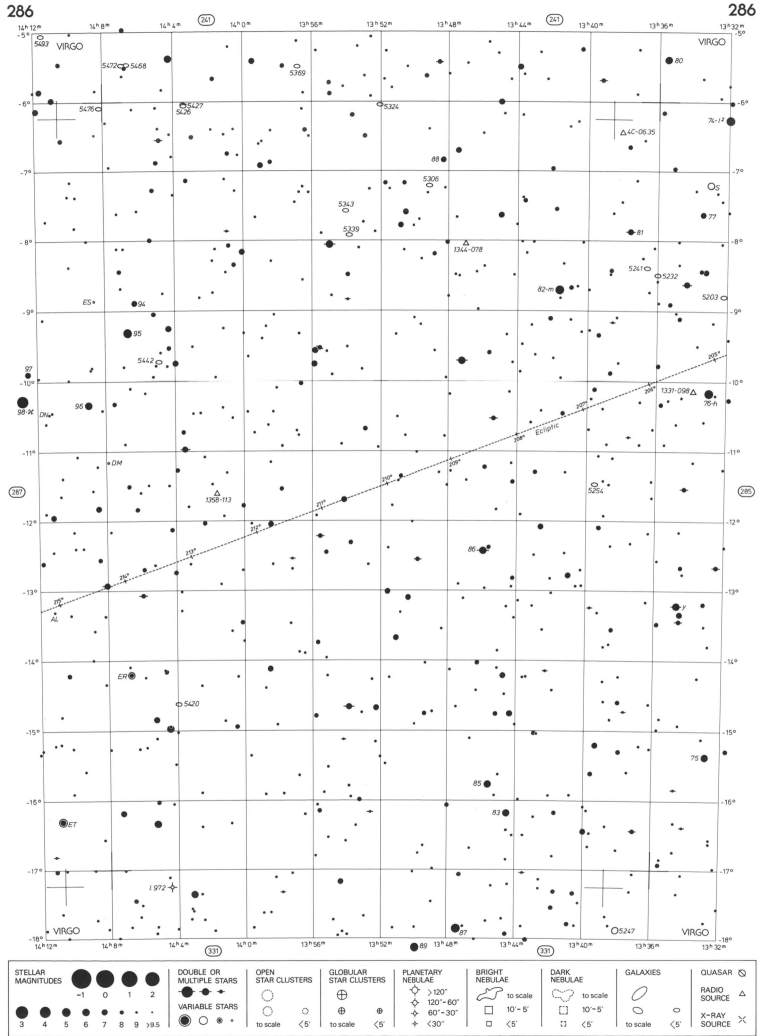

STELLAR MAGNITUDES
-1 0 1 2
3 4 5 6 7 8 9 >9.5

DOUBLE OR MULTIPLE STARS

VARIABLE STARS

OPEN STAR CLUSTERS
to scale <5'

GLOBULAR STAR CLUSTERS
to scale <5'

PLANETARY NEBULAE
>120"
120"-60"
60"-30"
<30"

BRIGHT NEBULAE
to scale
10'-5'
<5'

DARK NEBULAE
to scale
10'-5'
<5'

GALAXIES
to scale <5'

QUASAR

RADIO SOURCE

X-RAY SOURCE

© 1988 WILLMANN-BELL, INC.

Barry Rappaport & Wil Tirion

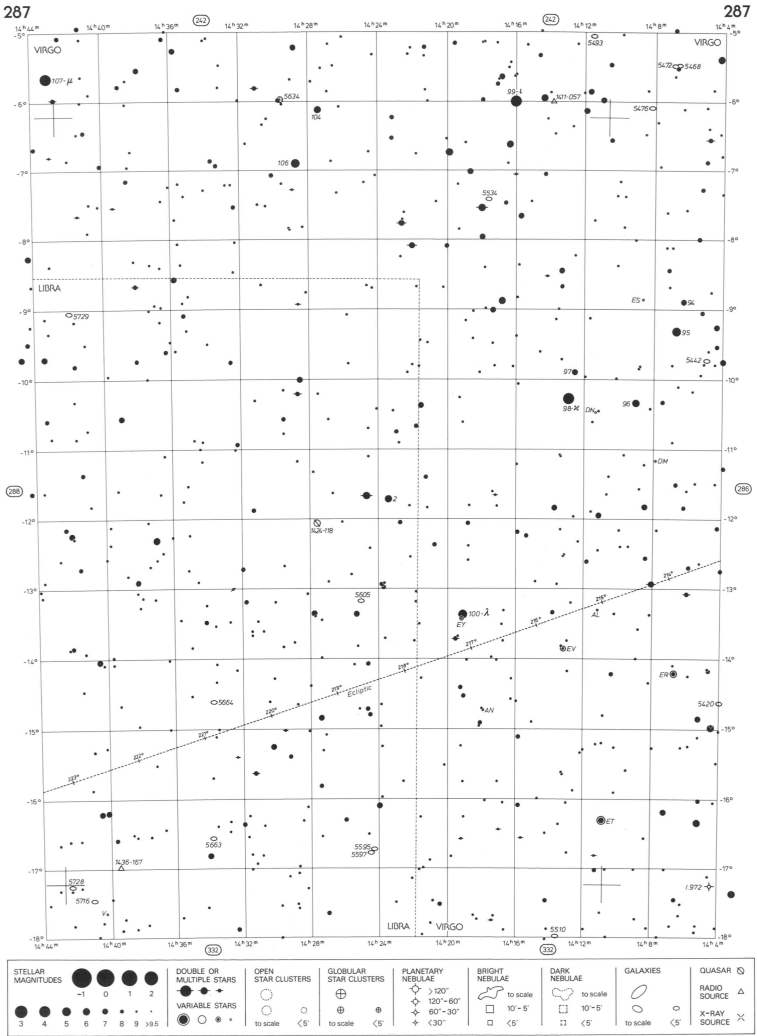

© 1988 WILLMANN-BELL, INC.

Barry Rappaport & Wil Tirion

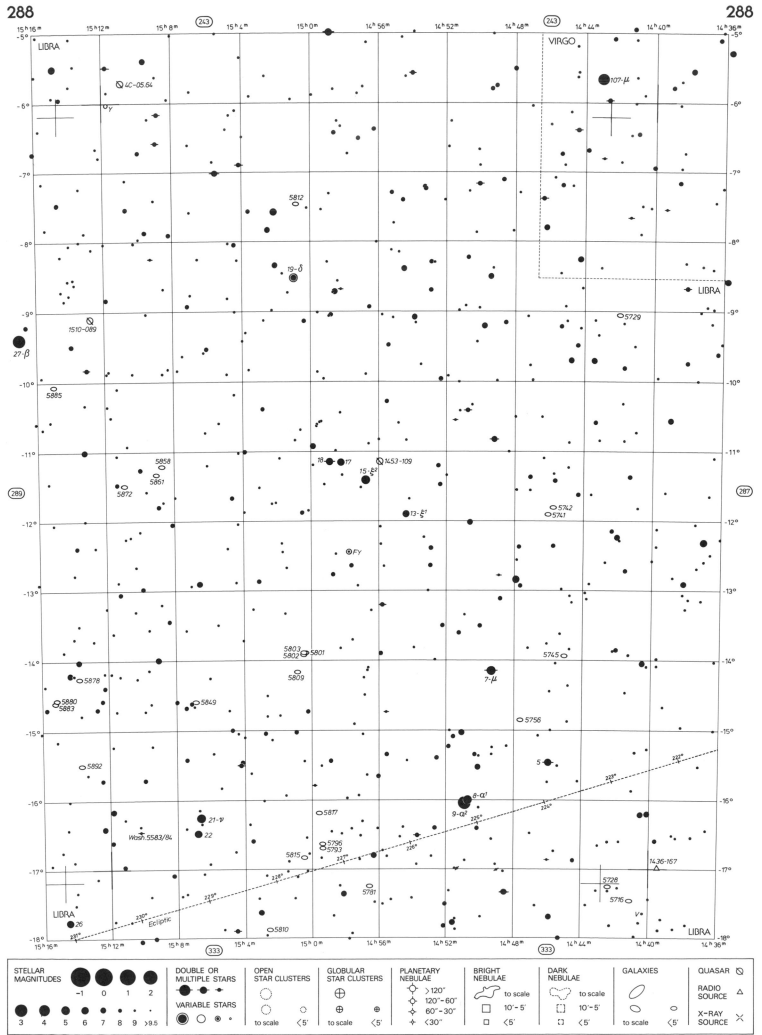

© 1988 WILLMANN-BELL, INC.

Barry Rappaport & Wil Tirion

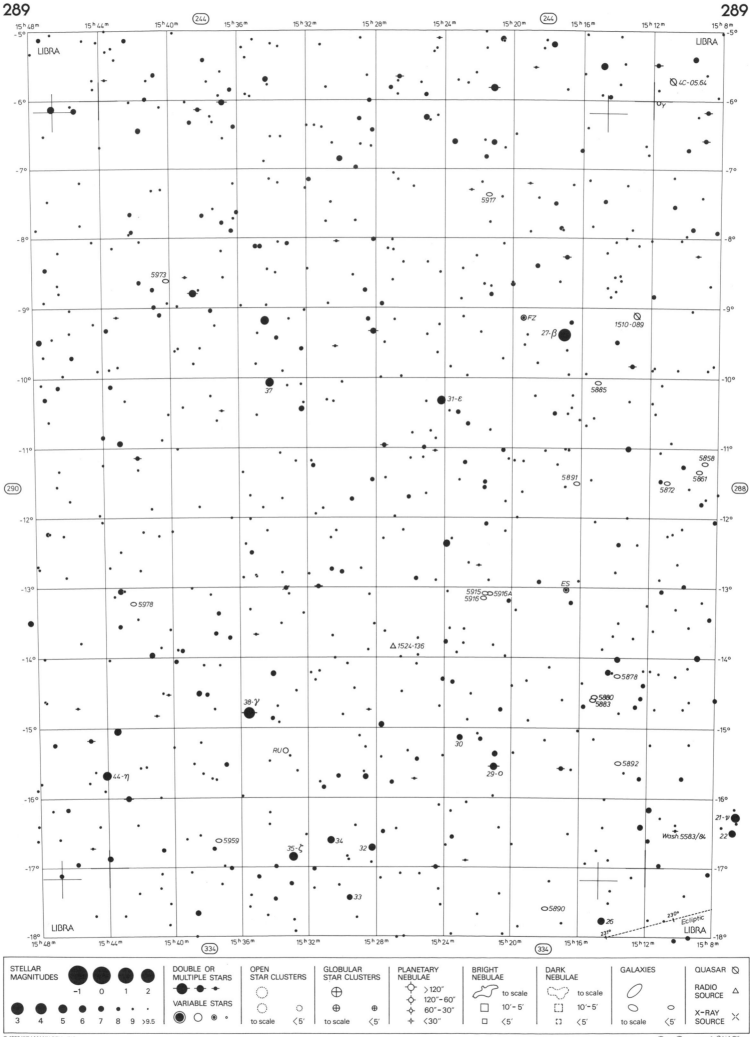

© 1988 WILLMANN-BELL, INC.

Barry Rappaport & Wil Tirion

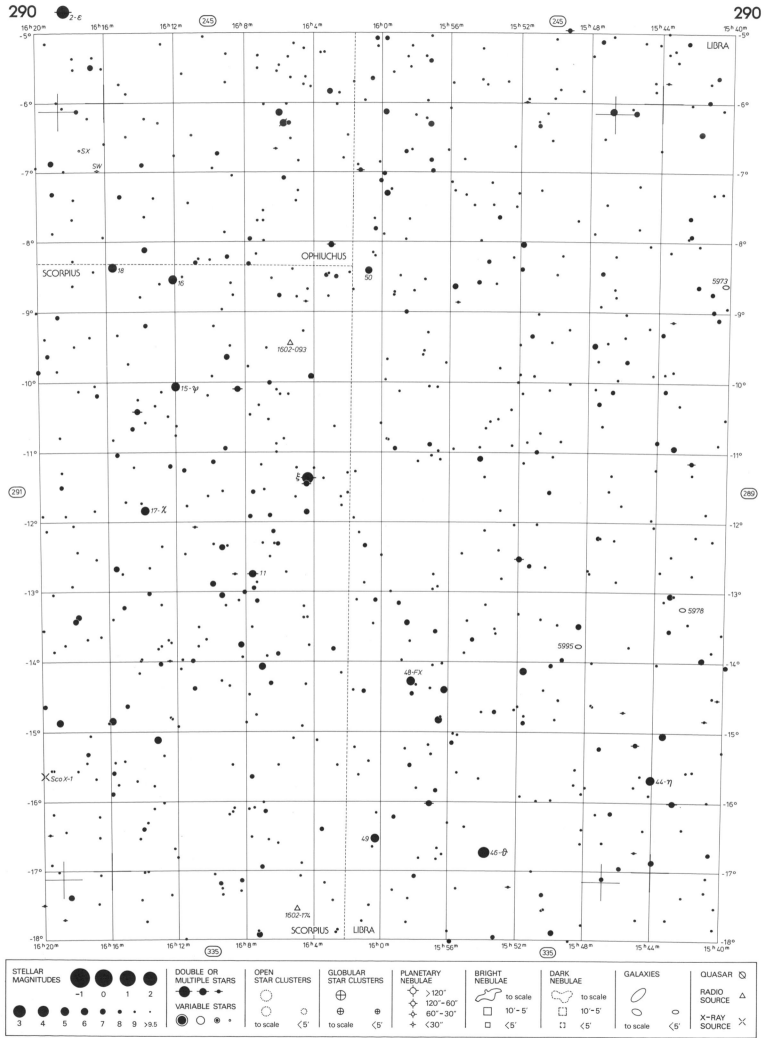

2-ε

245

LIBRA

SX

SW

SCORPIUS

18

16

OPHIUCHUS

50

5973

1602-093

15-ψ

291

289

17-χ

ξ

11

5978

5995

48-FX

Sco X-1

44-η

49

46-ϑ

1602-174

SCORPIUS

LIBRA

335

335

STELLAR MAGNITUDES
-1 0 1 2
3 4 5 6 7 8 9 >9.5

DOUBLE OR MULTIPLE STARS

VARIABLE STARS

OPEN STAR CLUSTERS
to scale <5'

GLOBULAR STAR CLUSTERS
⊕ ⊕
to scale <5'

PLANETARY NEBULAE
◇ >120"
◇ 120"-60"
◇ 60"-30"
✦ <30"

BRIGHT NEBULAE
to scale
□ 10'-5'
□ <5'

DARK NEBULAE
to scale
⌐⌐ 10'-5'
⌐⌐ <5'

GALAXIES
to scale <5'

QUASAR ⊘

RADIO SOURCE △

X-RAY SOURCE ✕

© 1988 WILLMANN-BELL, INC.

Barry Rappaport & Wil Tirion

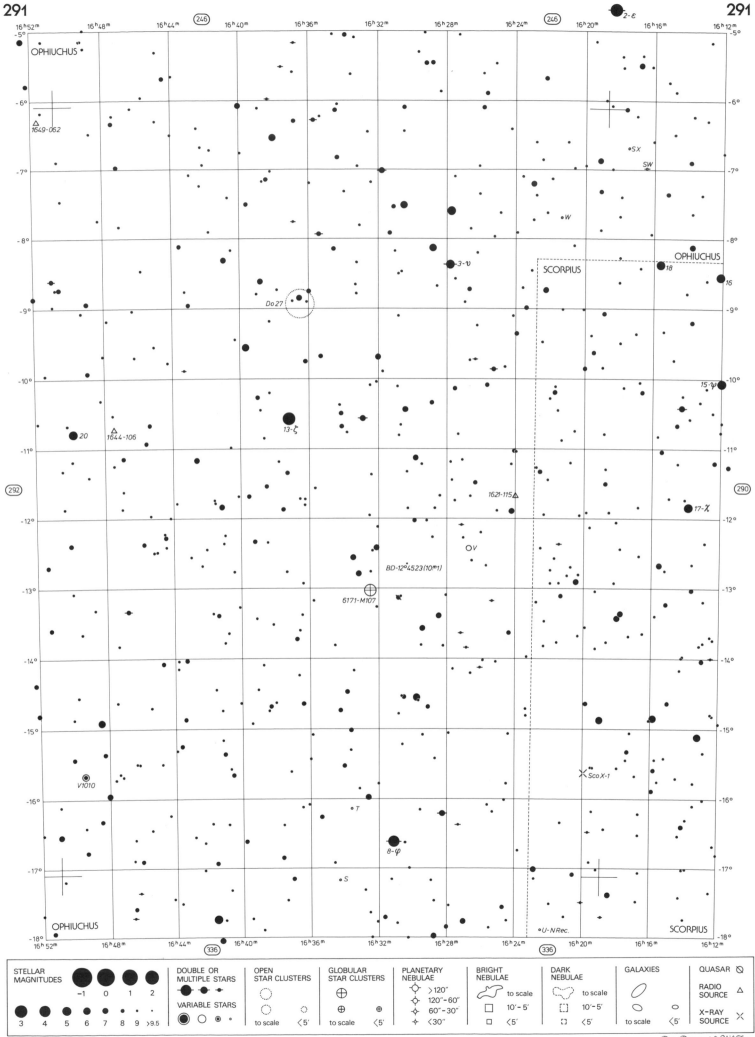

OPHIUCHUS

SCORPIUS

OPHIUCHUS

SCORPIUS

1649-062

1644-106

1621-115

6171-M107

BD-12°4523(10ᵐ1)

Do 27

13-ζ

3-υ

2-ε

18

16

15-ψ

17-χ

20

SX

SW

W

V

T

S

8-φ

V1010

Sco X-1

U-N Rec.

246

246

292

290

336

336

© 1988 WILLMANN-BELL, INC.

Barry Rappaport & Wil Tirion

STELLAR MAGNITUDES					DOUBLE OR MULTIPLE STARS	OPEN STAR CLUSTERS	GLOBULAR STAR CLUSTERS	PLANETARY NEBULAE		BRIGHT NEBULAE		DARK NEBULAE		GALAXIES		QUASAR
-1	0	1	2					>120"		to scale		to scale				
								120"-60"		10'-5'		10'-5'				RADIO SOURCE
3	4	5 6 7 8 9	>9.5		VARIABLE STARS	to scale <5'	to scale <5'	60"-30" <30"		<5'		<5'		to scale <5'		X-RAY SOURCE

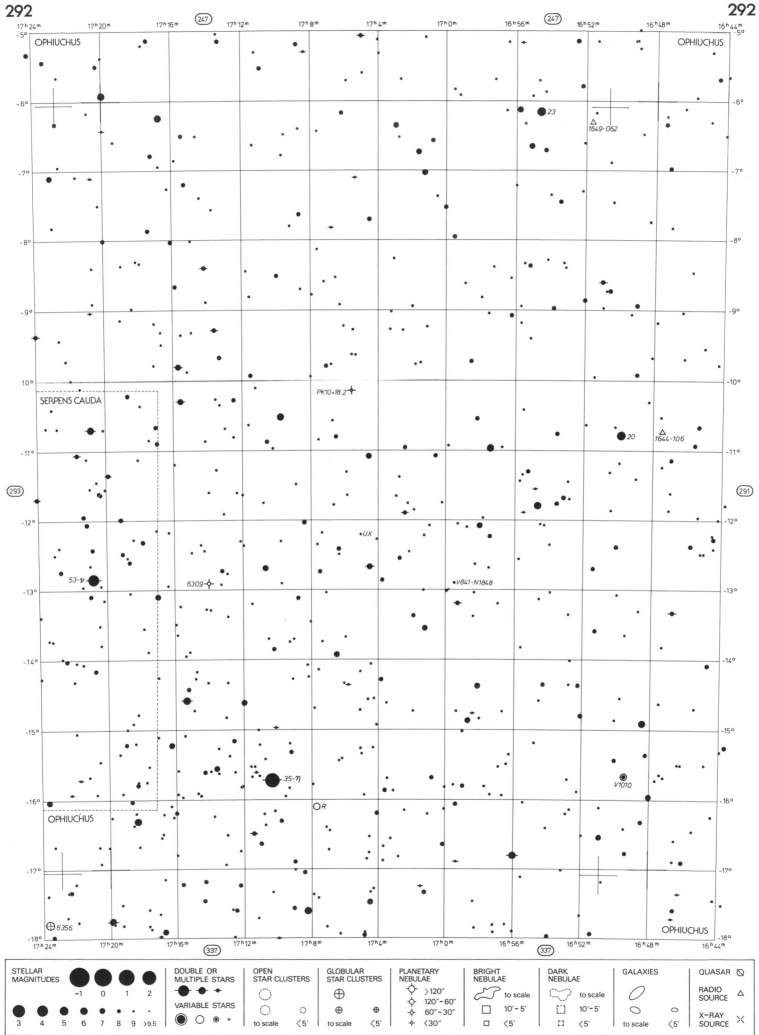

OPHIUCHUS

OPHIUCHUS

SERPENS CAUDA

OPHIUCHUS

OPHIUCHUS

PK10+18.2

53-ν

6309

UX

V841-N1848

20

1644-106

23

1649-062

V1010

35-η

R

6356

© 1988 WILLMANN-BELL, INC.

Barry Rappaport & Wil Tirion

STELLAR MAGNITUDES		DOUBLE OR MULTIPLE STARS	OPEN STAR CLUSTERS	GLOBULAR STAR CLUSTERS	PLANETARY NEBULAE	BRIGHT NEBULAE	DARK NEBULAE	GALAXIES	QUASAR
-1 0 1 2		VARIABLE STARS	to scale <5'	<5'	>120" 120"-60" 60"-30" <30"	to scale 10'-5' <5'	to scale 10'-5' <5'	to scale <5'	RADIO SOURCE X-RAY SOURCE
3 4 5 6 7 8 9 >9.5									

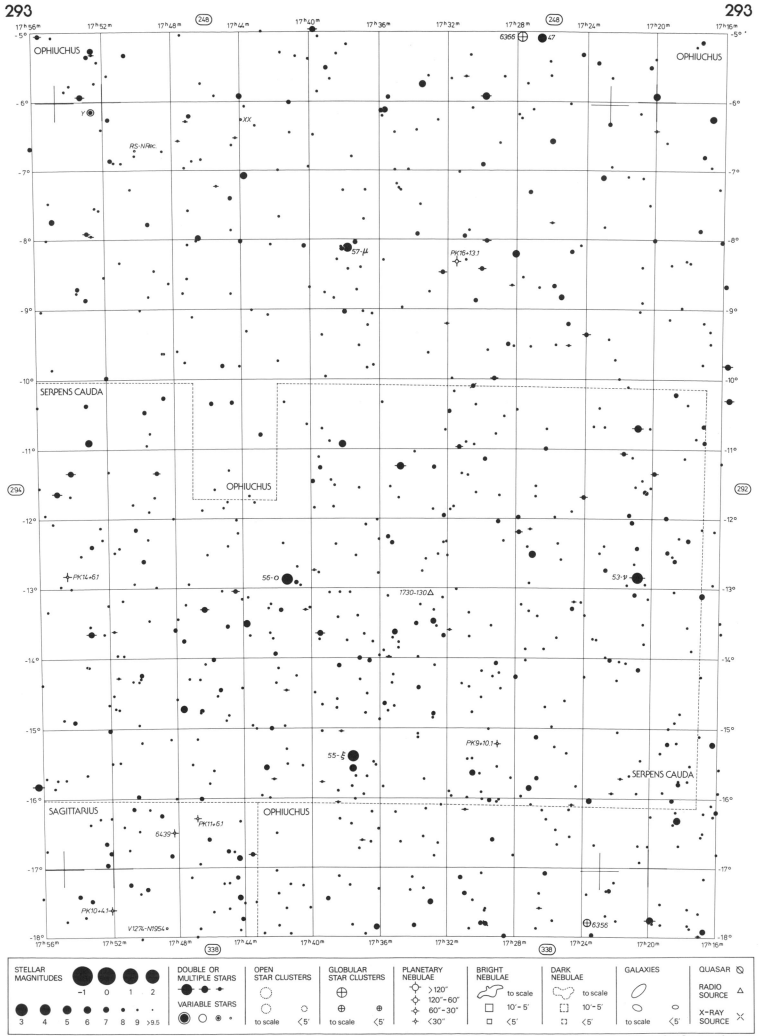

© 1988 WILLMANN-BELL, INC.

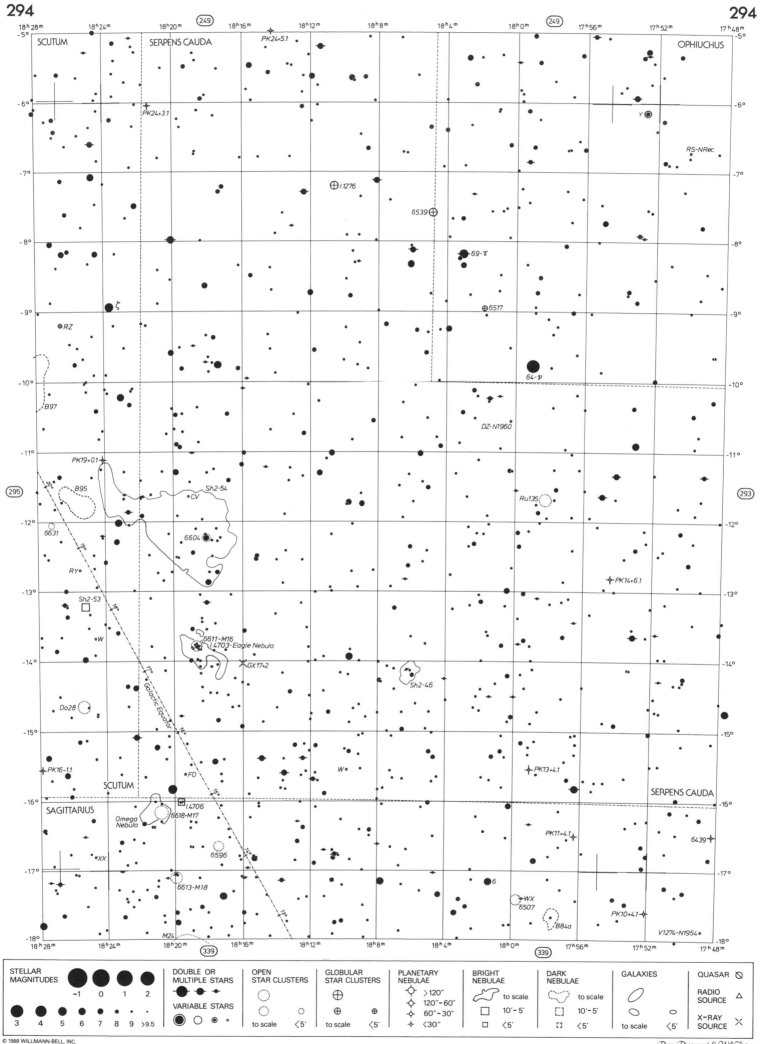

© 1988 WILLMANN-BELL, INC.

Barry Rappaport & Wil Tirion

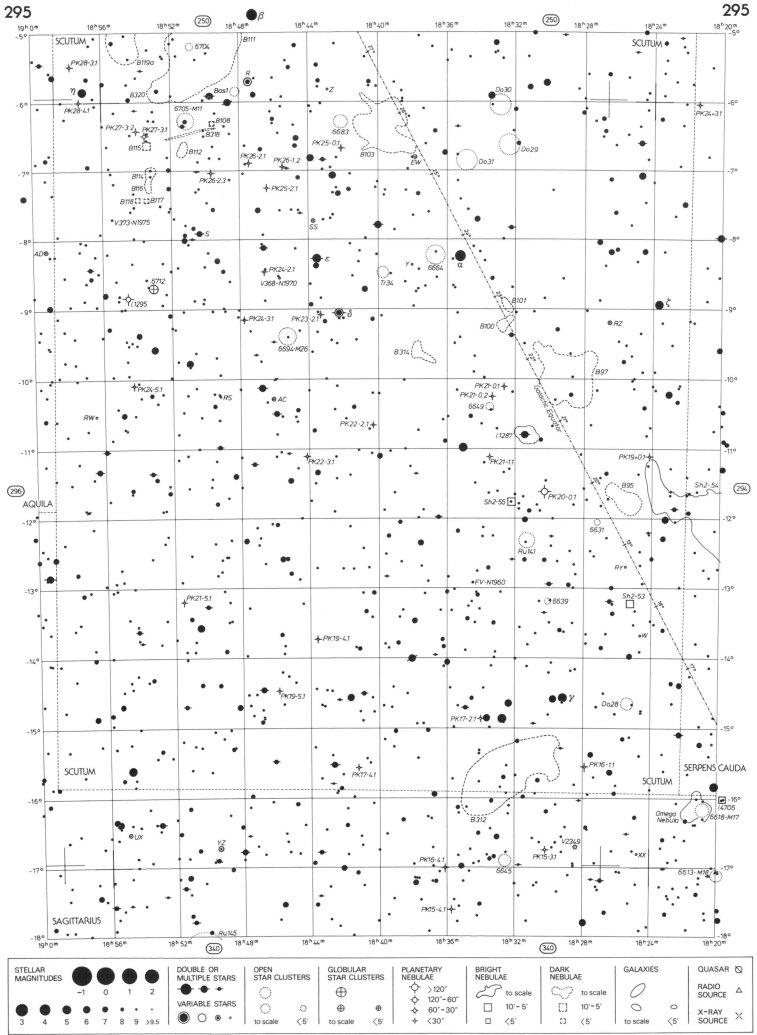

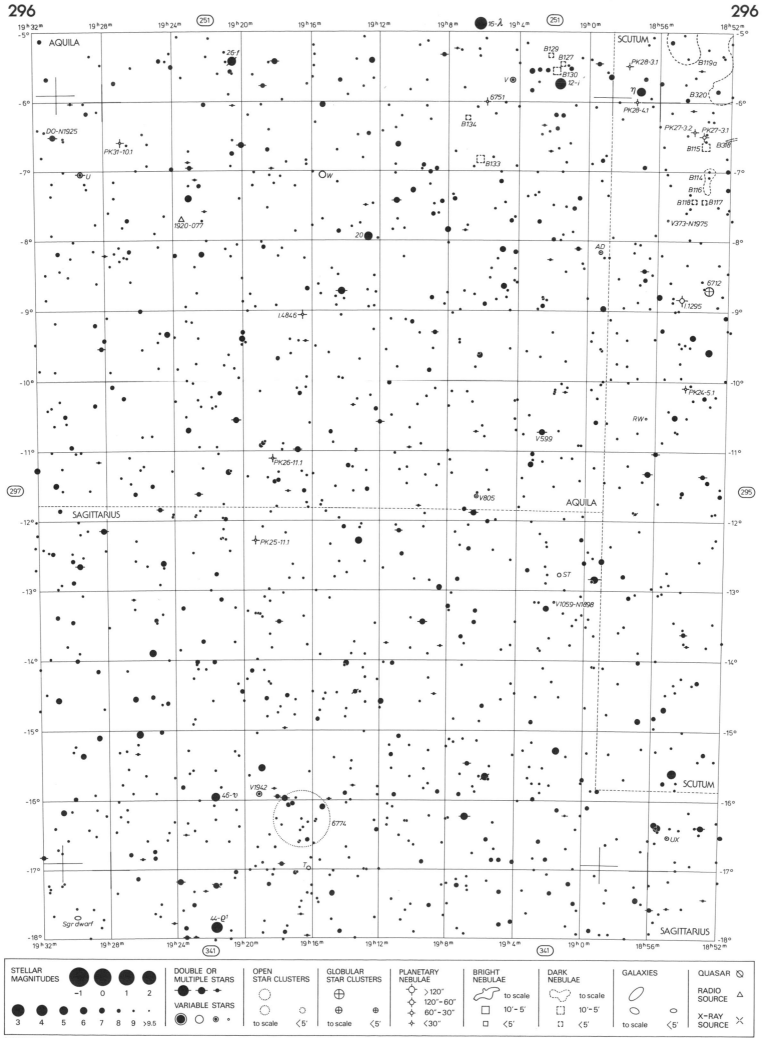

© 1988 WILLMANN-BELL, INC.

Barry Rappaport & Wil Tirion

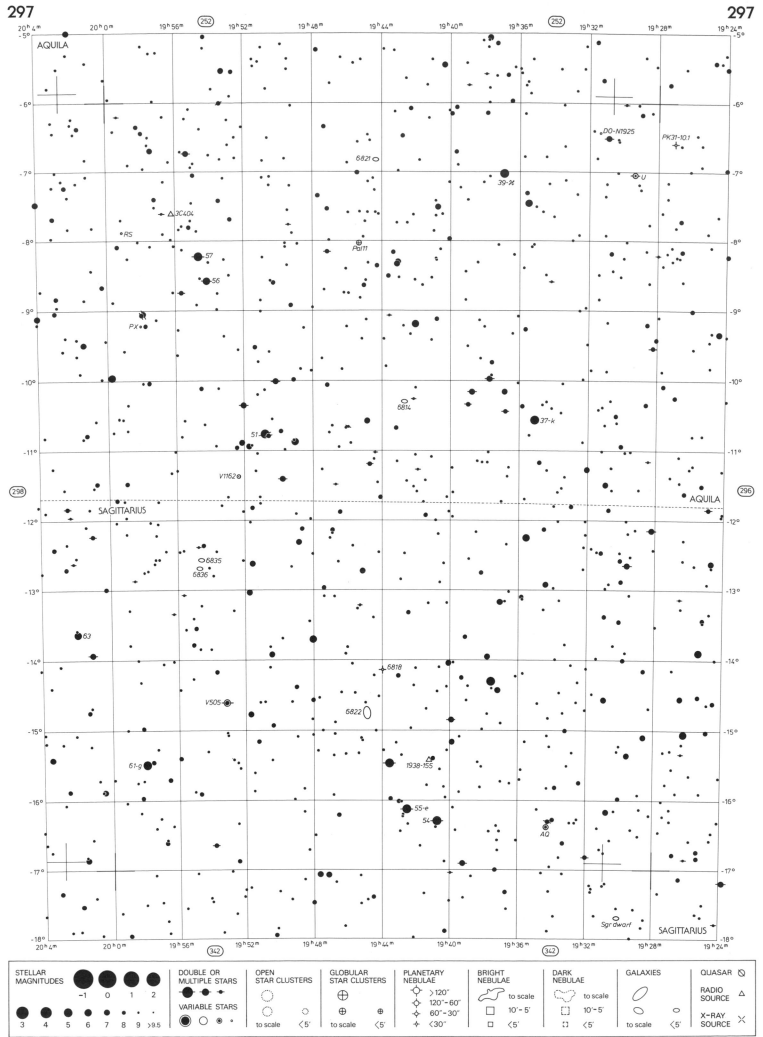

Barry Rappaport & Wil Tirion

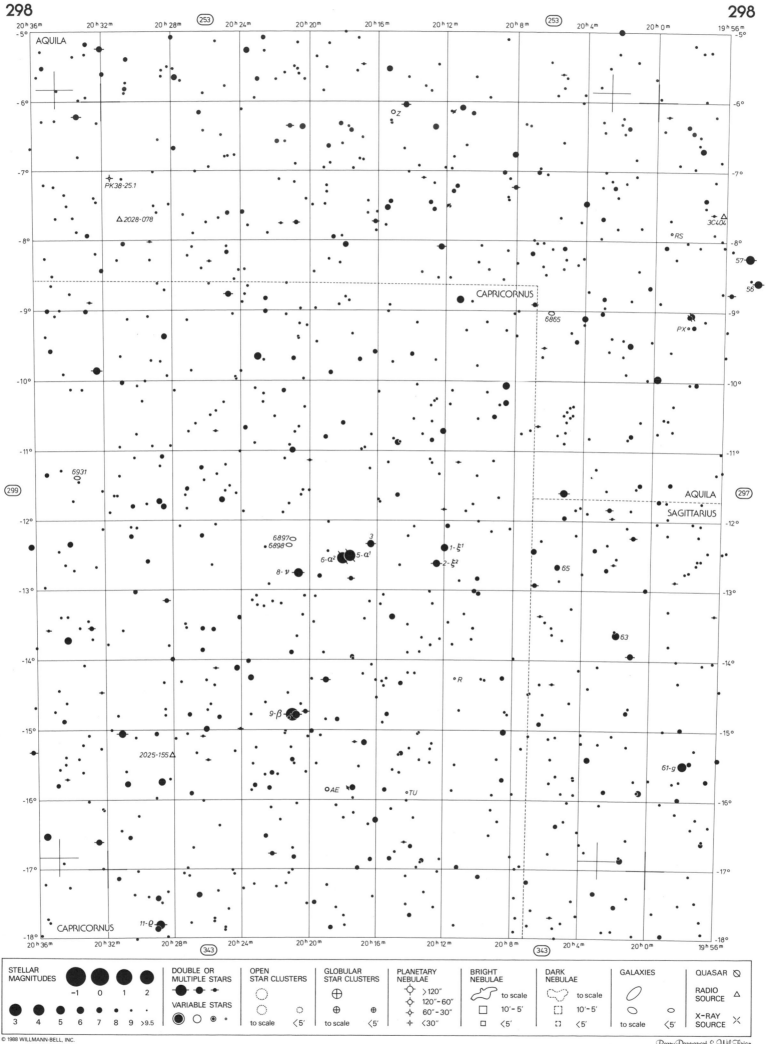

AQUILA

PK38-25.1

△ 2028-078

Z

CAPRICORNUS

6865

PX

RS

3C404

57

56

6931

AQUILA

SAGITTARIUS

6897
6898

3

6- α²   5- α¹

8- ν

1- ξ¹

2- ξ²

65

63

R

9- β

2025-155 △

AE   TU

61-g

11- ρ

CAPRICORNUS

© 1988 WILLMANN-BELL, INC.

Barry Rappaport & Wil Tirion

STELLAR
MAGNITUDES
-1 0 1 2
3 4 5 6 7 8 9 >9.5

DOUBLE OR
MULTIPLE STARS

VARIABLE STARS

OPEN
STAR CLUSTERS
to scale   <5'

GLOBULAR
STAR CLUSTERS
to scale   <5'

PLANETARY
NEBULAE
>120"
120"-60"
60"-30"
<30"

BRIGHT
NEBULAE
to scale
10'-5'
<5'

DARK
NEBULAE
to scale
10'-5'
<5'

GALAXIES
to scale   <5'

QUASAR

RADIO
SOURCE

X-RAY
SOURCE

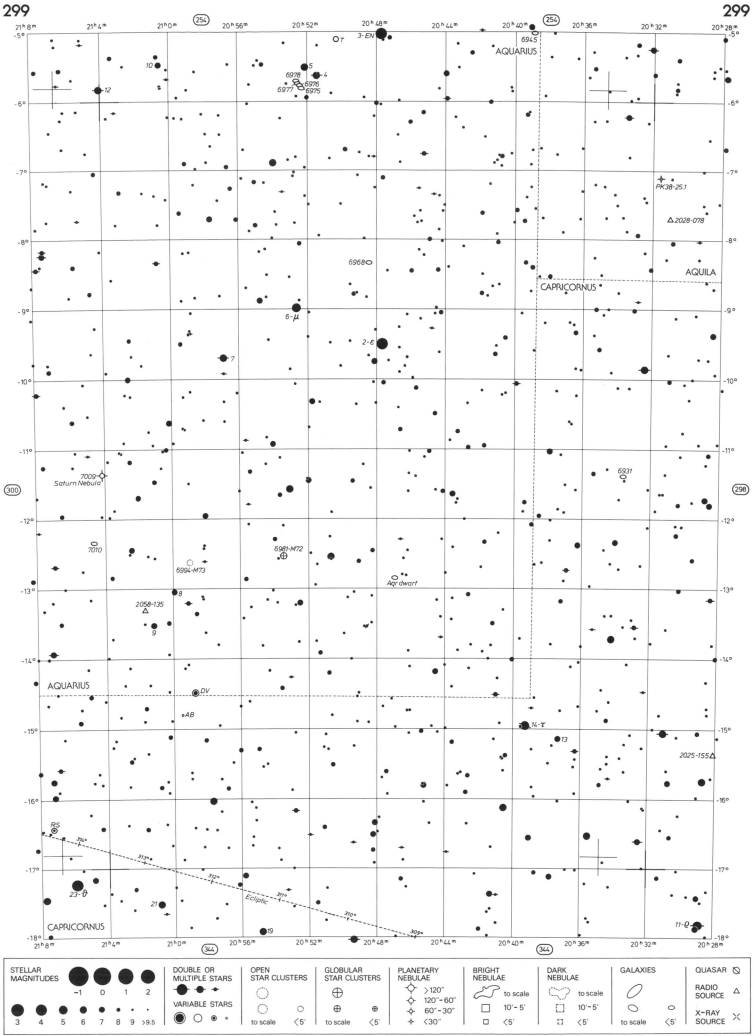

© 1988 WILLMANN-BELL, INC.

Barry Rappaport & Wil Tirion

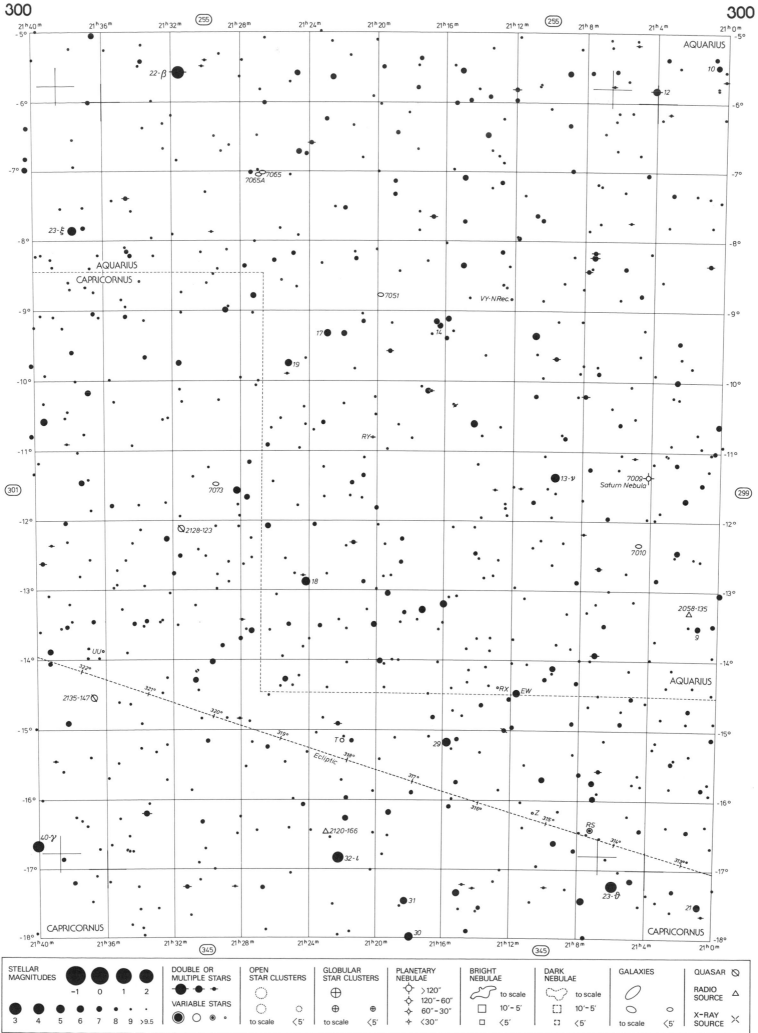

© 1988 WILLMANN-BELL, INC.

Barry Rappaport & Wil Tirion

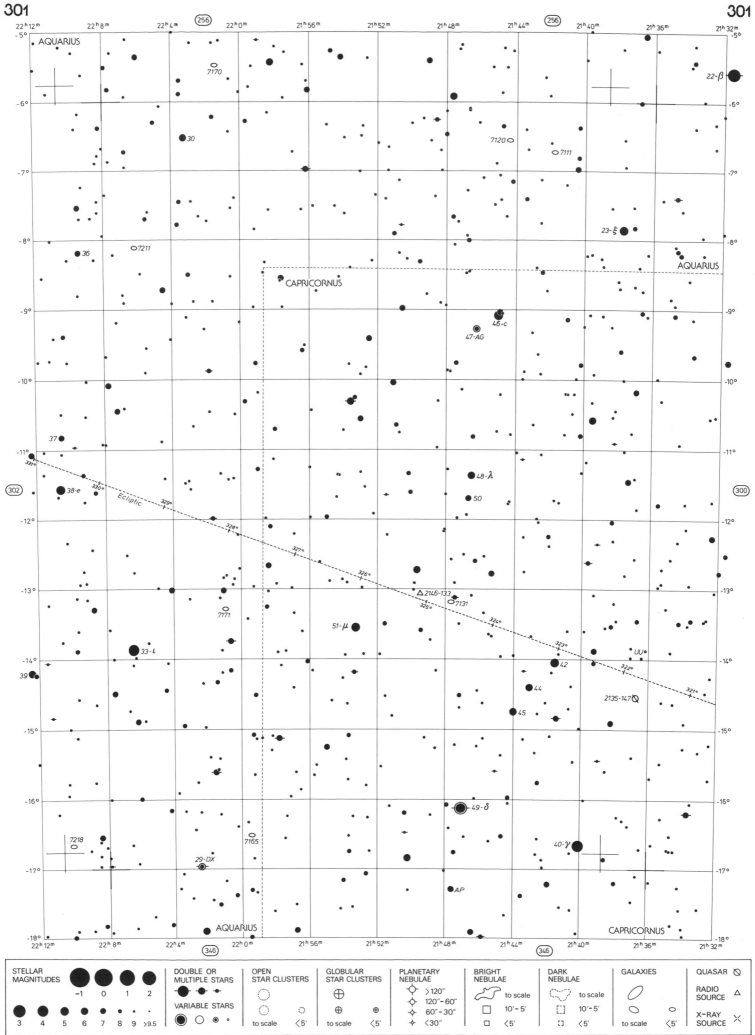

AQUARIUS

22-β

30

7170

7120

7111

23-ξ

36

7211

CAPRICORNUS

AQUARIUS

46-c

47-AG

37

48-λ

50

38-e

Ecliptic

331°

330°

329°

328°

327°

326°

325°

2146-133

7131

7171

324°

51-μ

323°

322°

UU

33-ι

42

321°

39

44

2135-147

45

49-δ

7218

40-γ

7165

29-DX

AP

AQUARIUS

CAPRICORNUS

STELLAR MAGNITUDES					
-1	0	1	2		
3	4	5	6	7 8 9 >9.5	

DOUBLE OR MULTIPLE STARS

VARIABLE STARS

OPEN STAR CLUSTERS

to scale   <5'

GLOBULAR STAR CLUSTERS

to scale   <5'

PLANETARY NEBULAE

>120"
120"-60"
60"-30"
<30"

BRIGHT NEBULAE

to scale
10'-5'
<5'

DARK NEBULAE

to scale
10'-5'
<5'

GALAXIES

to scale   <5'

QUASAR

RADIO SOURCE

X-RAY SOURCE

© 1988 WILLMANN-BELL, INC.

Barry Rappaport & Wil Tirion

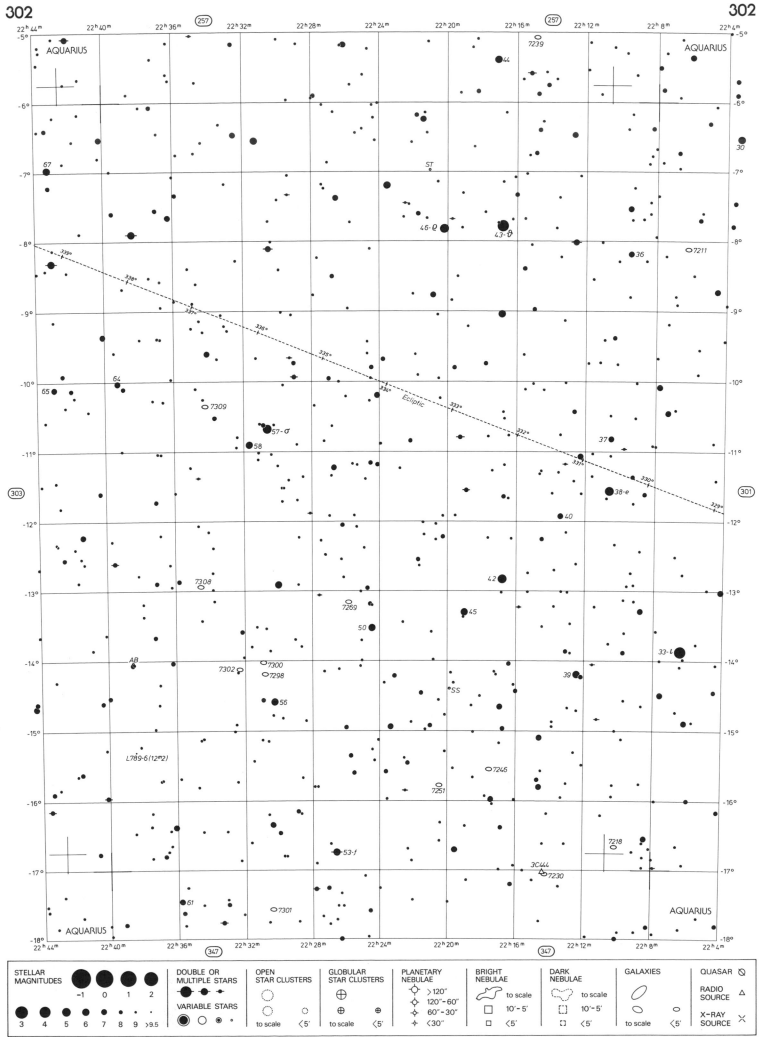

STELLAR MAGNITUDES
-1 0 1 2
3 4 5 6 7 8 9 >9.5

DOUBLE OR MULTIPLE STARS

VARIABLE STARS

OPEN STAR CLUSTERS
to scale <5'

GLOBULAR STAR CLUSTERS
to scale <5'

PLANETARY NEBULAE
>120"
120"-60"
60"-30"
<30"

BRIGHT NEBULAE
to scale
10'-5'
<5'

DARK NEBULAE
to scale
10'-5'
<5'

GALAXIES
to scale <5'

QUASAR

RADIO SOURCE

X-RAY SOURCE

© 1988 WILLMANN-BELL, INC.

Barry Rappaport & Wil Tirion

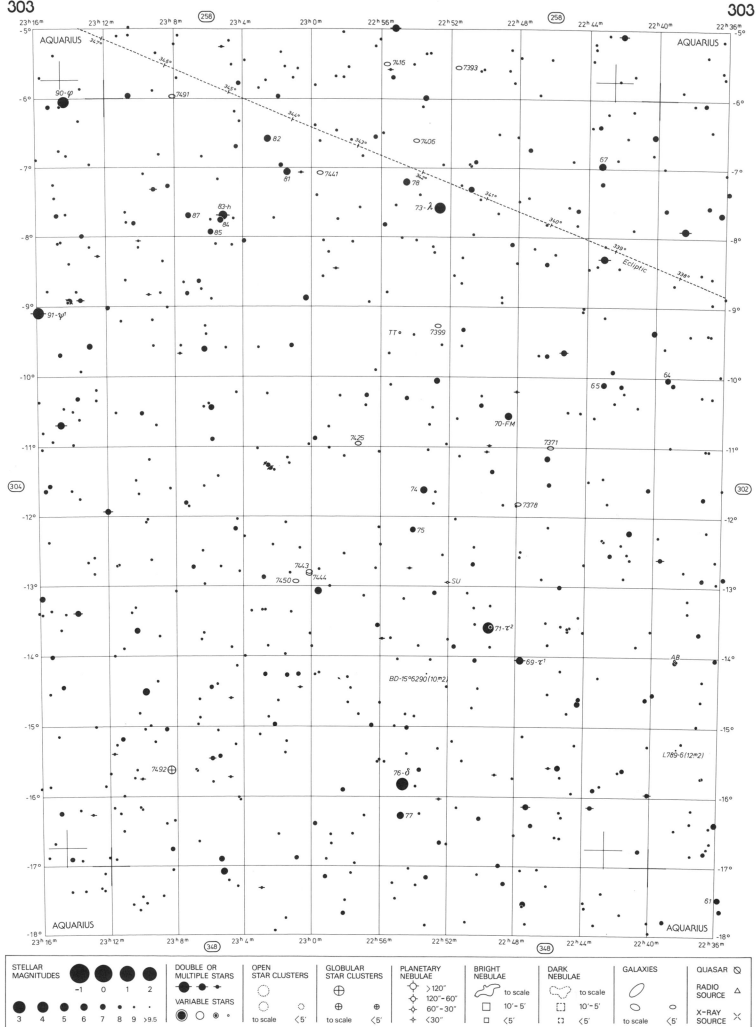

© 1988 WILLMANN-BELL, INC.

Barry Rappaport & Wil Tirion

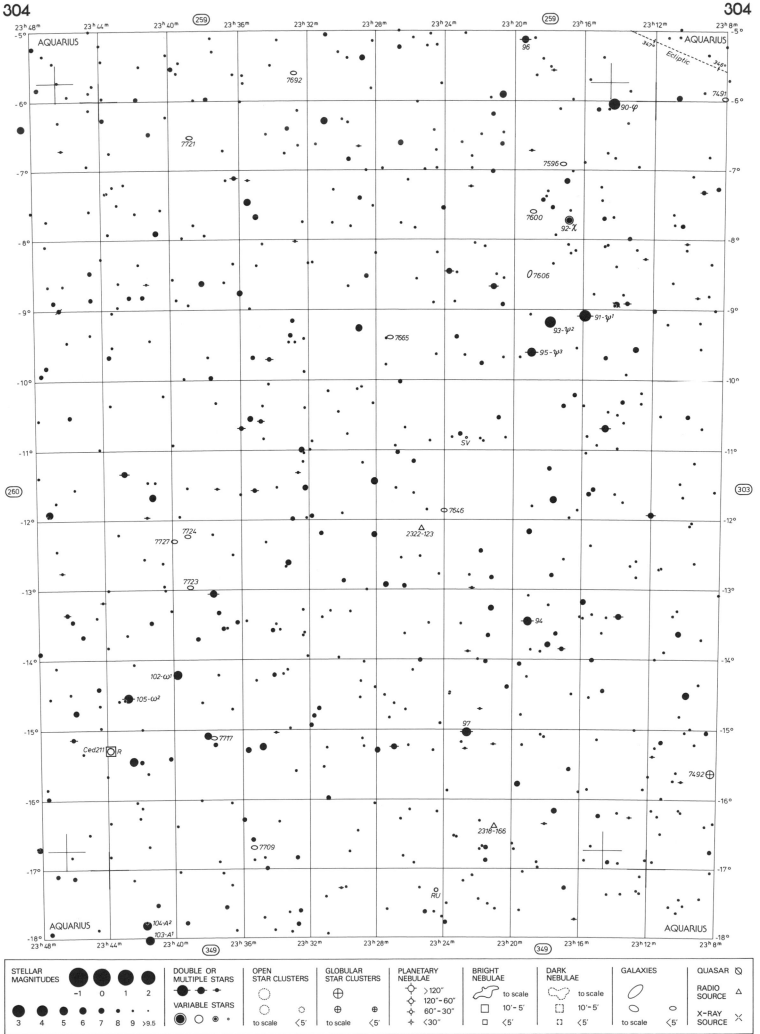

© 1988 WILLMANN-BELL, INC.

Barry Rappaport & Wil Tirion

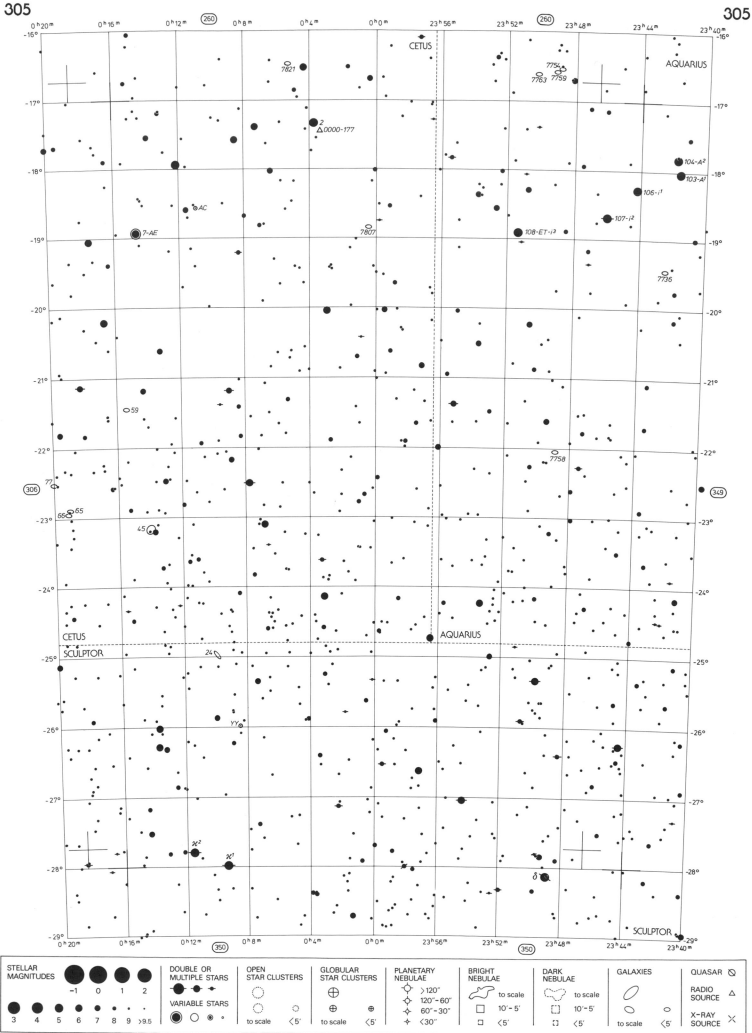

© 1988 WILLMANN-BELL, INC.

Barry Rappaport & Wil Tirion

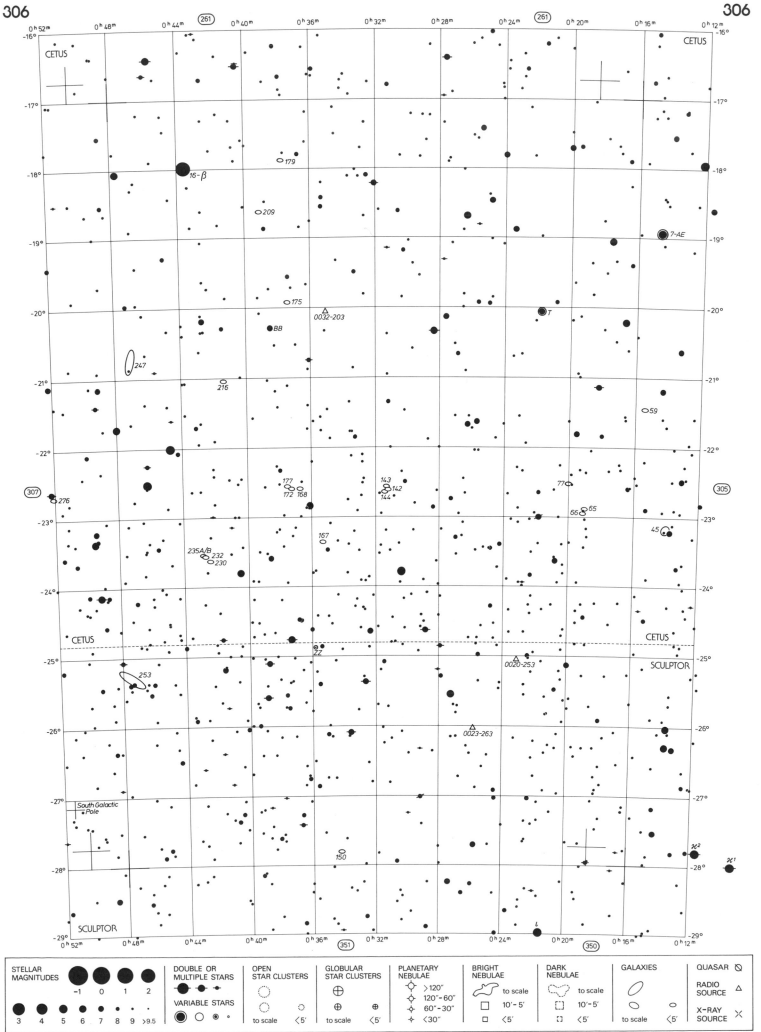

STELLAR MAGNITUDES

-1 0 1 2

3 4 5 6 7 8 9 >9.5

DOUBLE OR MULTIPLE STARS

VARIABLE STARS

OPEN STAR CLUSTERS

to scale <5'

GLOBULAR STAR CLUSTERS

to scale <5'

PLANETARY NEBULAE

>120"
120"-60"
60"-30"
<30"

BRIGHT NEBULAE

to scale
10'-5'
<5'

DARK NEBULAE

to scale
10'-5'
<5'

GALAXIES

to scale <5'

QUASAR

RADIO SOURCE

X-RAY SOURCE

© 1988 WILLMANN-BELL, INC.

Barry Rappaport & Wil Tirion

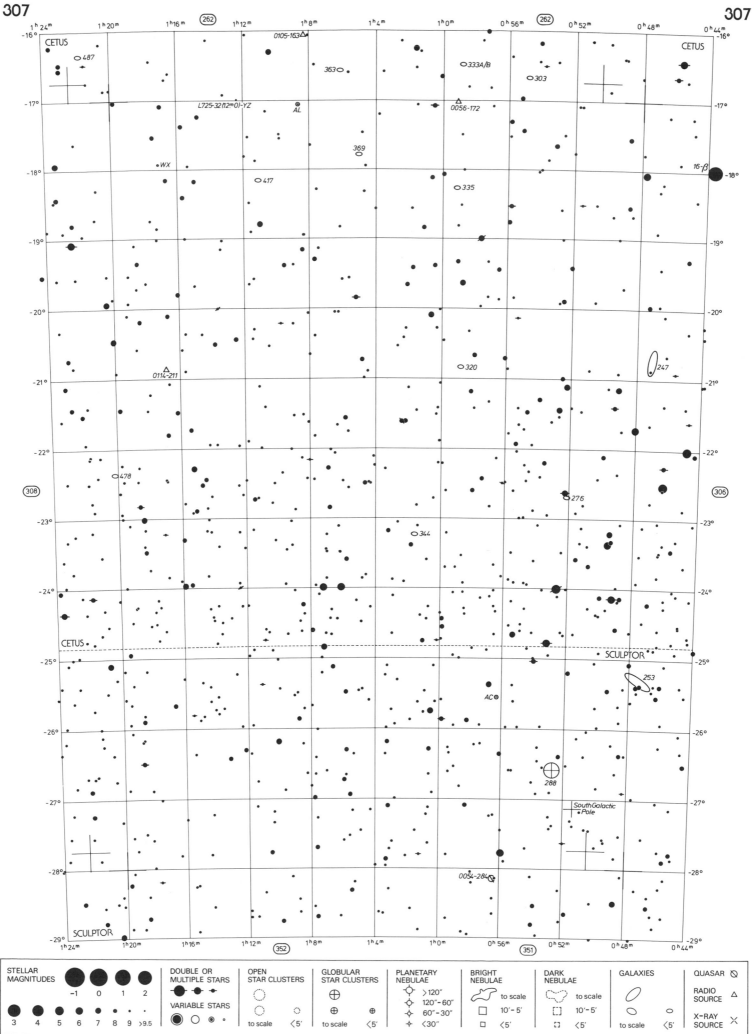

© 1988 WILLMANN-BELL, INC.

Barry Rappaport & Wil Tirion

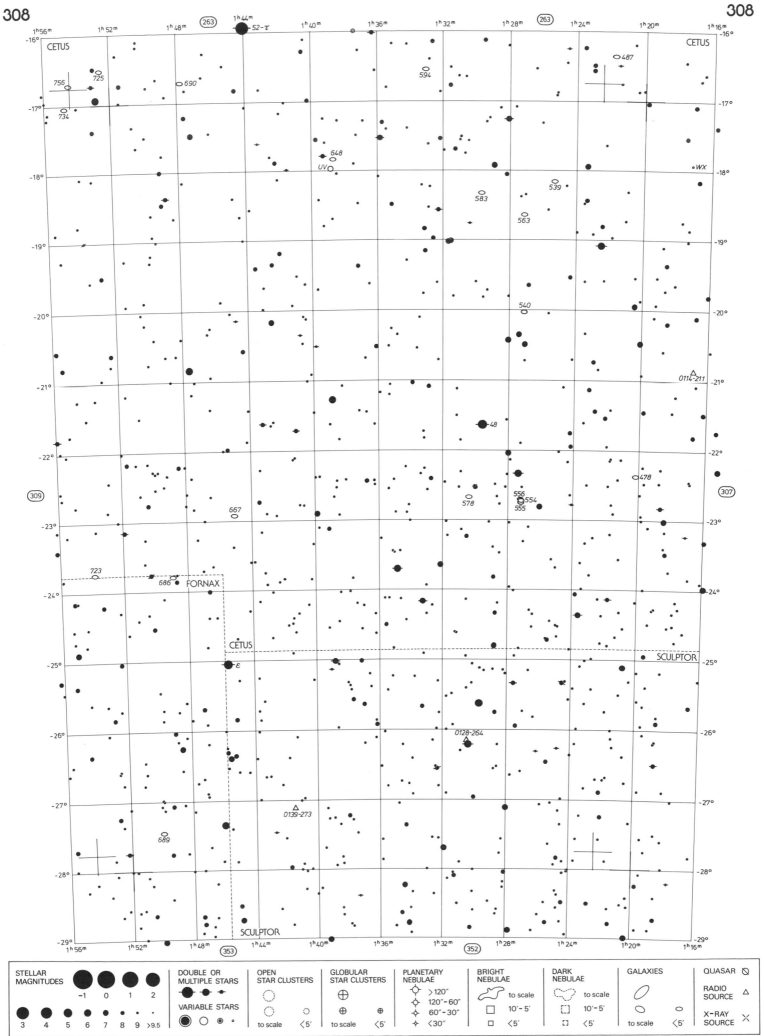

CETUS

CETUS

SCULPTOR

FORNAX

CETUS

SCULPTOR

SCULPTOR

STELLAR MAGNITUDES	DOUBLE OR MULTIPLE STARS	OPEN STAR CLUSTERS	GLOBULAR STAR CLUSTERS	PLANETARY NEBULAE	BRIGHT NEBULAE	DARK NEBULAE	GALAXIES	QUASAR
−1 0 1 2			⊕	◇ >120″	to scale	to scale		RADIO SOURCE
3 4 5 6 7 8 9 >9.5	VARIABLE STARS	to scale <5′	to scale <5′	◇ 120″−60″ ◇ 60″−30″ + <30″	10′−5′ <5′	10′−5′ <5′	to scale <5′	X−RAY SOURCE

© 1988 WILLMANN-BELL, INC.

Barry Rappaport & Wil Tirion

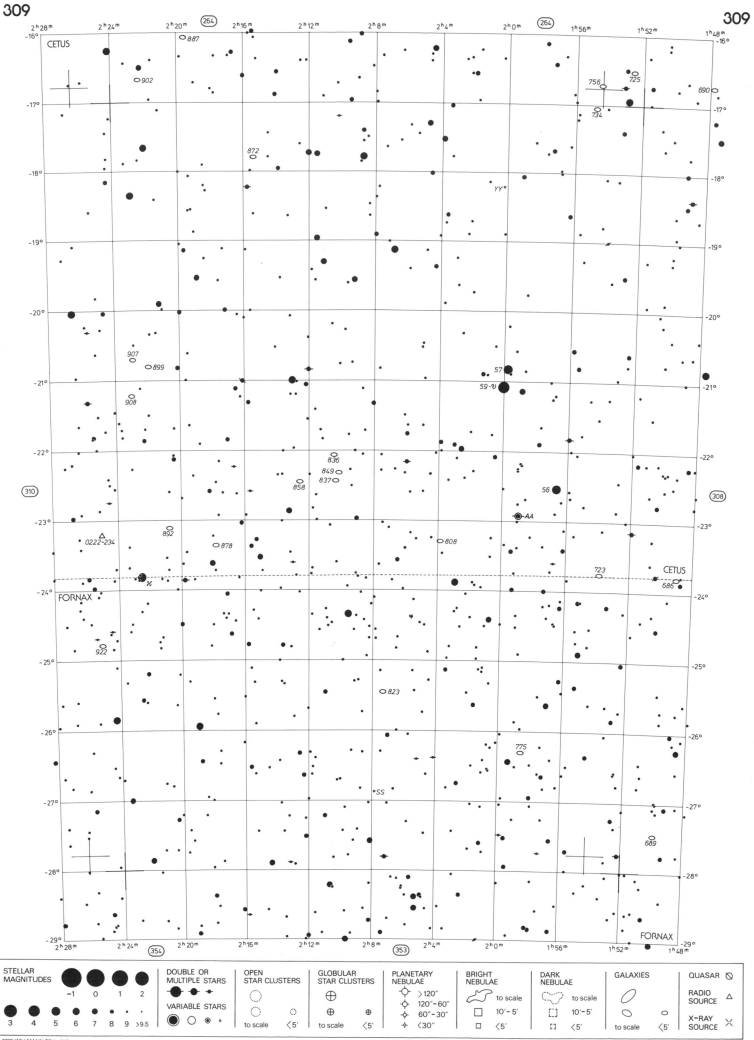

CETUS

CETUS

FORNAX

FORNAX

STELLAR MAGNITUDES	DOUBLE OR MULTIPLE STARS	OPEN STAR CLUSTERS	GLOBULAR STAR CLUSTERS	PLANETARY NEBULAE	BRIGHT NEBULAE	DARK NEBULAE	GALAXIES	QUASAR

© 1988 WILLMANN-BELL, INC.

Barry Rappaport & Wil Tirion

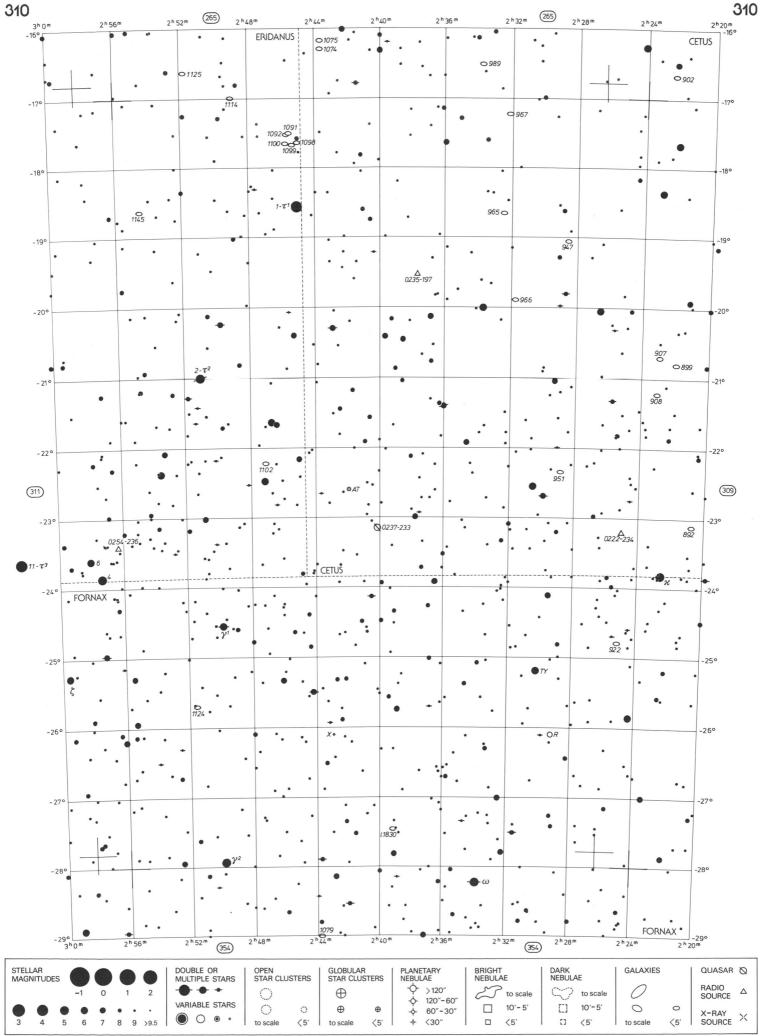

© 1988 WILLMANN-BELL, INC.

Barry Rappaport & Wil Tirion

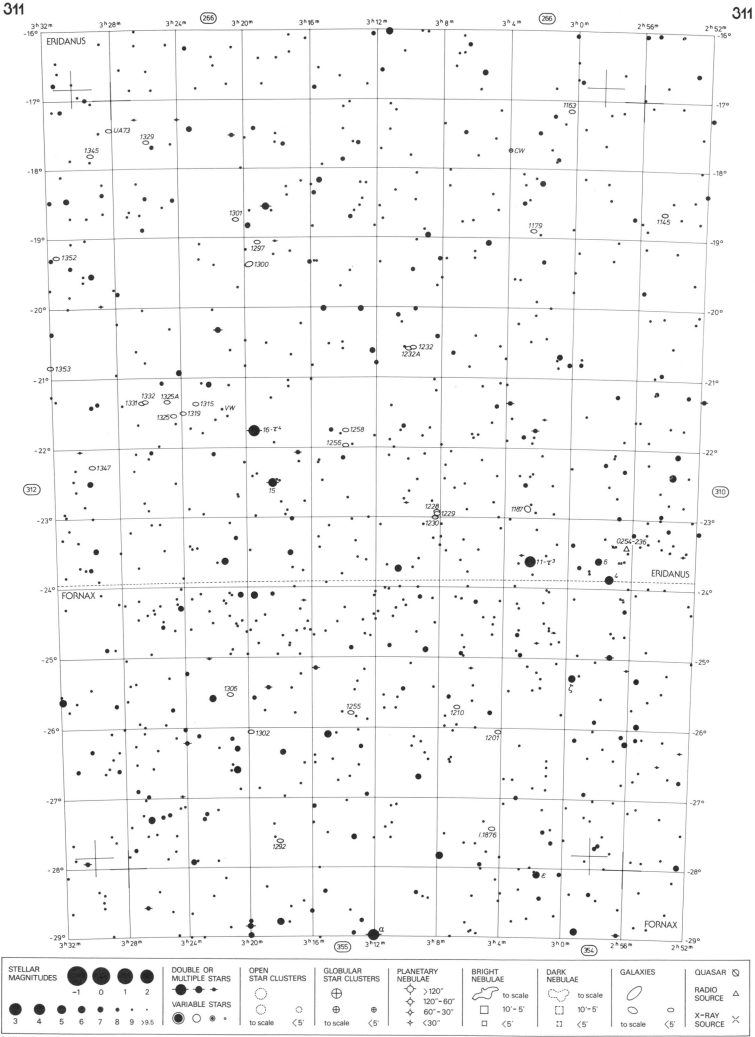

© 1988 WILLMANN-BELL, INC.

Barry Rappaport & Wil Tirion

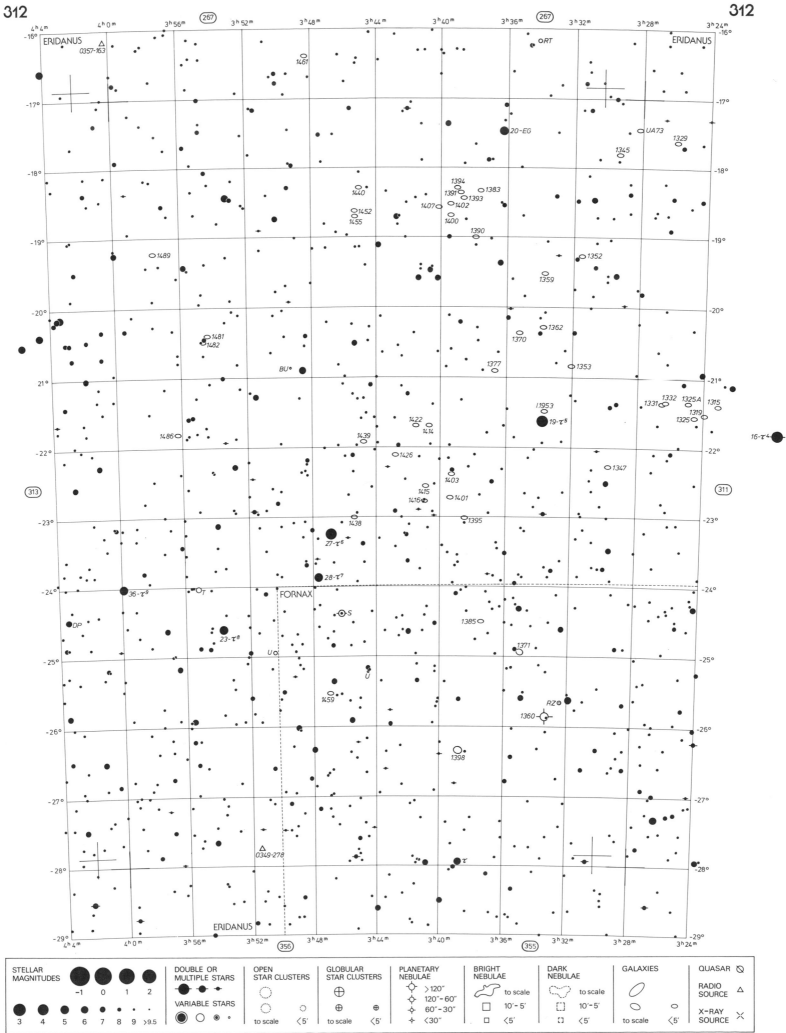

ERIDANUS
ERIDANUS
FORNAX
ERIDANUS

© 1988 WILLMANN-BELL, INC.

Barry Rappaport & Wil Tirion

STELLAR MAGNITUDES
-1 0 1 2
3 4 5 6 7 8 9 >9.5

DOUBLE OR MULTIPLE STARS
VARIABLE STARS

OPEN STAR CLUSTERS
to scale   <5'

GLOBULAR STAR CLUSTERS
to scale   <5'

PLANETARY NEBULAE
>120"
120"-60"
60"-30"
<30"

BRIGHT NEBULAE
to scale
10'-5'
<5'

DARK NEBULAE
to scale
10'-5'
<5'

GALAXIES
to scale   <5'

QUASAR

RADIO SOURCE

X-RAY SOURCE

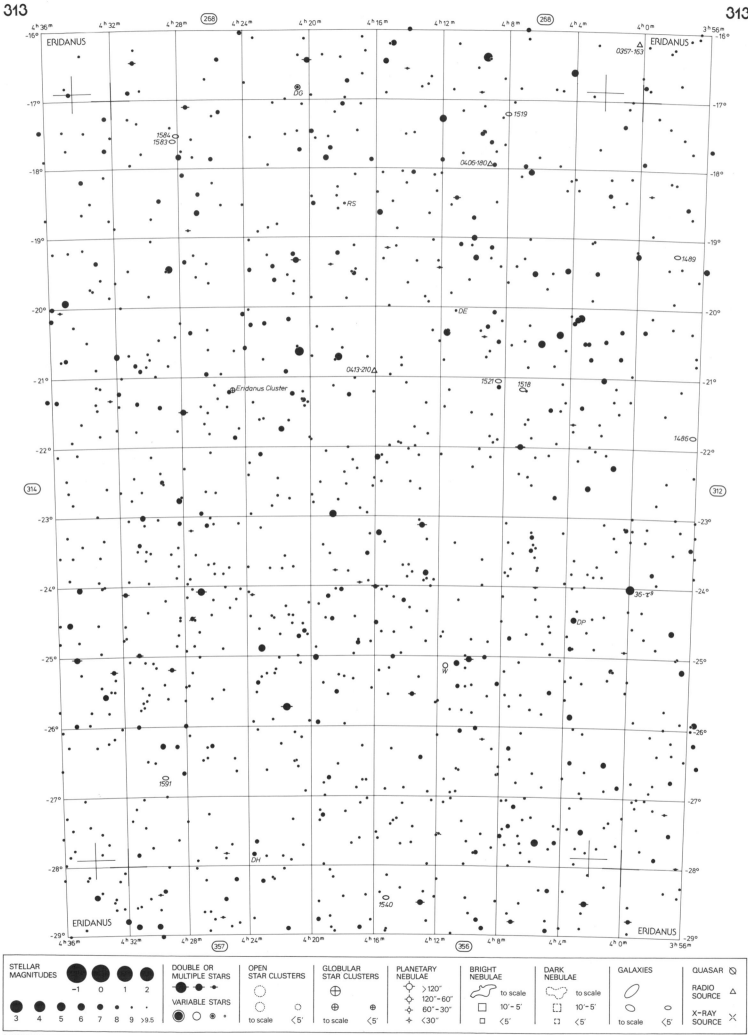

ERIDANUS

ERIDANUS

0357-163

DG

1519

1584
1583

0406-180

RS

1489

DE

0413-210

1521   1518

Eridanus Cluster

1486

314

312

36-τ⁹

DP

W

1591

DH

1540

ERIDANUS

ERIDANUS

268   268

314   312

357   356

STELLAR MAGNITUDES					DOUBLE OR MULTIPLE STARS	OPEN STAR CLUSTERS	GLOBULAR STAR CLUSTERS	PLANETARY NEBULAE	BRIGHT NEBULAE	DARK NEBULAE	GALAXIES	QUASAR
-1	0	1	2					>120″	to scale	to scale		RADIO SOURCE
3	4	5	6 7 8 9 >9.5		VARIABLE STARS	to scale <5′	to scale <5′	120″-60″ 60″-30″ <30″	10′-5′ <5′	10′-5′ <5′	to scale <5′	X-RAY SOURCE

© 1988 WILLMANN-BELL, INC.

Barry Rappaport & Wil Tirion

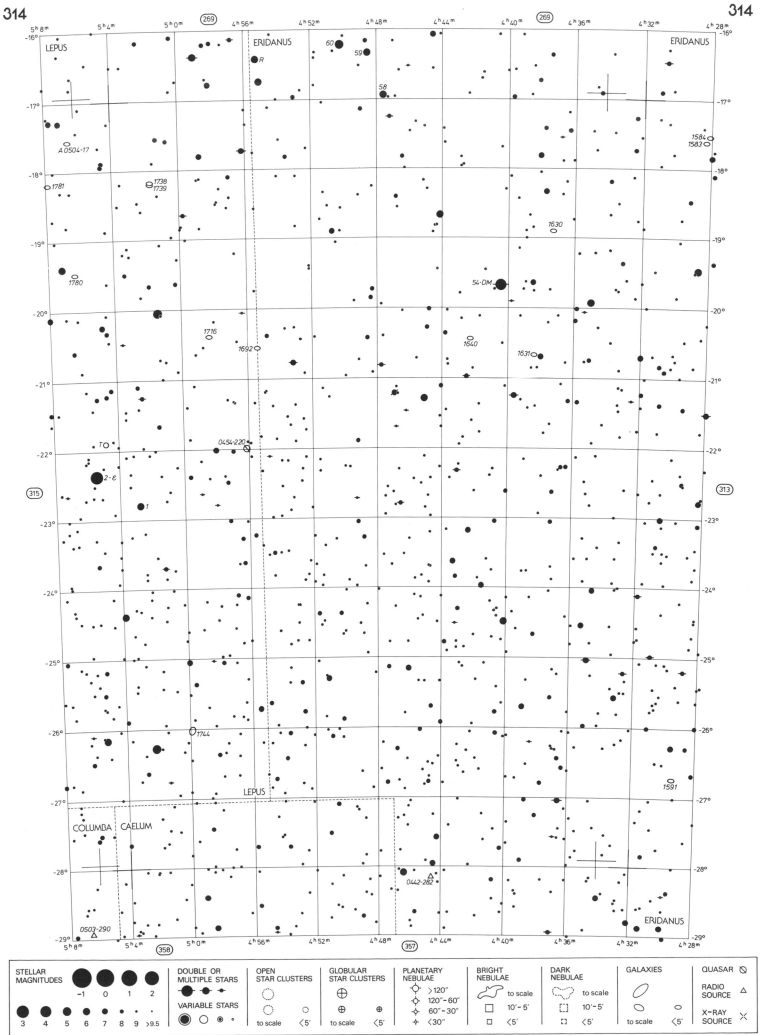

© 1988 WILLMANN-BELL, INC.

Barry Rappaport & Wil Tirion

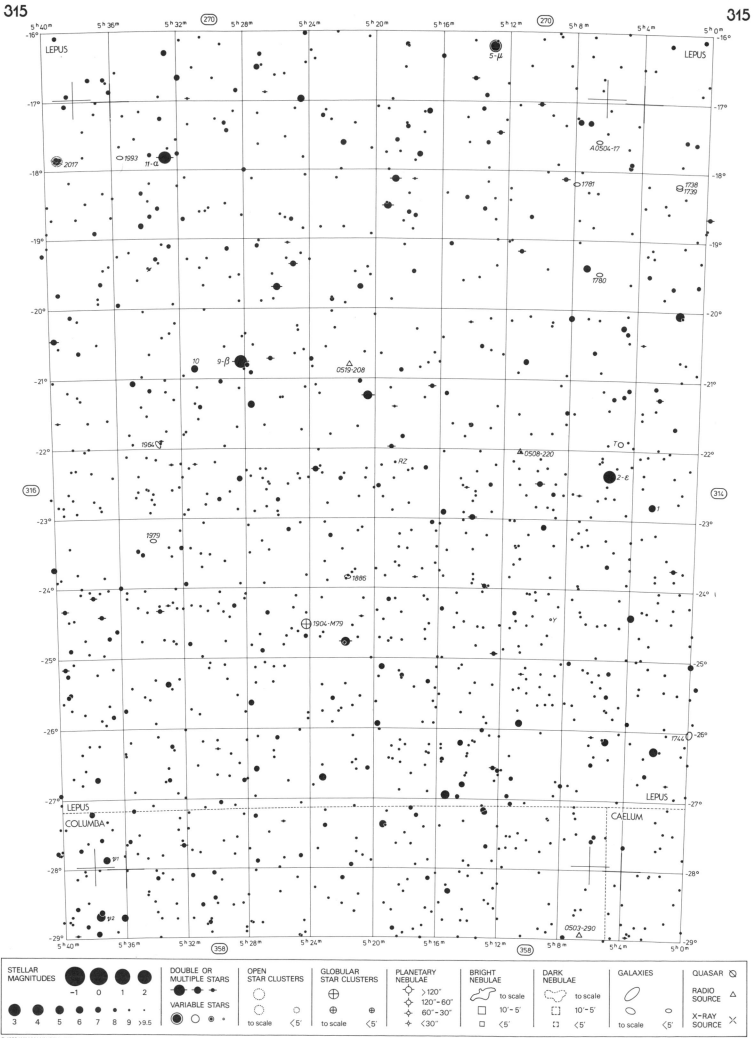

© 1988 WILLMANN-BELL, INC.

Barry Rappaport & Wil Tirion

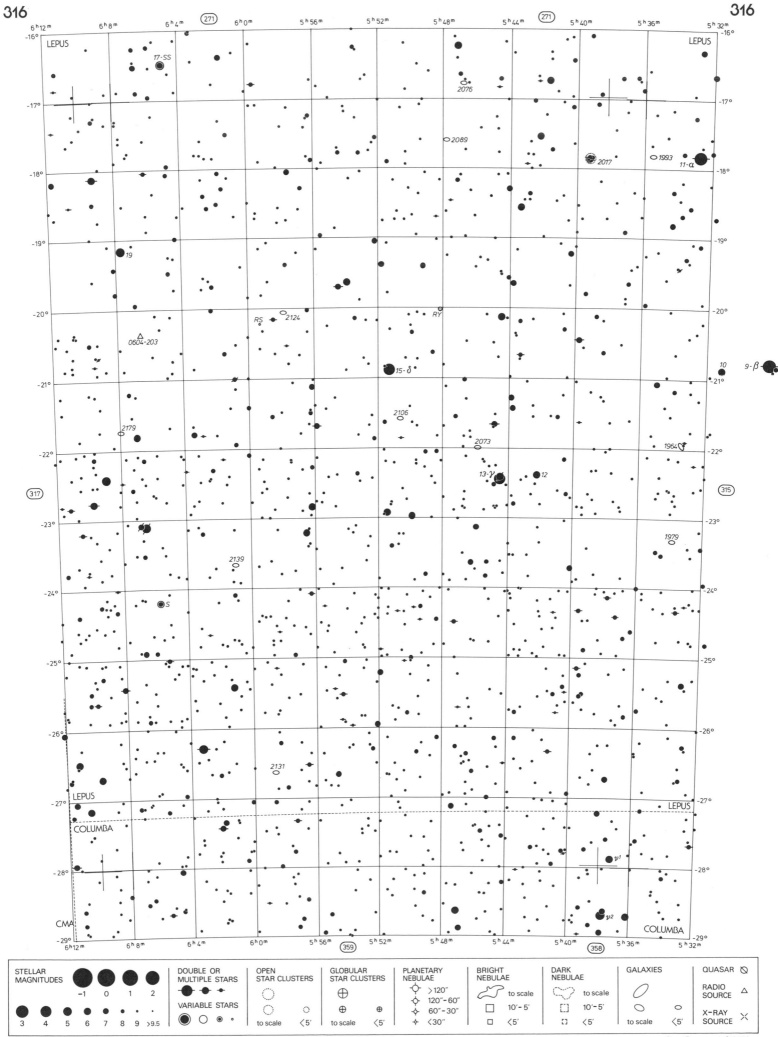

STELLAR MAGNITUDES	DOUBLE OR MULTIPLE STARS	OPEN STAR CLUSTERS	GLOBULAR STAR CLUSTERS	PLANETARY NEBULAE	BRIGHT NEBULAE	DARK NEBULAE	GALAXIES	QUASAR

© 1988 WILLMANN-BELL, INC.

Barry Rappaport & Wil Tirion

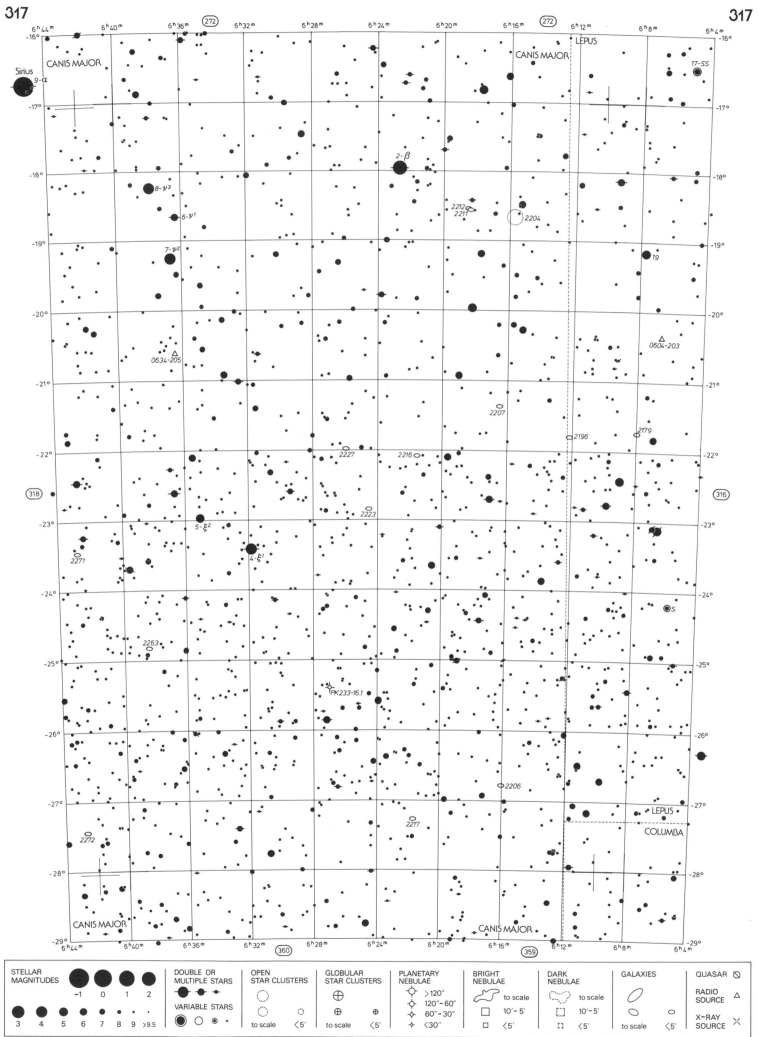

© 1988 WILLMANN-BELL, INC.

Barry Rappaport & Wil Tirion

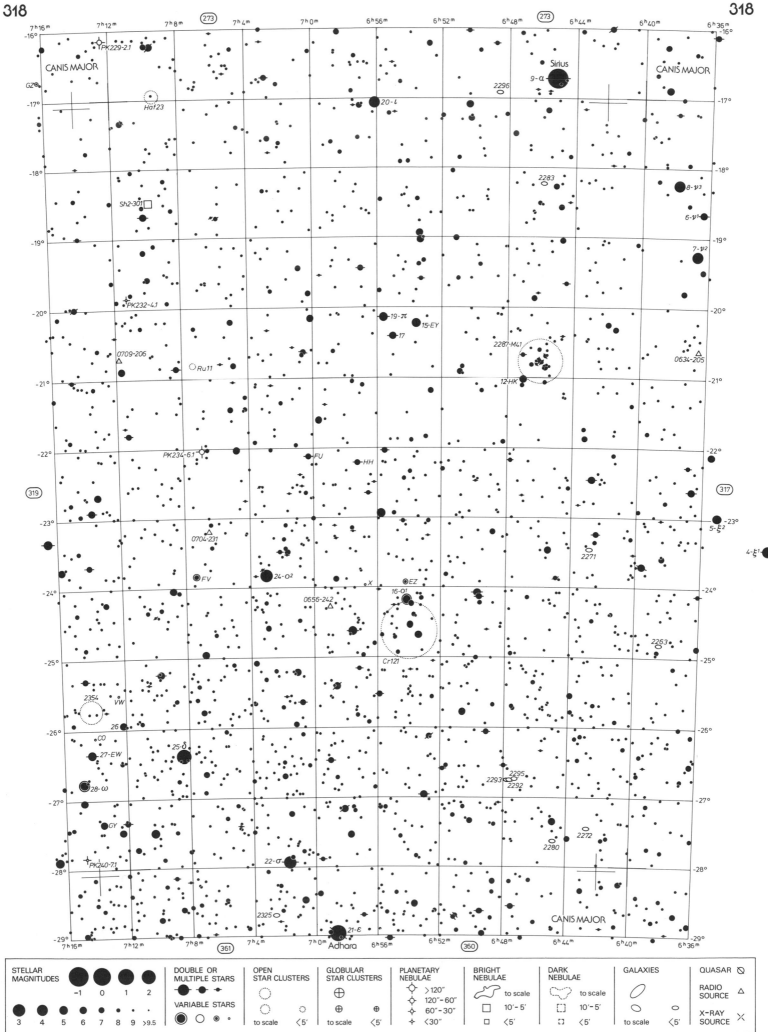

CANIS MAJOR

CANIS MAJOR

Sirius

9-α

2296

20-ι

2283

8-ν³

6-ν¹

7-ν²

Sh2-301

PK229-2.1

GZ

Haf 23

PK232-4.1

0709-206

Ru 11

19-π

15-EY

17

2287-M41

12-HK

0634-205

PK234-6.1

FU

HH

5-ξ²

319

317

0704-231

2271

4-ξ¹

FV

24-O²

X

EZ

16-O¹

0656-242

2263

Cr 121

2354

VW

26

CO

27-EW

25-δ

2295

2293

2292

GY

2272

2280

PK240-7.1

22-σ

2325

21-ε

Adhara

CANIS MAJOR

© 1988 WILLMANN-BELL, INC.

Barry Rappaport & Wil Tirion

STELLAR MAGNITUDES				DOUBLE OR MULTIPLE STARS	OPEN STAR CLUSTERS	GLOBULAR STAR CLUSTERS	PLANETARY NEBULAE	BRIGHT NEBULAE	DARK NEBULAE	GALAXIES	QUASAR
−1	0	1	2	VARIABLE STARS			>120"	to scale	to scale		RADIO SOURCE
3 4 5 6 7 8 9 >9.5					to scale <5'	to scale <5'	120"−60" 60"−30" <30"	10'−5' <5'	10'−5' <5'	to scale <5'	X-RAY SOURCE

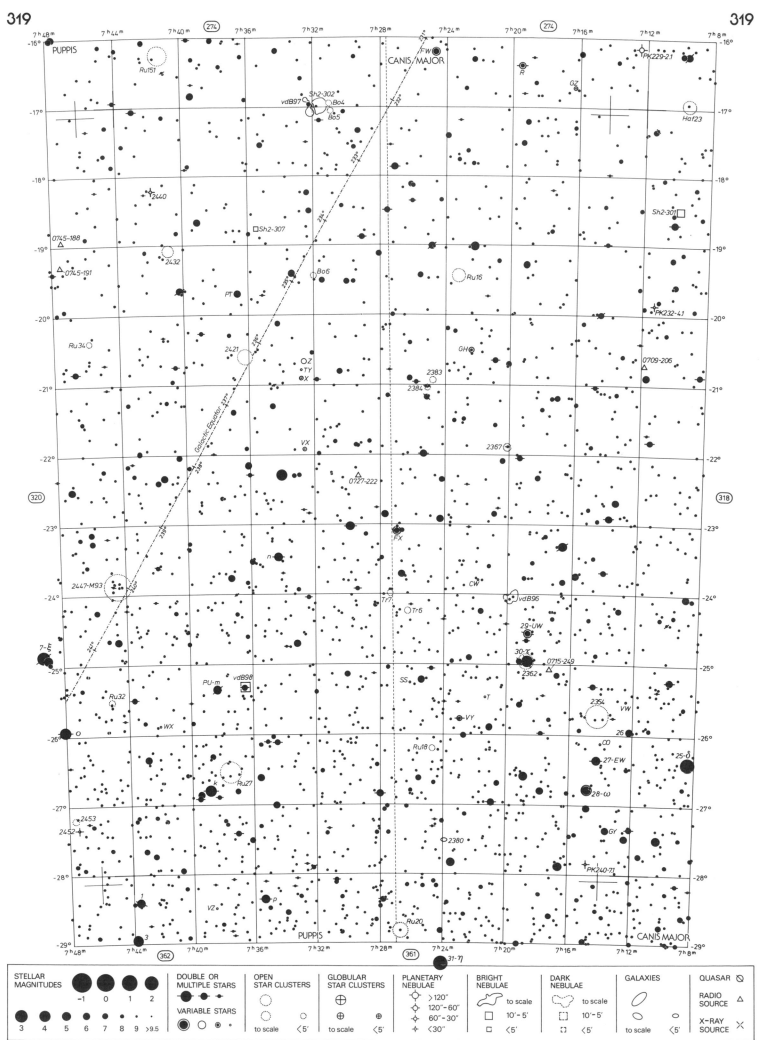

© 1988 WILLMANN-BELL, INC.

Barry Rappaport & Wil Tirion

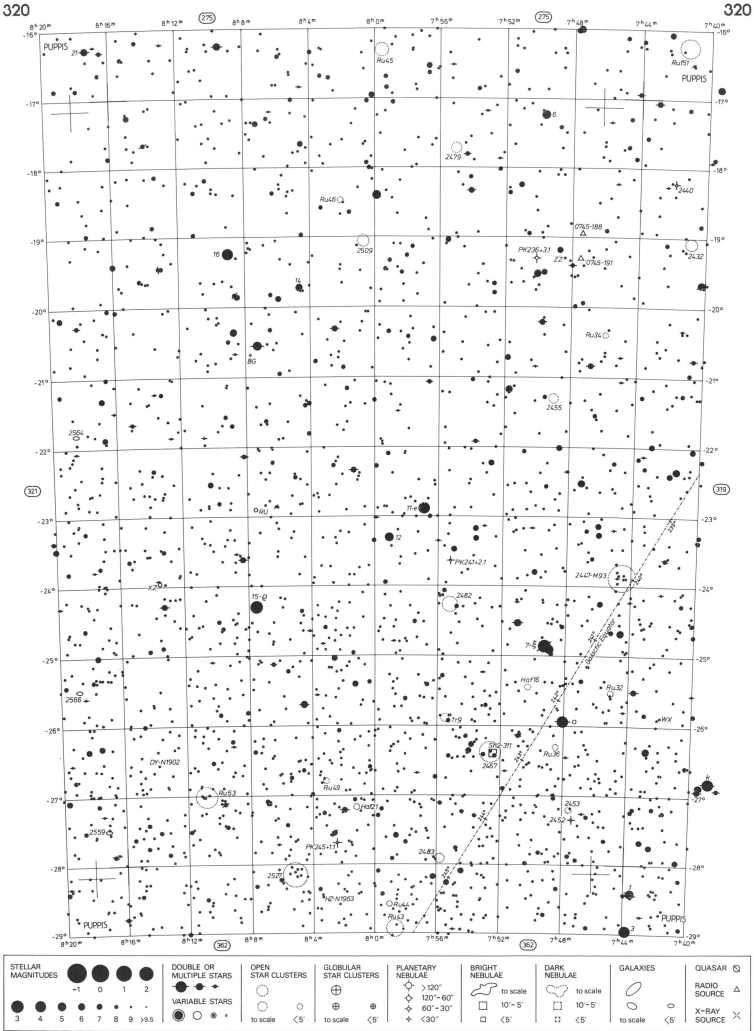

© 1988 WILLMANN-BELL, INC.

Barry Rappaport & Wil Tirion

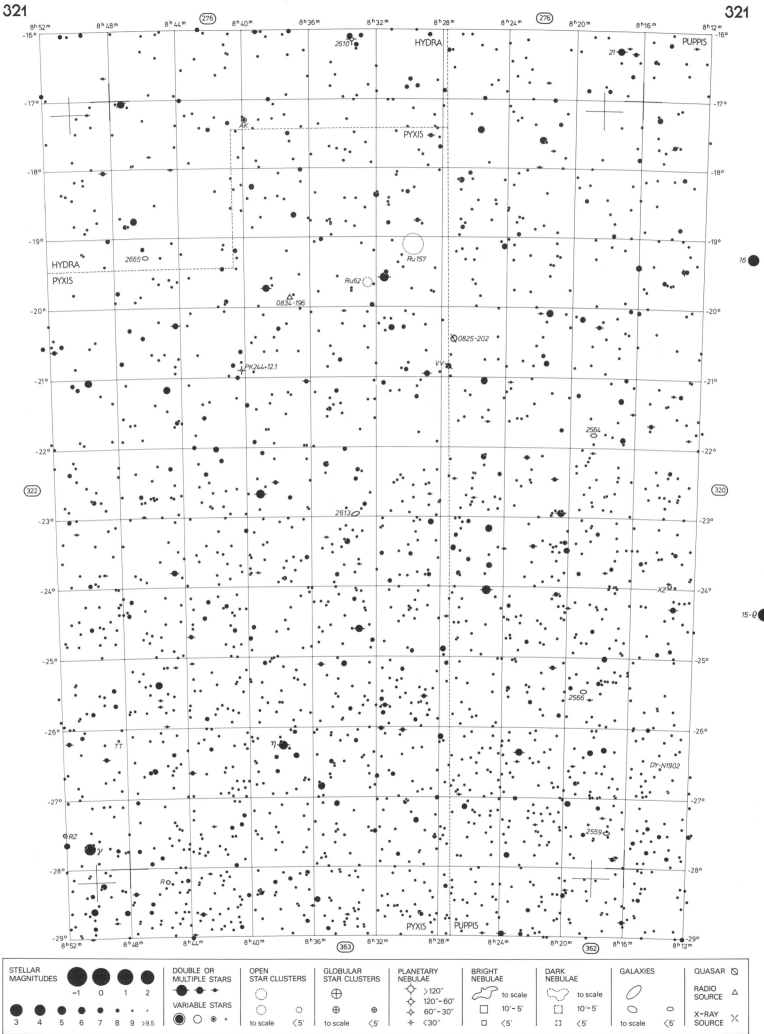

© 1988 WILLMANN-BELL, INC.

Barry Rappaport & Wil Tirion

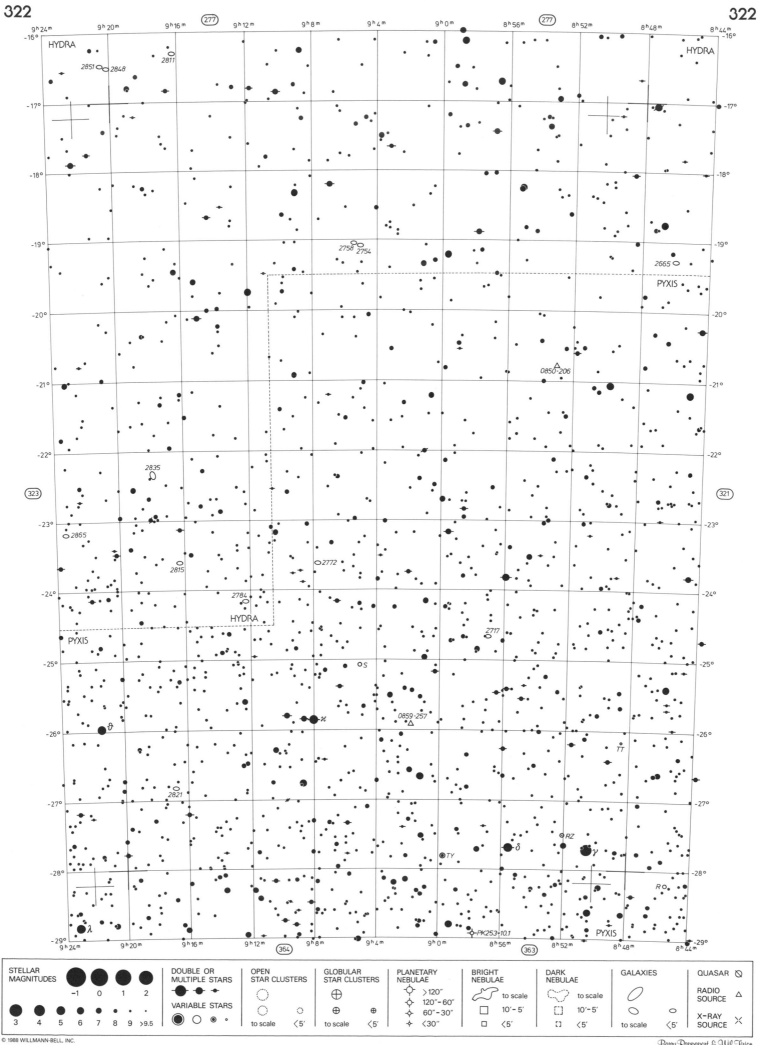

© 1988 WILLMANN-BELL, INC.

Barry Rappaport & Wil Tirion

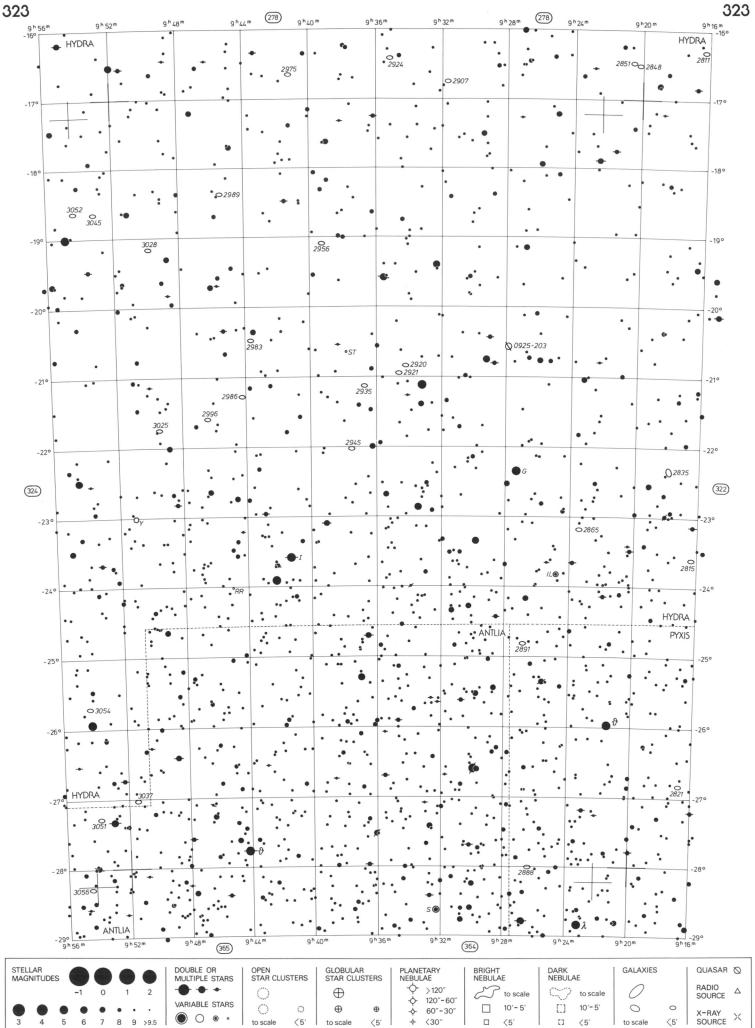

© 1988 WILLMANN-BELL, INC.

Barry Rappaport & Wil Tirion

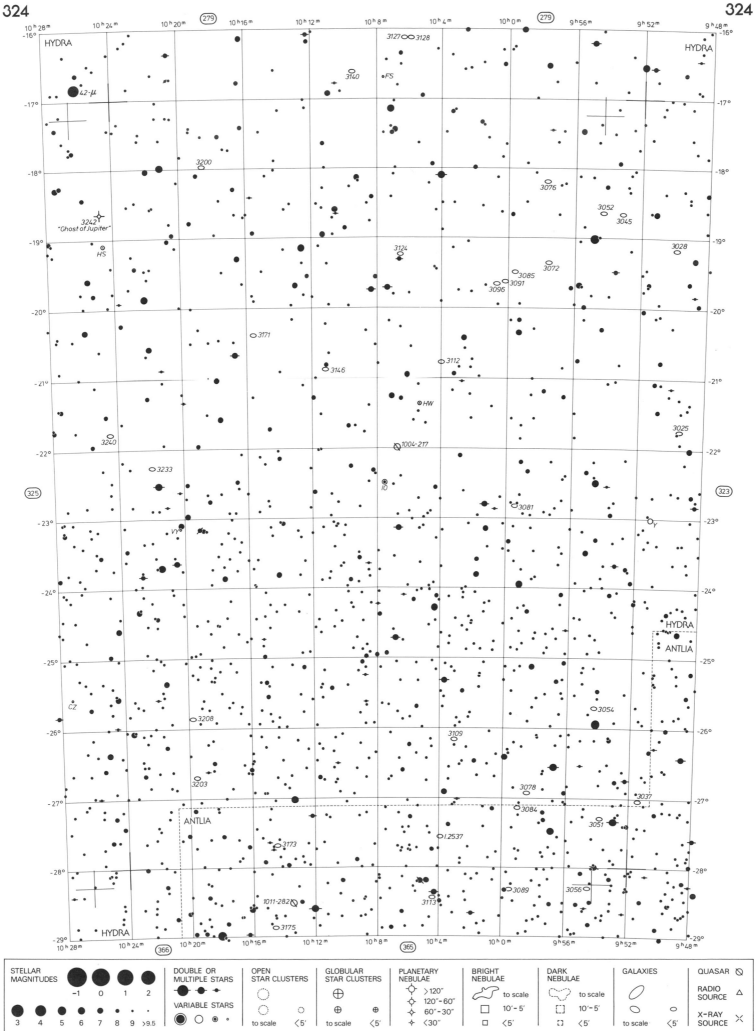

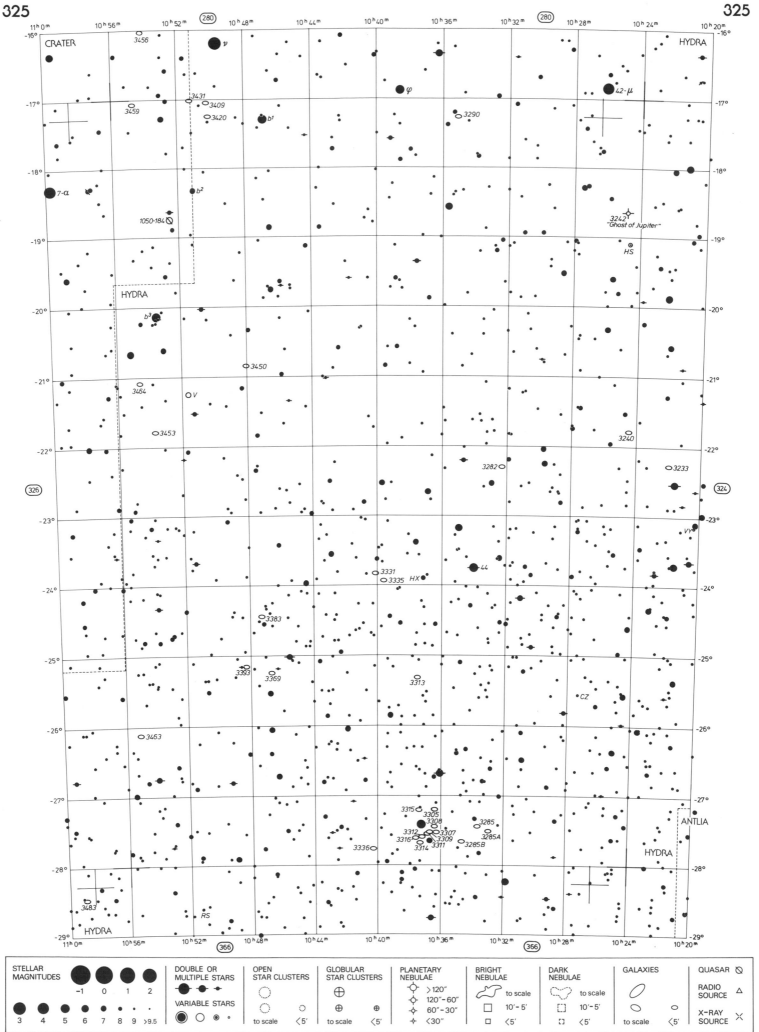

Barry Rappaport & Wil Tirion

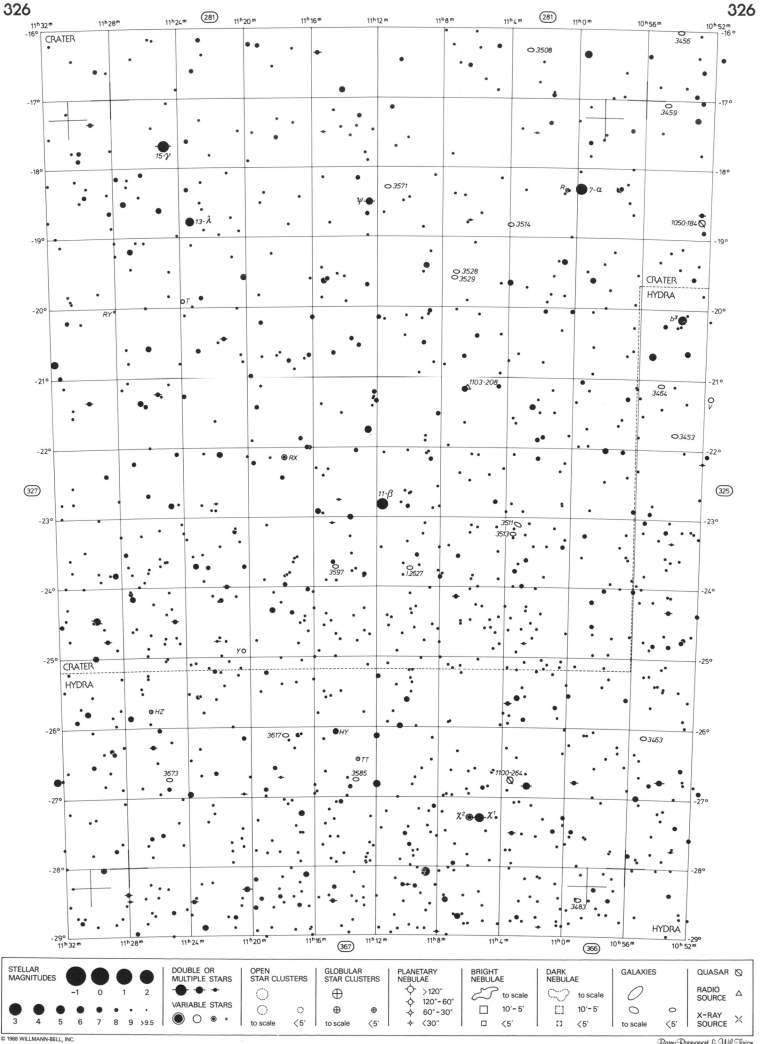

© 1988 WILLMANN-BELL, INC.

Barry Rappaport & Wil Tirion

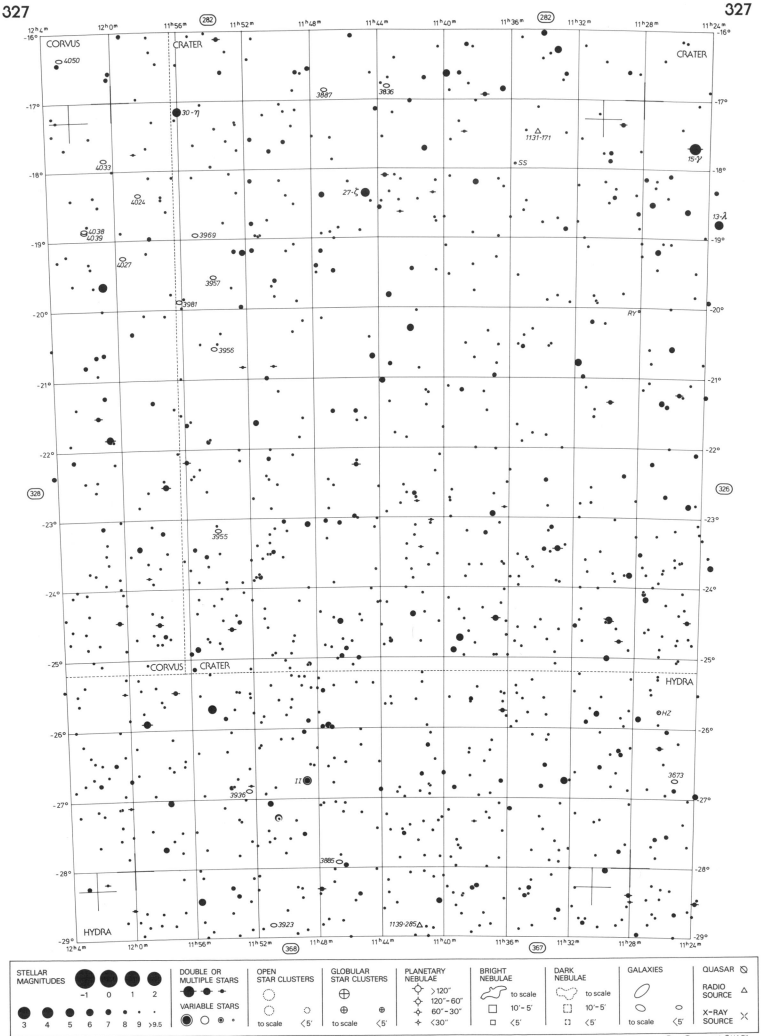

Barry Rappaport & Wil Tirion

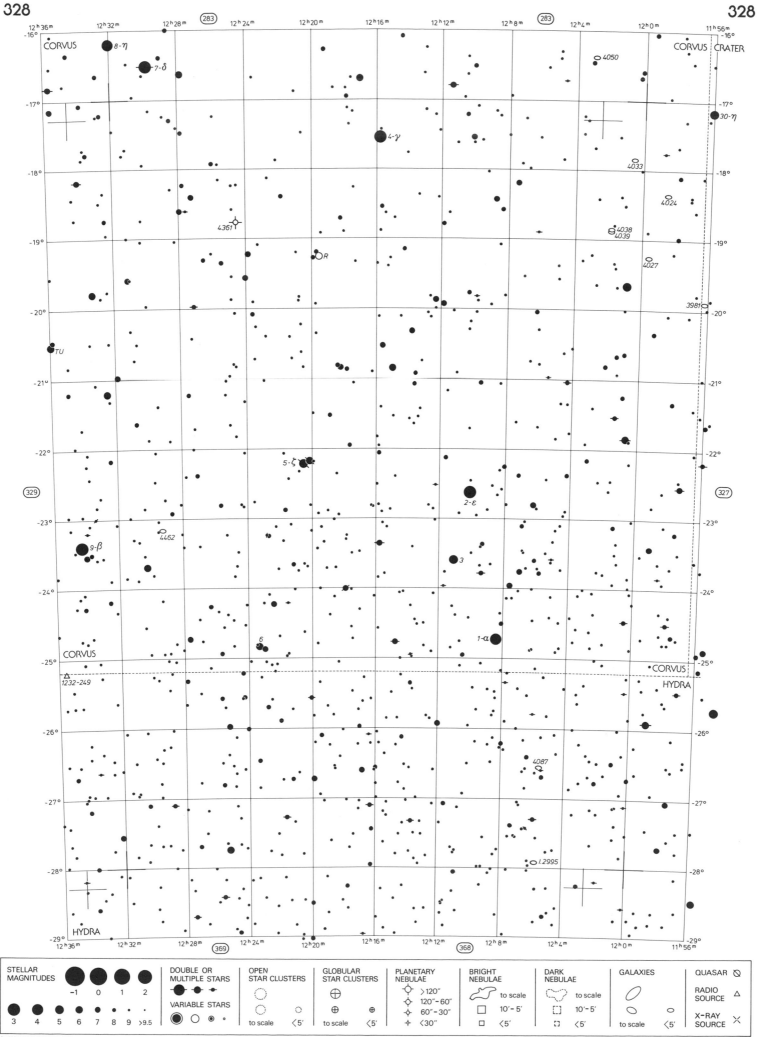

© 1988 WILLMANN-BELL, INC.

Barry Rappaport & Wil Tirion

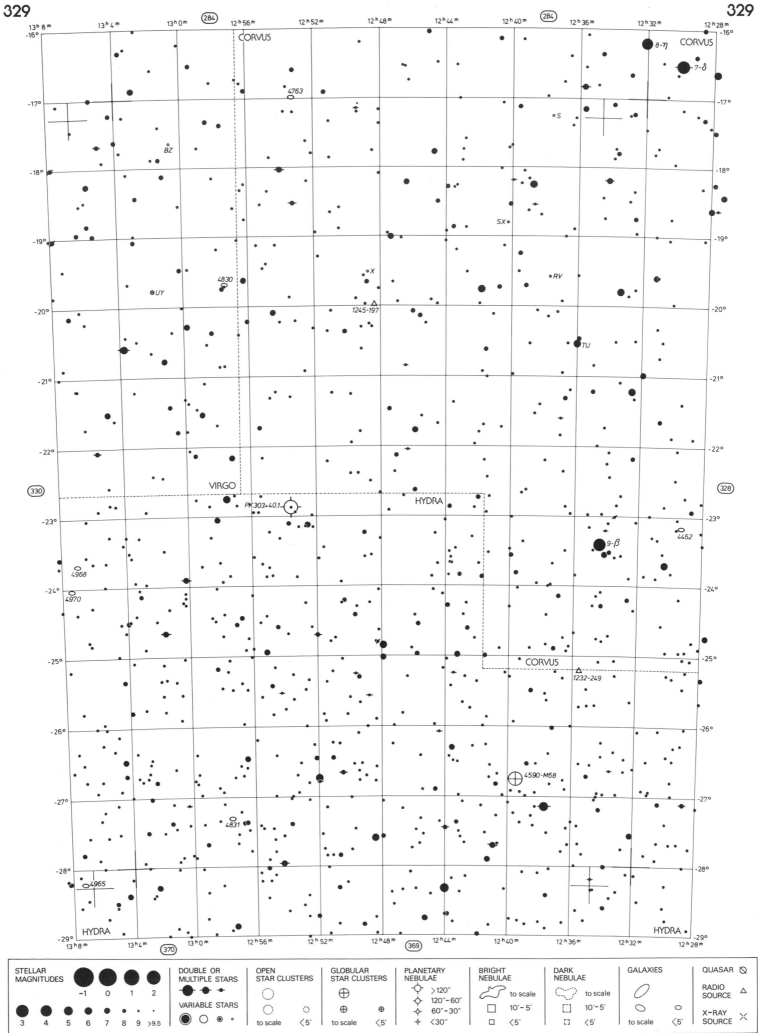

© 1988 WILLMANN-BELL, INC.

Barry Rappaport & Wil Tirion

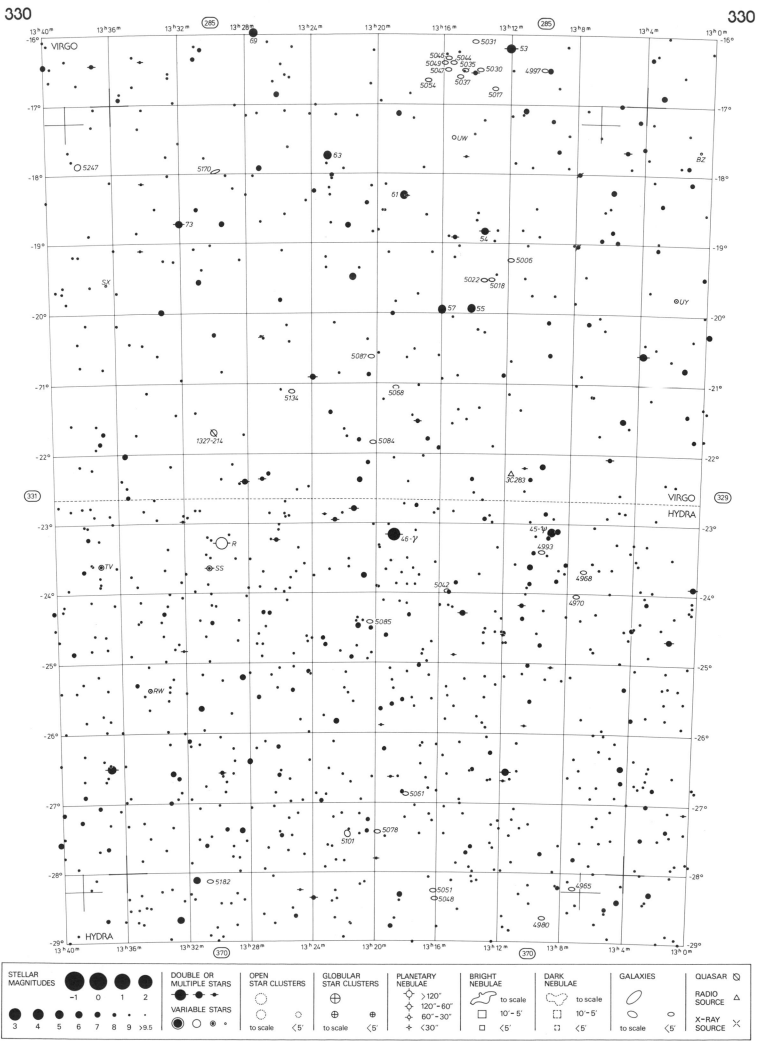

© 1988 WILLMANN-BELL, INC.

Barry Rappaport & Wil Tirion

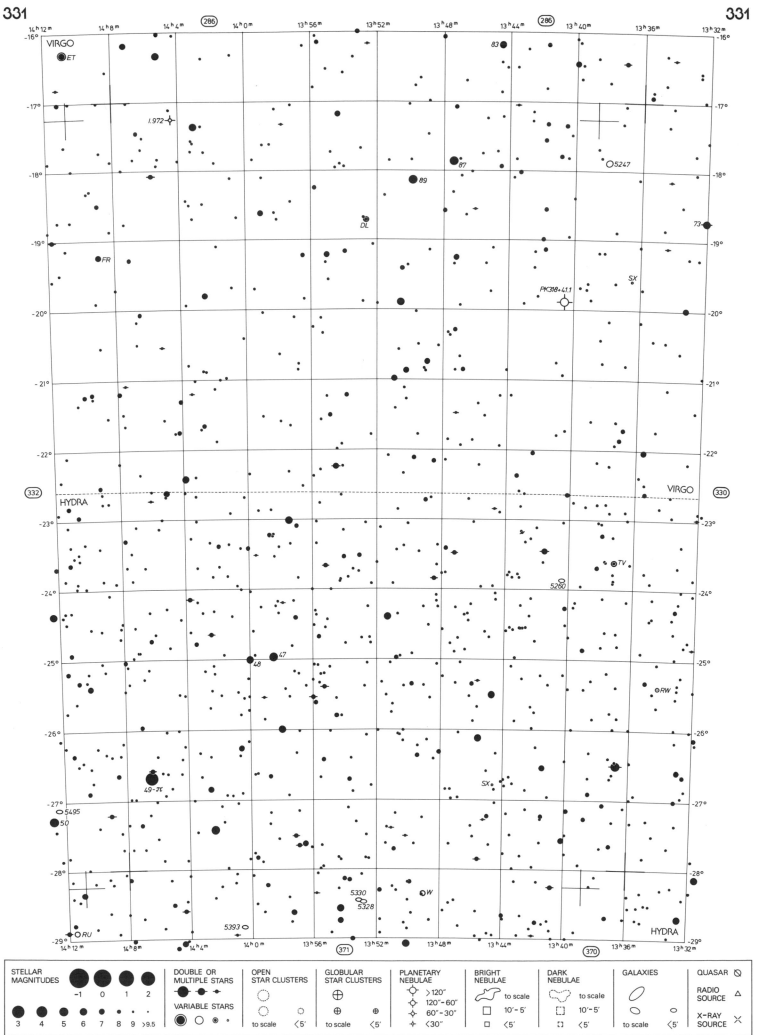

© 1988 WILLMANN-BELL, INC.

Barry Rappaport & Wil Tirion

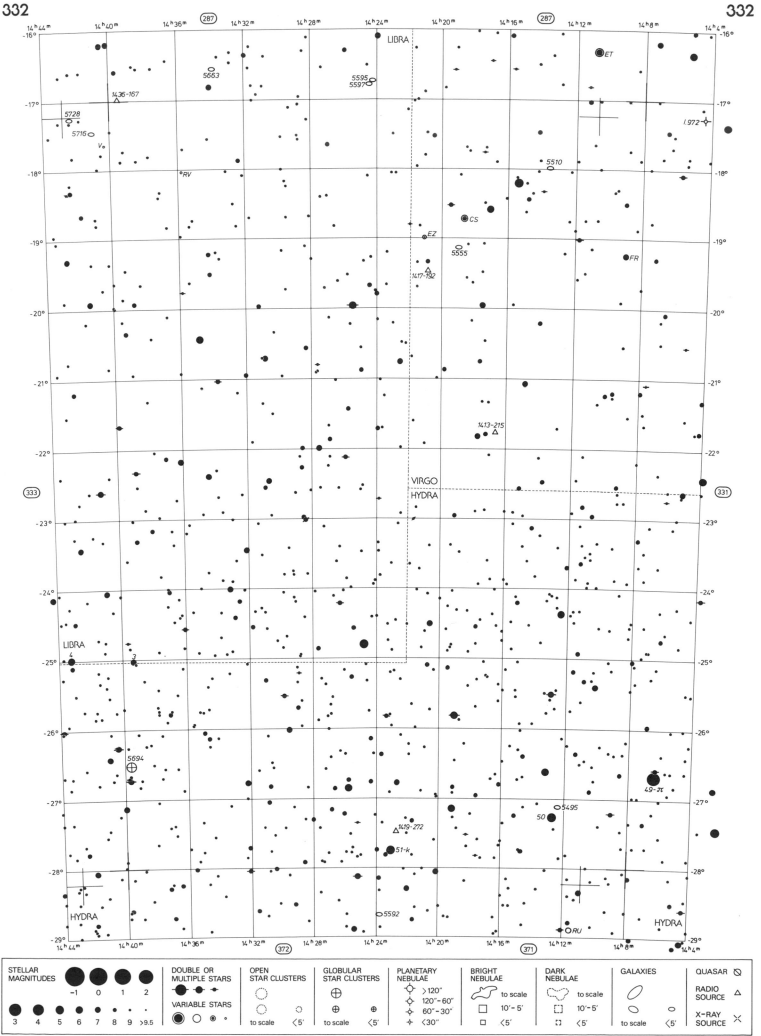

Barry Rappaport & Wil Tirion

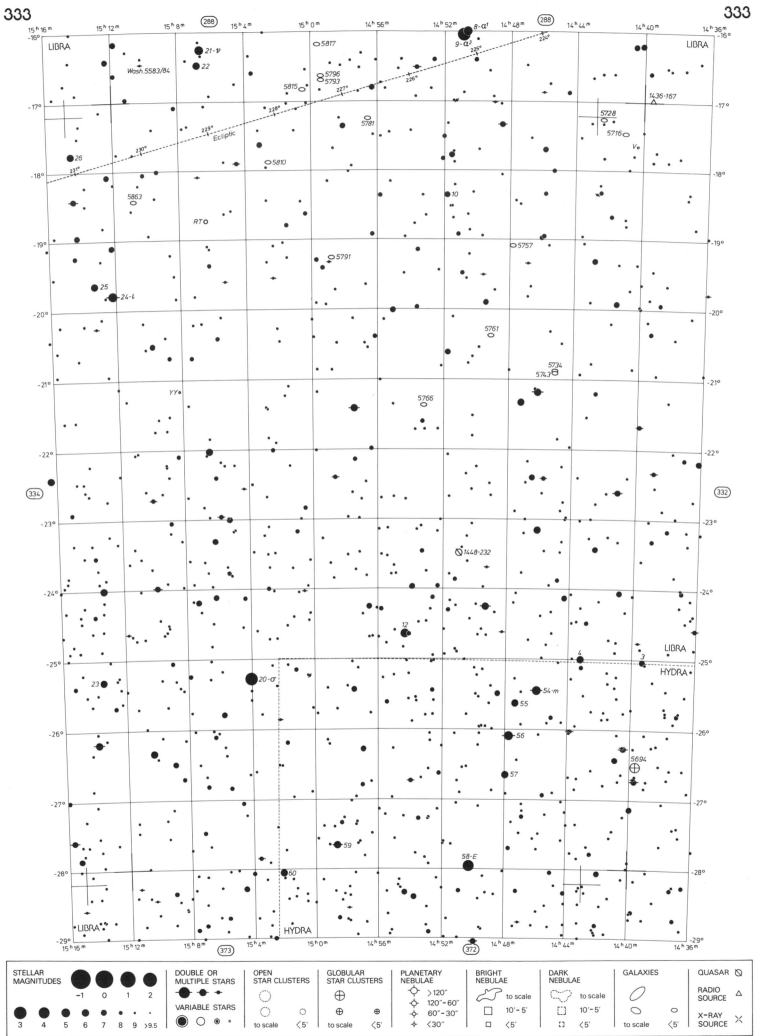

© 1988 WILLMANN-BELL, INC.

Barry Rappaport & Wil Tirion

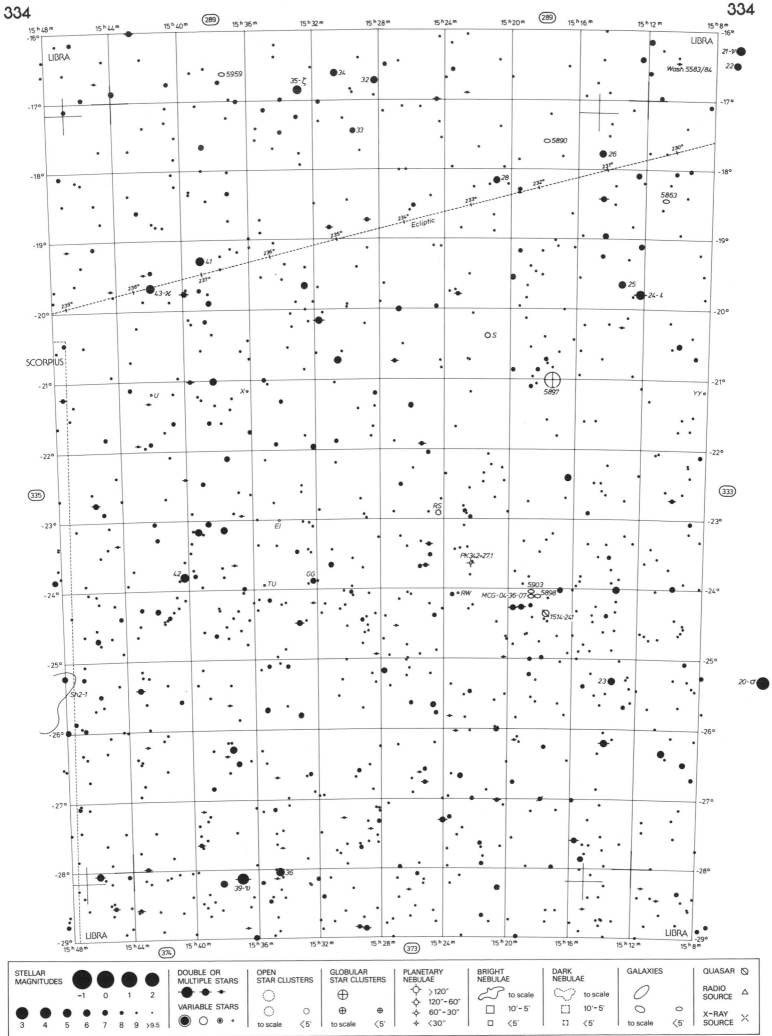

STELLAR MAGNITUDES

−1	0	1	2

3	4	5	6	7	8	9 >9.5

DOUBLE OR MULTIPLE STARS

VARIABLE STARS

OPEN STAR CLUSTERS

to scale <5'

GLOBULAR STAR CLUSTERS

to scale <5'

PLANETARY NEBULAE

>120"
120"−60"
60"−30"
<30"

BRIGHT NEBULAE

to scale
10'−5'
<5'

DARK NEBULAE

to scale
10'−5'
<5'

GALAXIES

to scale <5'

QUASAR

RADIO SOURCE

X-RAY SOURCE

© 1988 WILLMANN-BELL, INC.

Barry Rappaport & Wil Tirion

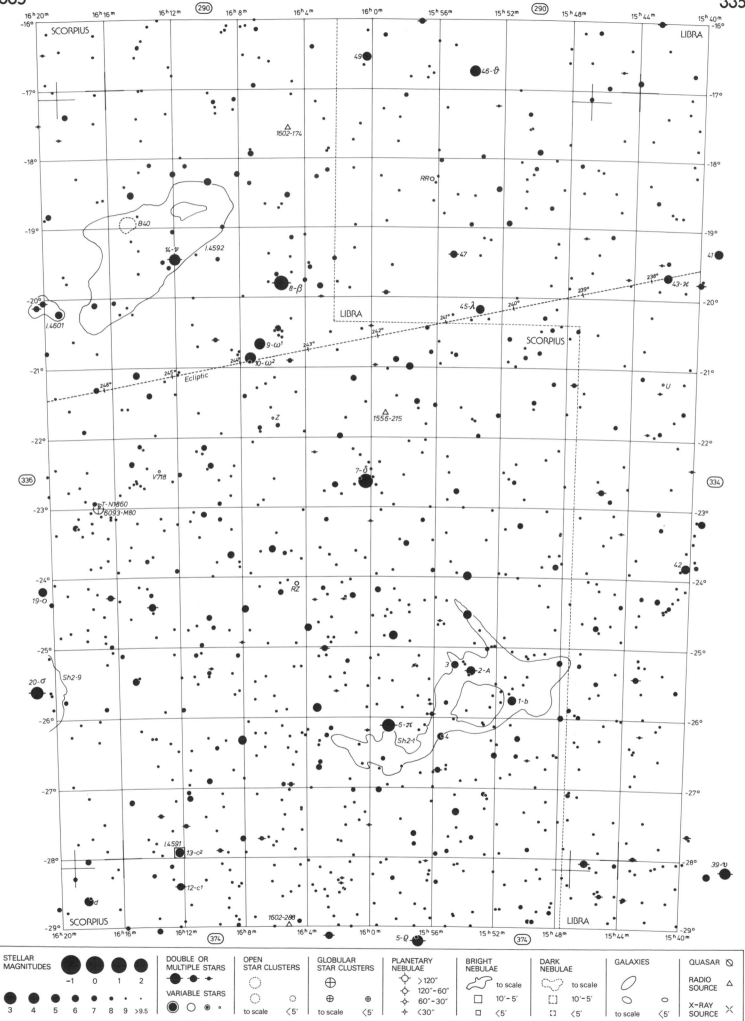

© 1988 WILLMANN-BELL, INC.

Barry Rappaport & Wil Tirion

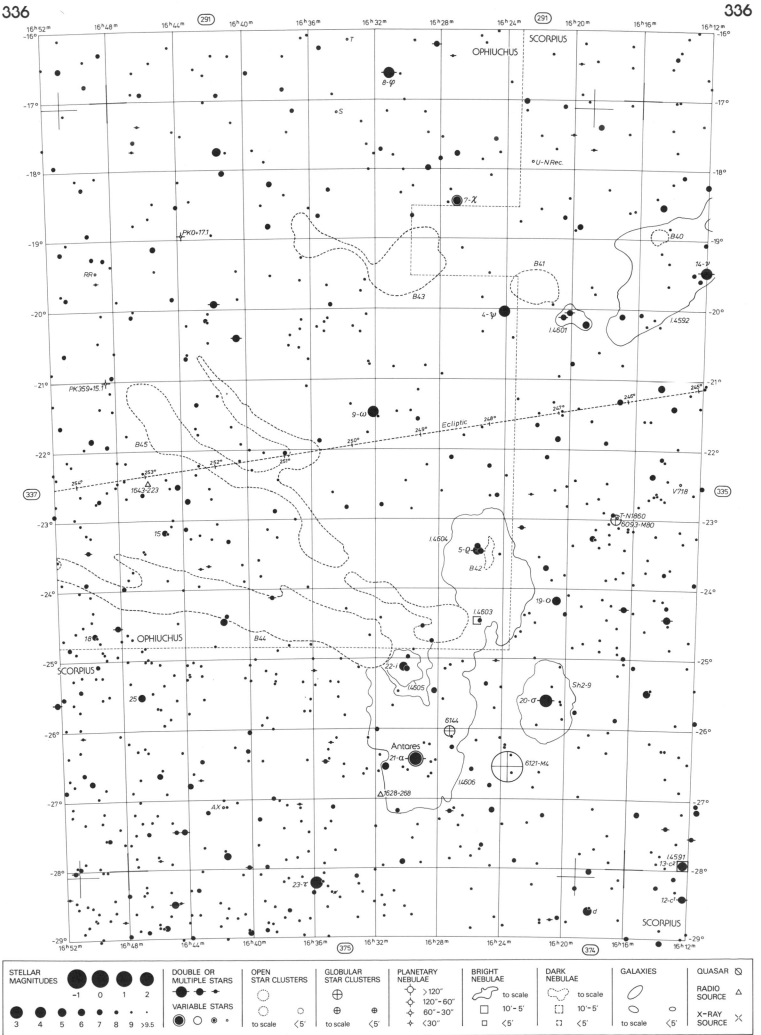

© 1988 WILLMANN-BELL, INC.

Barry Rappaport & Wil Tirion

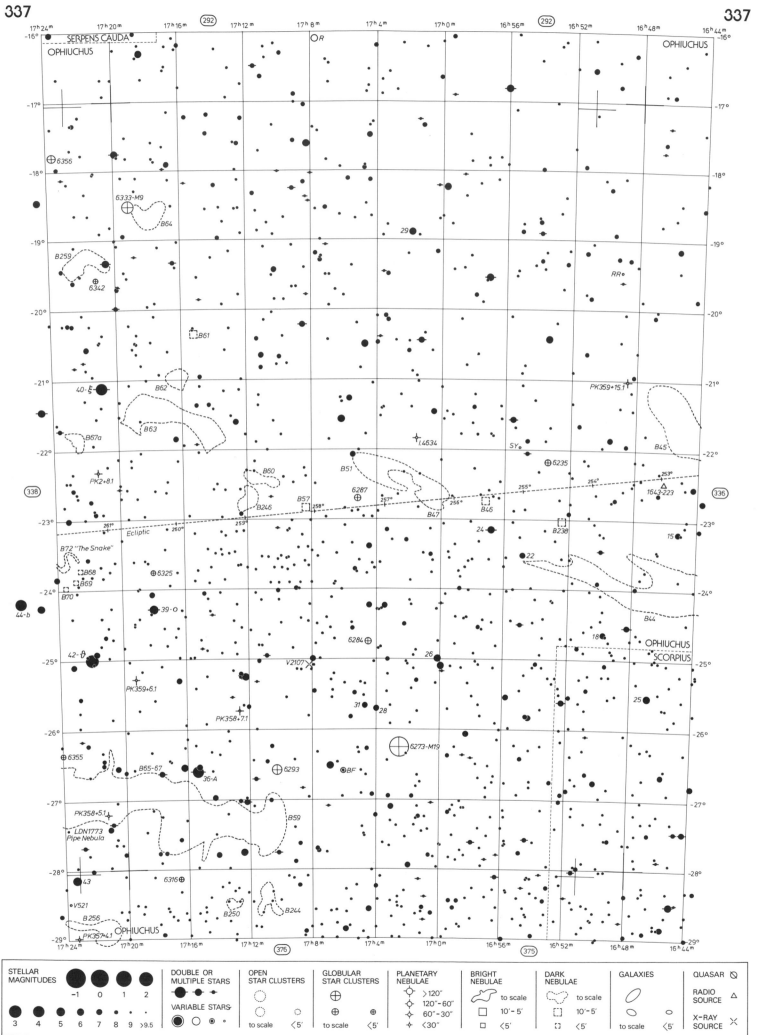

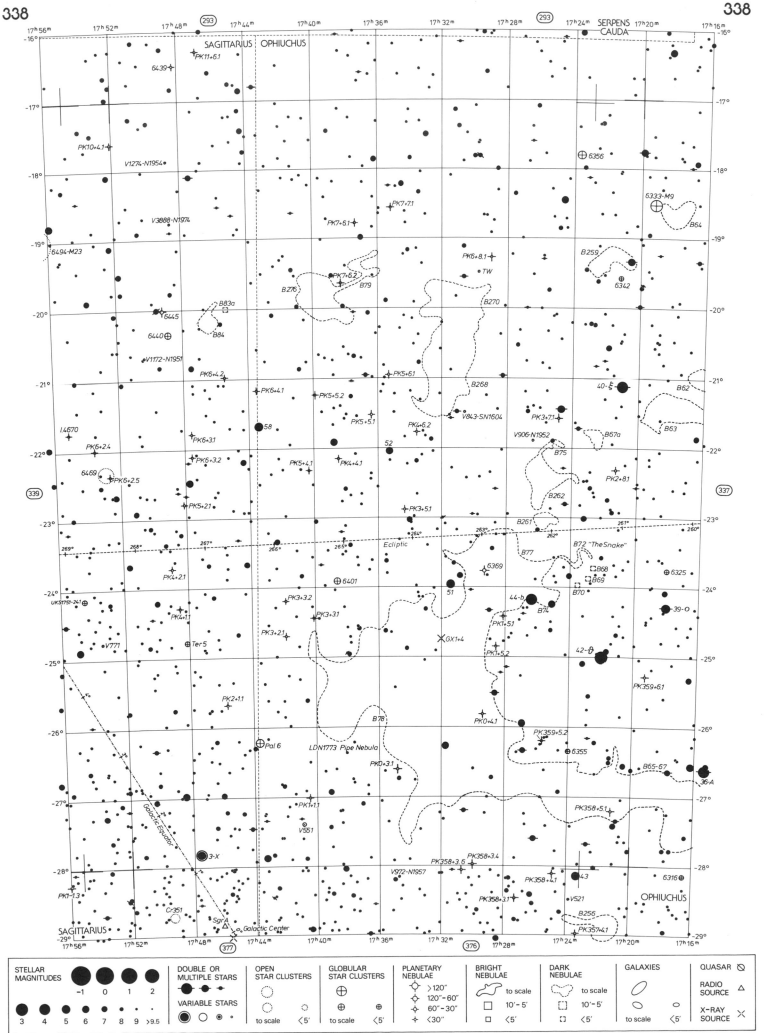

© 1988 WILLMANN-BELL, INC.

Barry Rappaport & Wil Tirion

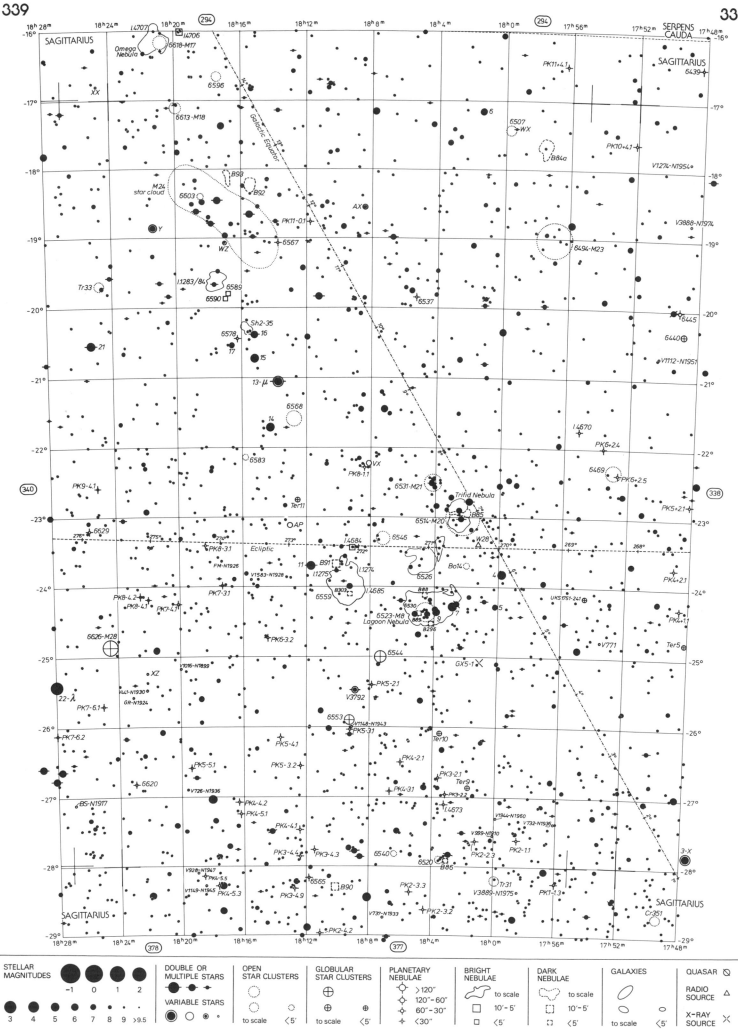

© 1988 WILLMANN-BELL, INC.

Barry Rappaport & Wil Tirion

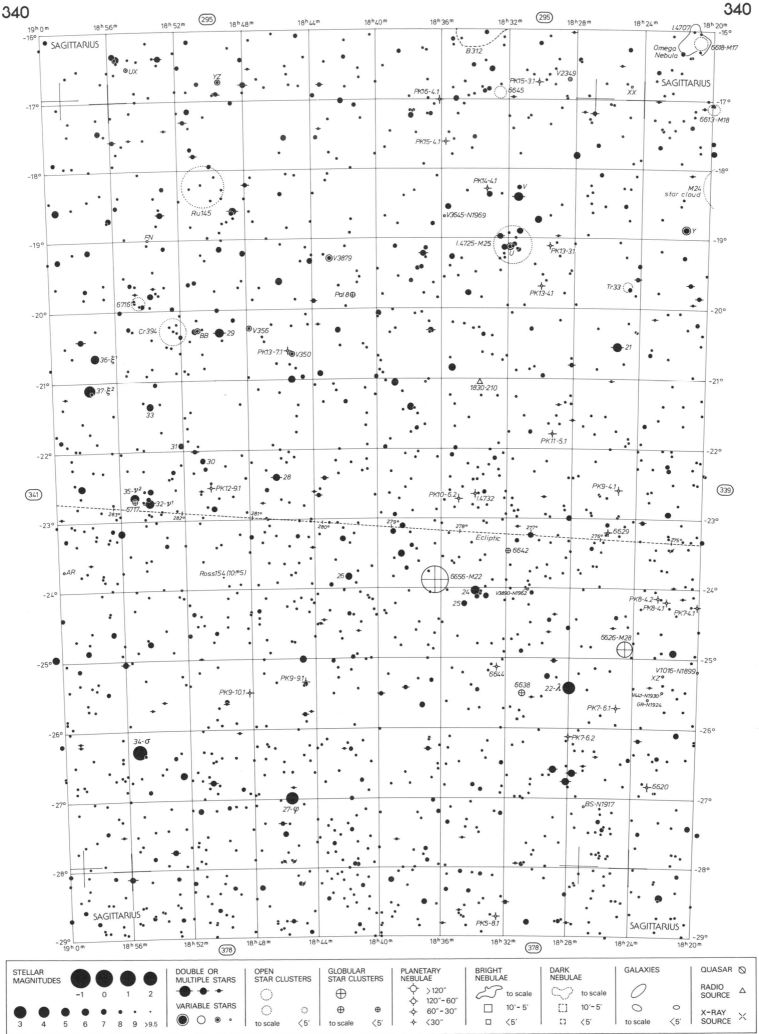

Barry Rappaport & Wil Tirion

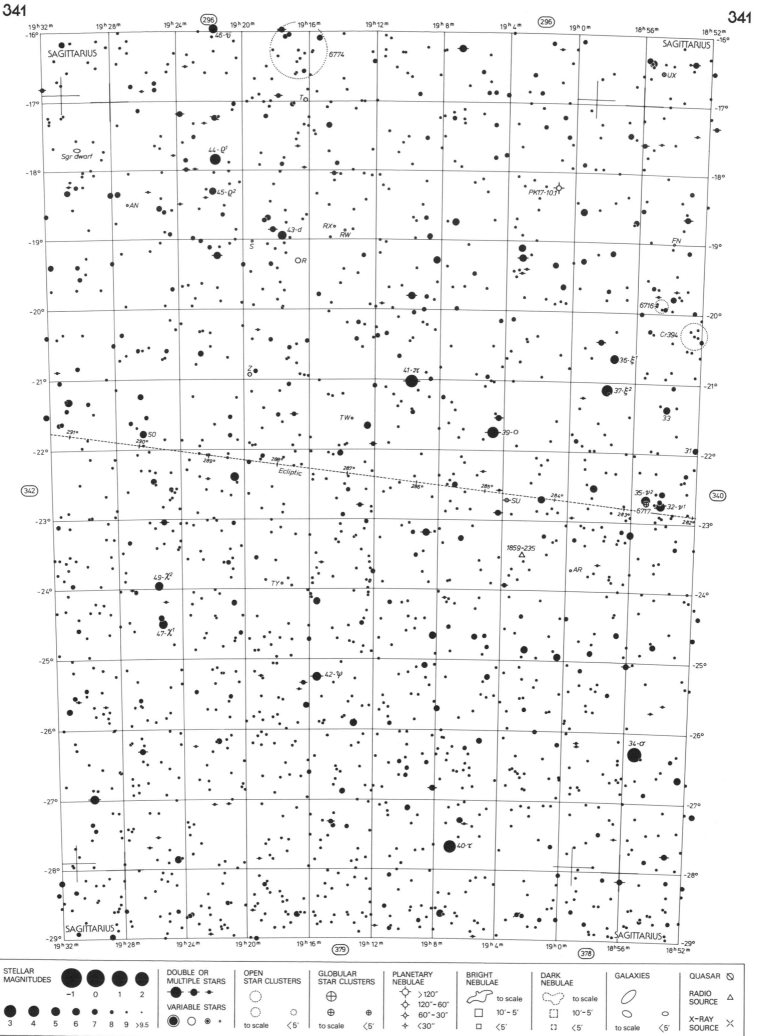

STELLAR MAGNITUDES		DOUBLE OR MULTIPLE STARS	OPEN STAR CLUSTERS	GLOBULAR STAR CLUSTERS	PLANETARY NEBULAE	BRIGHT NEBULAE	DARK NEBULAE	GALAXIES	QUASAR

© 1988 WILLMANN-BELL, INC.

Barry Rappaport & Wil Tirion

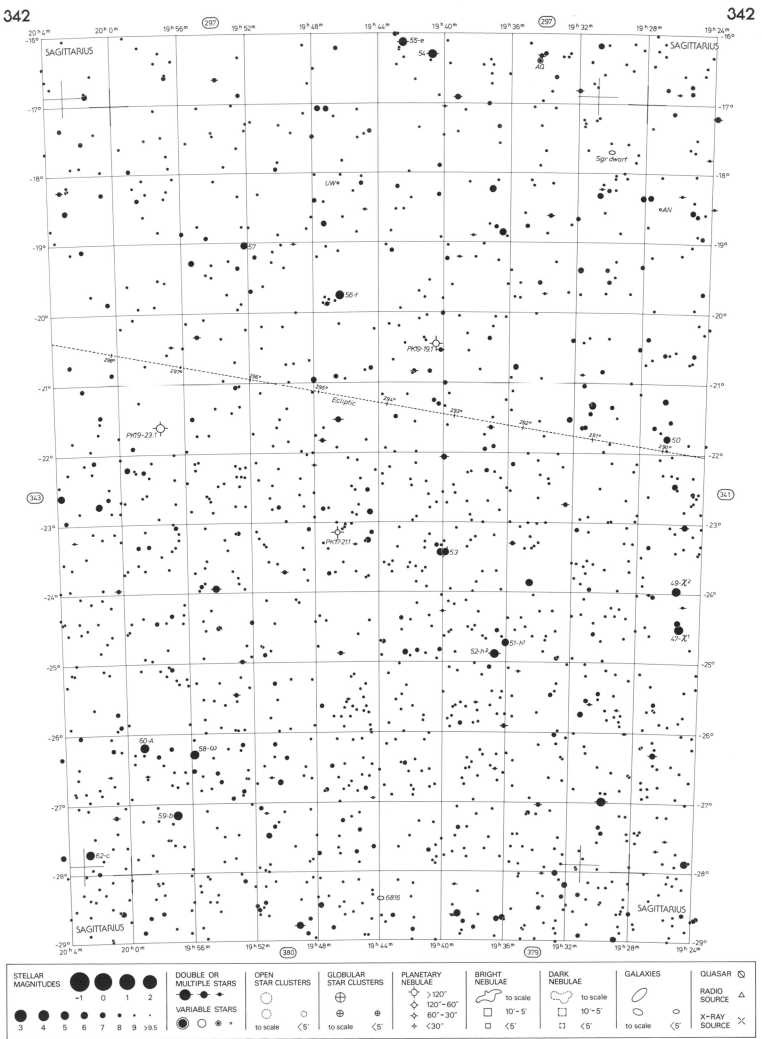

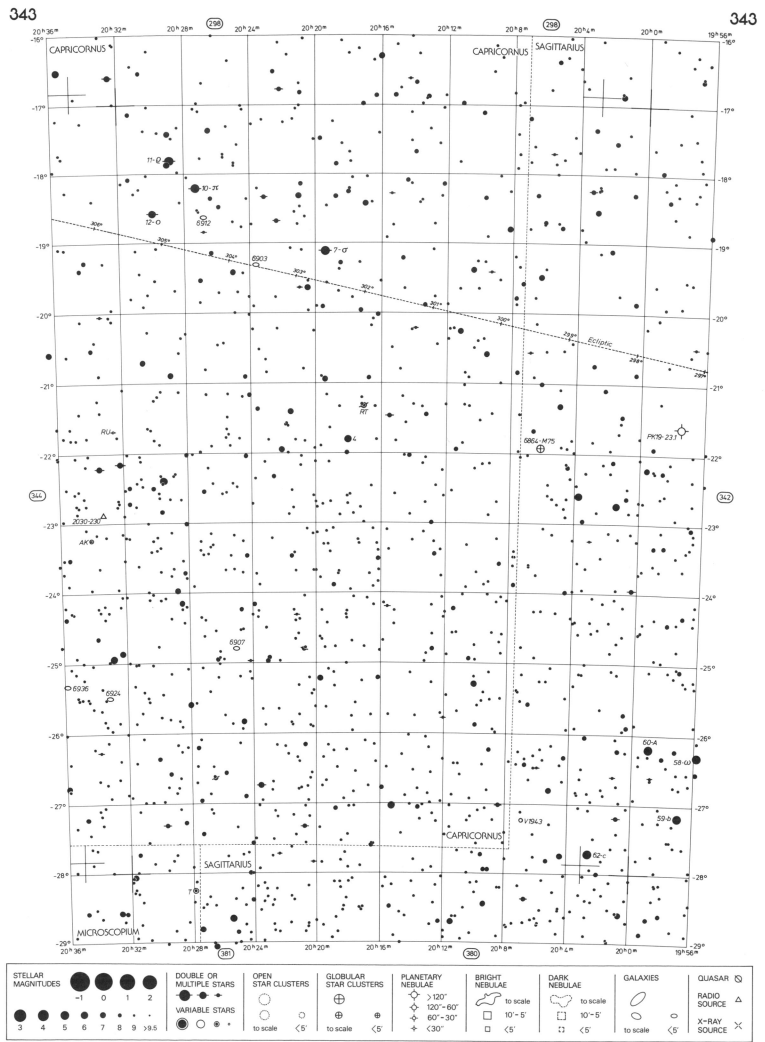

© 1988 WILLMANN-BELL, INC.

Barry Rappaport & Wil Tirion

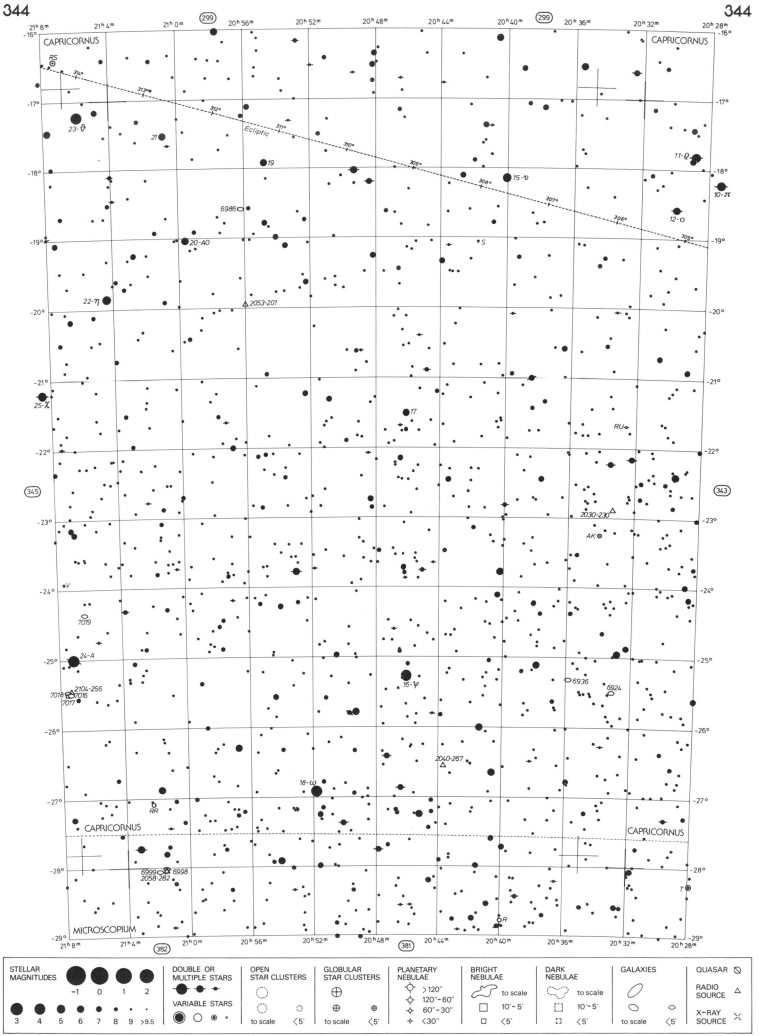

© 1988 WILLMANN-BELL, INC.

Barry Rappaport & Wil Tirion

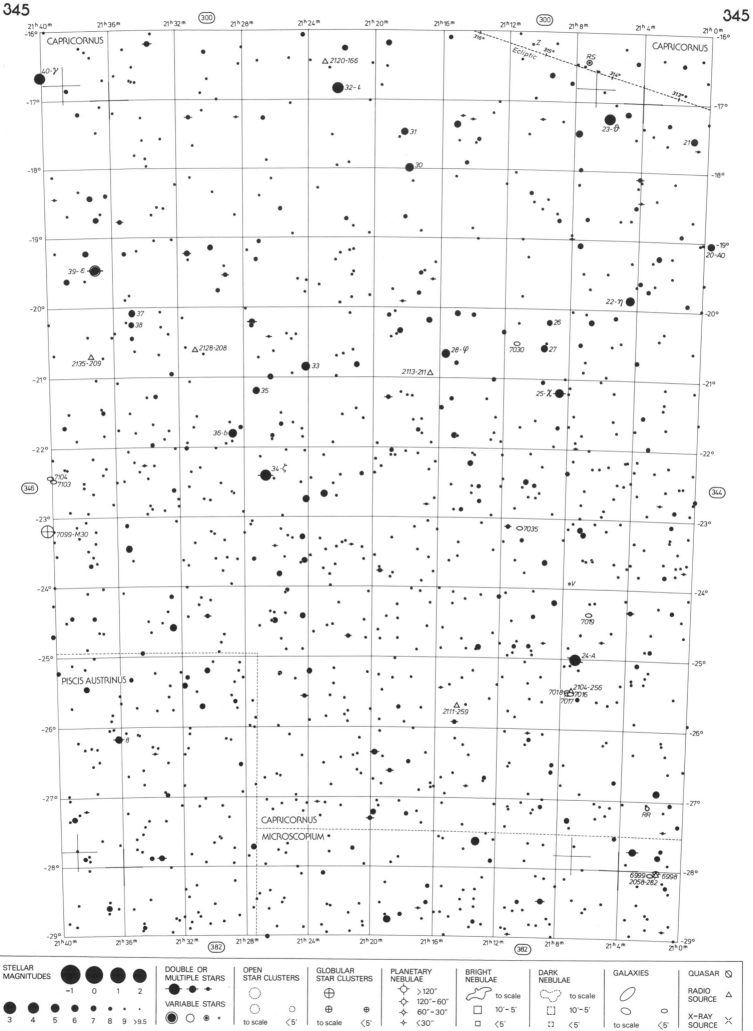

CAPRICORNUS

CAPRICORNUS

PISCIS AUSTRINUS

CAPRICORNUS

MICROSCOPIUM

STELLAR MAGNITUDES		DOUBLE OR MULTIPLE STARS	OPEN STAR CLUSTERS	GLOBULAR STAR CLUSTERS	PLANETARY NEBULAE	BRIGHT NEBULAE	DARK NEBULAE	GALAXIES	QUASAR

© 1988 WILLMANN-BELL, INC.

Barry Rappaport & Wil Tirion

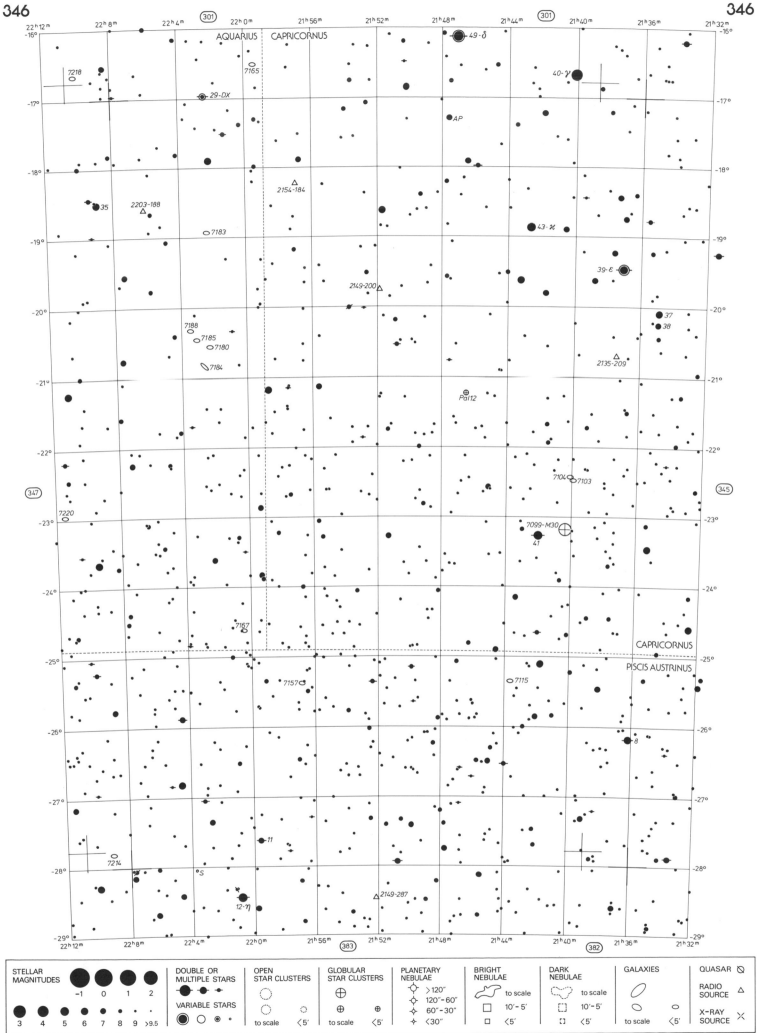

© 1988 WILLMANN-BELL, INC.

Barry Rappaport & Wil Tirion

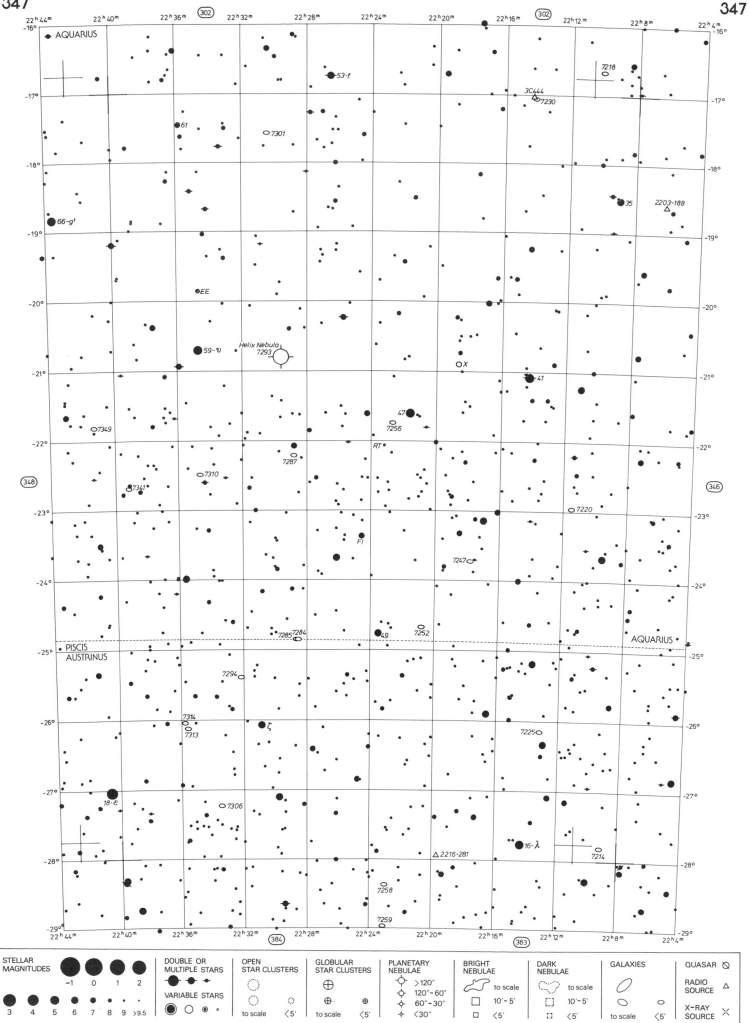

© 1988 WILLMANN-BELL, INC.

Barry Rappaport & Wil Tirion

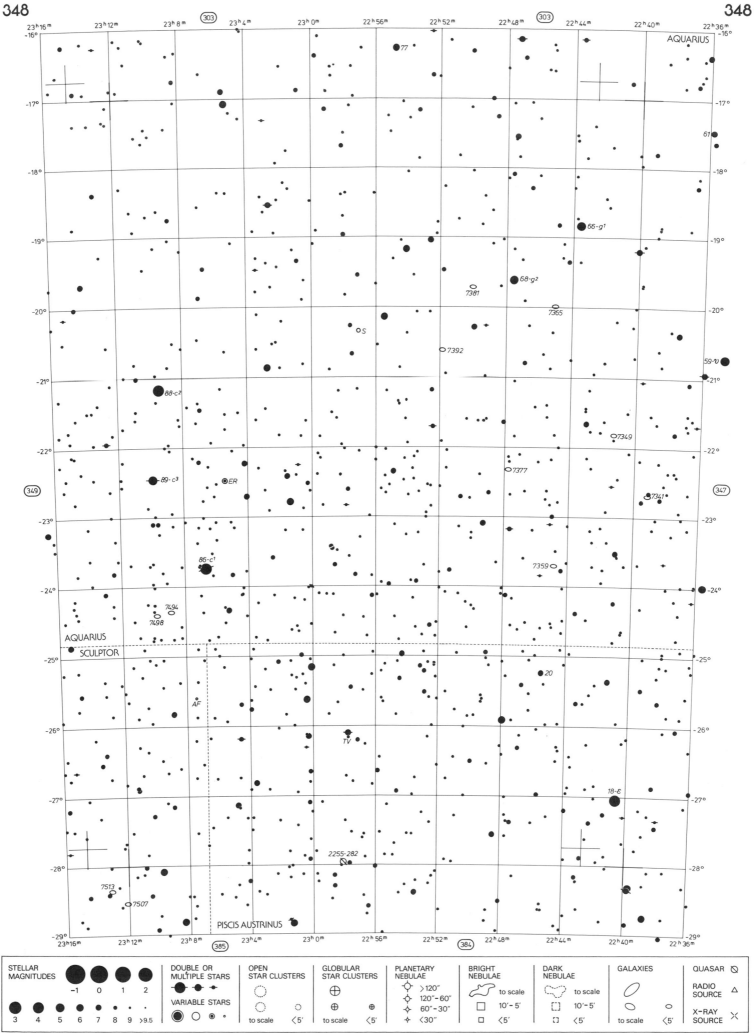

AQUARIUS

AQUARIUS
SCULPTOR

PISCIS AUSTRINUS

STELLAR MAGNITUDES

DOUBLE OR MULTIPLE STARS

VARIABLE STARS

OPEN STAR CLUSTERS

GLOBULAR STAR CLUSTERS

PLANETARY NEBULAE

BRIGHT NEBULAE

DARK NEBULAE

GALAXIES

QUASAR

RADIO SOURCE

X-RAY SOURCE

© 1988 WILLMANN-BELL, INC.

Barry Rappaport & Wil Tirion

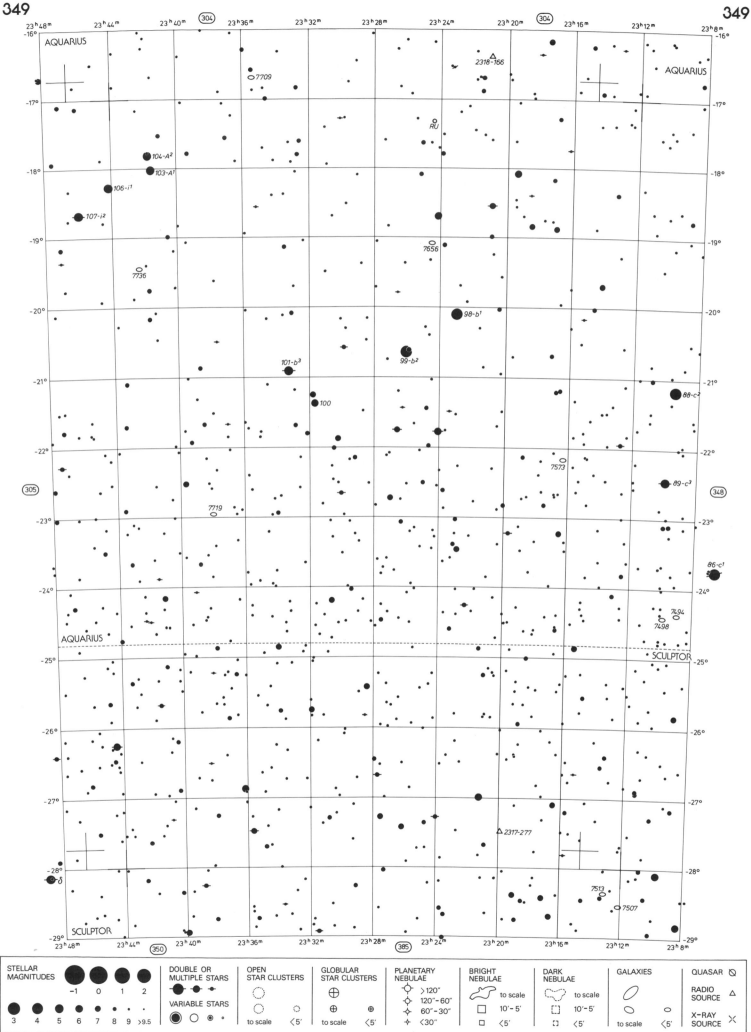

© 1988 WILLMANN-BELL, INC.

Barry Rappaport & Wil Tirion

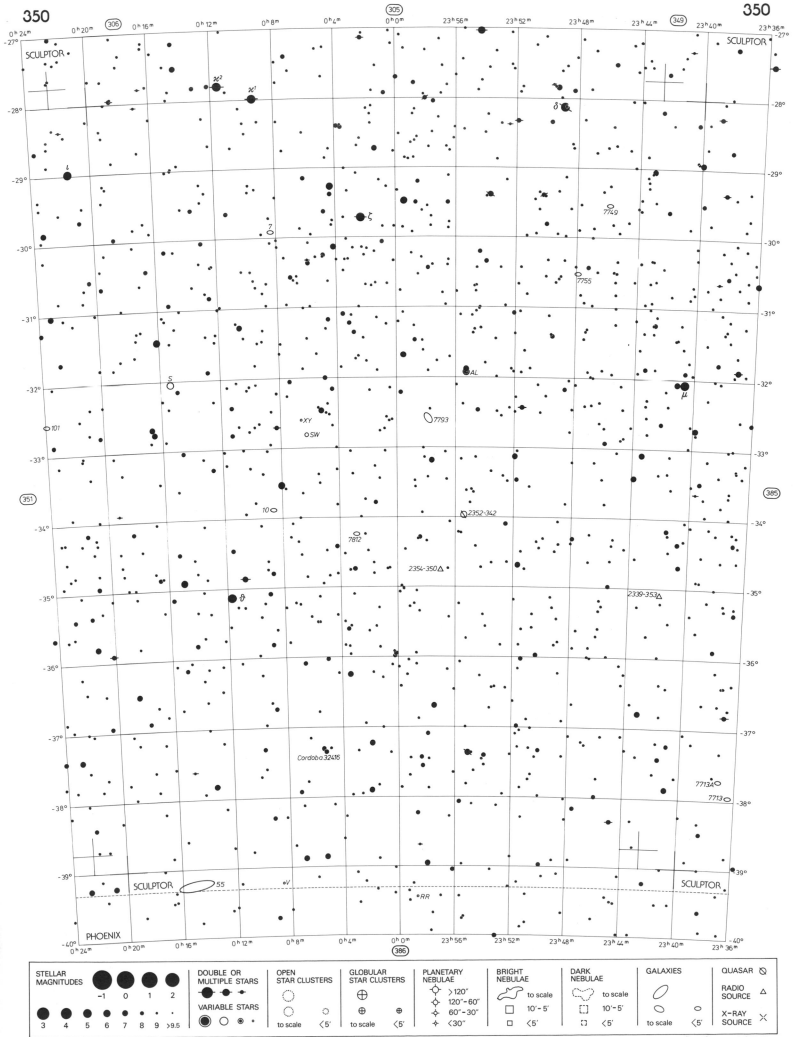

© 1988 WILLMANN-BELL, INC.

Barry Rappaport & Wil Tirion

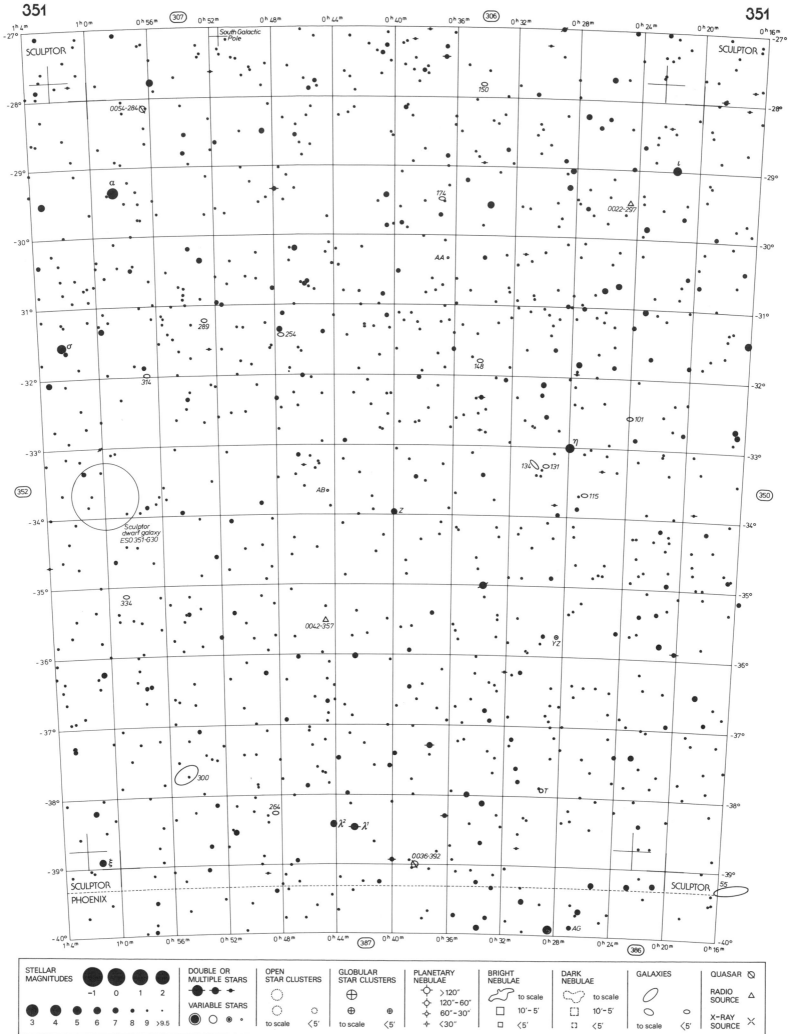

SCULPTOR

SCULPTOR

South Galactic Pole

0054-284

α

150

174

0022-297

AA

289

254

σ

148

314

101

η

134 131

352

350

AB

115

z

Sculptor
dwarf galaxy
ESO 351-G30

334

0042-357

YZ

T

300

264

λ² λ¹

0036-392

ξ

SCULPTOR
PHOENIX

SCULPTOR
55

AG

STELLAR MAGNITUDES					DOUBLE OR MULTIPLE STARS	OPEN STAR CLUSTERS		GLOBULAR STAR CLUSTERS		PLANETARY NEBULAE		BRIGHT NEBULAE		DARK NEBULAE		GALAXIES		QUASAR
	−1	0	1	2				⊕		◇ >120"		⌇ to scale		⌐⌐ to scale		⬭		⊘
					VARIABLE STARS					◇ 120"-60"		□ 10'-5'		[:] 10'-5'				RADIO SOURCE △
3	4	5	6	7	8	9	>9.5	⊕ to scale	⊕ <5'	◇ 60"-30"		□ <5'		:: <5'		⬯ to scale	⬯ <5'	X-RAY SOURCE ✕
								to scale	<5'	✧ <30"								

© 1988 WILLMANN-BELL, INC.

Barry Rappaport & Wil Tirion

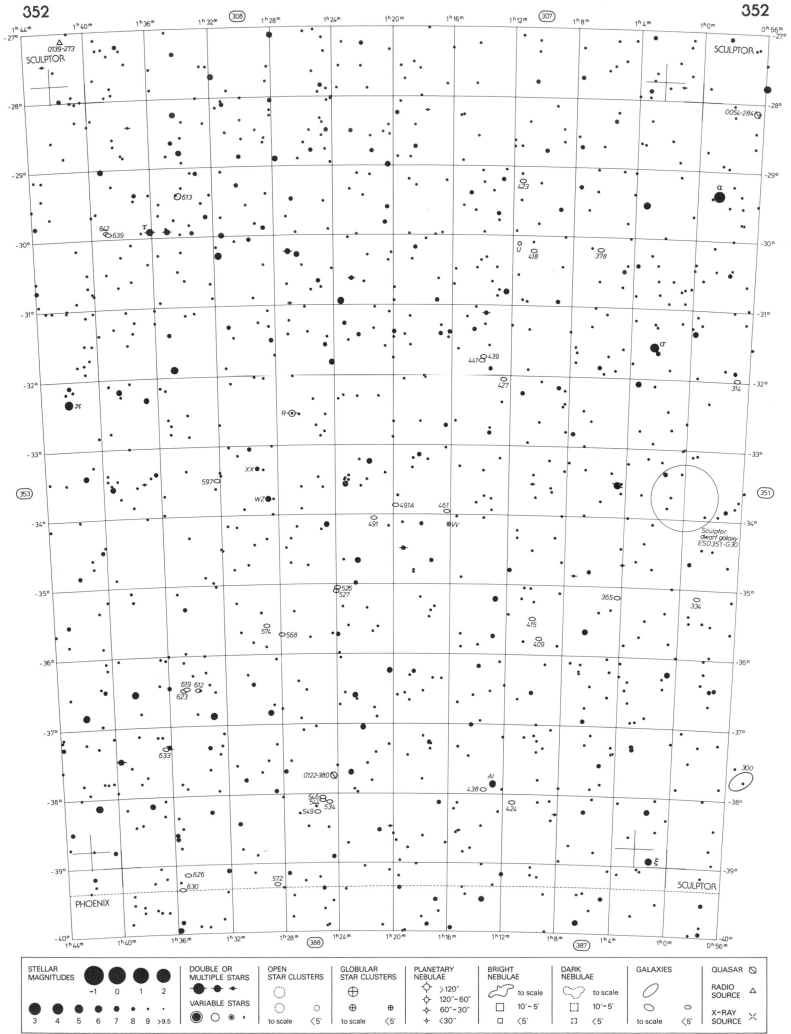

© 1988 WILLMANN-BELL, INC.

Barry Rappaport & Wil Tirion

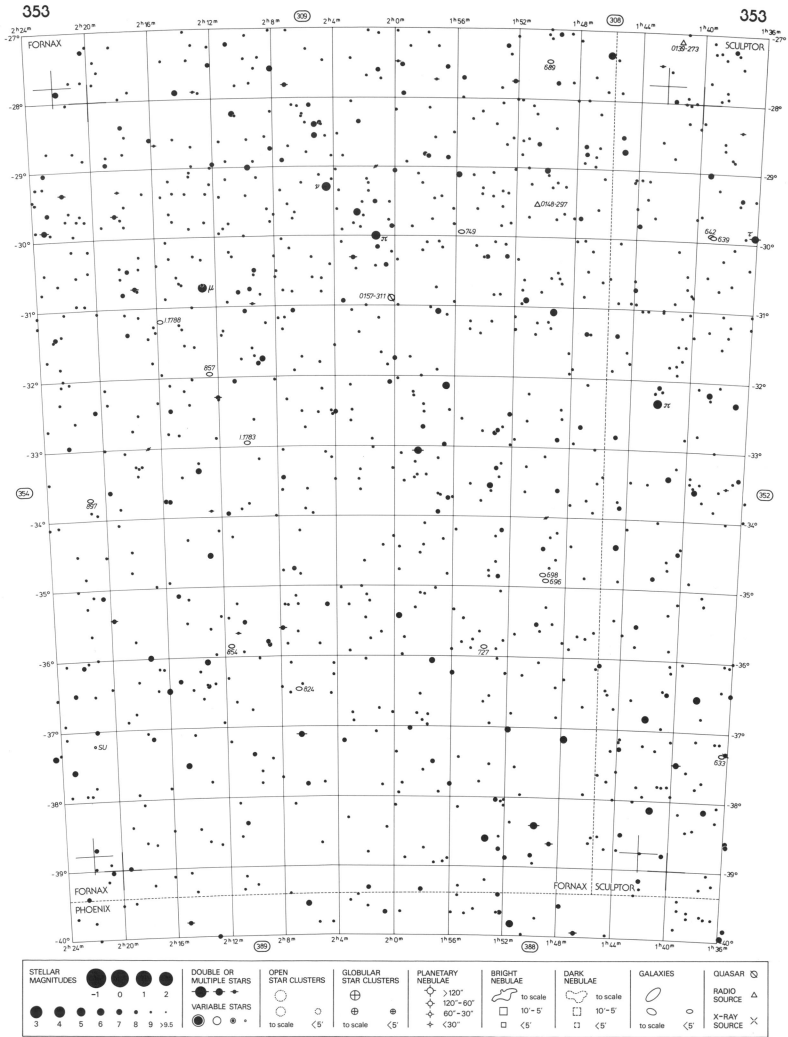

© 1988 WILLMANN-BELL, INC.

Barry Rappaport & Wil Tirion

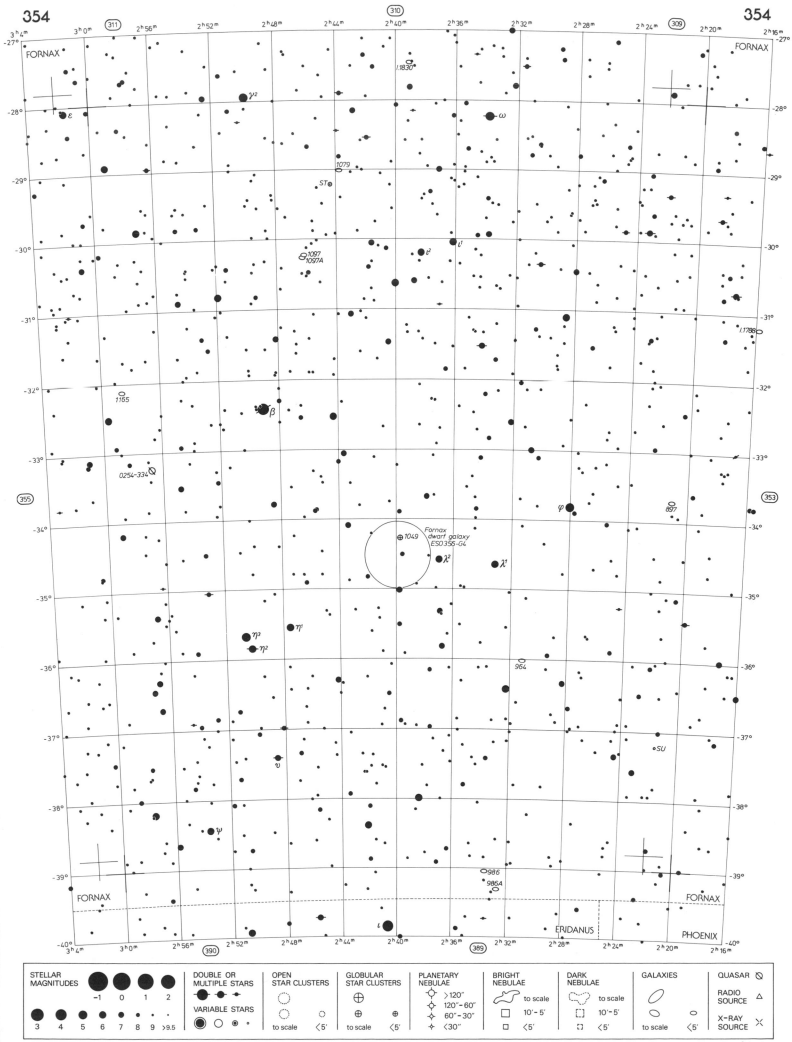

STELLAR MAGNITUDES
−1 0 1 2
3 4 5 6 7 8 9 >9.5

DOUBLE OR MULTIPLE STARS
VARIABLE STARS

OPEN STAR CLUSTERS
to scale <5′

GLOBULAR STAR CLUSTERS
⊕ ⊕ ⊕
to scale <5′

PLANETARY NEBULAE
>120″
120″–60″
60″–30″
<30″

BRIGHT NEBULAE
to scale
10′–5′
<5′

DARK NEBULAE
to scale
10′–5′
<5′

GALAXIES
to scale <5′

QUASAR

RADIO SOURCE

X-RAY SOURCE

© 1988 WILLMANN-BELL, INC.

Barry Rappaport & Wil Tirion

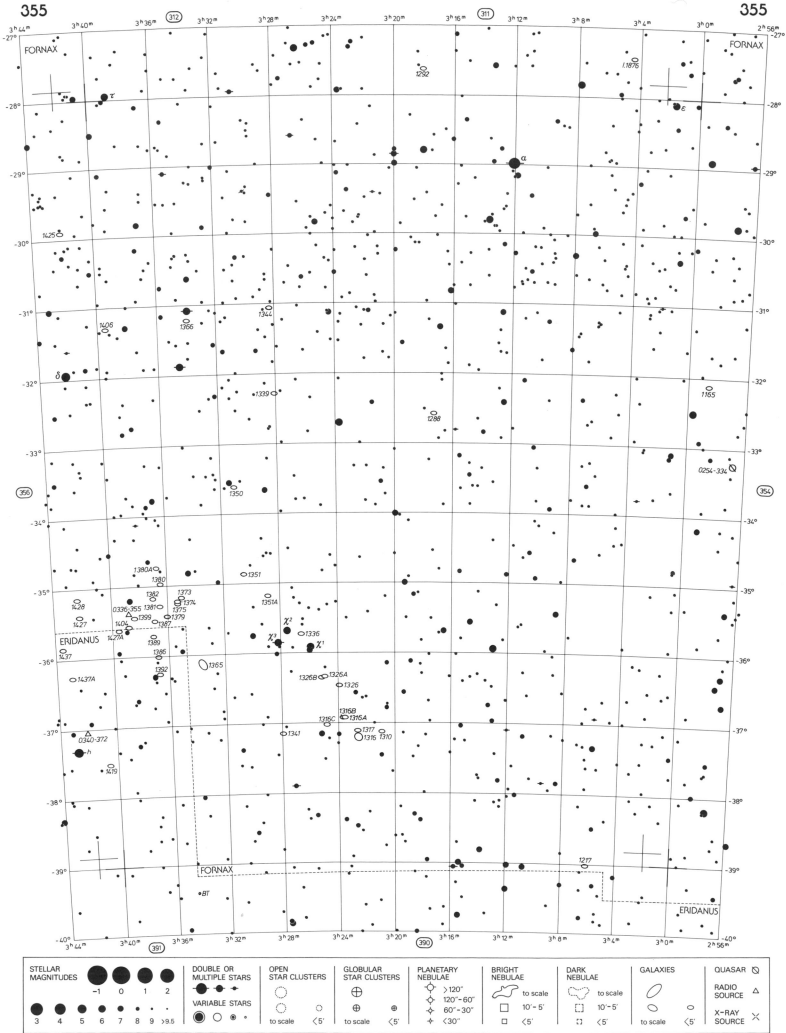

© 1988 WILLMANN-BELL, INC.

Barry Rappaport & Wil Tirion

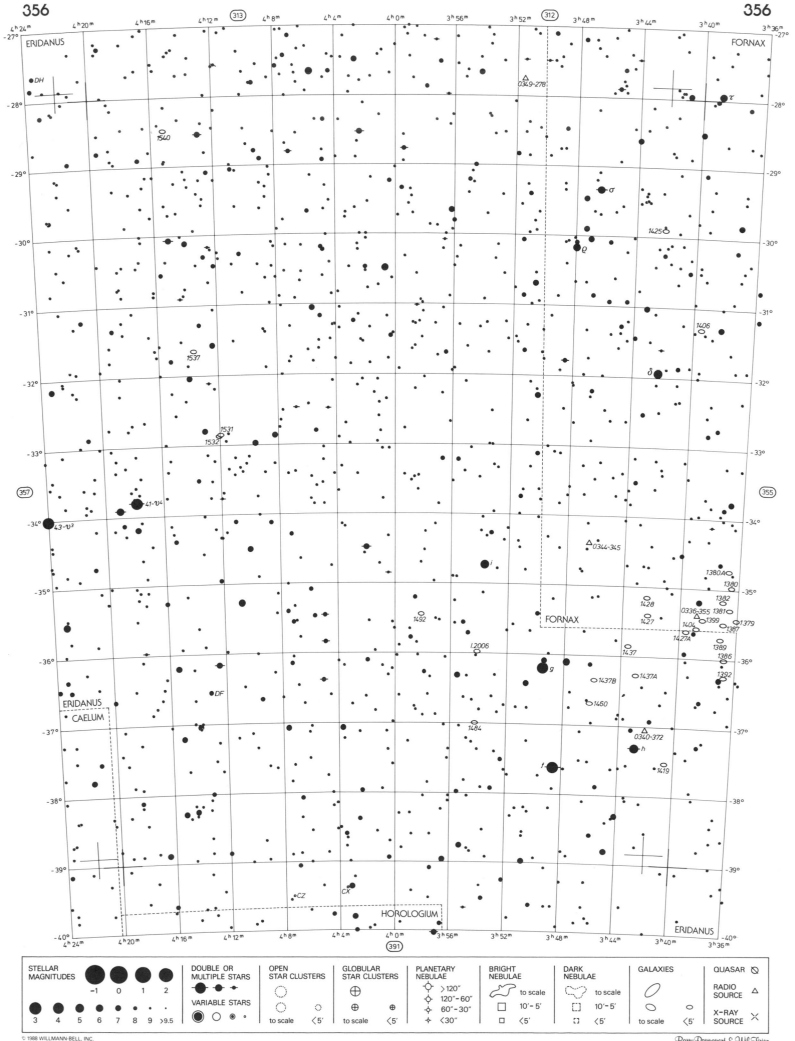

ERIDANUS

FORNAX

ERIDANUS

CAELUM

FORNAX

HOROLOGIUM

ERIDANUS

STELLAR MAGNITUDES					DOUBLE OR MULTIPLE STARS	OPEN STAR CLUSTERS	GLOBULAR STAR CLUSTERS	PLANETARY NEBULAE	BRIGHT NEBULAE	DARK NEBULAE	GALAXIES	QUASAR

© 1988 WILLMANN-BELL, INC.

Barry Rappaport & Wil Tirion

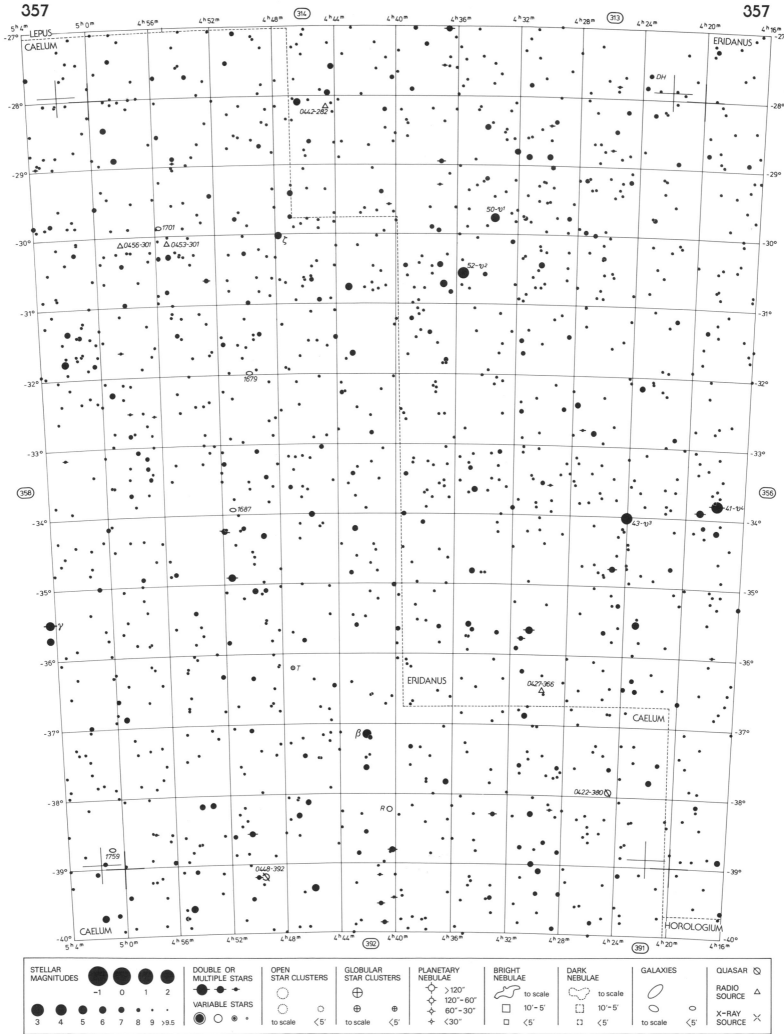

© 1988 WILLMANN-BELL, INC.

Barry Rappaport & Wil Tirion

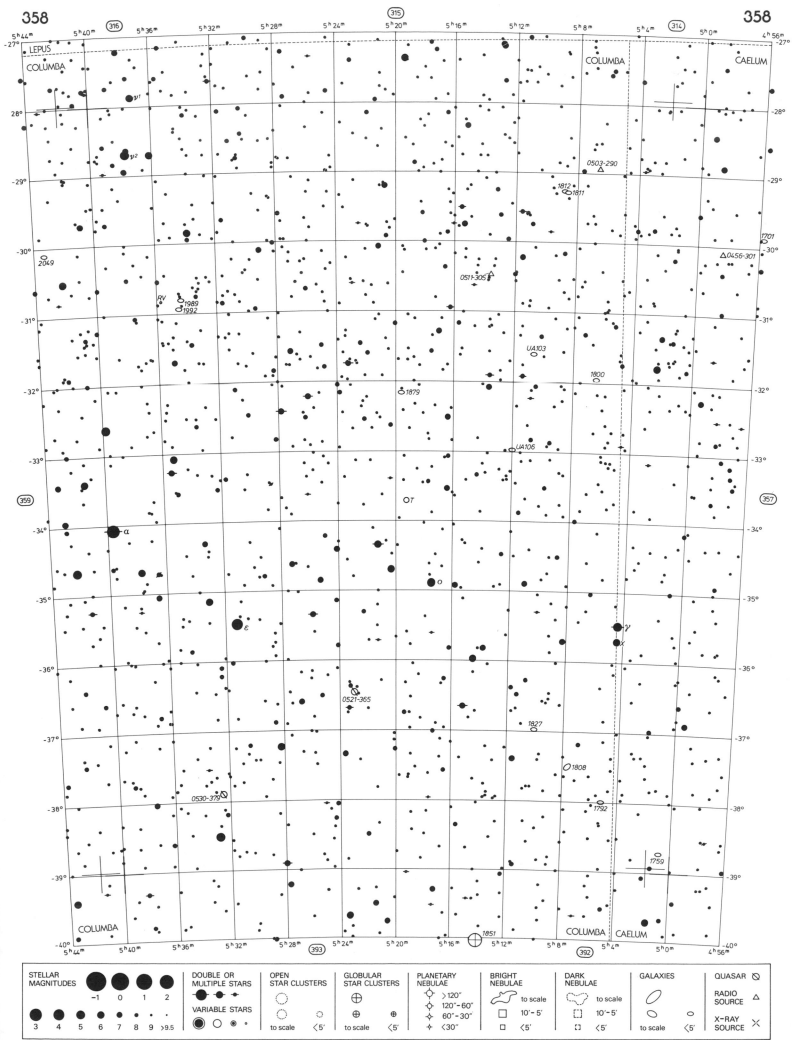

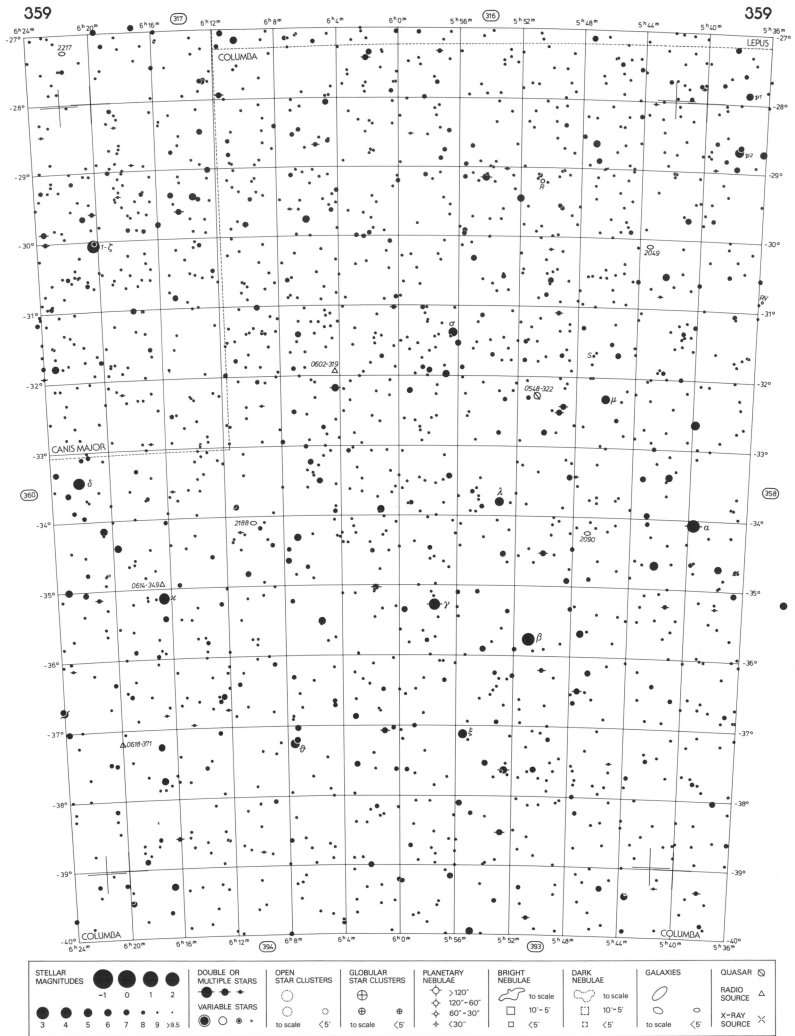

© 1988 WILLMANN-BELL, INC.

Barry Rappaport & Wil Tirion

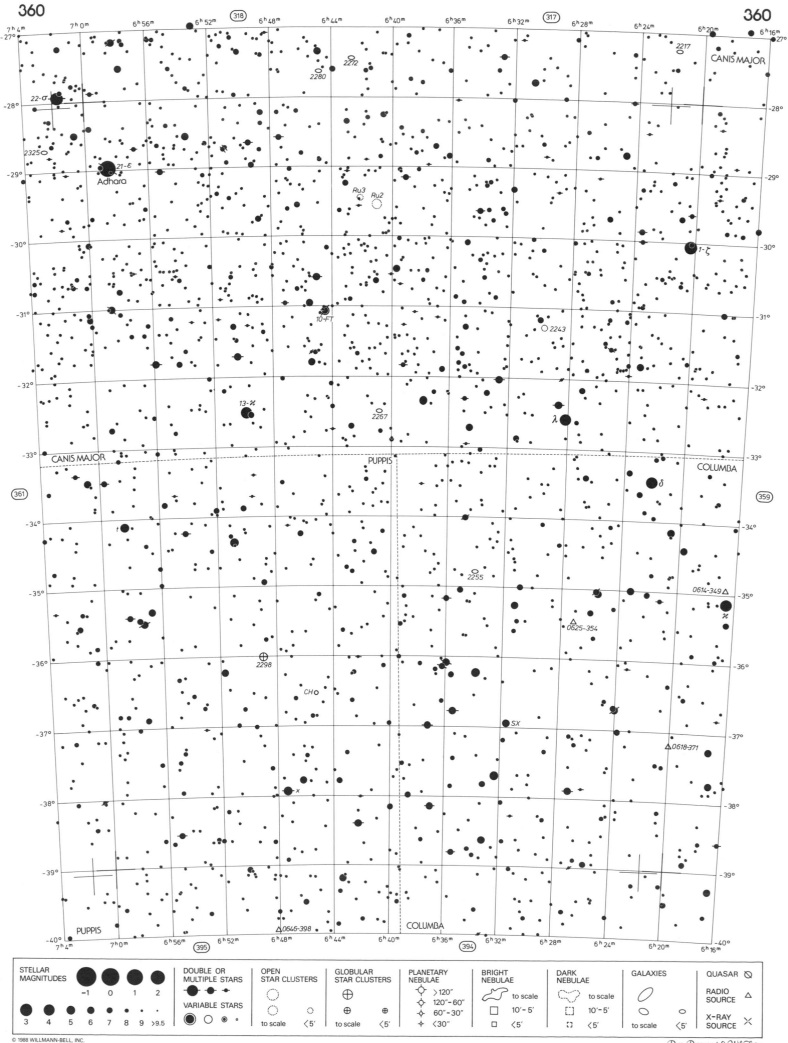

CANIS MAJOR

PUPPIS

COLUMBA

CANIS MAJOR

PUPPIS

COLUMBA

Adhara

21-ε

22-σ

2325

2272

2280

Ru3

Ru2

1-ζ

10-FT

2243

13-κ

2267

λ

δ

t

2255

0614-349

κ

0625-354

2298

CH

0618-371

SX

x

0646-398

STELLAR MAGNITUDES	DOUBLE OR MULTIPLE STARS	OPEN STAR CLUSTERS	GLOBULAR STAR CLUSTERS	PLANETARY NEBULAE	BRIGHT NEBULAE	DARK NEBULAE	GALAXIES	QUASAR
-1 0 1 2				> 120″	to scale	to scale		RADIO SOURCE
	VARIABLE STARS	to scale		120″-60″				X-RAY
3 4 5 6 7 8 9 >9.5		< 5′	to scale	< 5′	60″-30″	10′-5′	10′-5′	to scale	< 5′	SOURCE
				< 30″	< 5′	< 5′		

© 1988 WILLMANN-BELL, INC.

Barry Rappaport & Wil Tirion

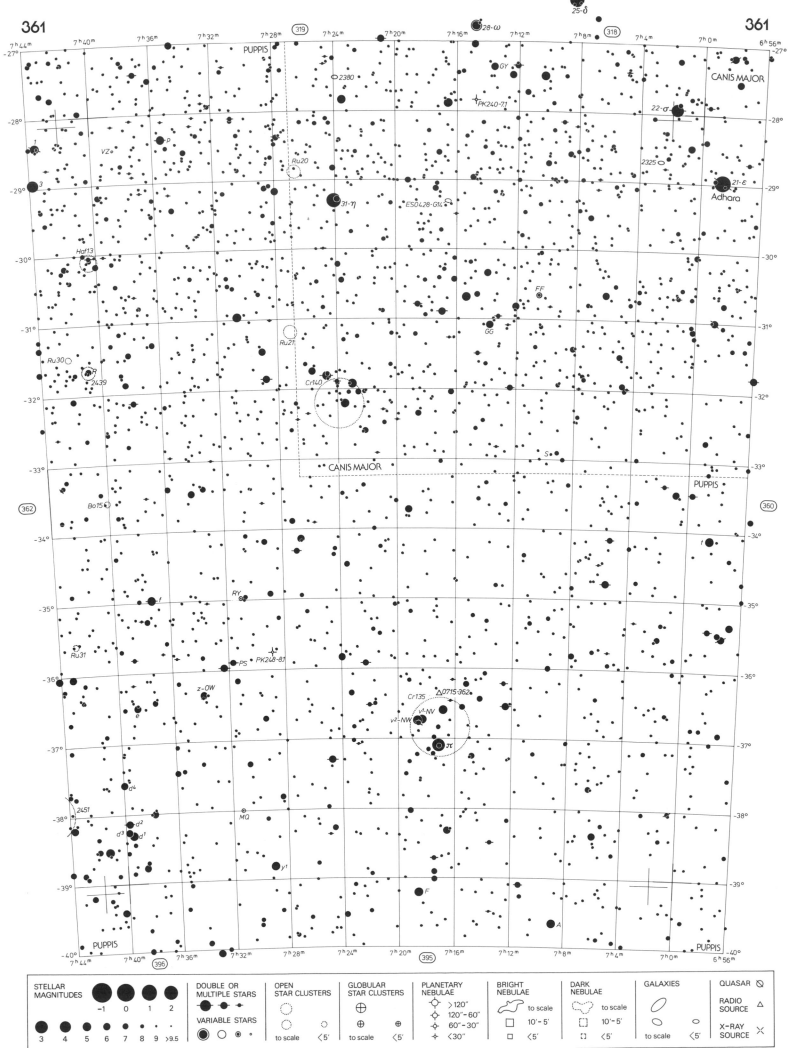

© 1988 WILLMANN-BELL, INC.

Barry Rappaport & Wil Tirion

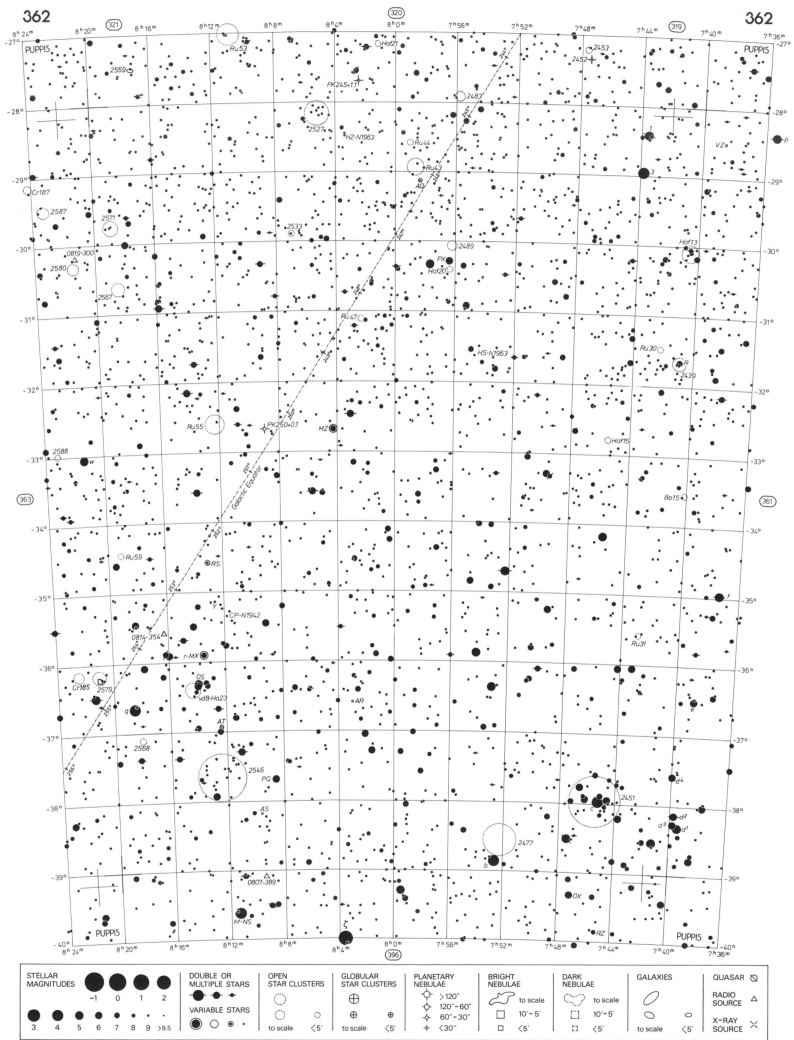

© 1988 WILLMANN-BELL, INC.

Barry Rappaport & Wil Tirion

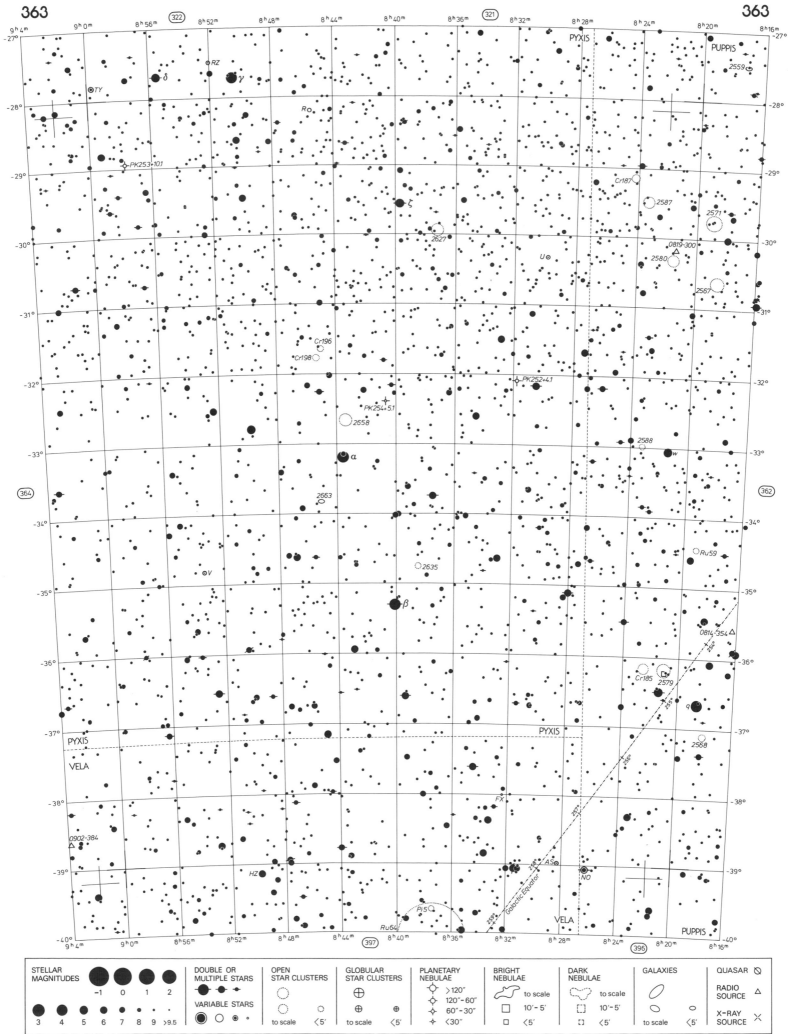

© 1988 WILLMANN-BELL, INC.

Barry Rappaport & Wil Tirion

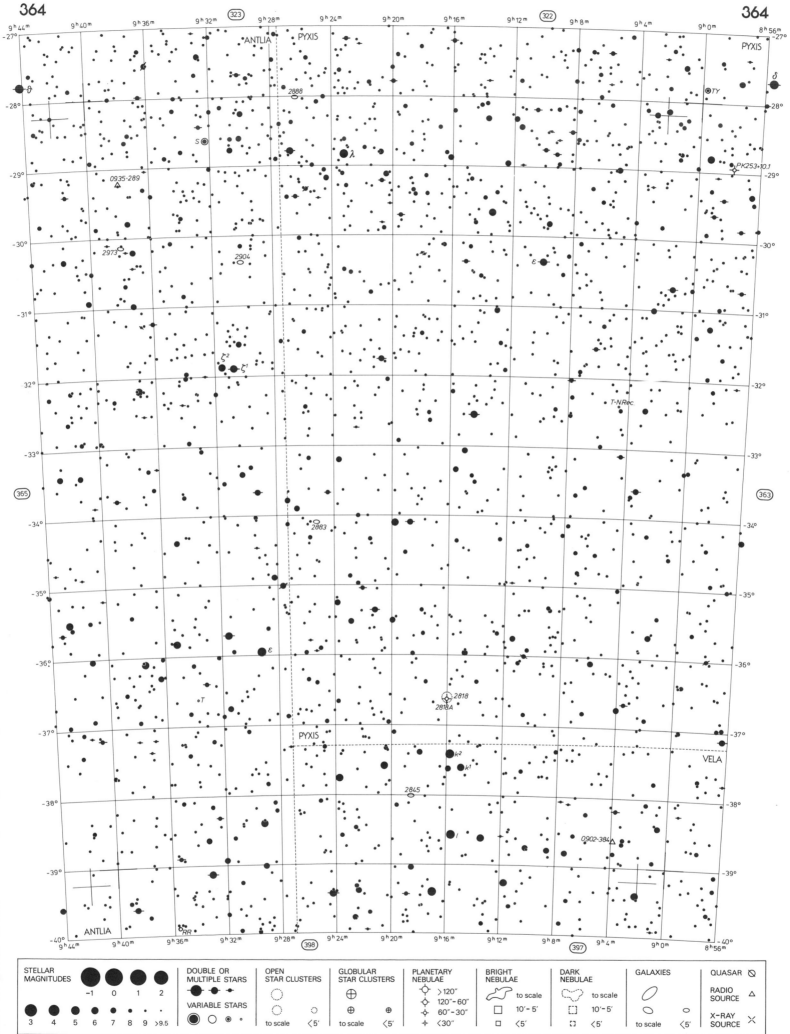

© 1988 WILLMANN-BELL, INC.

Barry Rappaport & Wil Tirion

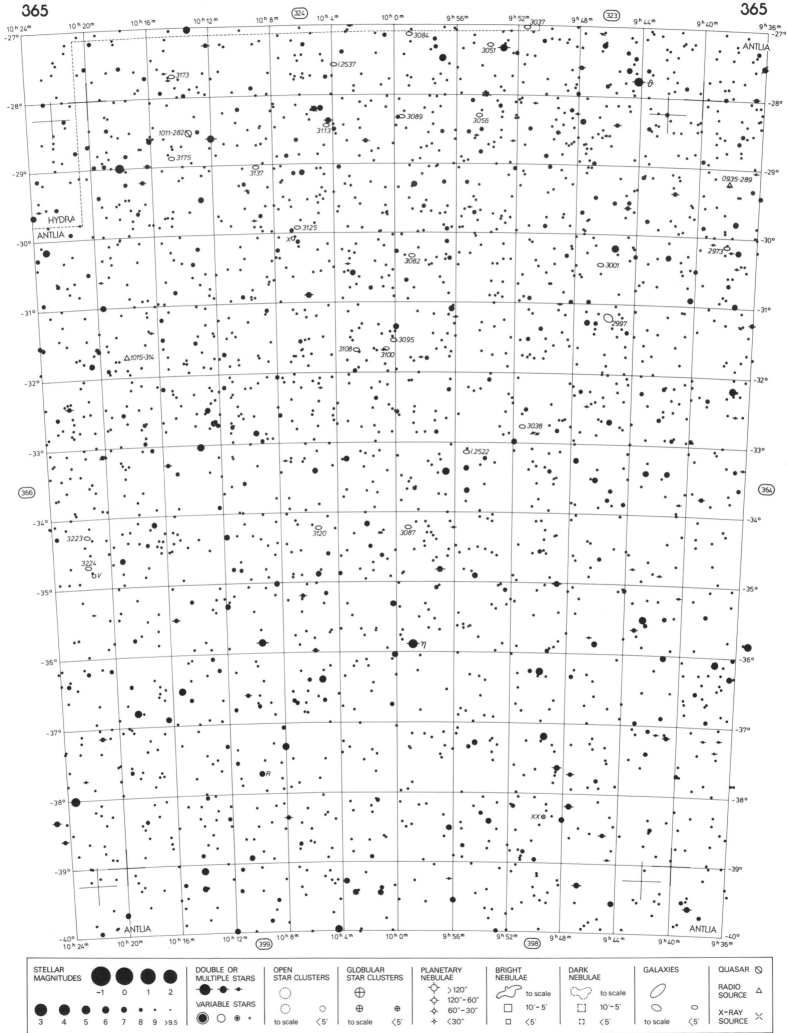

© 1988 WILLMANN-BELL, INC.

Barry Rappaport & Wil Tirion

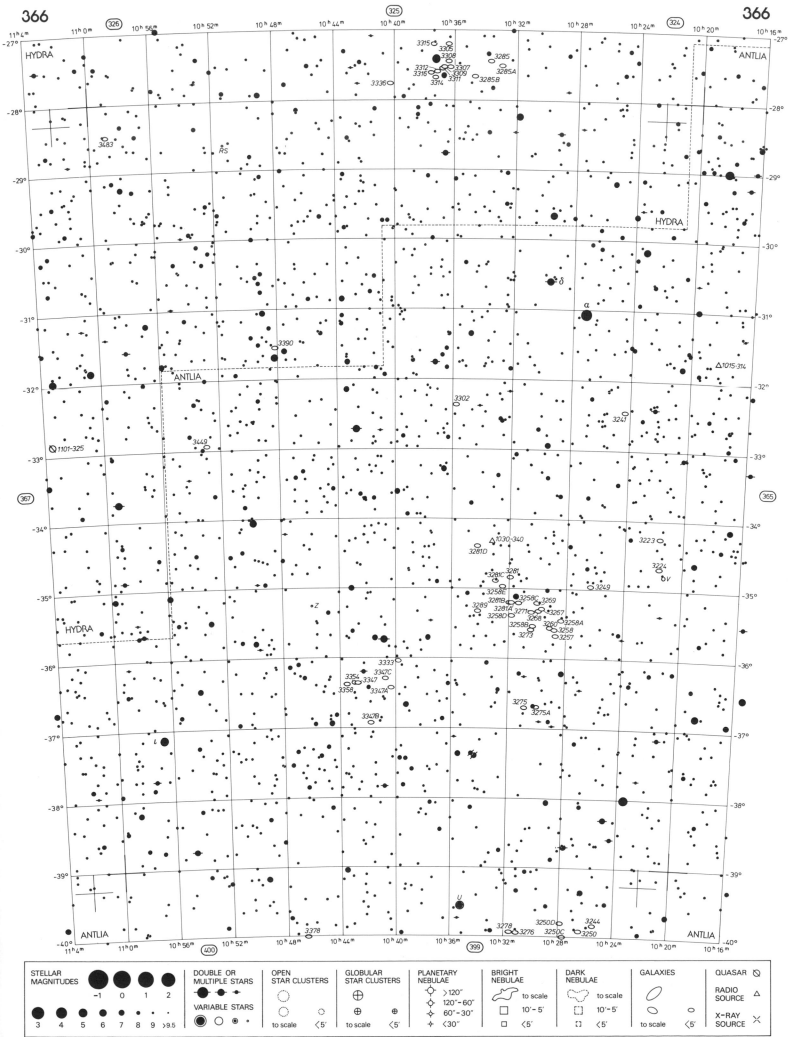

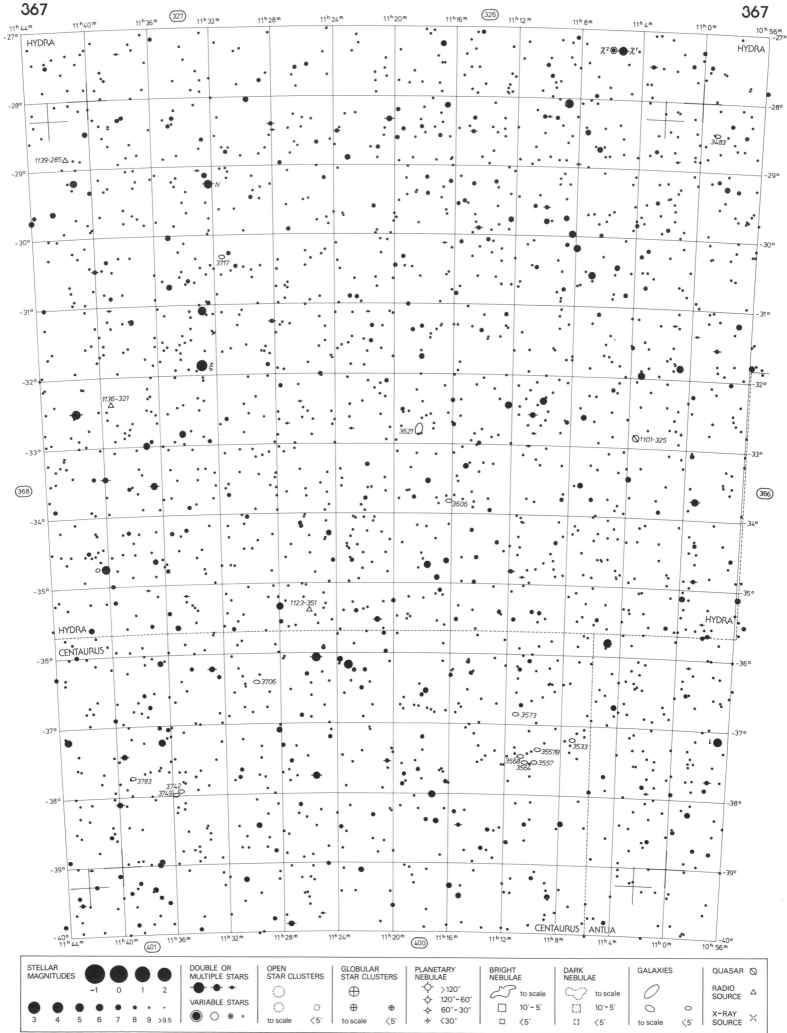

© 1988 WILLMANN-BELL, INC.

Barry Rappaport & Wil Tirion

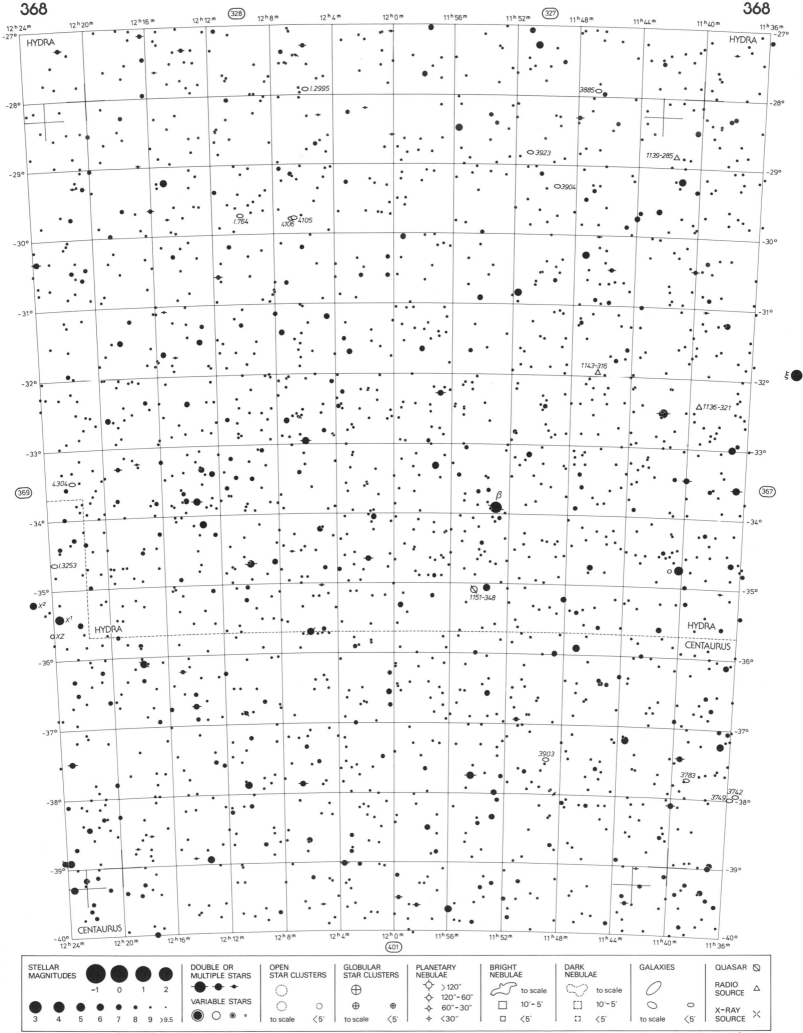

© 1988 WILLMANN-BELL, INC.

Barry Rappaport & Wil Tirion

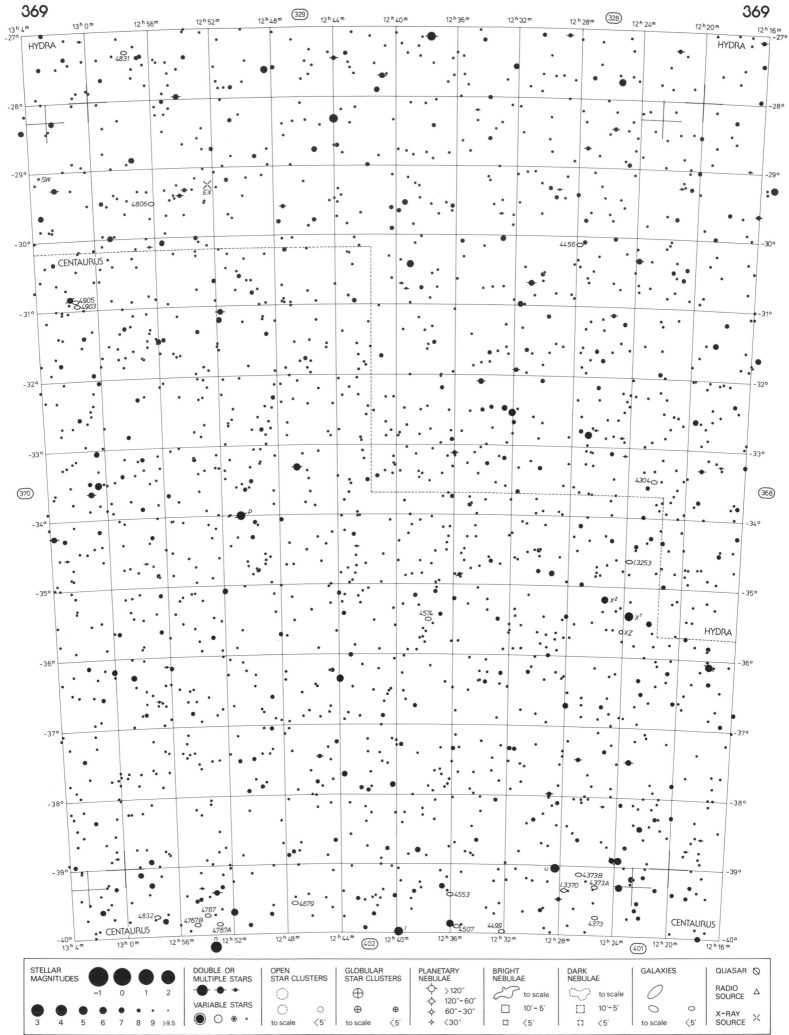

© 1988 WILLMANN-BELL, INC.

Barry Rappaport & Wil Tirion

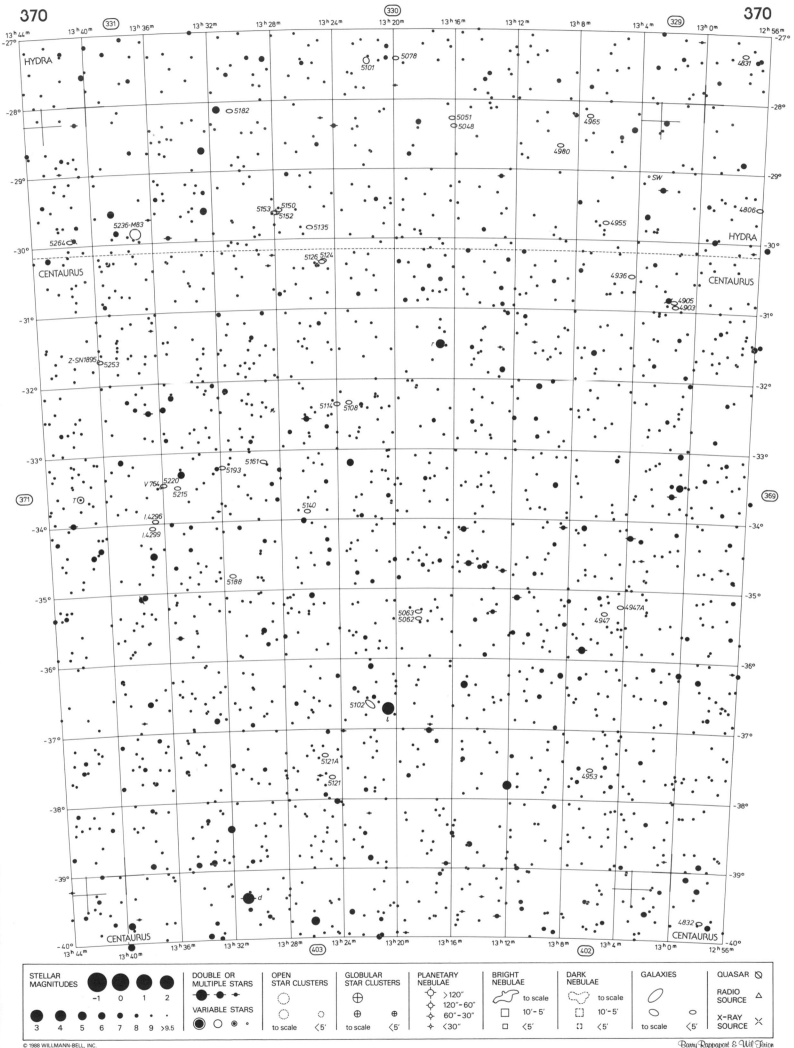

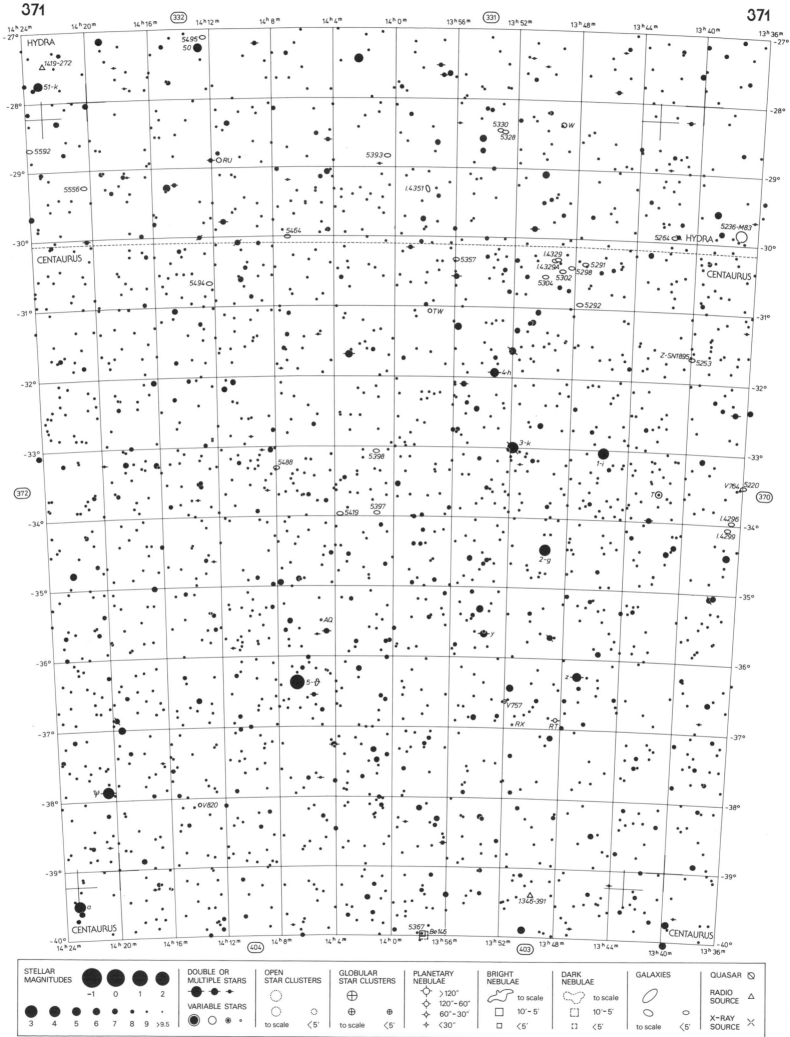

© 1988 WILLMANN-BELL, INC.

Barry Rappaport & Wil Tirion

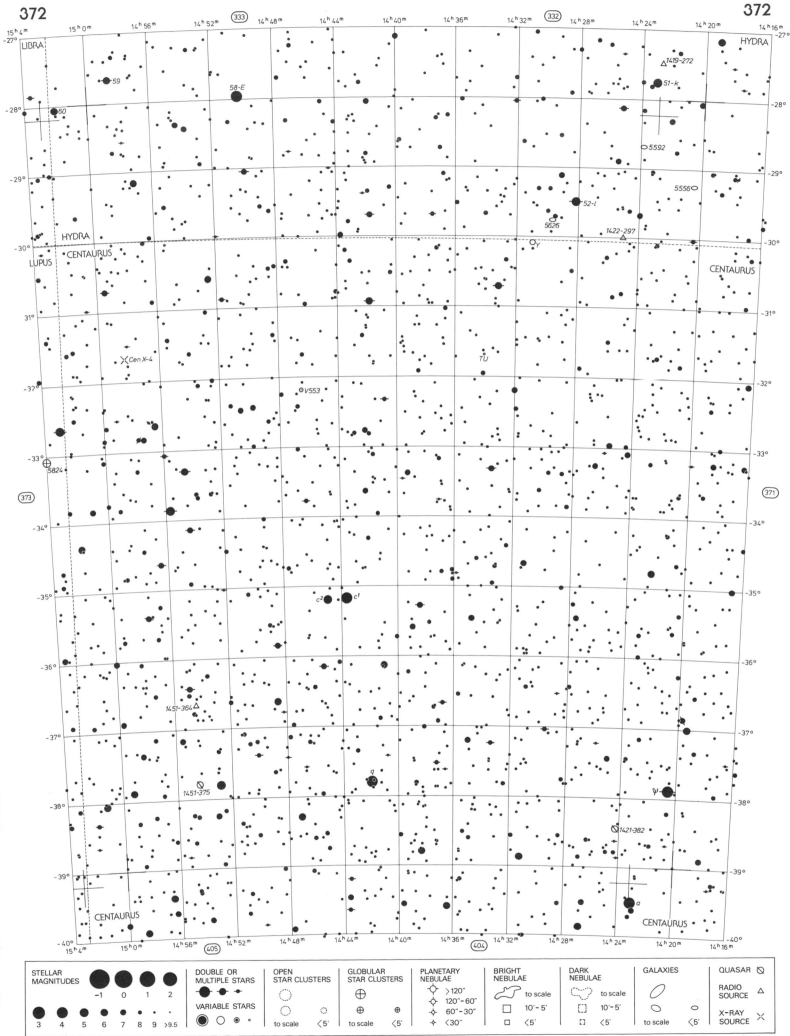

© 1988 WILLMANN-BELL, INC.

Barry Rappaport & Wil Tirion

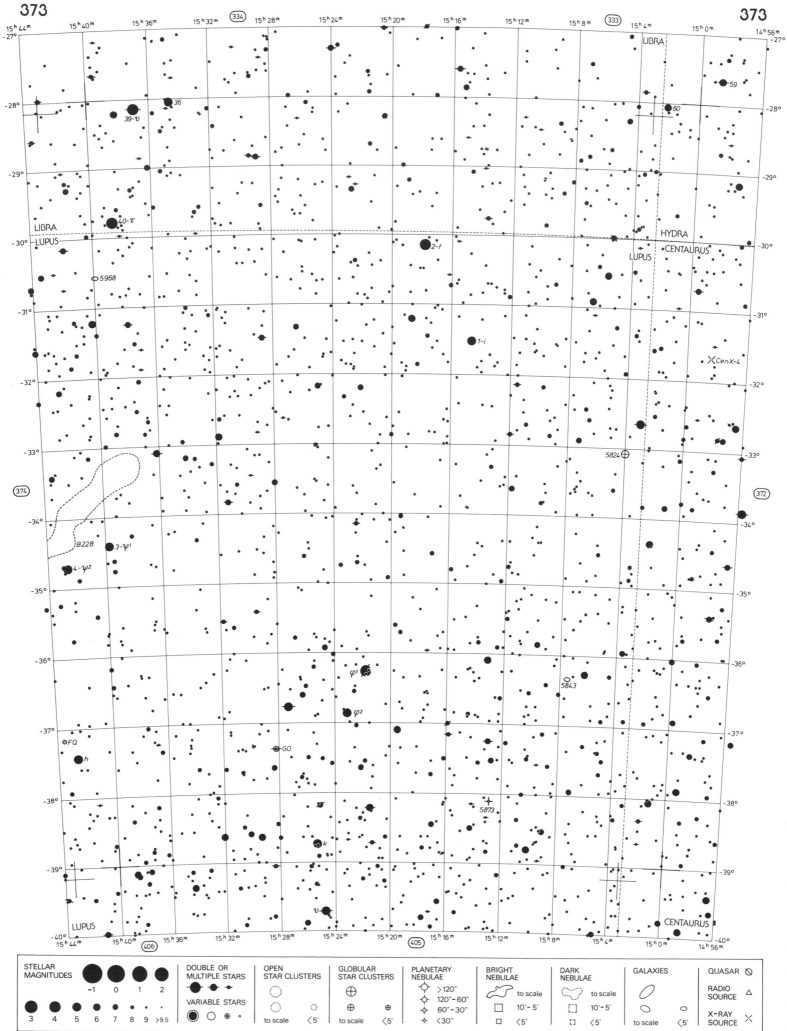

Barry Rappaport & Wil Tirion

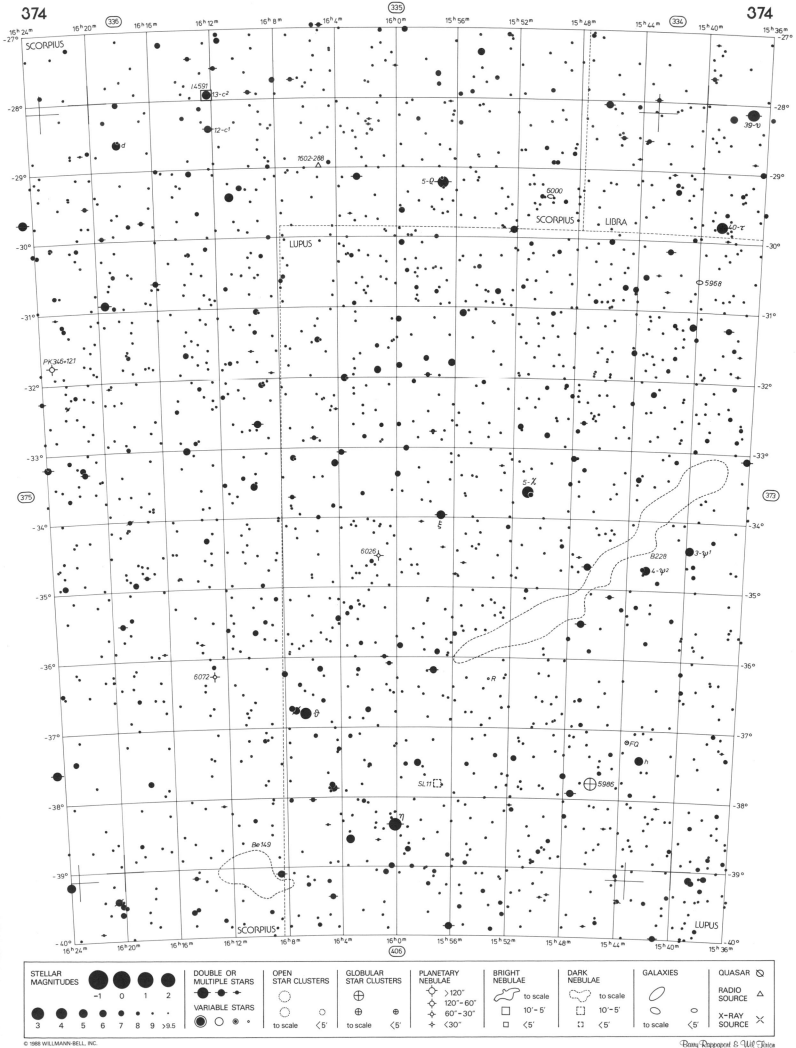

© 1988 WILLMANN-BELL, INC.

Barry Rappaport & Wil Tirion

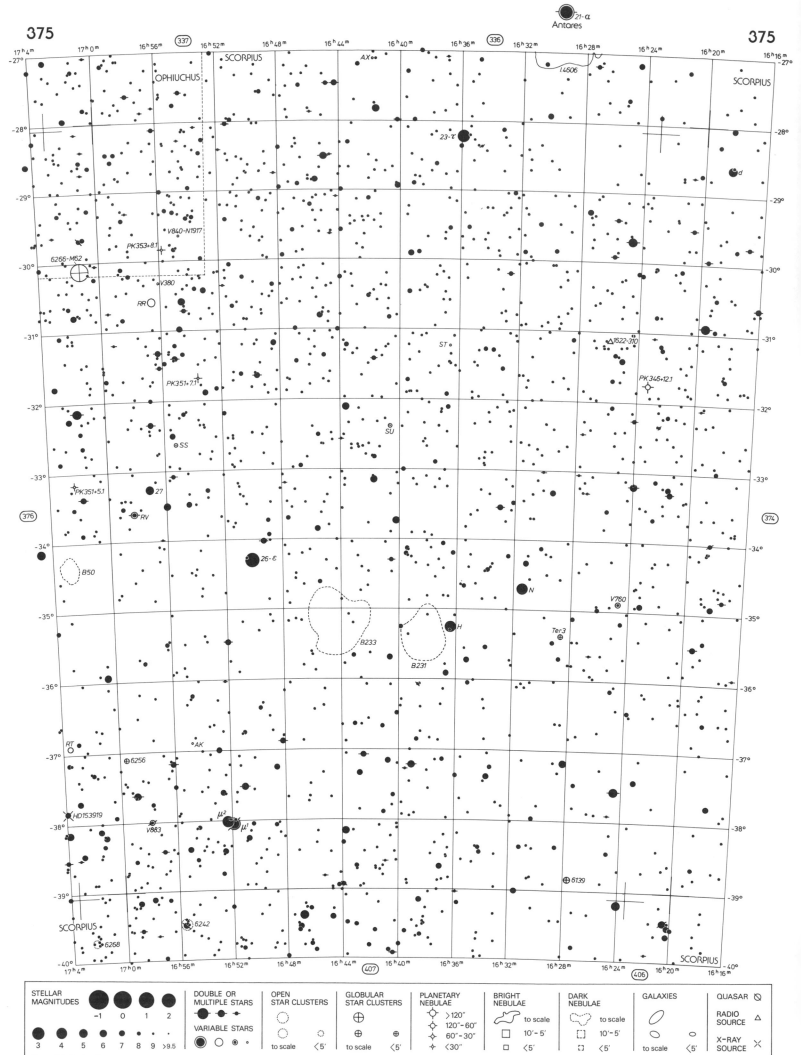

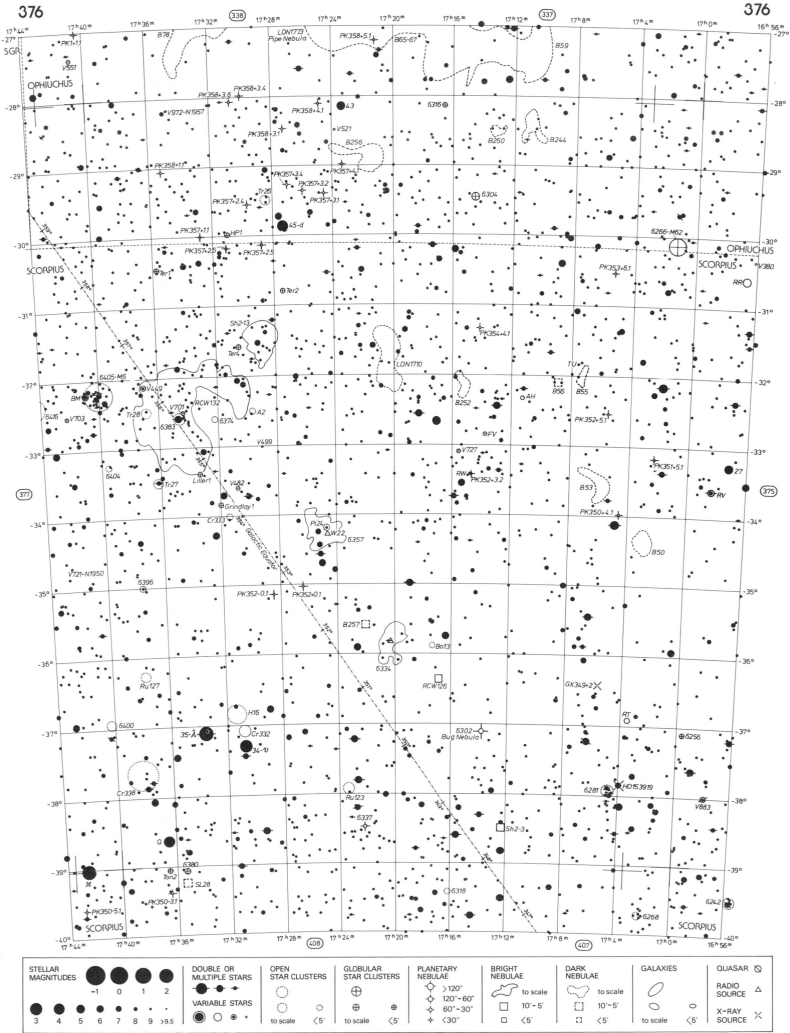

© 1988 WILLMANN-BELL, INC.

Barry Rappaport & Wil Tirion

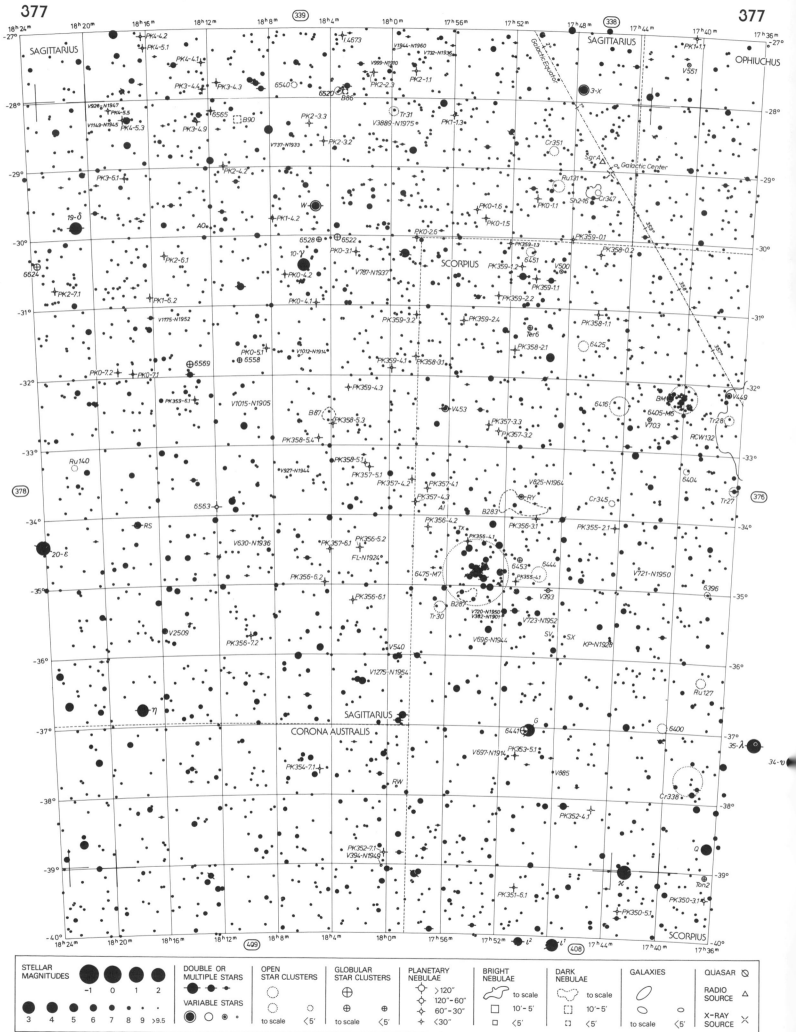

© 1988 WILLMANN-BELL, INC.

Barry Rappaport & Wil Tirion

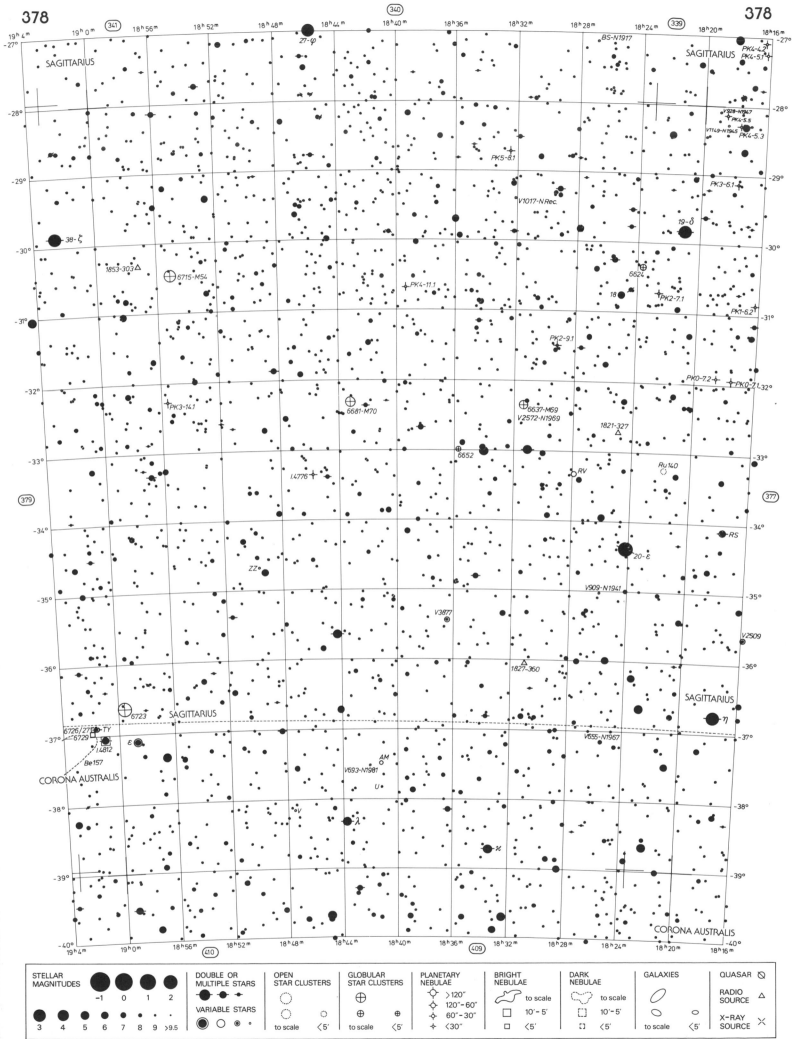

© 1988 WILLMANN-BELL, INC.

Barry Rappaport & Wil Tirion

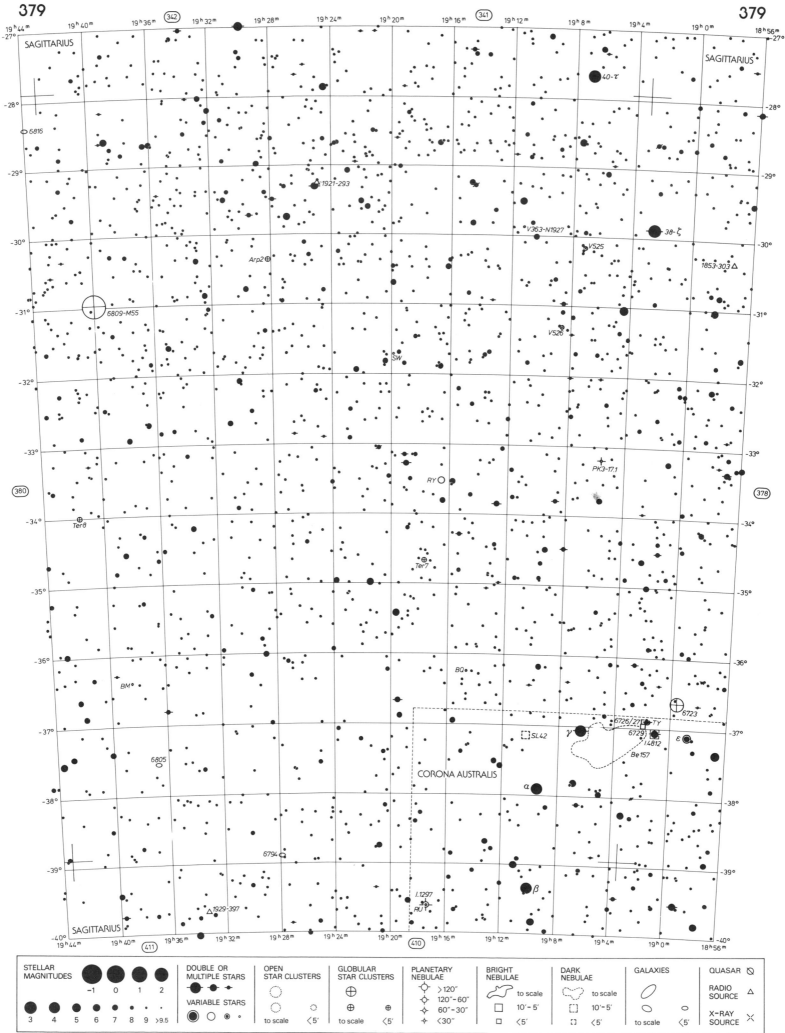

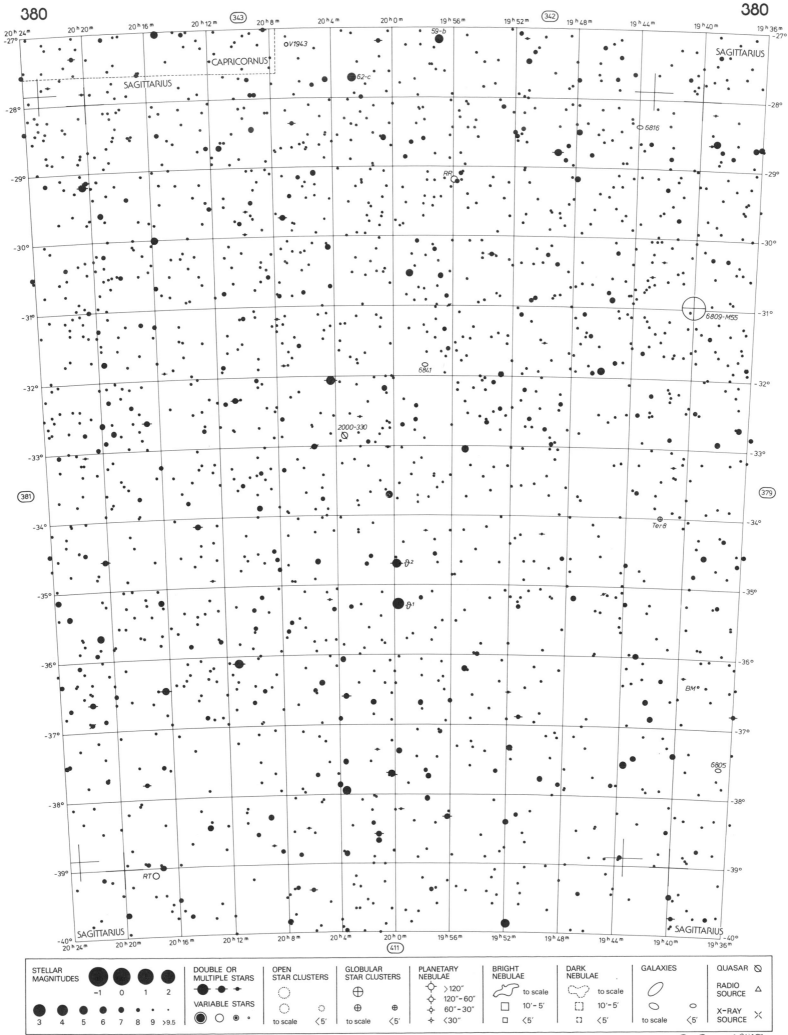

© 1988 WILLMANN-BELL, INC.

Barry Rappaport & Wil Tirion

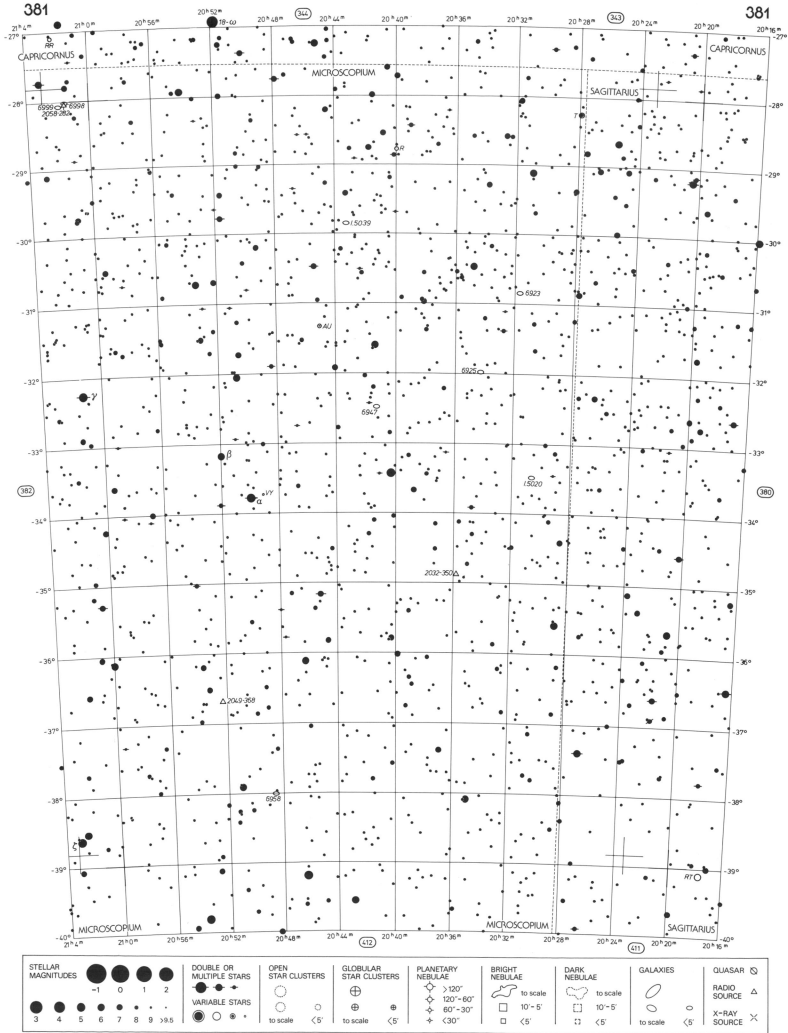

© 1988 WILLMANN-BELL, INC.

Barry Rappaport & Wil Tirion

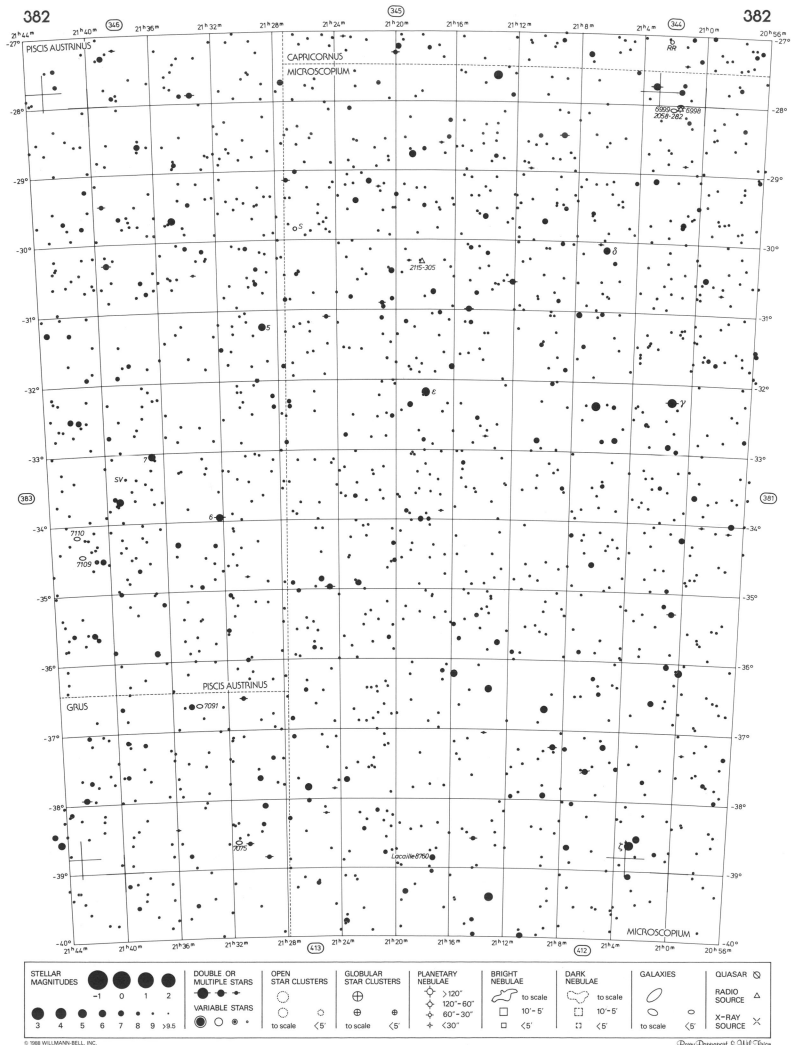

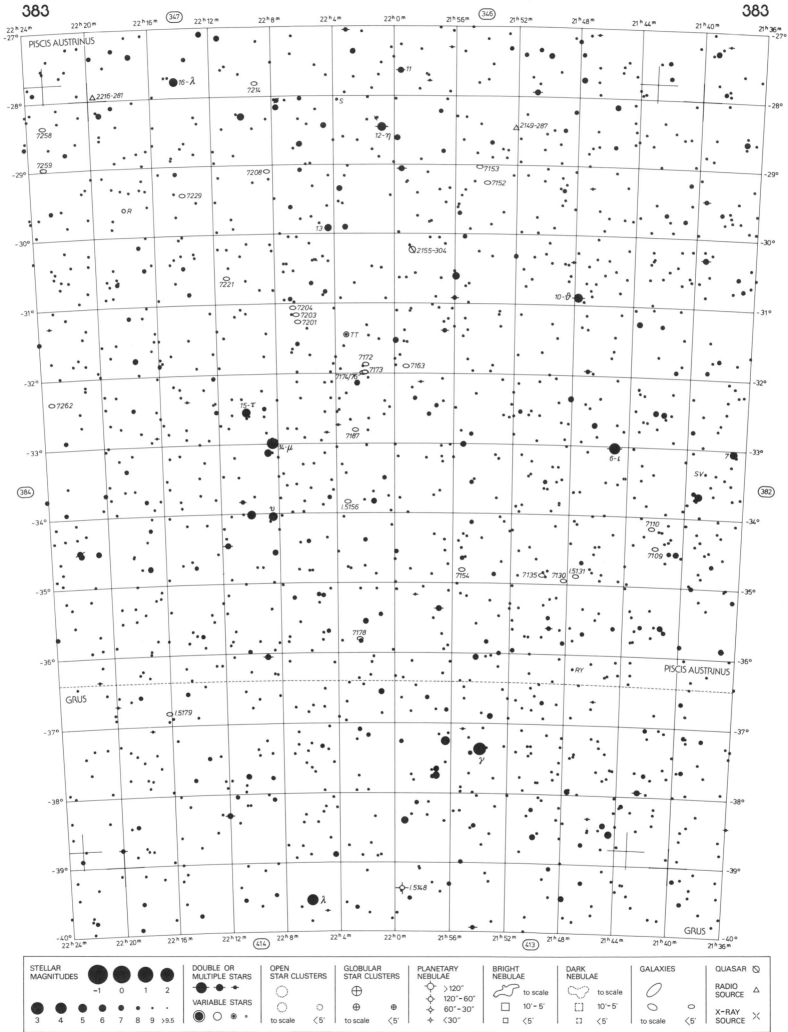

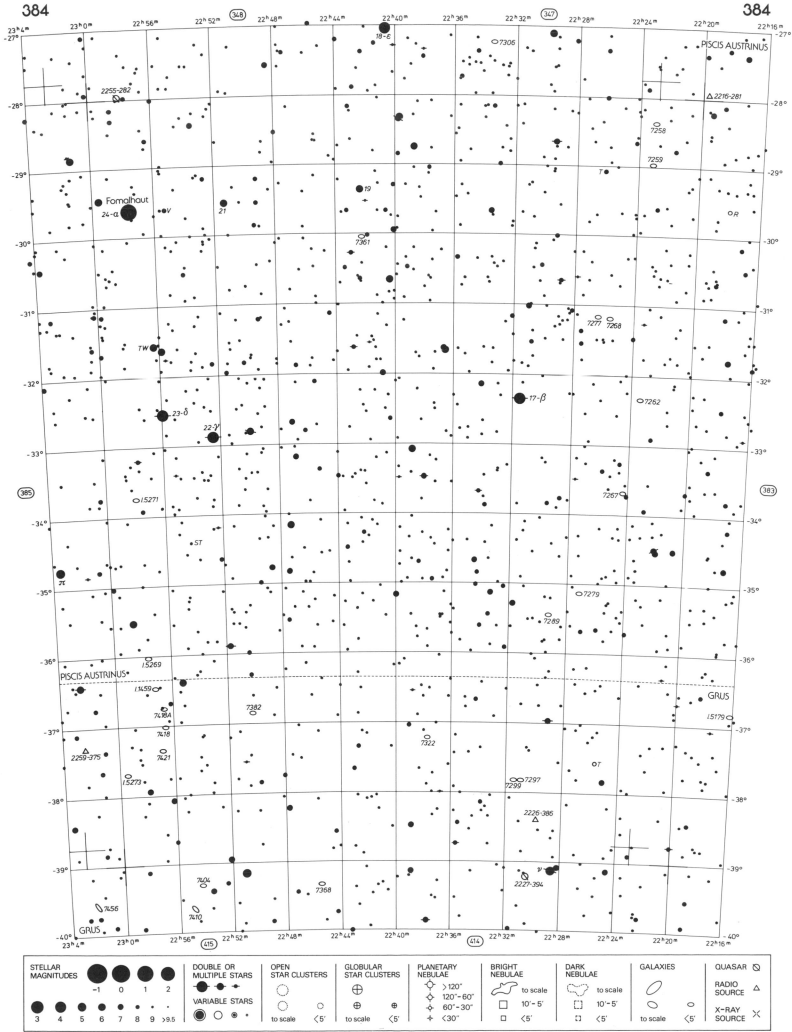

PISCIS AUSTRINUS

GRUS

PISCIS AUSTRINUS

GRUS

STELLAR MAGNITUDES	DOUBLE OR MULTIPLE STARS	OPEN STAR CLUSTERS	GLOBULAR STAR CLUSTERS	PLANETARY NEBULAE	BRIGHT NEBULAE	DARK NEBULAE	GALAXIES	QUASAR

© 1988 WILLMANN-BELL, INC.

Barry Rappaport & Wil Tirion

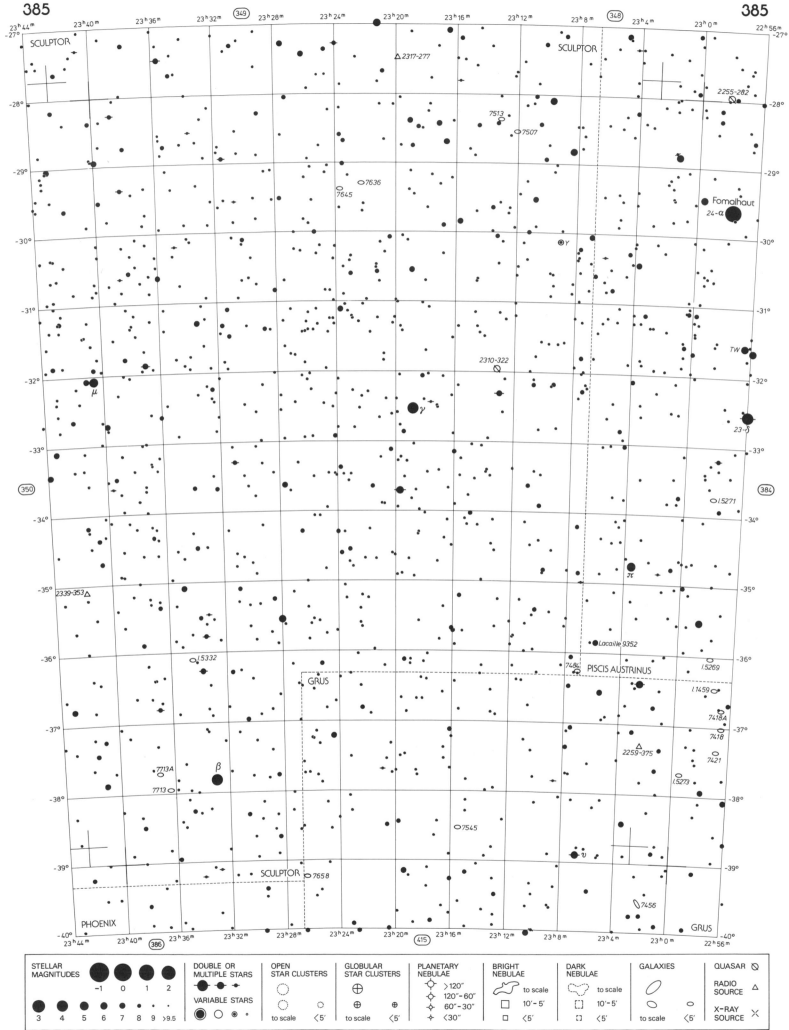

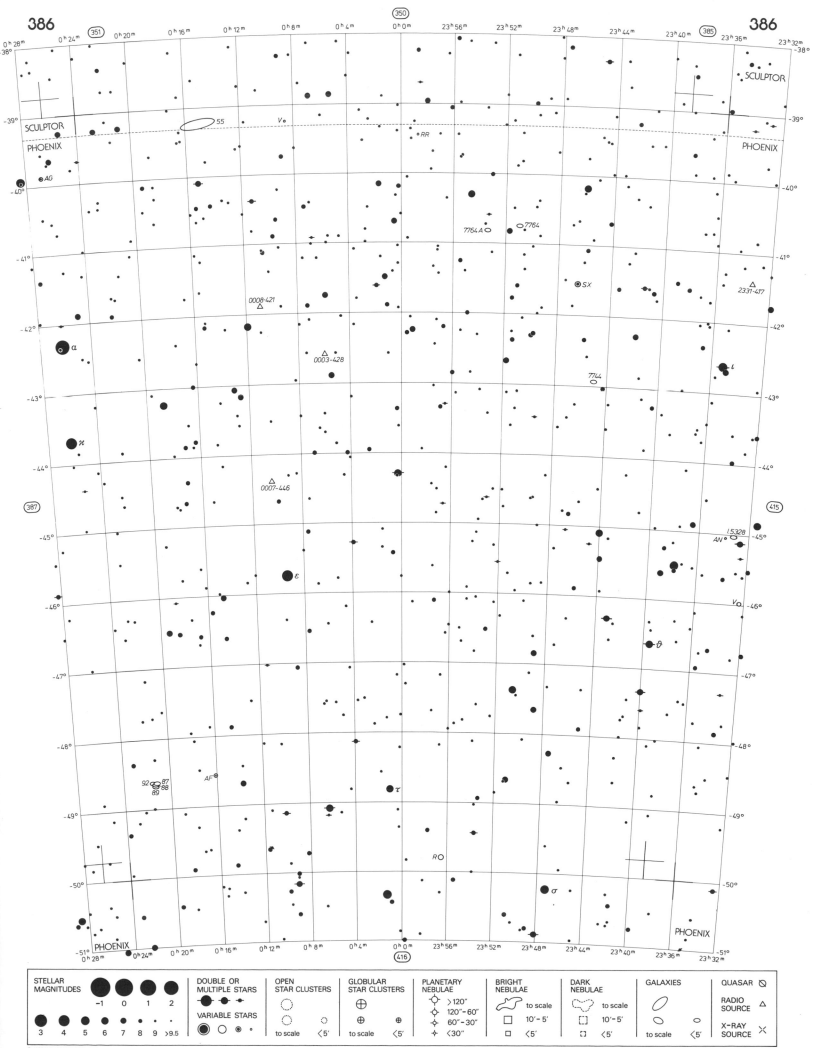

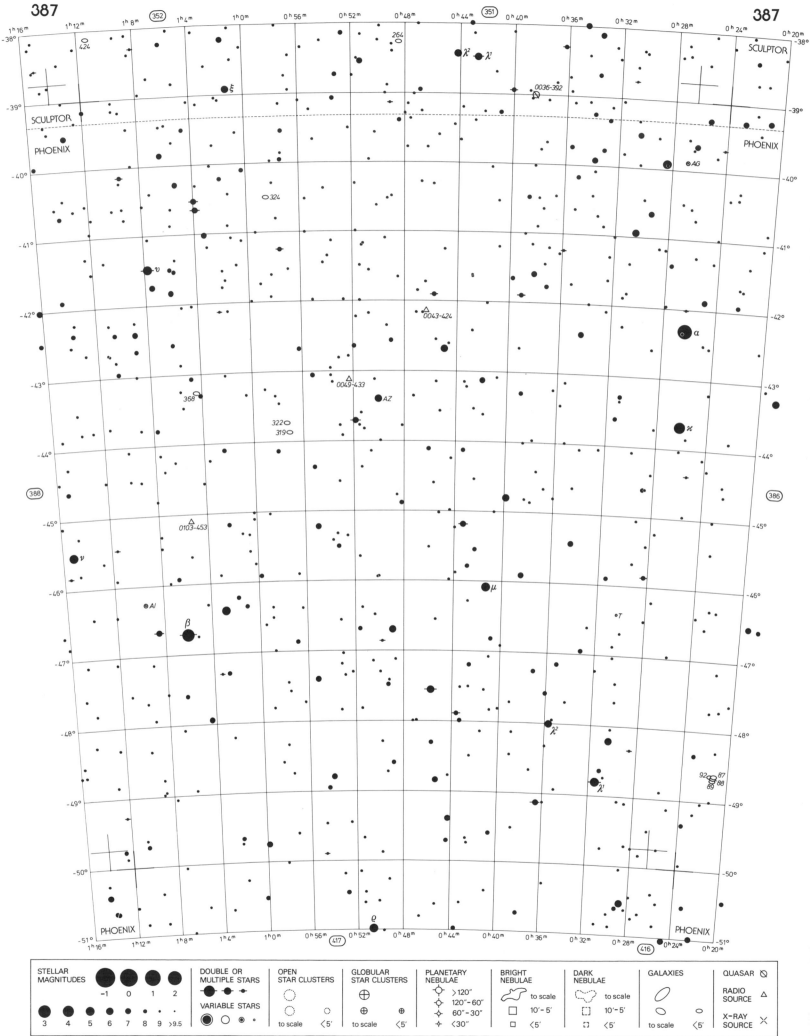

© 1988 WILLMANN-BELL, INC.

Barry Rappaport & Wil Tirion

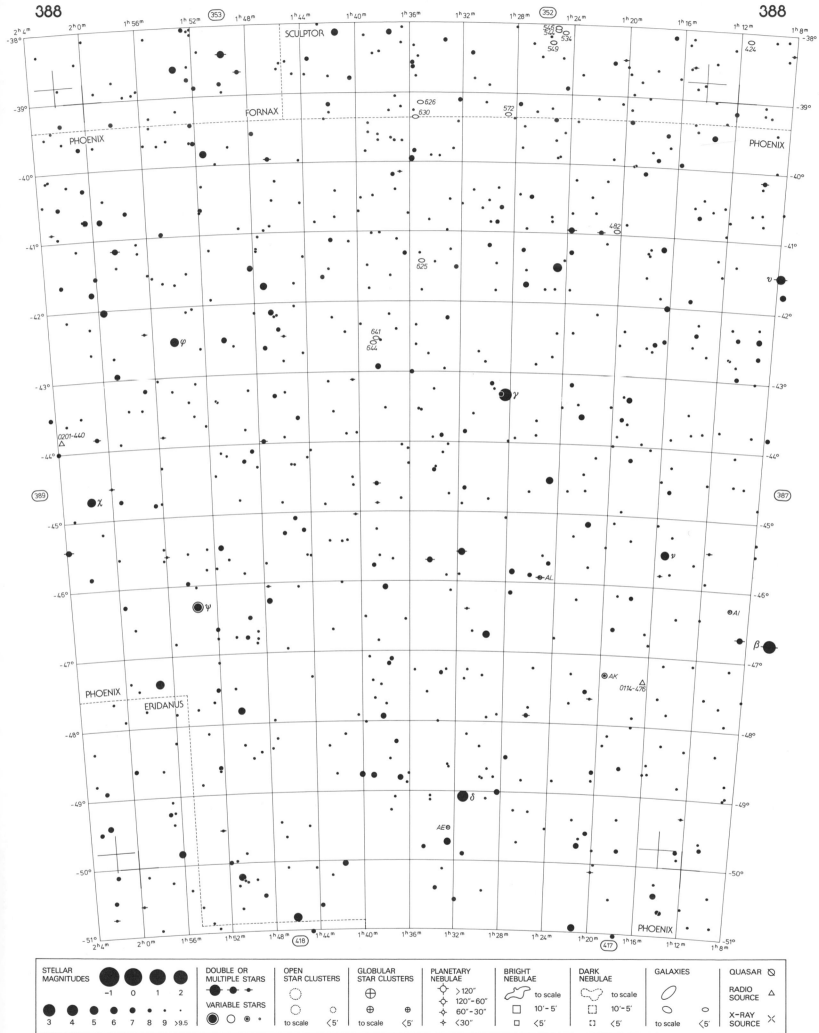

STELLAR
MAGNITUDES

-1   0   1   2

3   4   5   6   7   8   9 >9.5

DOUBLE OR
MULTIPLE STARS

VARIABLE STARS

OPEN
STAR CLUSTERS

to scale   <5'

GLOBULAR
STAR CLUSTERS

to scale   <5'

PLANETARY
NEBULAE

>120"
120"-60"
60"-30"
<30"

BRIGHT
NEBULAE

to scale
10'-5'
<5'

DARK
NEBULAE

to scale
10'-5'
<5'

GALAXIES

to scale   <5'

QUASAR

RADIO
SOURCE

X-RAY
SOURCE

© 1988 WILLMANN-BELL, INC.

Barry Rappaport & Wil Tirion

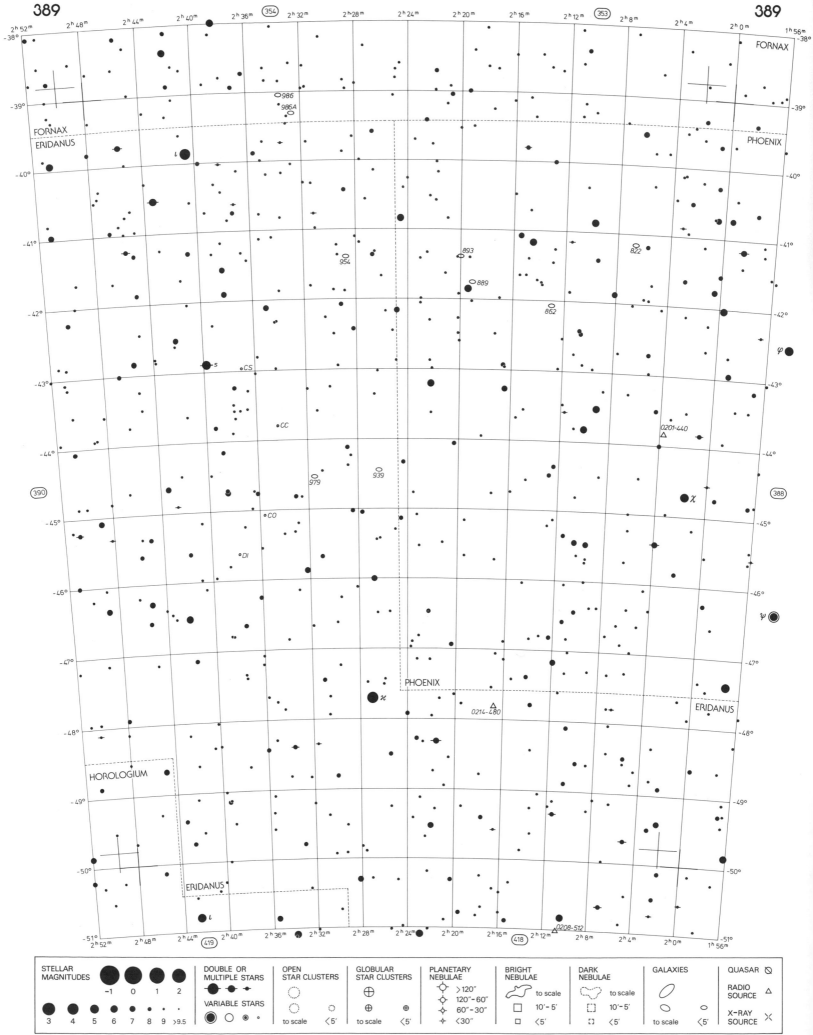

© 1988 WILLMANN-BELL, INC.

Barry Rappaport & Wil Tirion

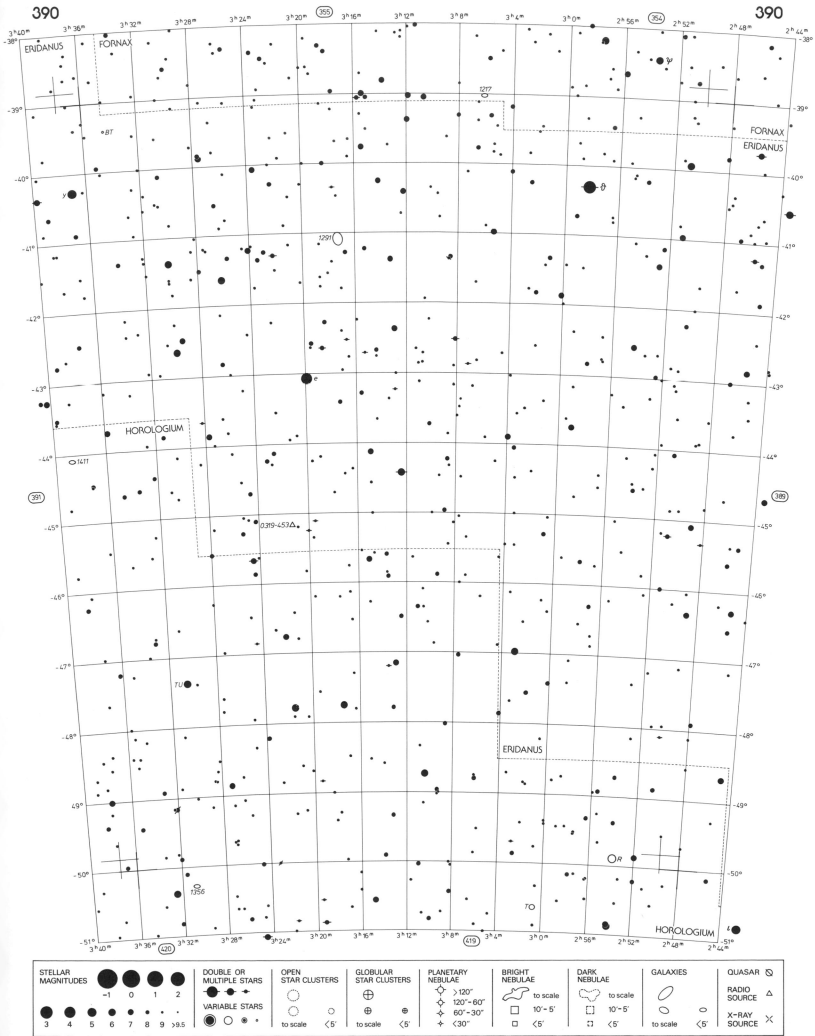

STELLAR MAGNITUDES

DOUBLE OR MULTIPLE STARS

VARIABLE STARS

OPEN STAR CLUSTERS
to scale <5'

GLOBULAR STAR CLUSTERS
to scale <5'

PLANETARY NEBULAE
>120"
120"-60"
60"-30"
<30"

BRIGHT NEBULAE
to scale
10'-5'
<5'

DARK NEBULAE
to scale
10'-5'
<5'

GALAXIES
to scale <5'

QUASAR

RADIO SOURCE

X-RAY SOURCE

© 1988 WILLMANN-BELL, INC.

Barry Rappaport & Wil Tirion

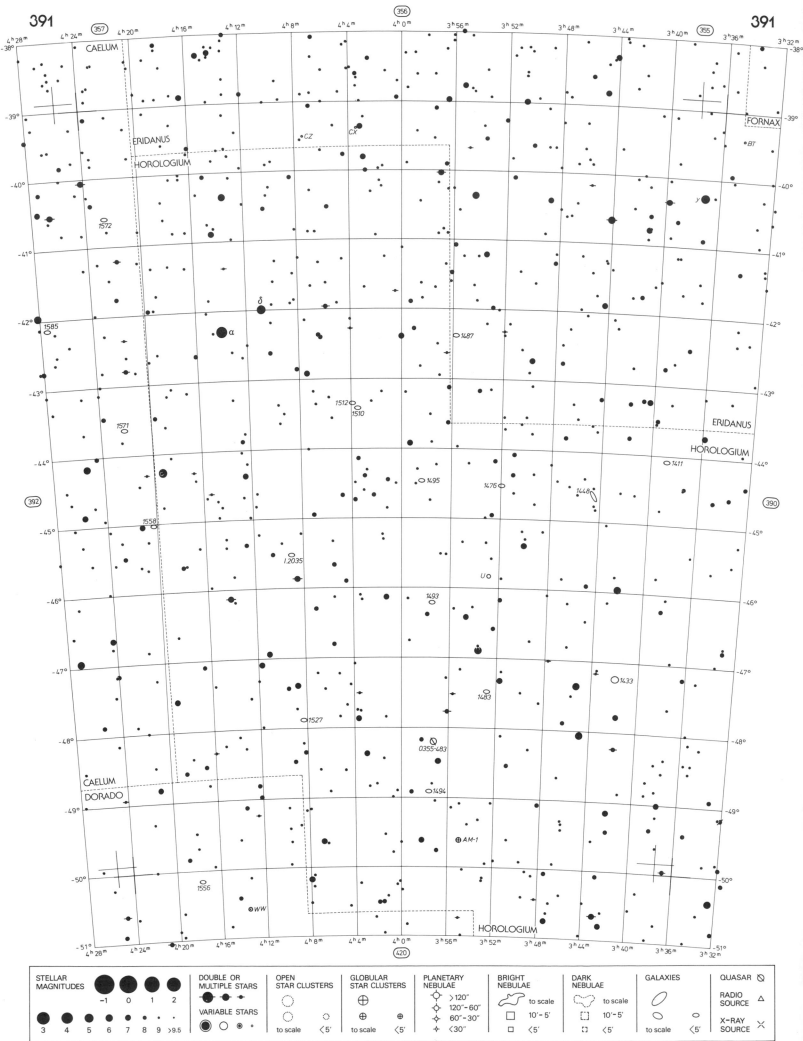

CAELUM

FORNAX

ERIDANUS

HOROLOGIUM

ERIDANUS

HOROLOGIUM

CAELUM

DORADO

HOROLOGIUM

STELLAR MAGNITUDES				DOUBLE OR MULTIPLE STARS	OPEN STAR CLUSTERS	GLOBULAR STAR CLUSTERS	PLANETARY NEBULAE	BRIGHT NEBULAE	DARK NEBULAE	GALAXIES	QUASAR

-1 0 1 2

VARIABLE STARS

3 4 5 6 7 8 9 >9.5

> 120"
120"- 60"
60"- 30"
< 30"

to scale   < 5'

to scale   < 5'

to scale   < 5'

to scale   < 5'

10'- 5'
< 5'

10'- 5'
< 5'

to scale   < 5'

RADIO SOURCE

X-RAY SOURCE

© 1988 WILLMANN-BELL, INC.

Barry Rappaport & Wil Tirion

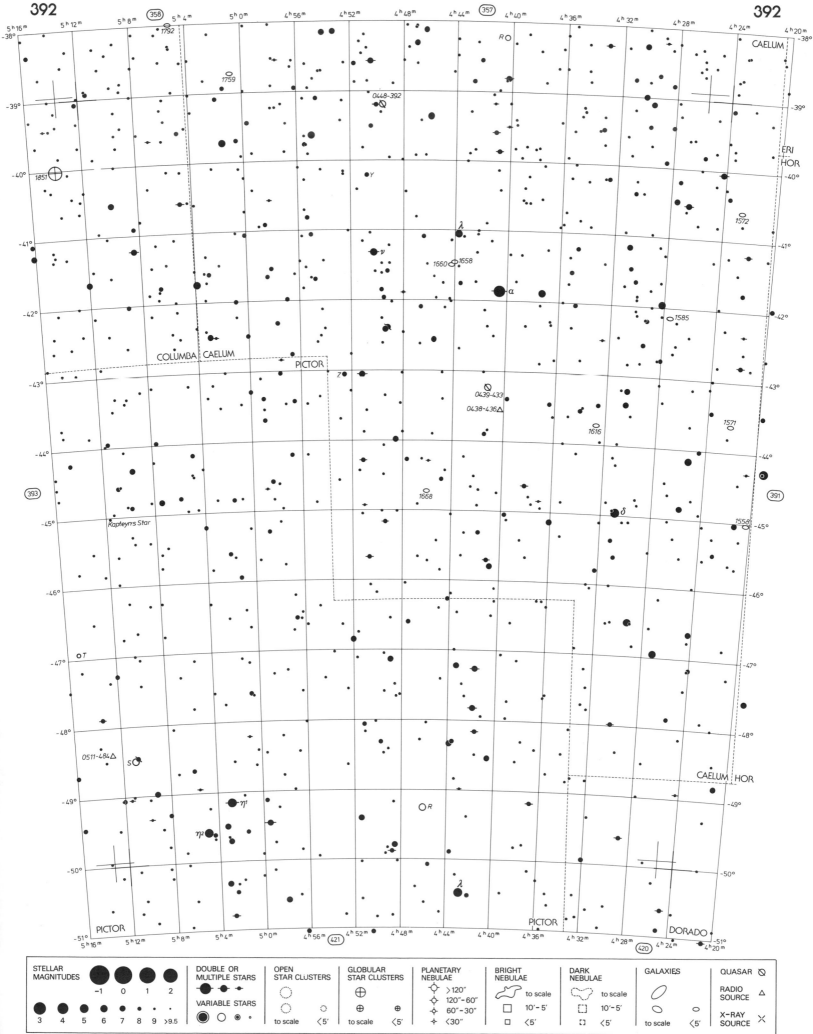

STELLAR MAGNITUDES		DOUBLE OR MULTIPLE STARS	OPEN STAR CLUSTERS	GLOBULAR STAR CLUSTERS	PLANETARY NEBULAE	BRIGHT NEBULAE	DARK NEBULAE	GALAXIES	QUASAR

© 1988 WILLMANN-BELL, INC.

Barry Rappaport & Wil Tirion

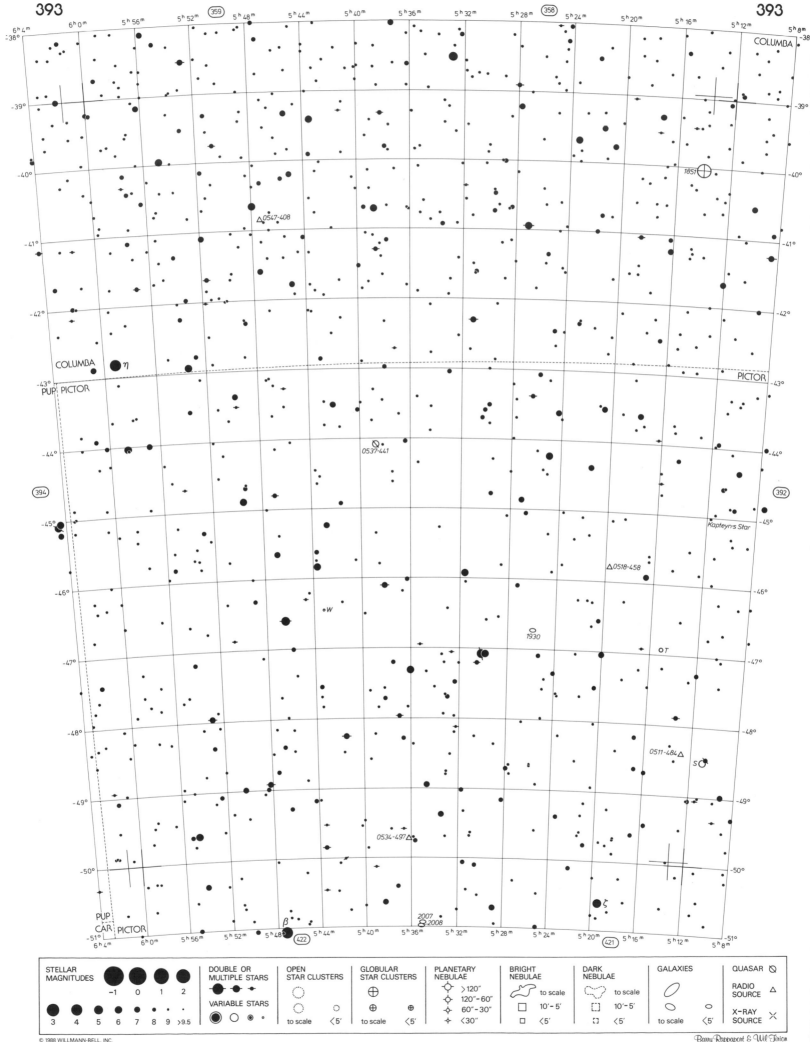

COLUMBA

0547-408

COLUMBA η

PUP PICTOR
PUP PICTOR

PICTOR

0537-441

394

392

Kapteyn's Star

0518-458

W

1930

T

0511-484 S

0534-497

2007
2008

β

ζ

PUP
CAR PICTOR

© 1988 WILLMANN-BELL, INC.

Barry Rappaport & Wil Tirion

STELLAR MAGNITUDES
-1 0 1 2
3 4 5 6 7 8 9 >9.5

DOUBLE OR MULTIPLE STARS

VARIABLE STARS

OPEN STAR CLUSTERS
to scale   <5'

GLOBULAR STAR CLUSTERS
to scale   <5'

PLANETARY NEBULAE
>120"
120"-60"
60"-30"
<30"

BRIGHT NEBULAE
to scale
10'-5'
<5'

DARK NEBULAE
to scale
10'-5'
<5'

GALAXIES
to scale
<5'

QUASAR

RADIO SOURCE

X-RAY SOURCE

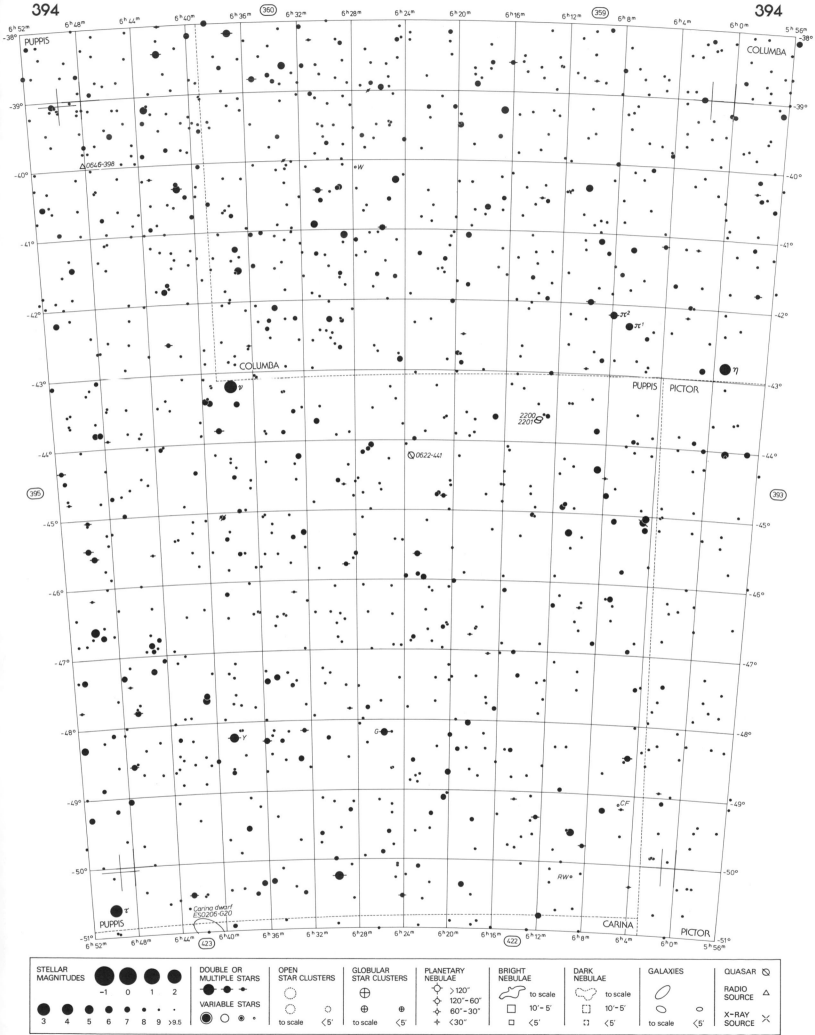

PUPPIS

COLUMBA

W

△ 0646-398

π²
π¹

η

COLUMBA
ν

PUPPIS PICTOR

2200
2201

⊘ 0622-441

PICTOR

Y

G

CF

RW

τ

Carina dwarf
ESO206-G20

PUPPIS

CARINA

PICTOR

STELLAR
MAGNITUDES

-1 0 1 2

3 4 5 6 7 8 9 >9.5

DOUBLE OR
MULTIPLE STARS

VARIABLE STARS

OPEN
STAR CLUSTERS

to scale   <5'

GLOBULAR
STAR CLUSTERS

⊕

⊕   ⊕

to scale   <5'

PLANETARY
NEBULAE

>120"
120"-60"
60"-30"
<30"

BRIGHT
NEBULAE

to scale

10'-5'

<5'

DARK
NEBULAE

to scale

10'-5'

<5'

GALAXIES

to scale   <5'

QUASAR ⊘

RADIO
SOURCE △

X-RAY
SOURCE ✕

© 1988 WILLMANN-BELL, INC.

Barry Rappaport & Wil Tirion

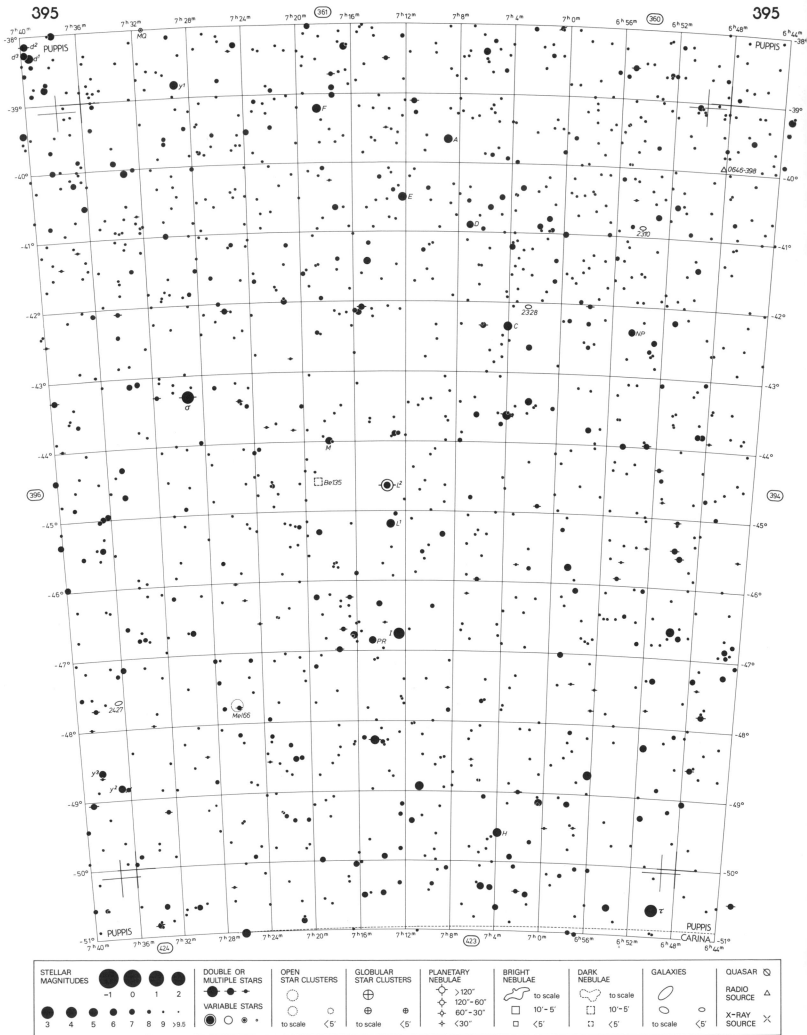

© 1988 WILLMANN-BELL, INC.

Barry Rappaport & Wil Tirion

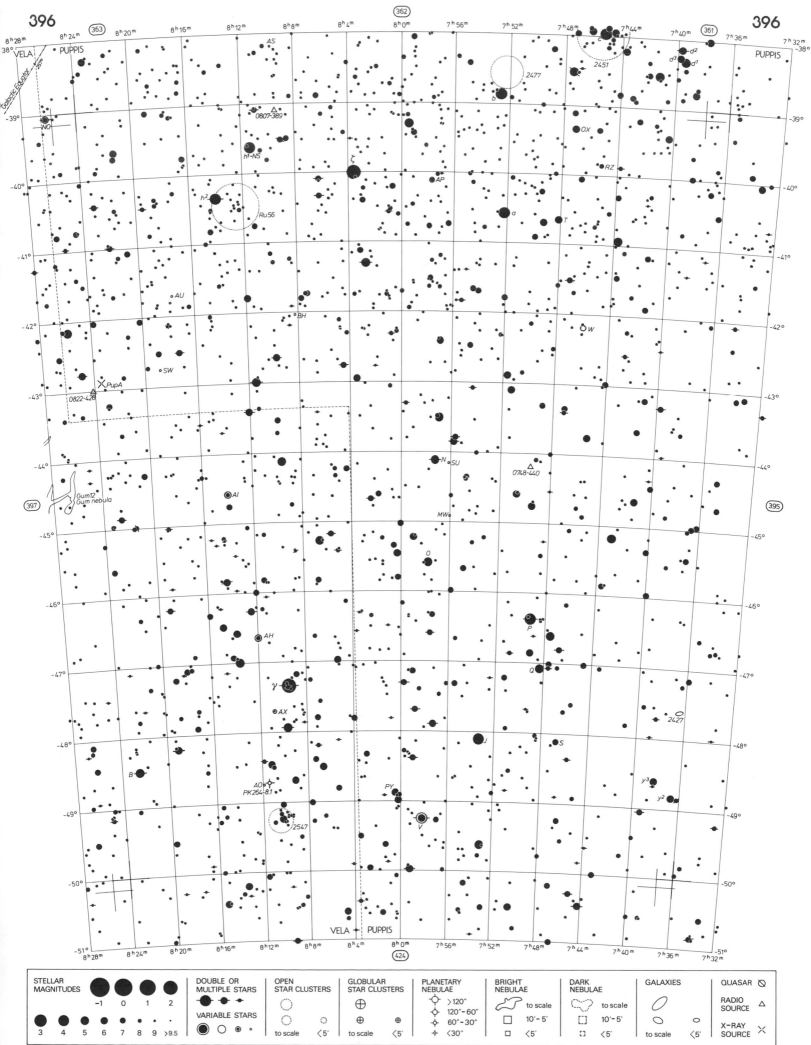

© 1988 WILLMANN-BELL, INC.

Barry Rappaport & Wil Tirion

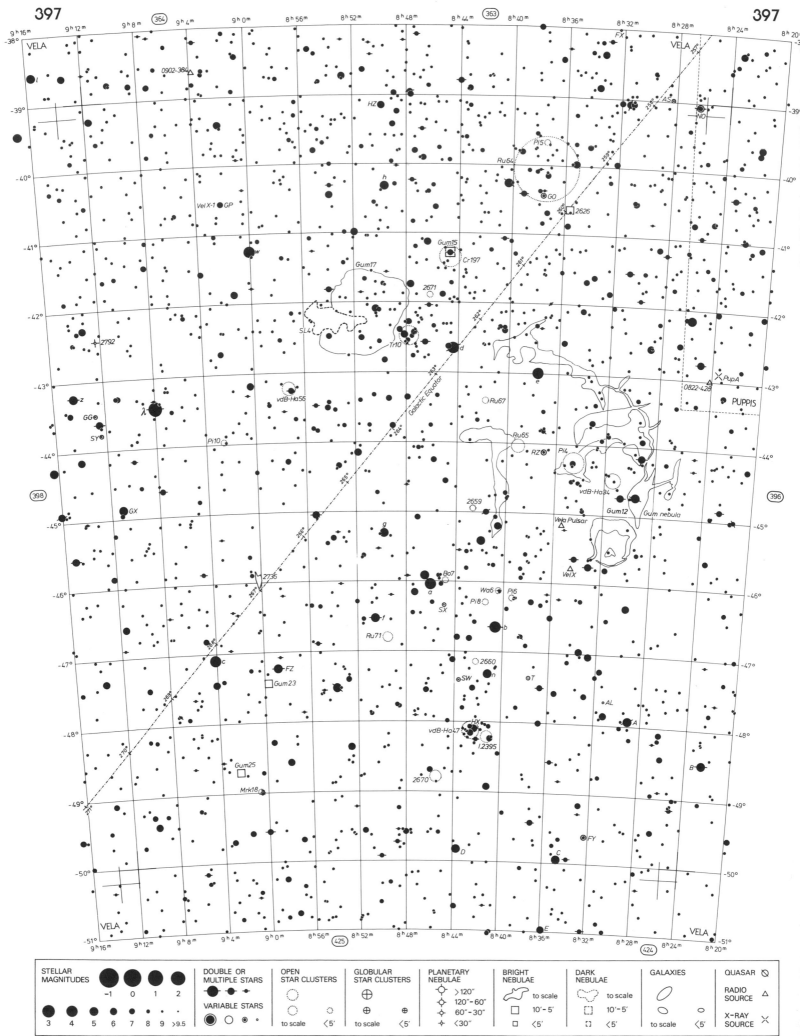

© 1988 WILLMANN-BELL, INC.

Barry Rappaport & Wil Tirion

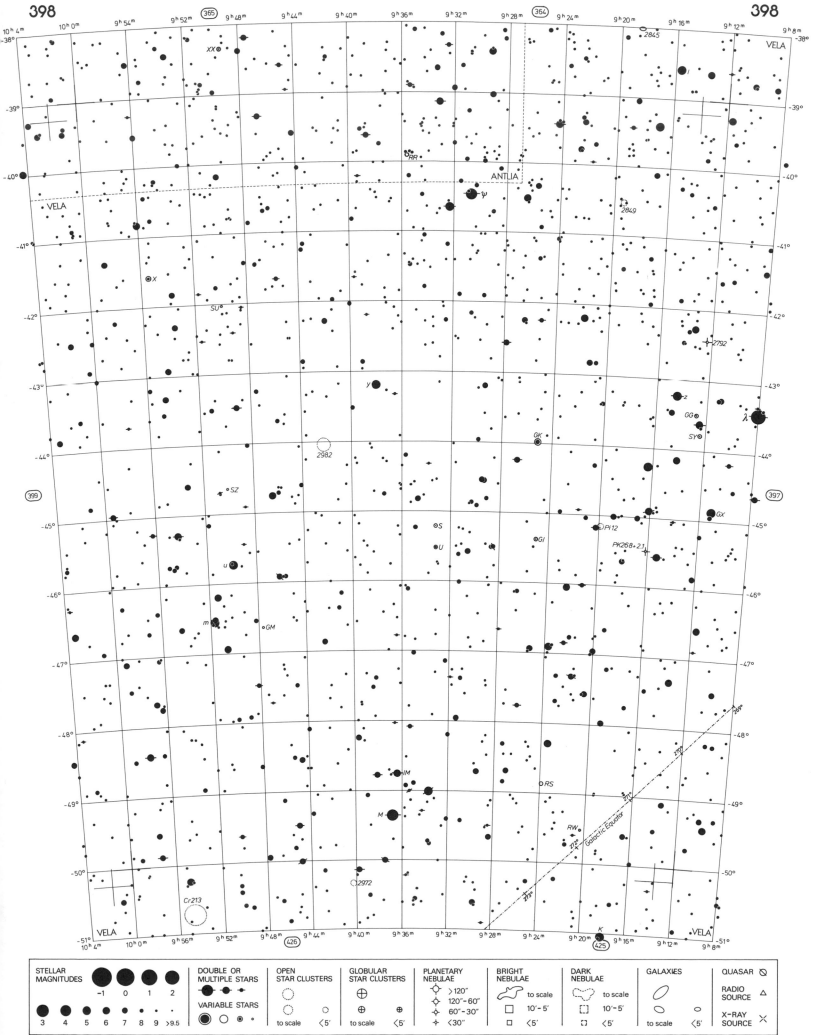

© 1988 WILLMANN-BELL, INC.

Barry Rappaport & Wil Tirion

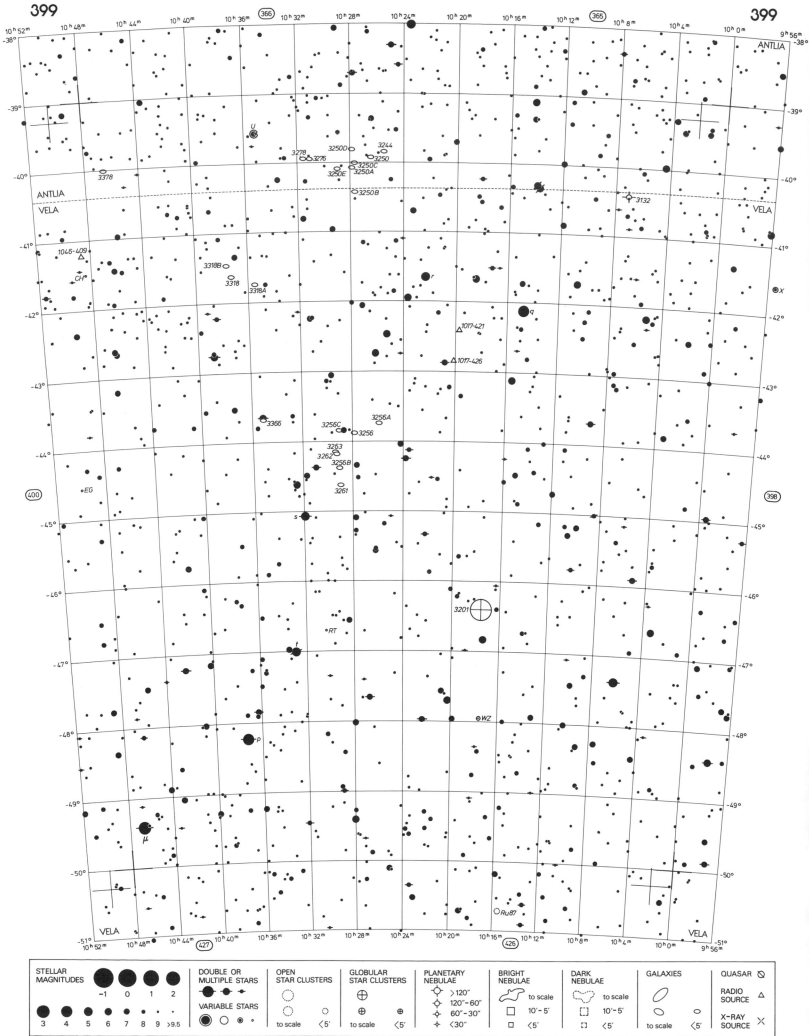

© 1988 WILLMANN-BELL, INC.

Barry Rappaport & Wil Tirion

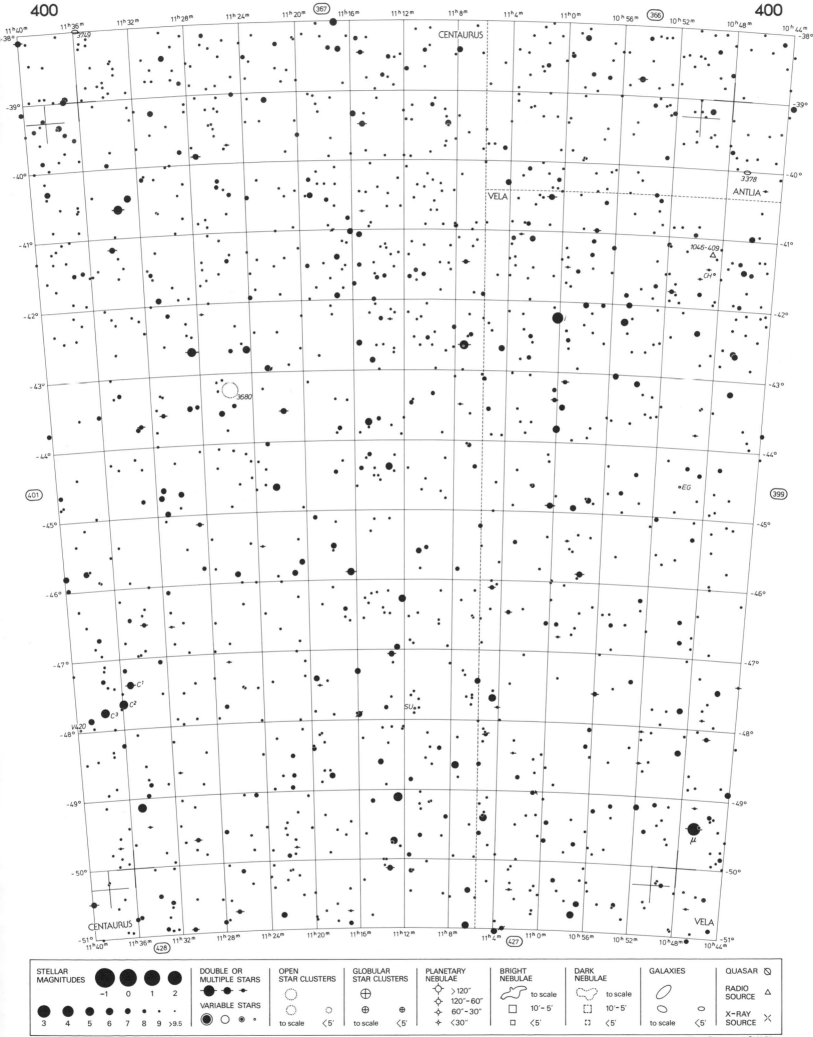

STELLAR MAGNITUDES

-1 0 1 2

3 4 5 6 7 8 9 >9.5

DOUBLE OR MULTIPLE STARS

VARIABLE STARS

OPEN STAR CLUSTERS

to scale   <5'

GLOBULAR STAR CLUSTERS

⊕   ⊕

to scale   <5'

PLANETARY NEBULAE

>120"
120"-60"
60"-30"
<30"

BRIGHT NEBULAE

to scale

10'-5'

<5'

DARK NEBULAE

to scale

10'-5'

<5'

GALAXIES

to scale   <5'

QUASAR

RADIO SOURCE △

X-RAY SOURCE ✕

© 1988 WILLMANN-BELL, INC.

Barry Rappaport & Wil Tirion

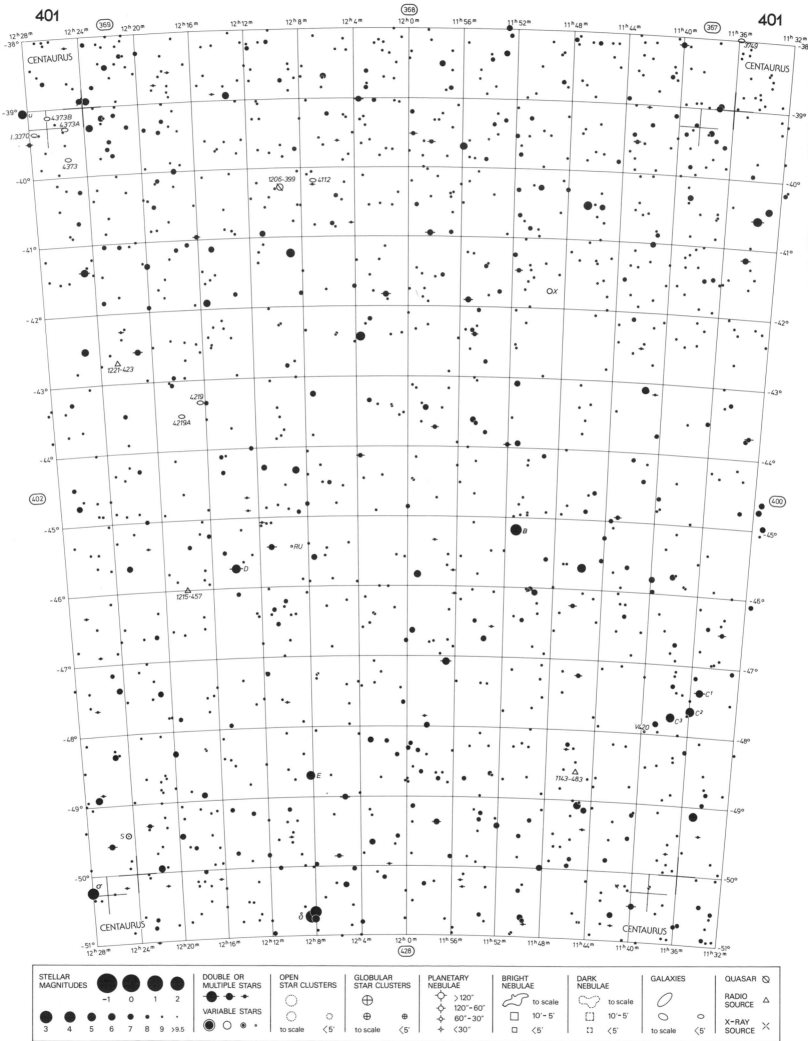

CENTAURUS

CENTAURUS

CENTAURUS

CENTAURUS

STELLAR MAGNITUDES		DOUBLE OR MULTIPLE STARS	OPEN STAR CLUSTERS	GLOBULAR STAR CLUSTERS	PLANETARY NEBULAE	BRIGHT NEBULAE	DARK NEBULAE	GALAXIES	QUASAR

© 1988 WILLMANN-BELL, INC.

Barry Rappaport & Wil Tirion

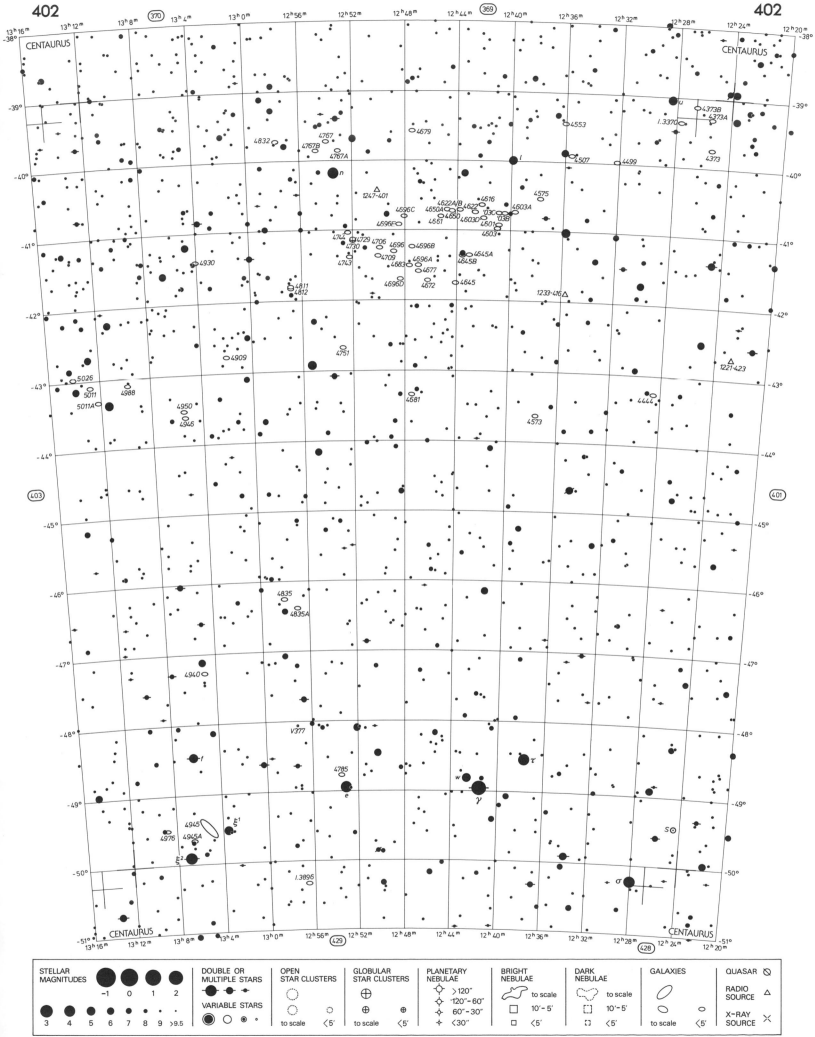

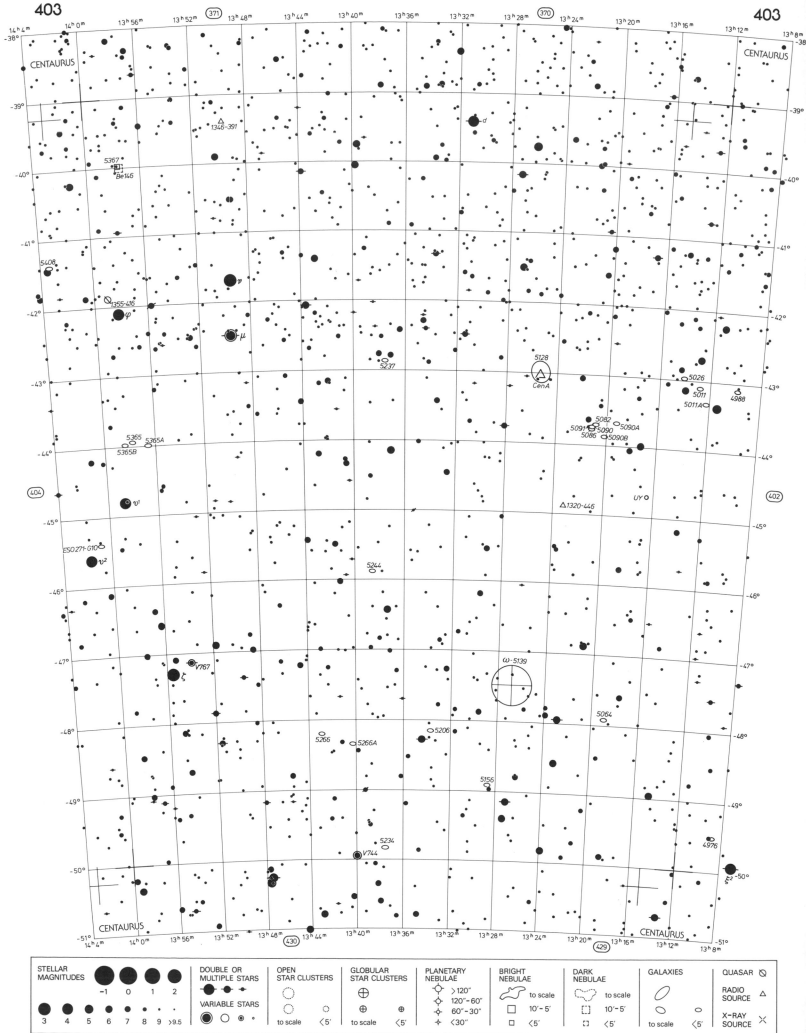

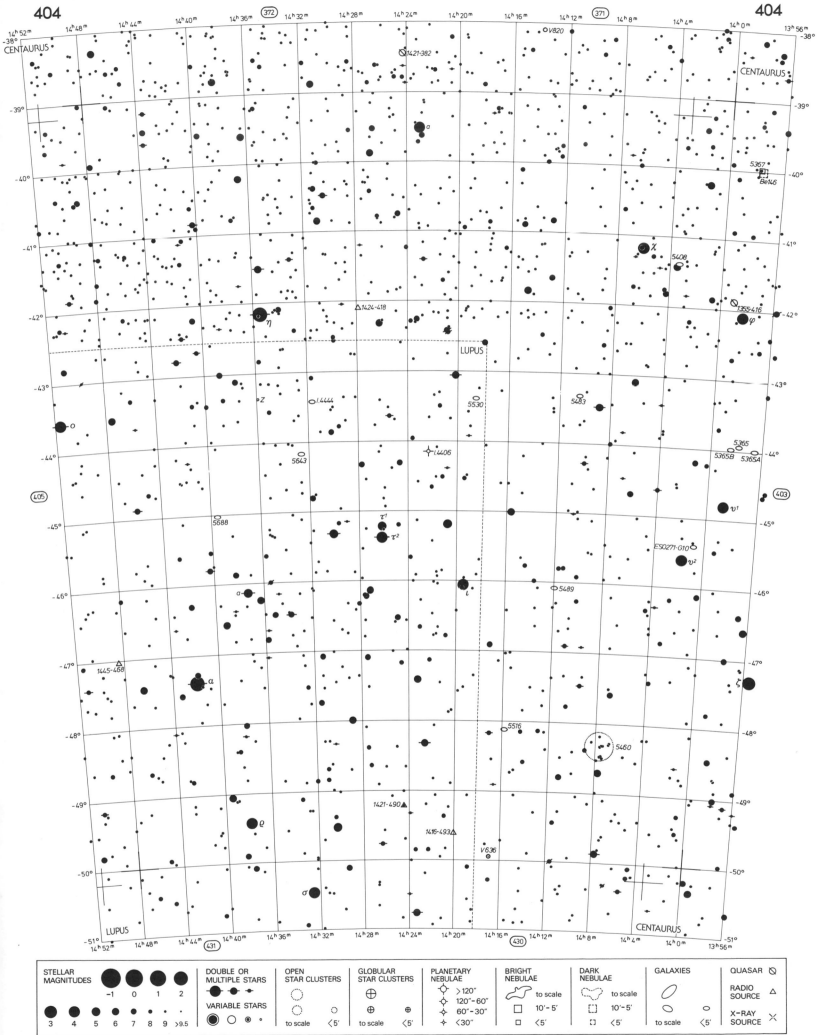

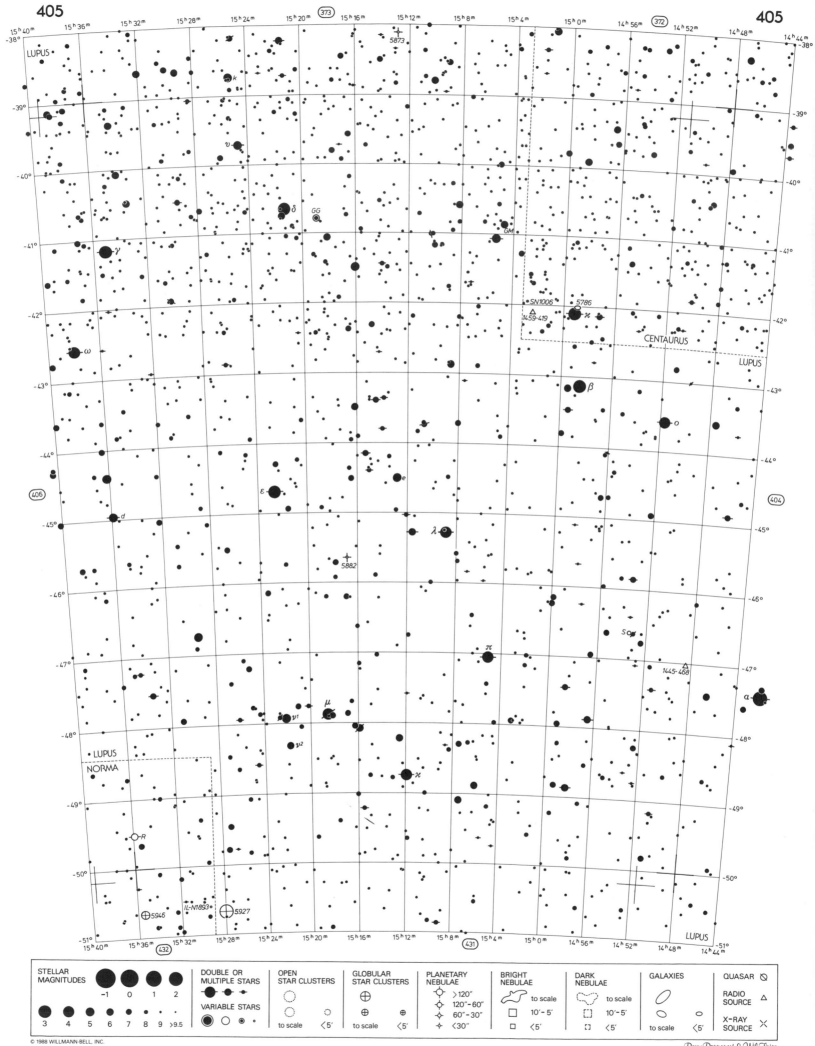

© 1988 WILLMANN-BELL, INC.

Barry Rappaport & Wil Tirion

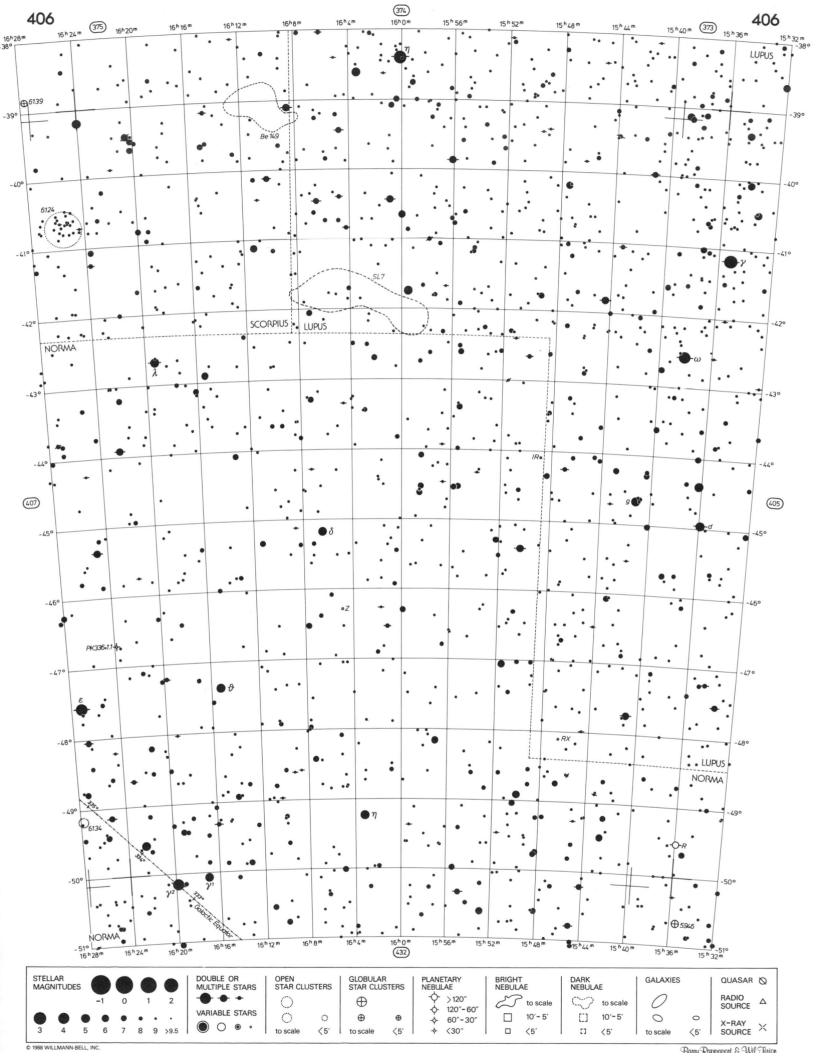

LUPUS

NORMA

SCORPIUS LUPUS

LUPUS
NORMA

NORMA

© 1988 WILLMANN-BELL, INC.

Barry Rappaport & Wil Tirion

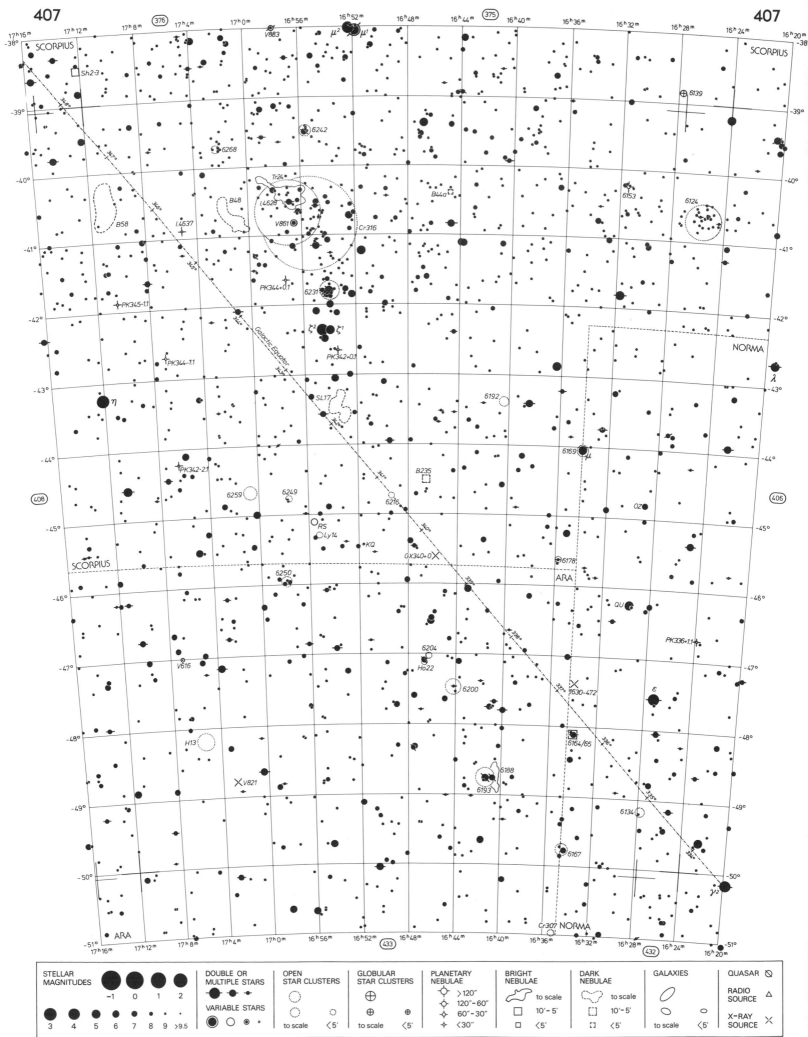

© 1988 WILLMANN-BELL, INC.

Barry Rappaport & Wil Tirion

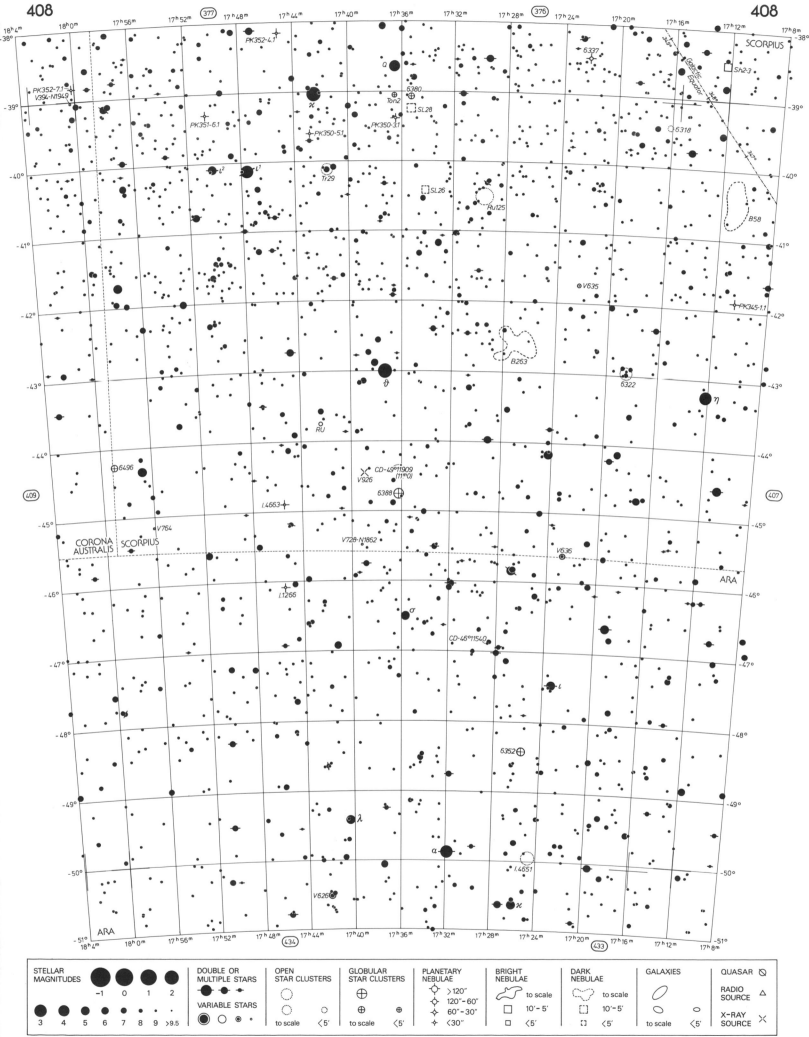

© 1988 WILLMANN-BELL, INC.

Barry Rappaport & Wil Tirion

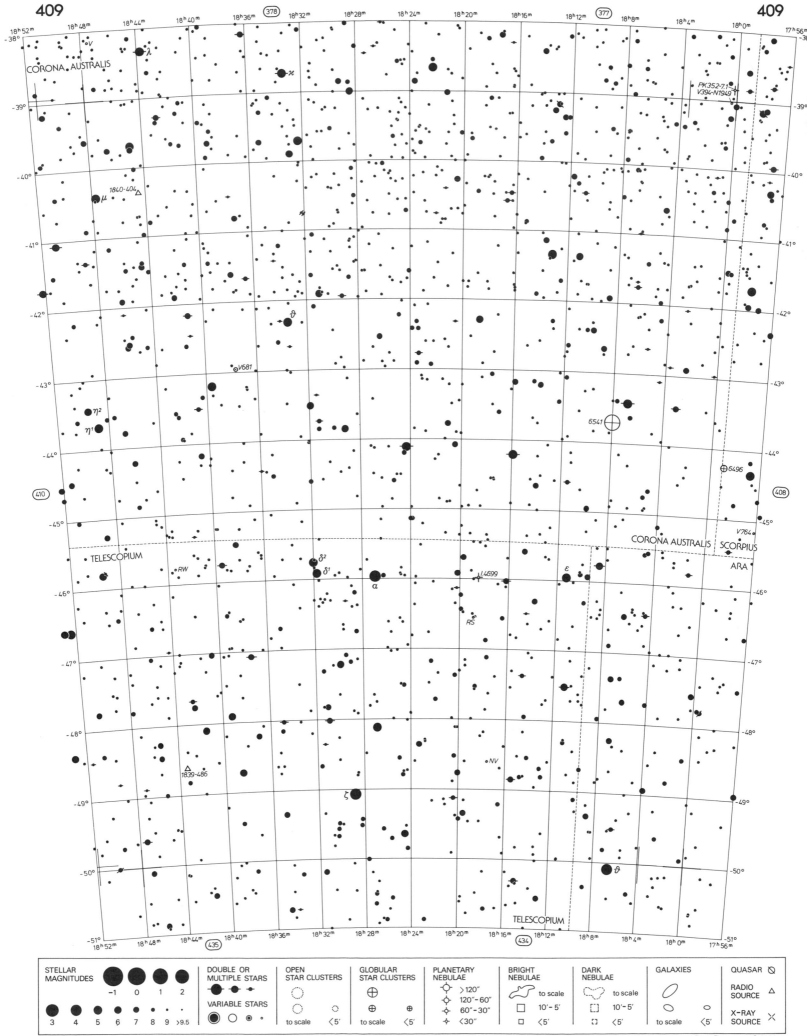

© 1988 WILLMANN-BELL, INC.

Barry Rappaport & Wil Tirion

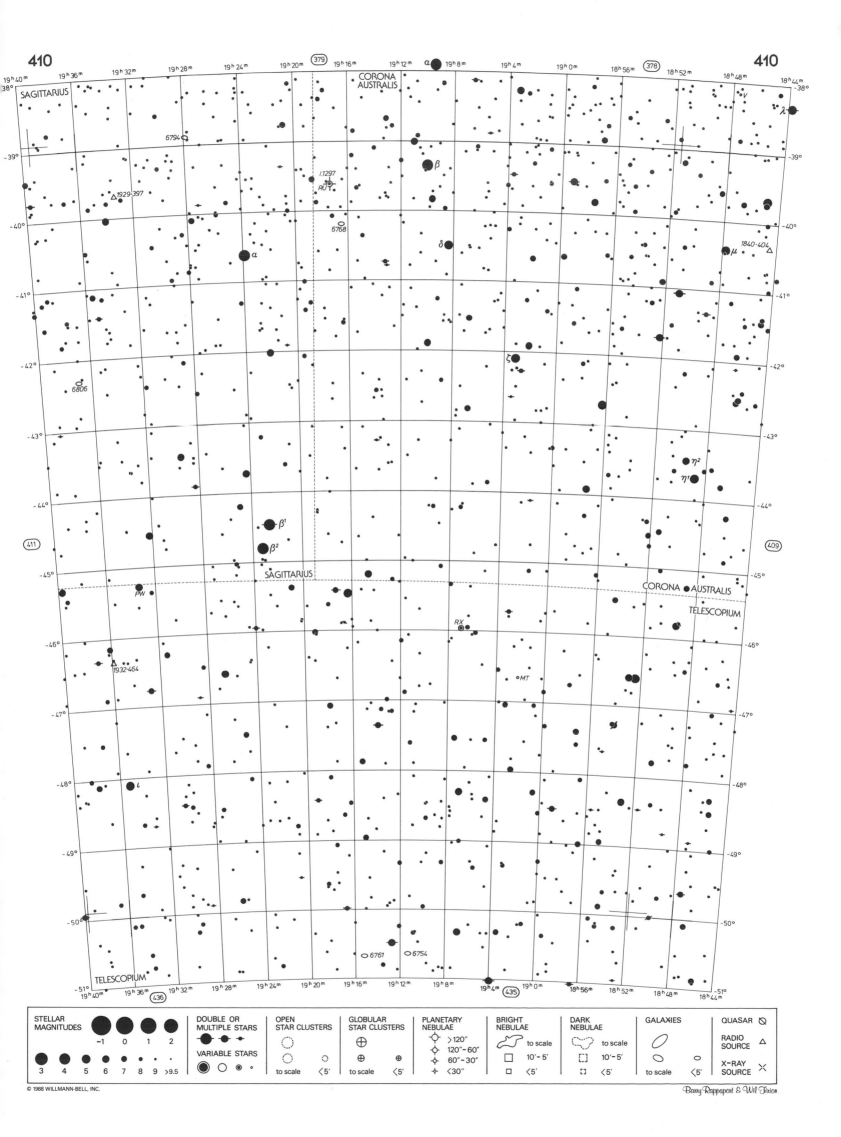

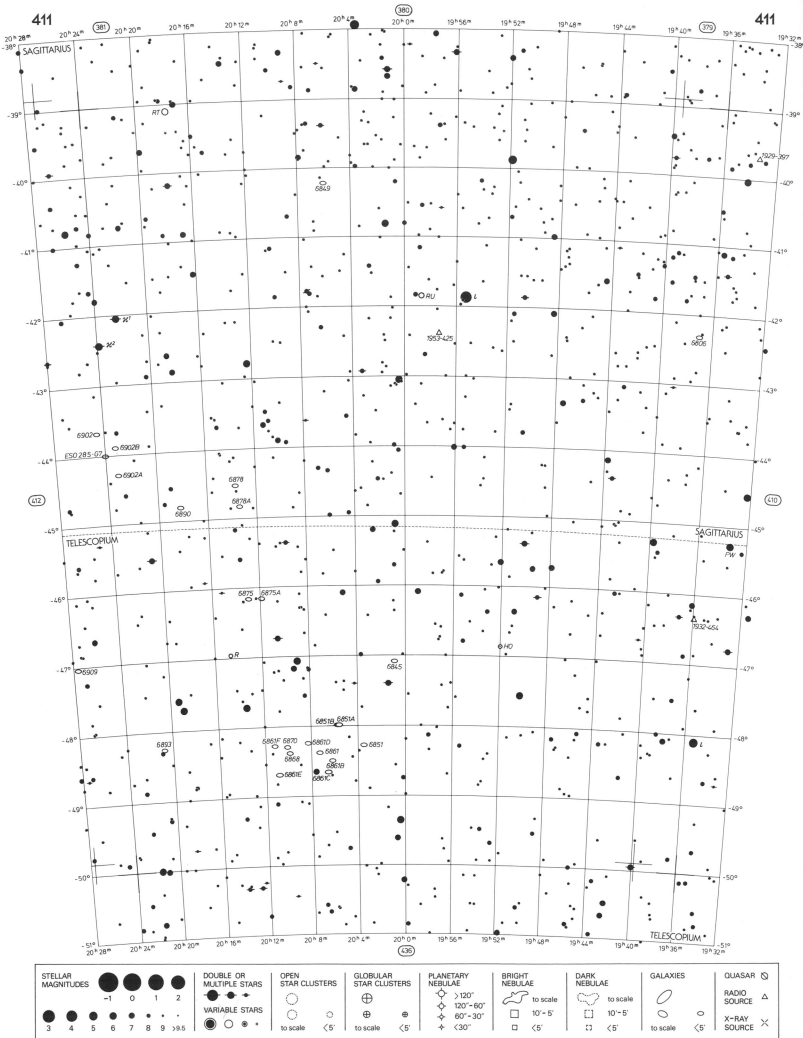

© 1988 WILLMANN-BELL, INC.

Barry Rappaport & Wil Tirion

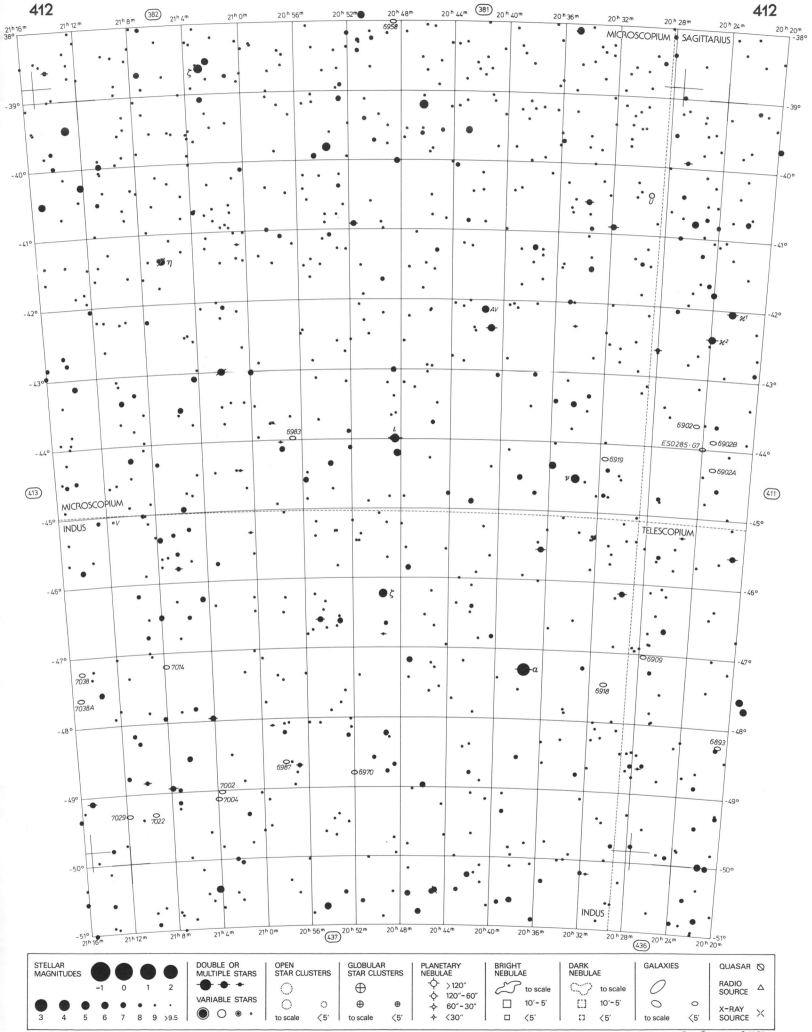

MICROSCOPIUM • SAGITTARIUS

MICROSCOPIUM

INDUS

TELESCOPIUM

INDUS

© 1988 WILLMANN-BELL, INC.

Barry Rappaport & Wil Tirion

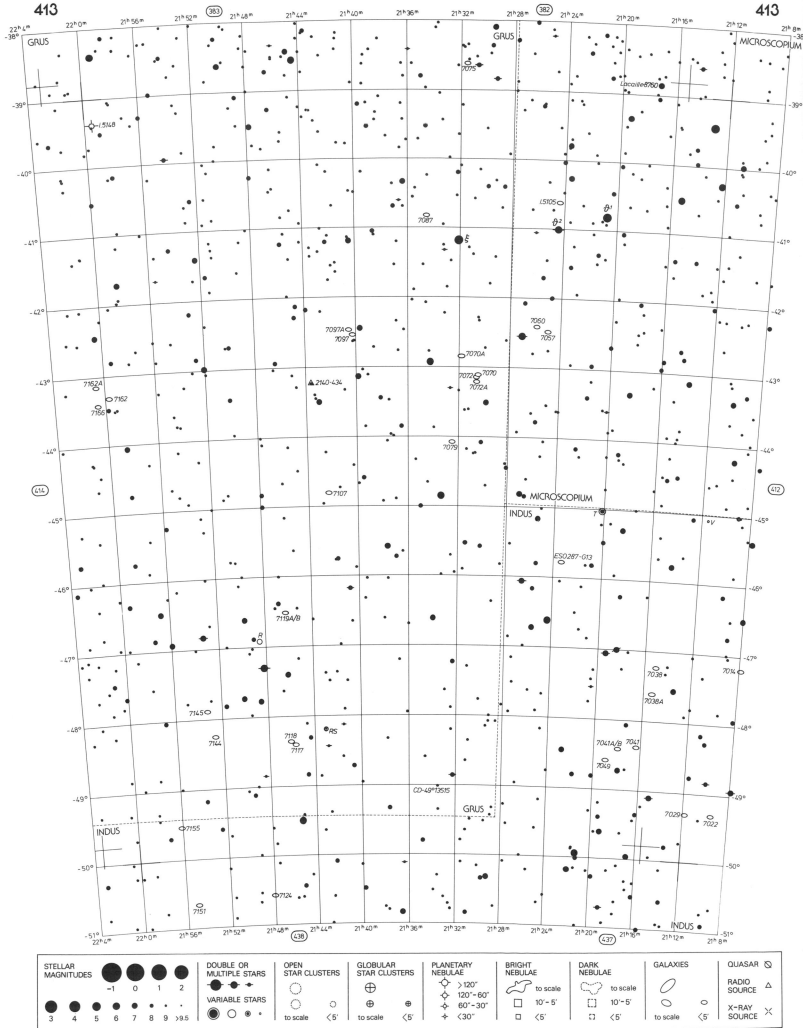

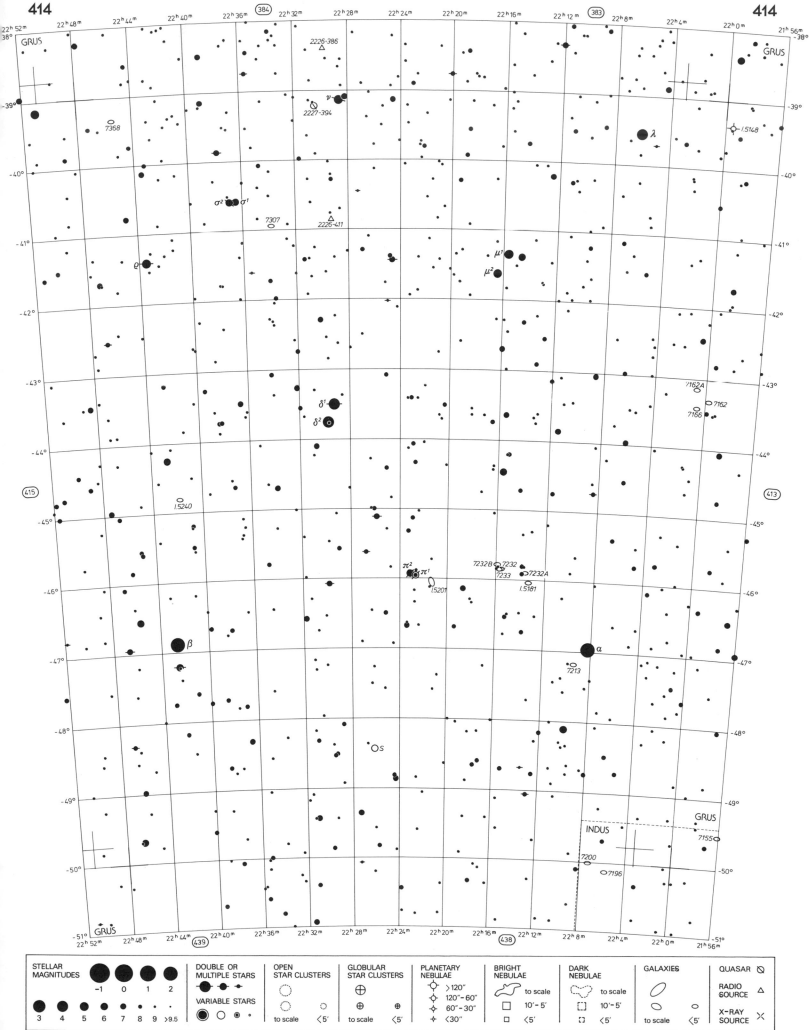

© 1988 WILLMANN-BELL, INC.

Barry Rappaport & Wil Tirion

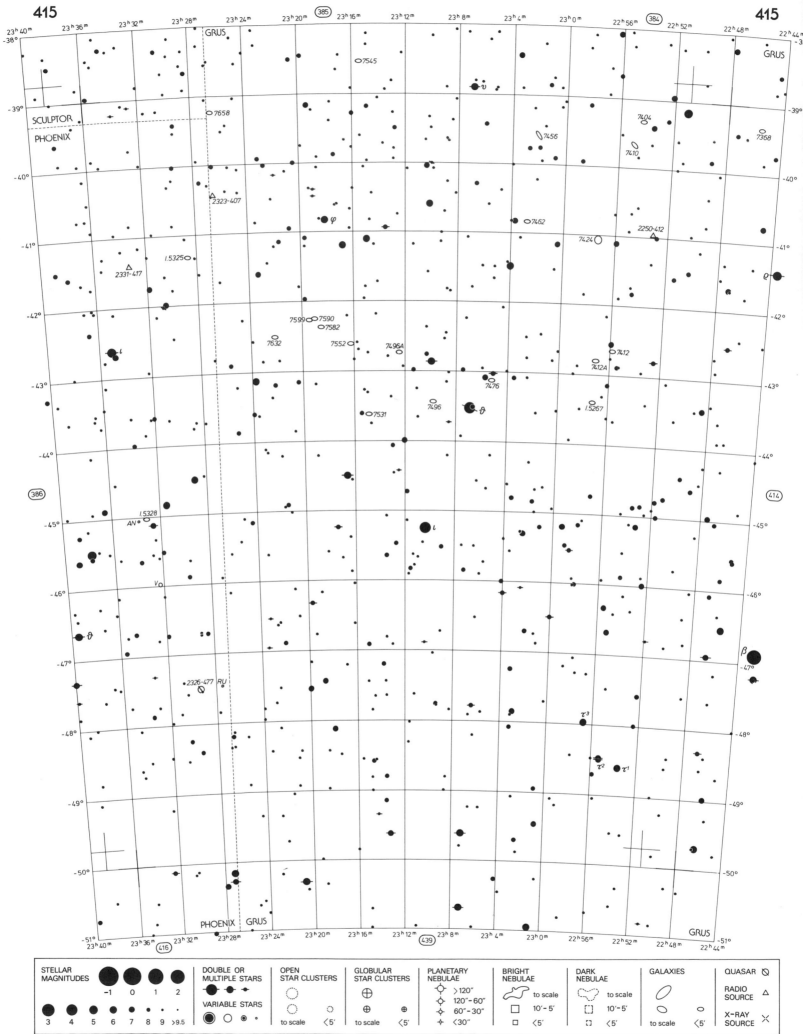

© 1988 WILLMANN-BELL, INC.

Barry Rappaport & Wil Tirion

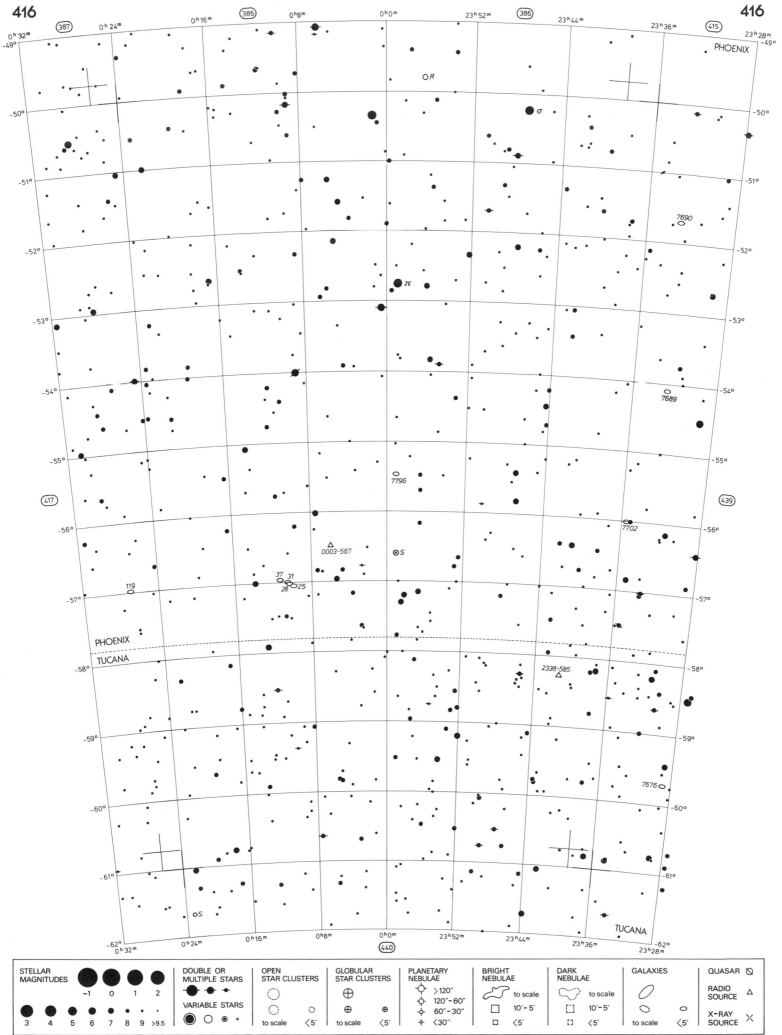

PHOENIX

TUCANA

© 1988 WILLMANN-BELL, INC.

Barry Rappaport & Wil Tirion

STELLAR MAGNITUDES

−1 0 1 2

3 4 5 6 7 8 9 >9.5

DOUBLE OR MULTIPLE STARS

VARIABLE STARS

OPEN STAR CLUSTERS

to scale   <5'

GLOBULAR STAR CLUSTERS

to scale   <5'

PLANETARY NEBULAE

>120"

120"−60"

60"−30"

<30"

BRIGHT NEBULAE

to scale

10'−5'

<5'

DARK NEBULAE

to scale

10'−5'

<5'

GALAXIES

to scale   <5'

QUASAR

RADIO SOURCE

X-RAY SOURCE

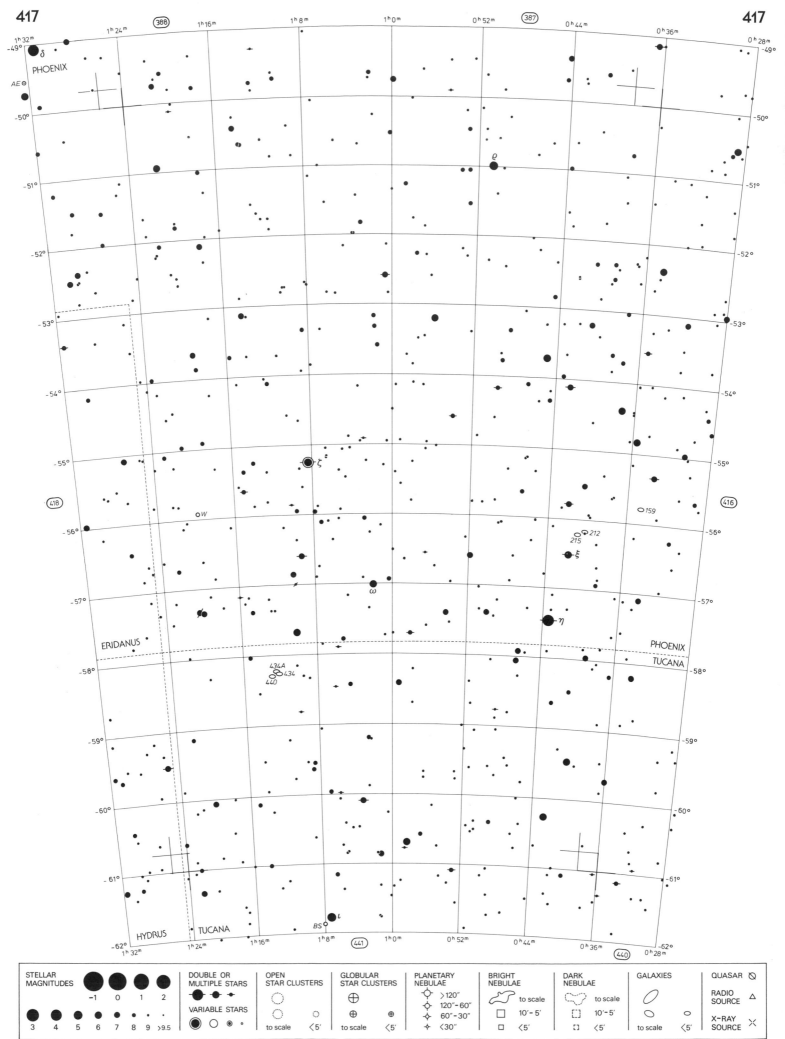

© 1988 WILLMANN-BELL, INC.

Barry Rappaport & Wil Tirion

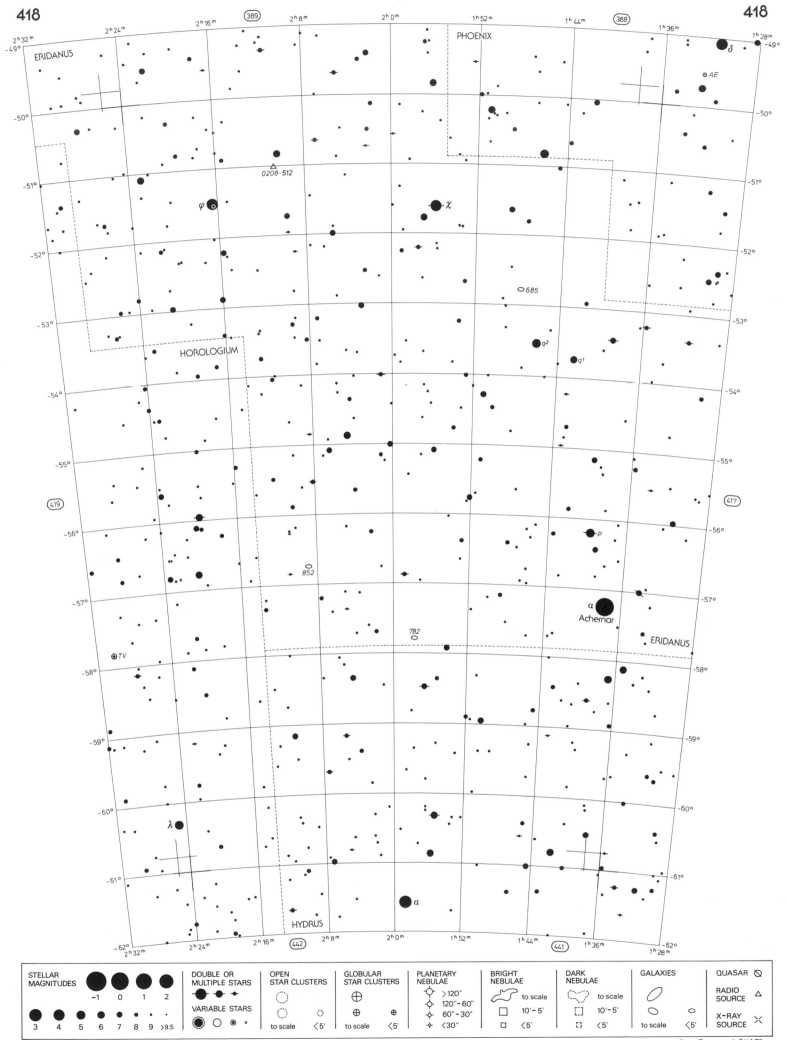

© 1988 WILLMANN-BELL, INC.

Barry Rappaport & Wil Tirion

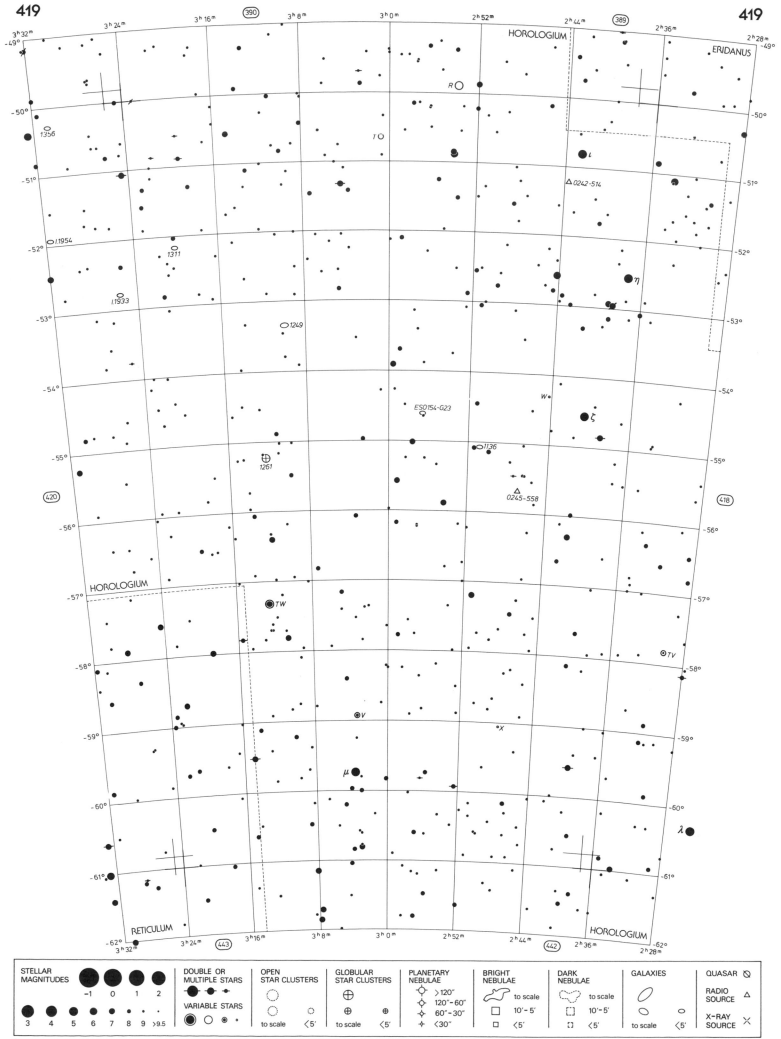

© 1988 WILLMANN-BELL, INC.

Barry Rappaport & Wil Tirion

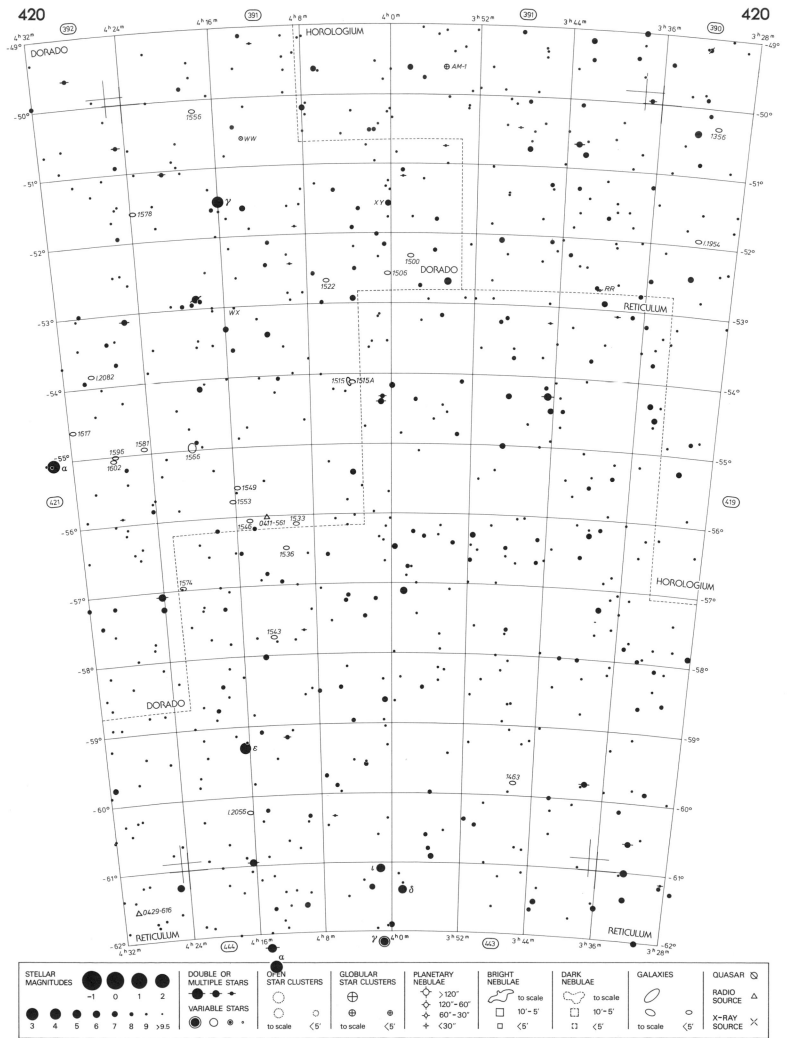

© 1988 WILLMANN-BELL, INC.

Barry Rappaport & Wil Tirion

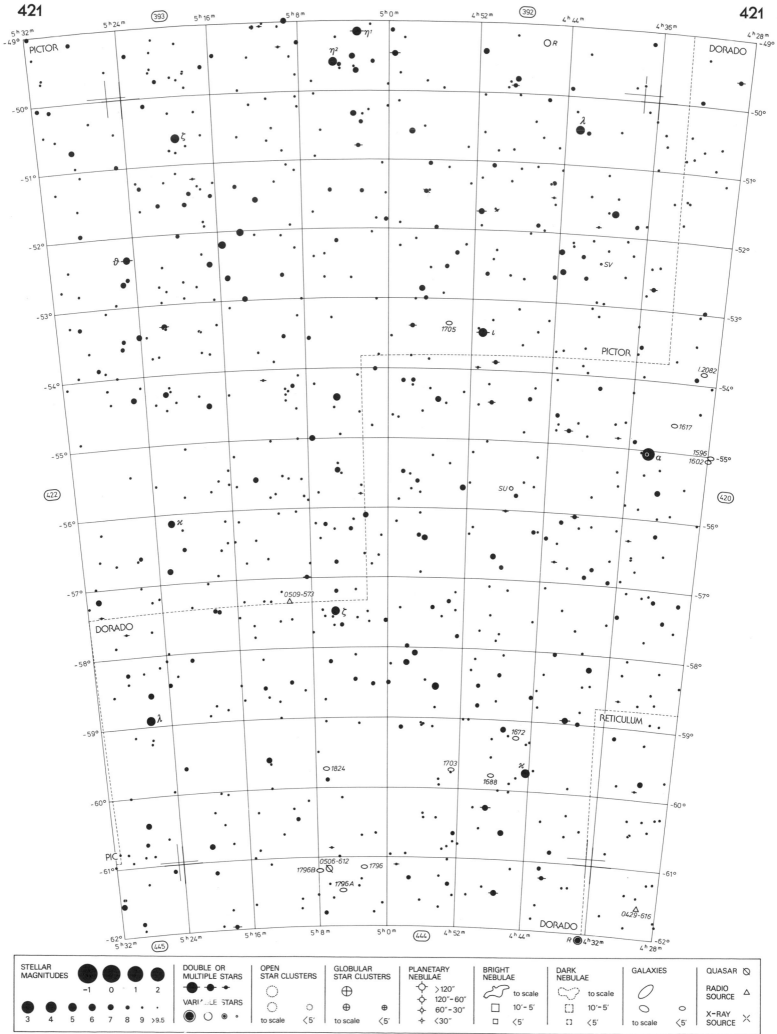

PICTOR

DORADO

PICTOR

DORADO

RETICULUM

DORADO

STELLAR MAGNITUDES				DOUBLE OR MULTIPLE STARS	OPEN STAR CLUSTERS	GLOBULAR STAR CLUSTERS	PLANETARY NEBULAE	BRIGHT NEBULAE	DARK NEBULAE	GALAXIES	QUASAR

© 1988 WILLMANN-BELL, INC.

Barry Rappaport & Wil Tirion

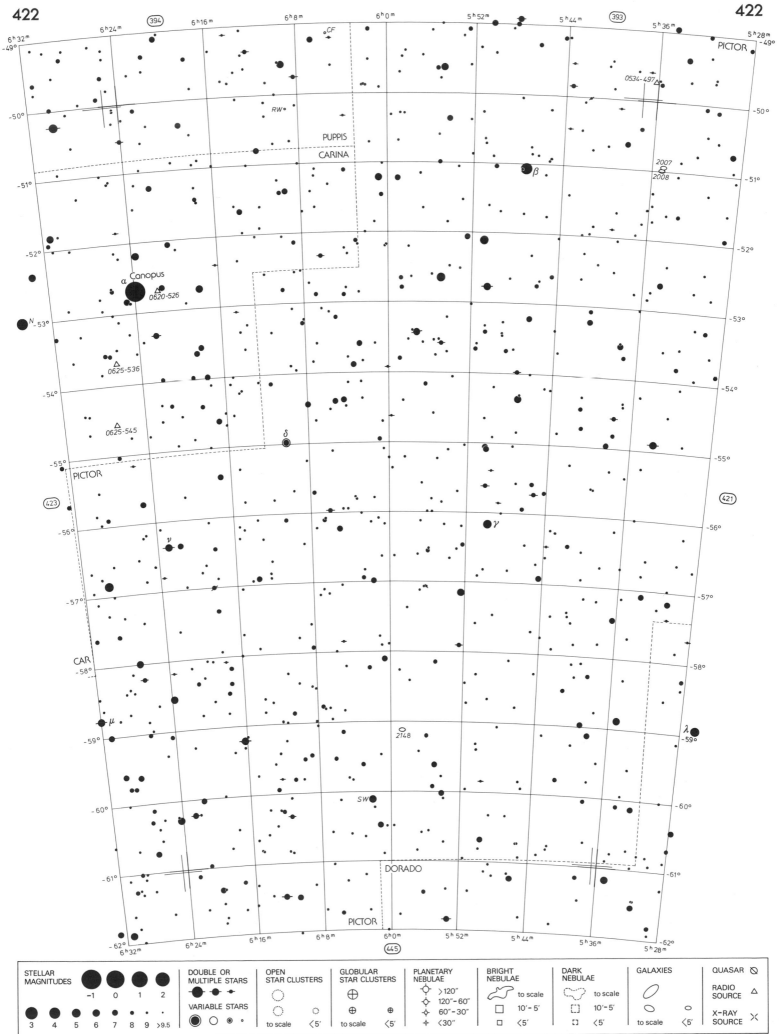

© 1988 WILLMANN-BELL, INC.

Barry Rappaport & Wil Tirion

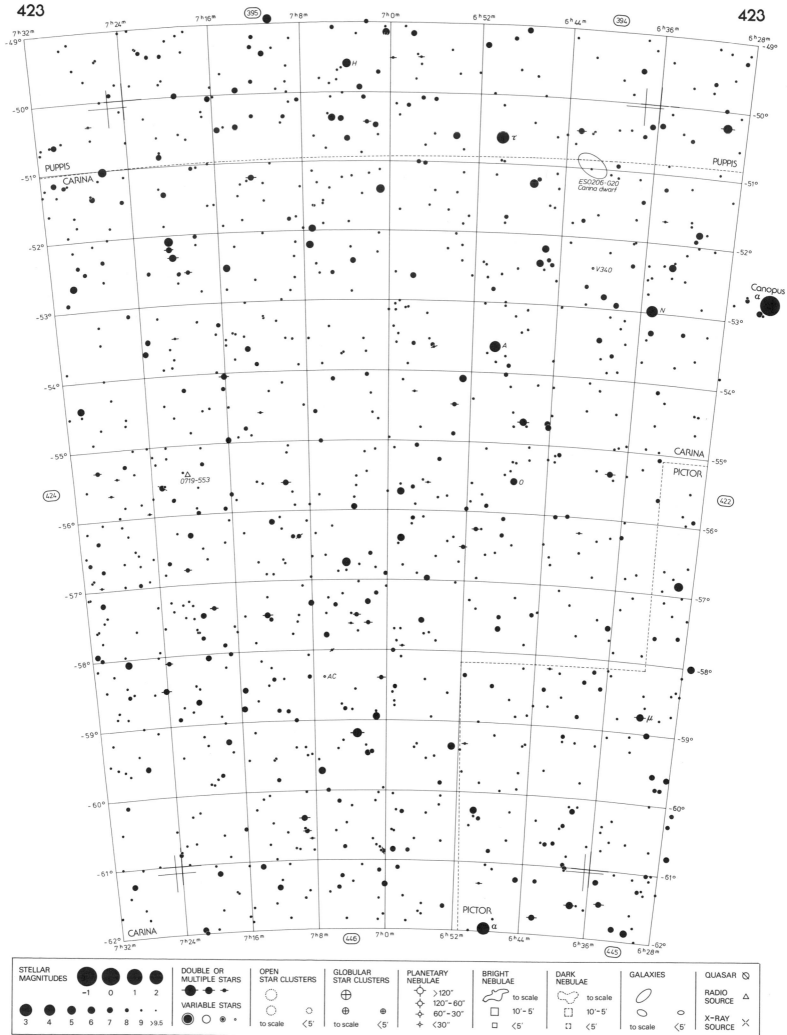

© 1988 WILLMANN-BELL, INC.

Barry Rappaport & Wil Tirion

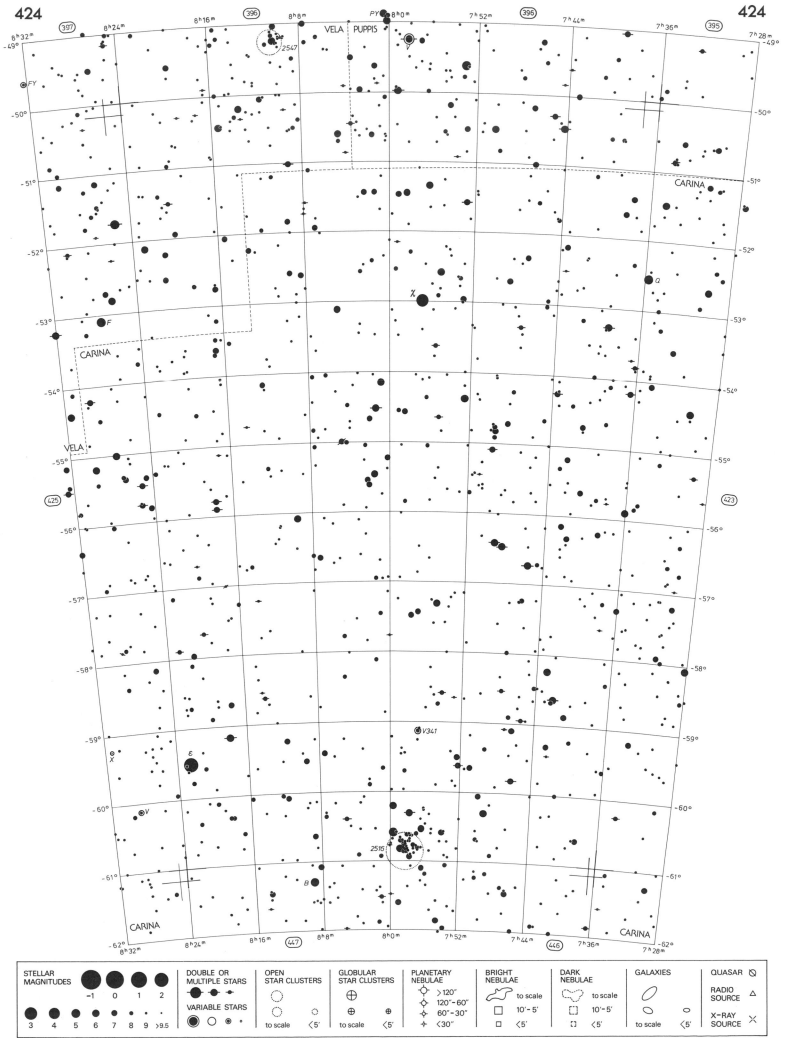

© 1988 WILLMANN-BELL, INC.

Barry Rappaport & Wil Tirion

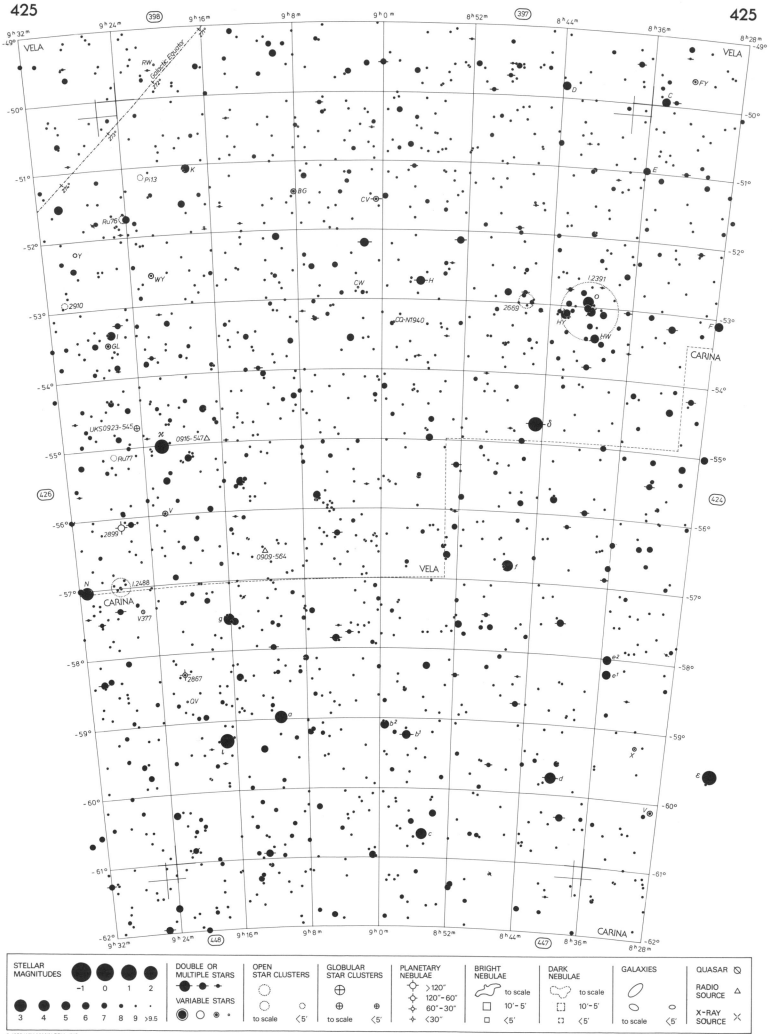

© 1988 WILLMANN-BELL, INC.

Barry Rappaport & Wil Tirion

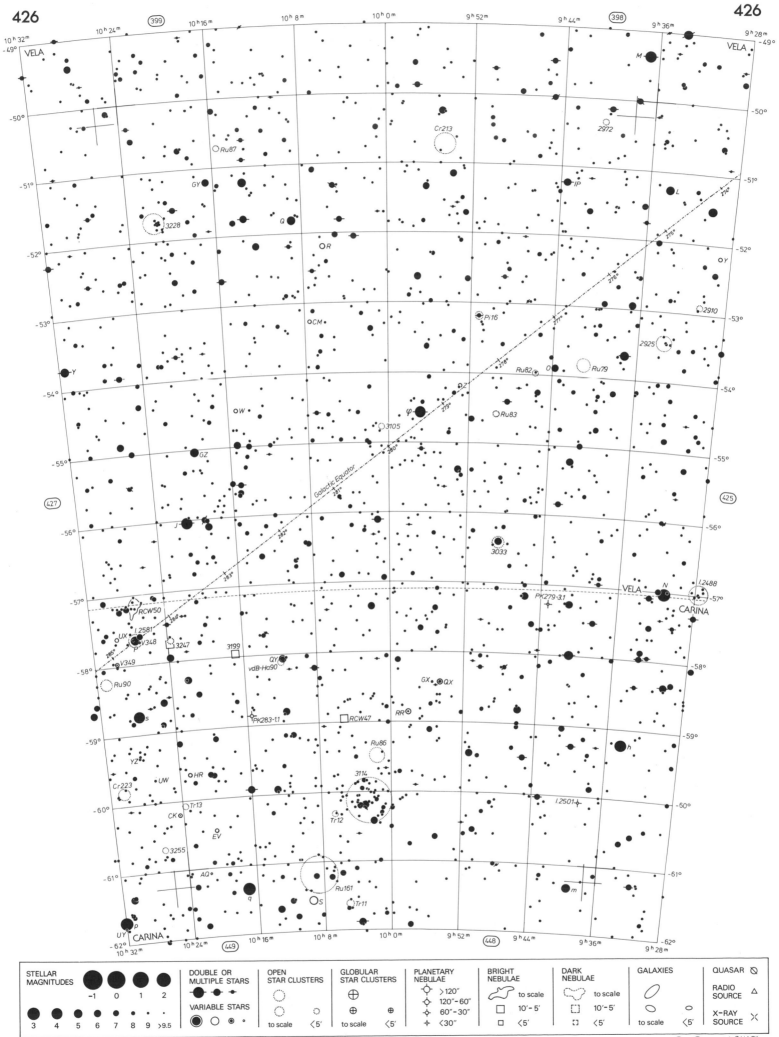

© 1988 WILLMANN-BELL, INC.

Barry Rappaport & Wil Tirion

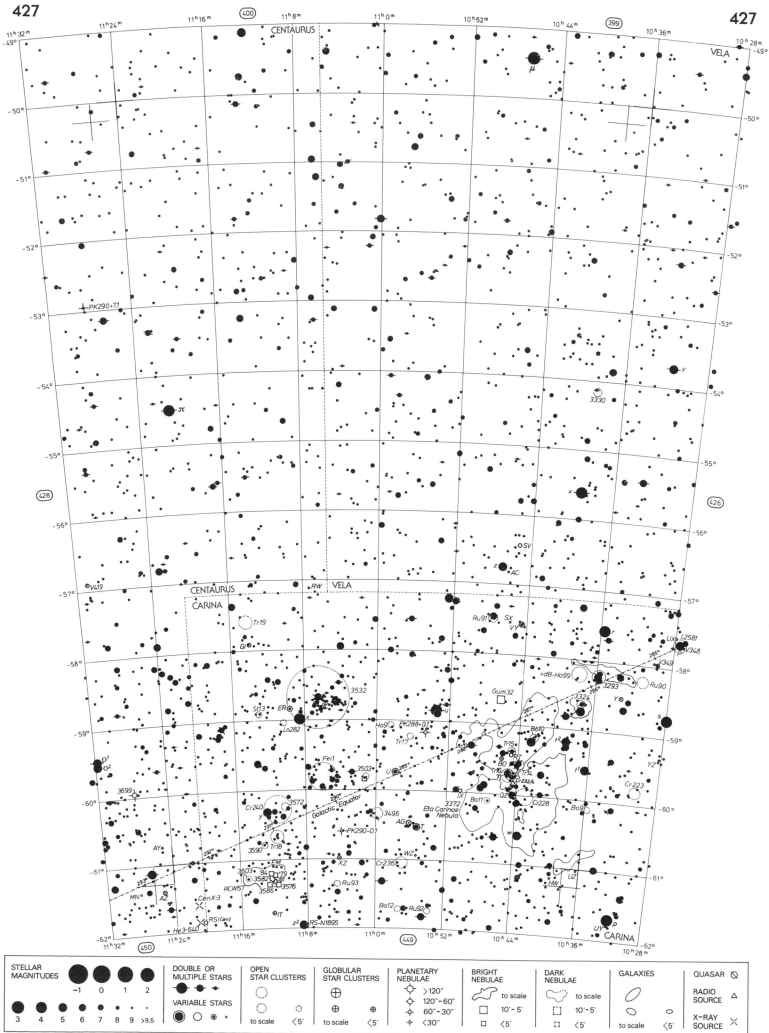

© 1988 WILLMANN-BELL, INC.

Barry Rappaport & Wil Tirion

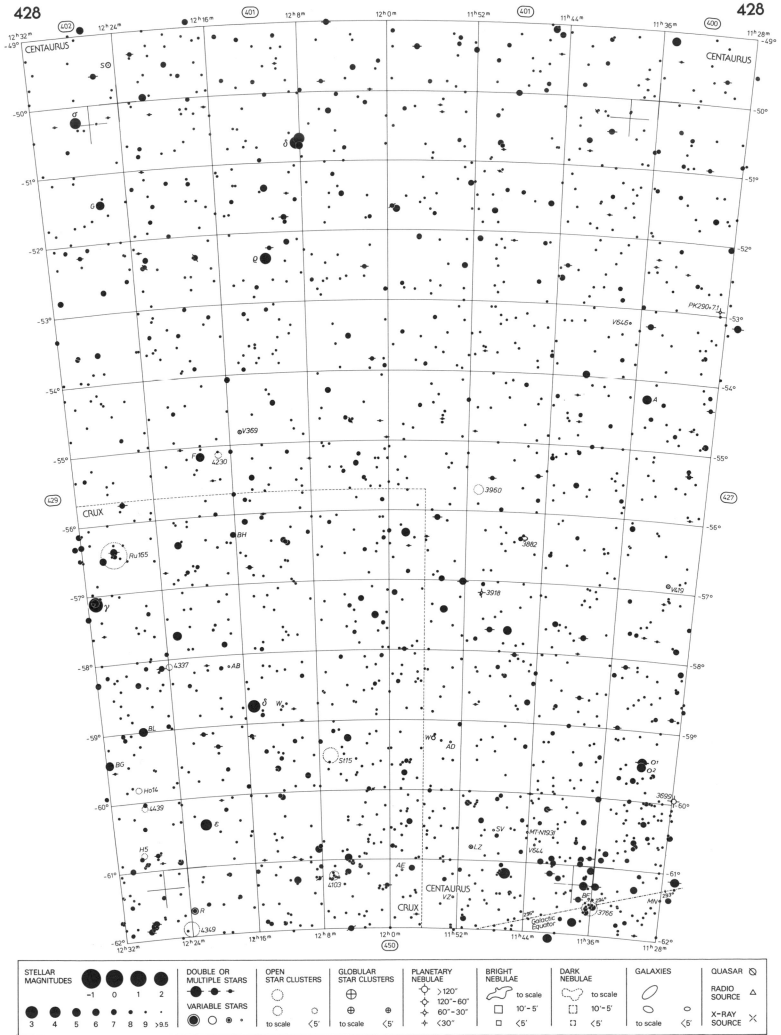

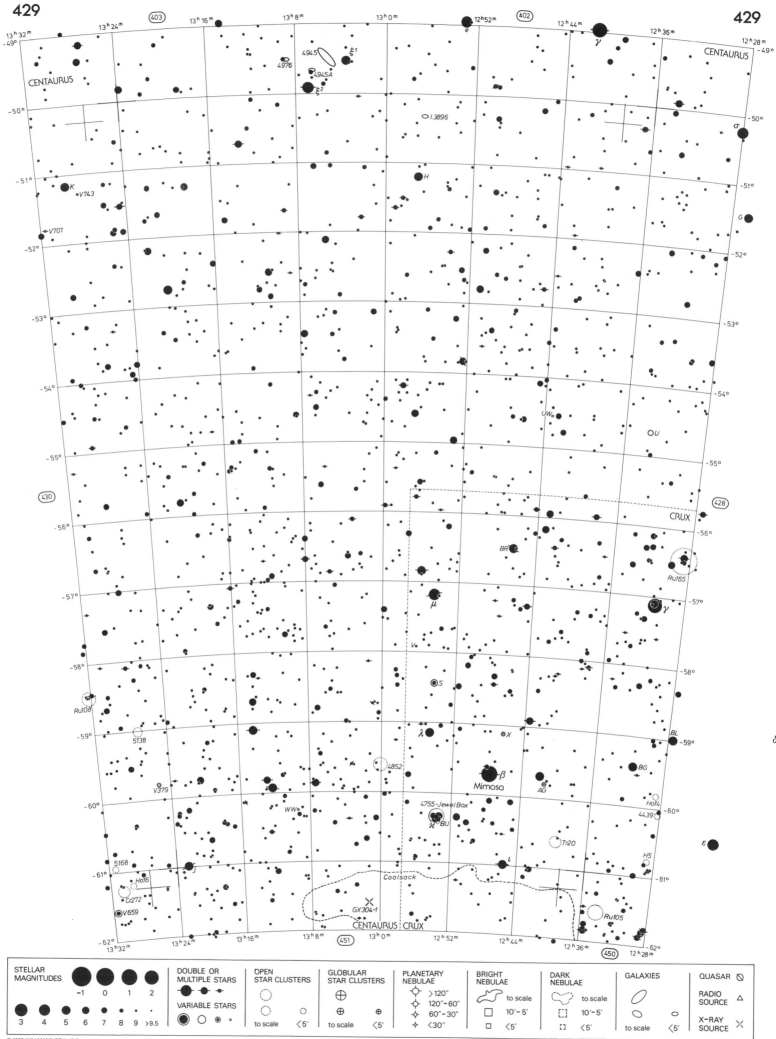

CENTAURUS

CENTAURUS

CRUX

Mimosa

4755-Jewel Box

Coalsack

CENTAURUS CRUX

STELLAR MAGNITUDES					DOUBLE OR MULTIPLE STARS	OPEN STAR CLUSTERS	GLOBULAR STAR CLUSTERS	PLANETARY NEBULAE	BRIGHT NEBULAE	DARK NEBULAE	GALAXIES	QUASAR

© 1988 WILLMANN-BELL, INC.

Barry Rappaport & Wil Tirion

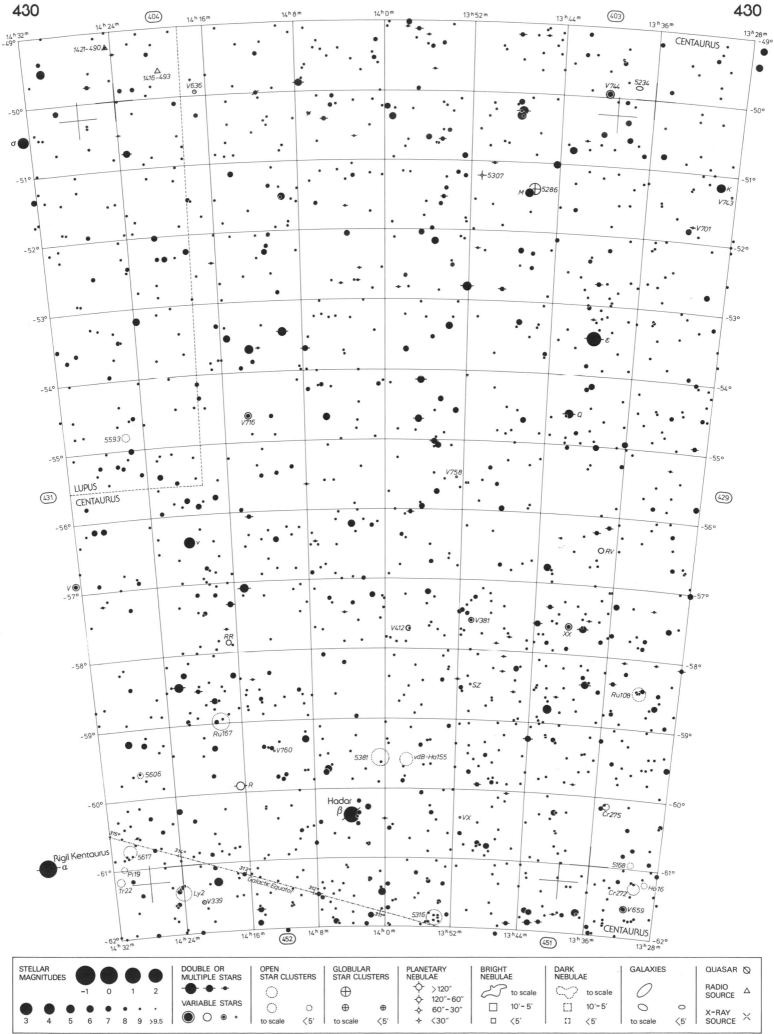

© 1988 WILLMANN-BELL, INC.

Barry Rappaport & Wil Tirion

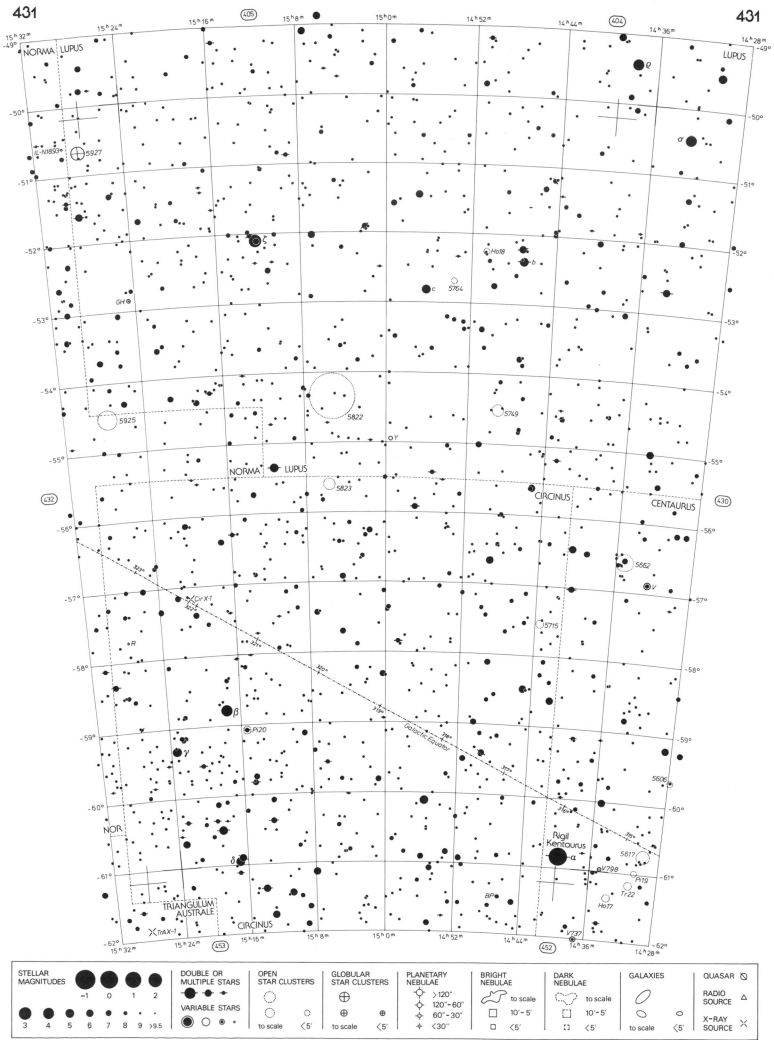

© 1988 WILLMANN-BELL, INC.

Barry Rappaport & Wil Tirion

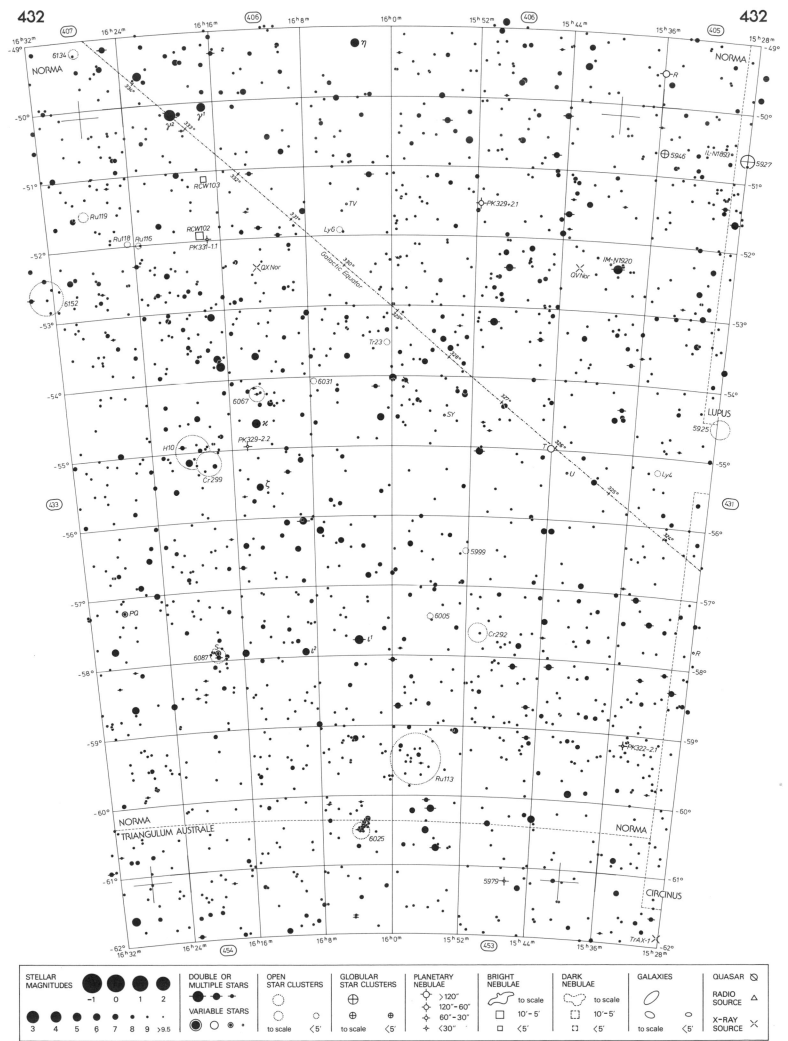

Barry Rappaport & Wil Tirion

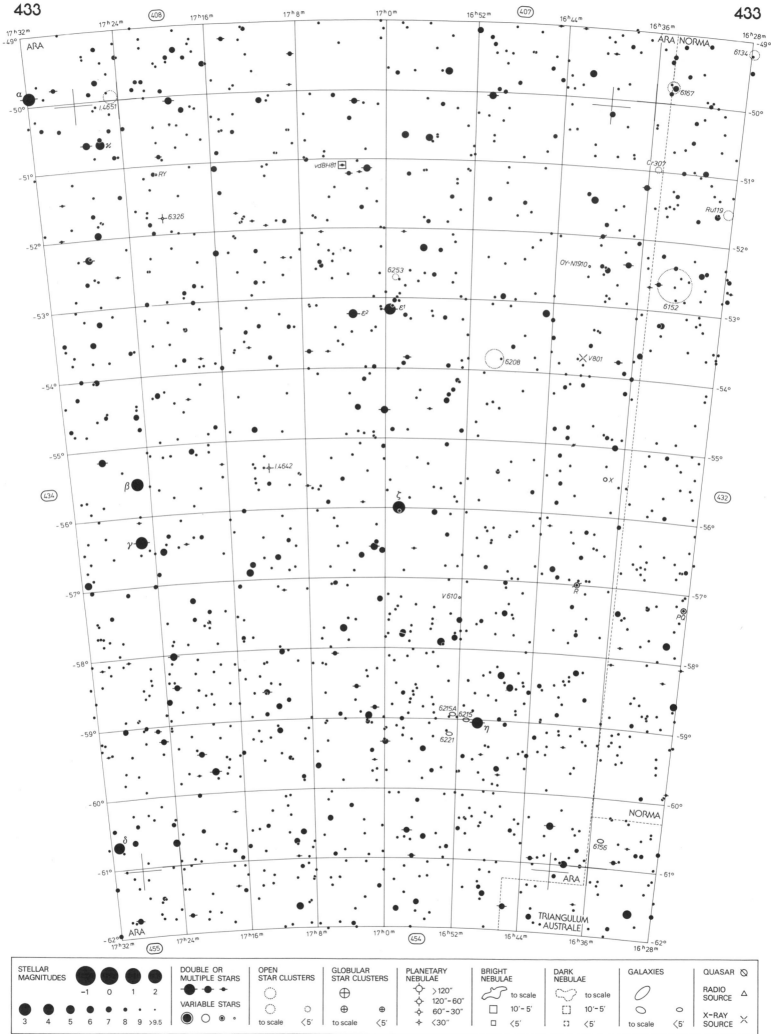

© 1988 WILLMANN-BELL, INC.

Barry Rappaport & Wil Tirion

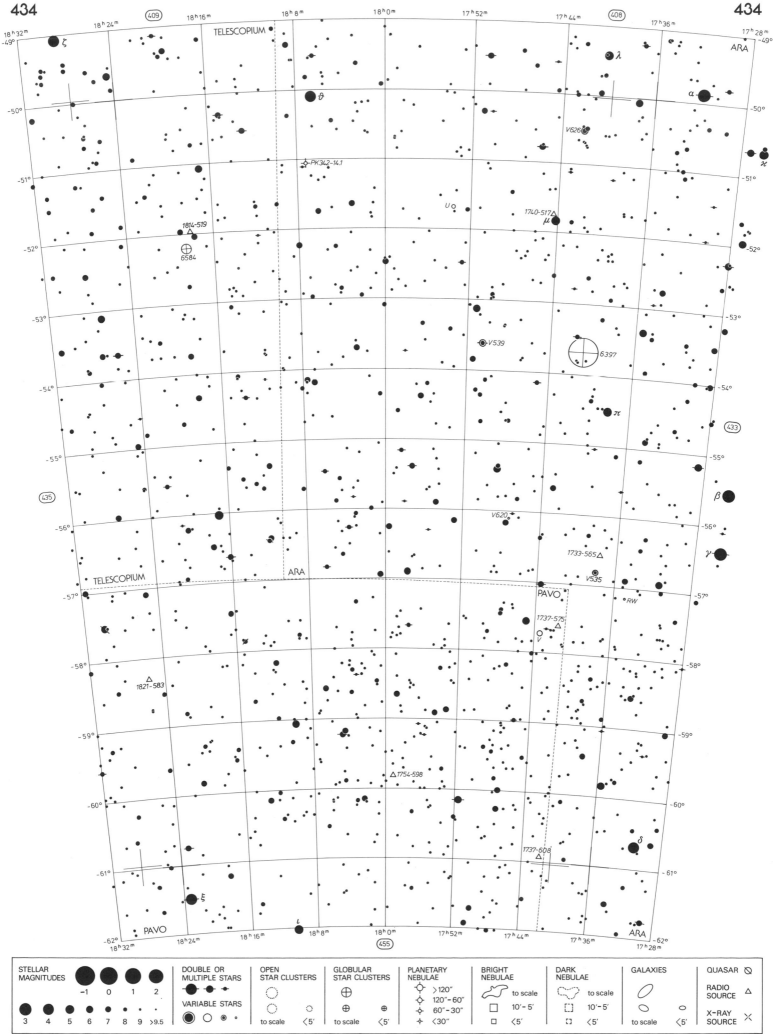

© 1988 WILLMANN-BELL, INC.

Barry Rappaport & Wil Tirion

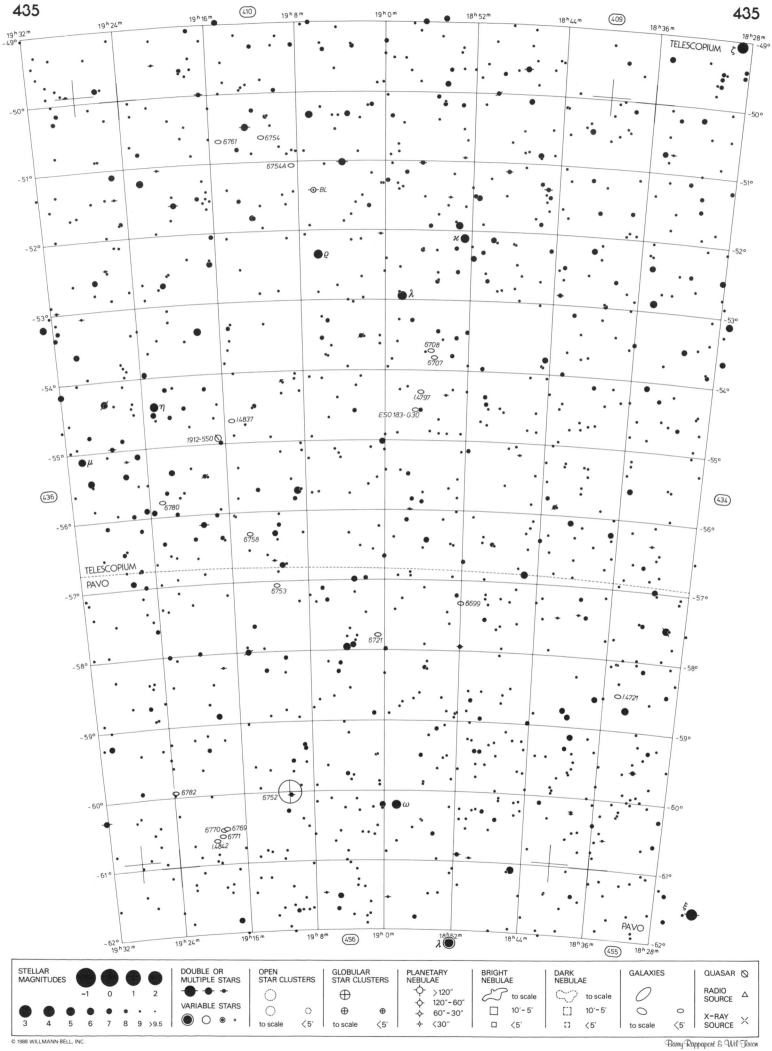

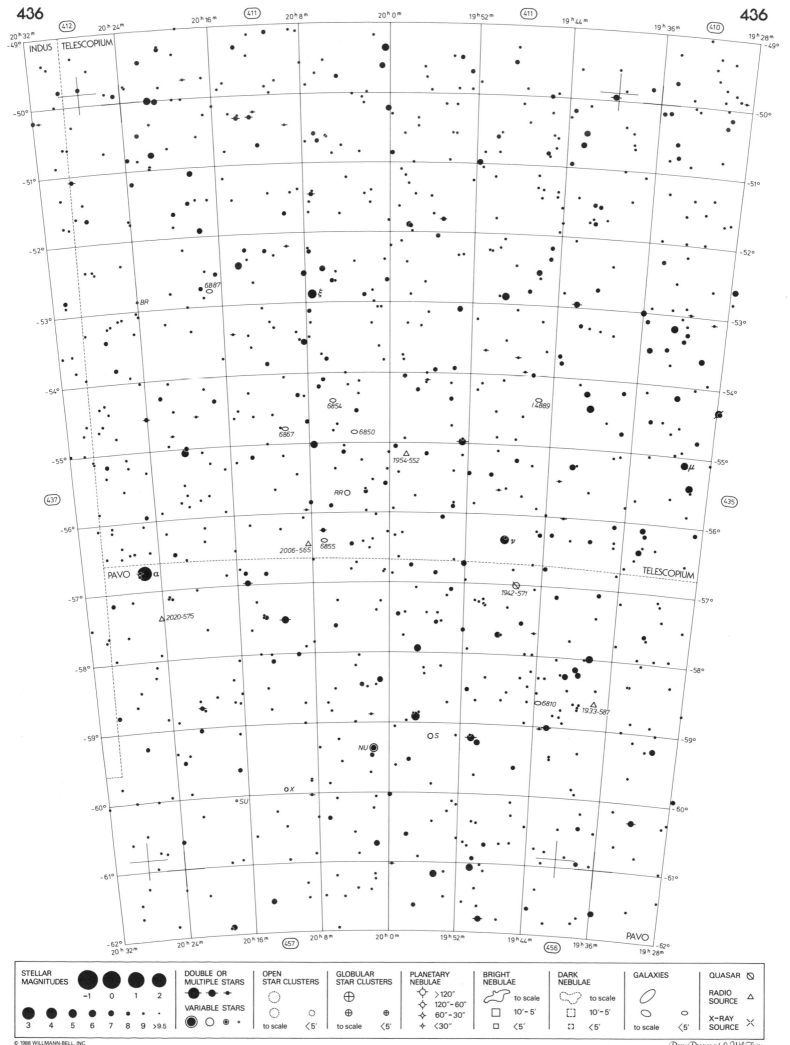

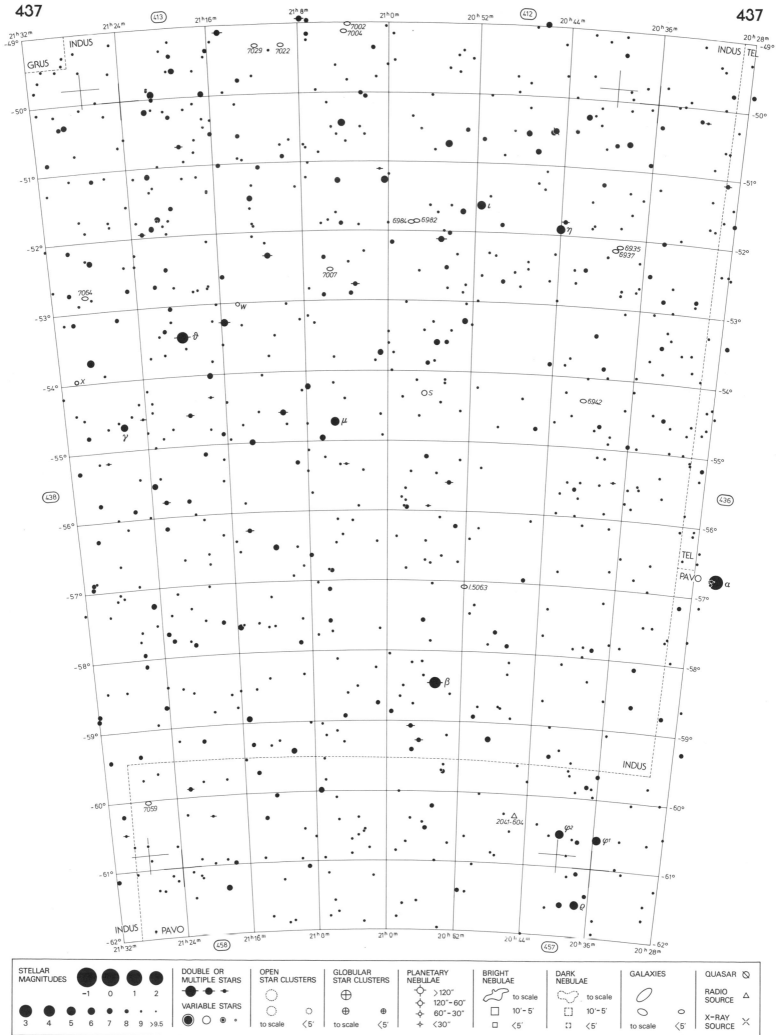

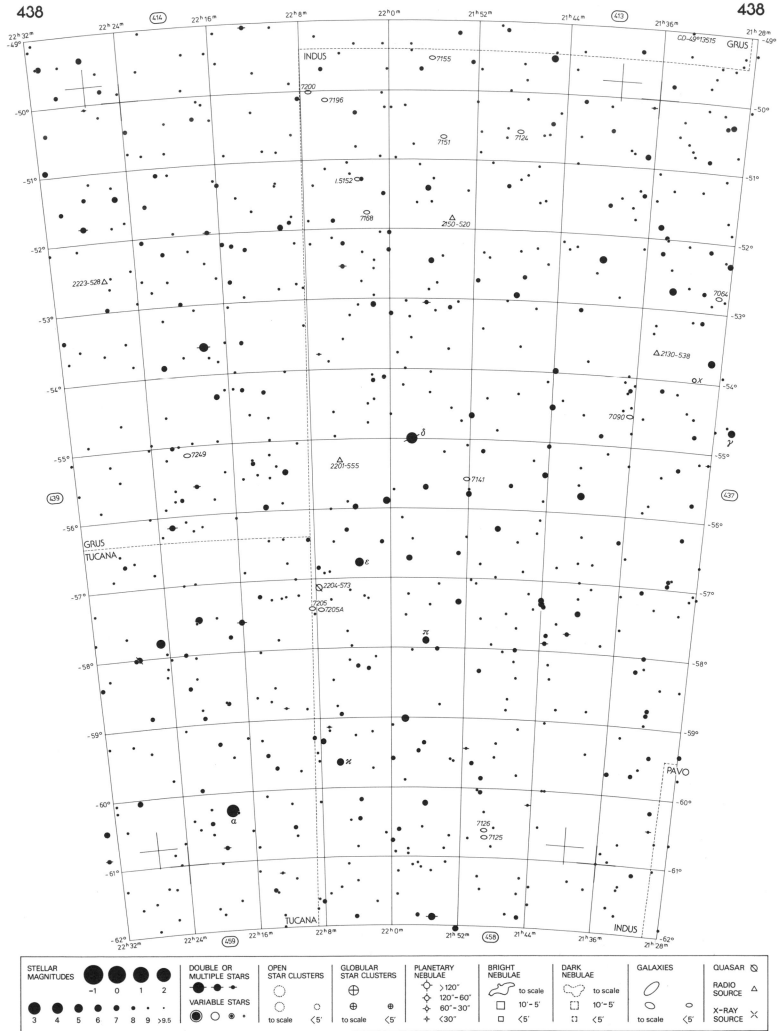

STELLAR MAGNITUDES

DOUBLE OR MULTIPLE STARS

VARIABLE STARS

OPEN STAR CLUSTERS
to scale   ⟨5'

GLOBULAR STAR CLUSTERS
to scale   ⟨5'

PLANETARY NEBULAE
⟩120"
120"–60"
60"–30"
⟨30"

BRIGHT NEBULAE
to scale
10'–5'
⟨5'

DARK NEBULAE
to scale
10'–5'
⟨5'

GALAXIES
to scale   ⟨5'

QUASAR

RADIO SOURCE

X–RAY SOURCE

© 1988 WILLMANN-BELL, INC.

Barry Rappaport & Wil Tirion

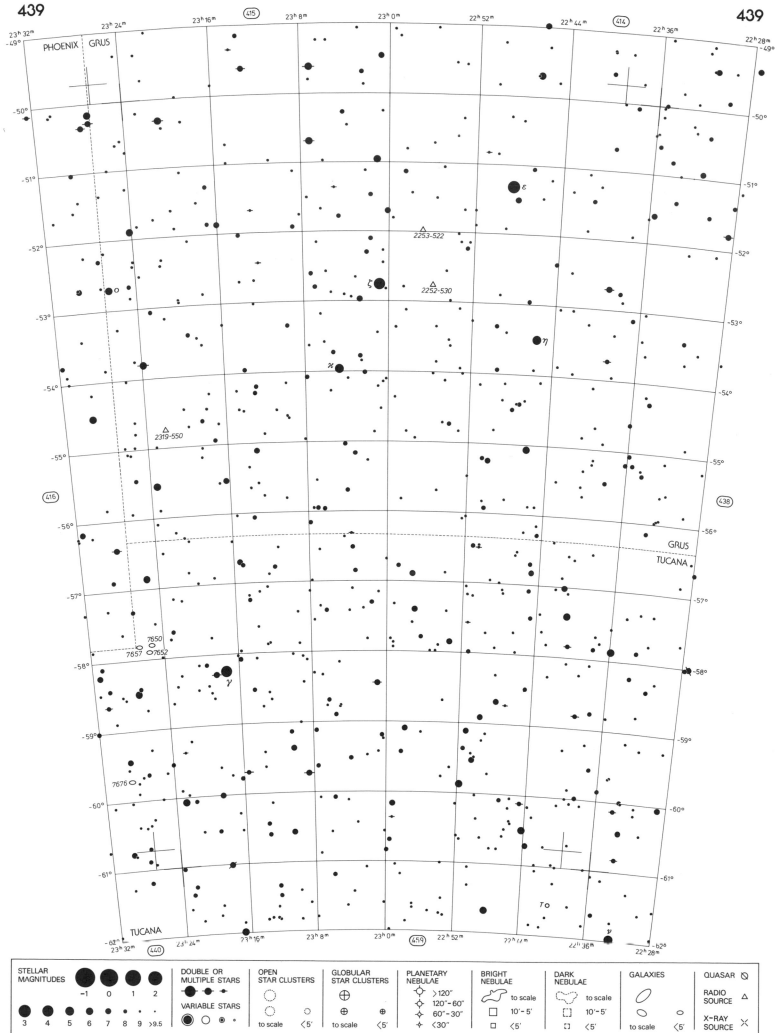

PHOENIX GRUS

415

414

416

438

GRUS

TUCANA

2253-522

2252-530

2319-550

7650
7657 7652

7676

γ

TUCANA

440 459

© 1988 WILLMANN-BELL, INC.

Barry Rappaport & Wil Tirion

STELLAR MAGNITUDES					DOUBLE OR MULTIPLE STARS		OPEN STAR CLUSTERS		GLOBULAR STAR CLUSTERS		PLANETARY NEBULAE		BRIGHT NEBULAE		DARK NEBULAE		GALAXIES		QUASAR	
	-1	0	1	2					⊕		>120″		to scale		to scale		to scale		RADIO SOURCE	
3	4 5	6 7	8 9	>9.5	VARIABLE STARS		to scale	<5′	⊕	⊕	120″-60″ 60″-30″ <30″		10′-5′ <5′		10′-5′ <5′		to scale <5′		X-RAY SOURCE	

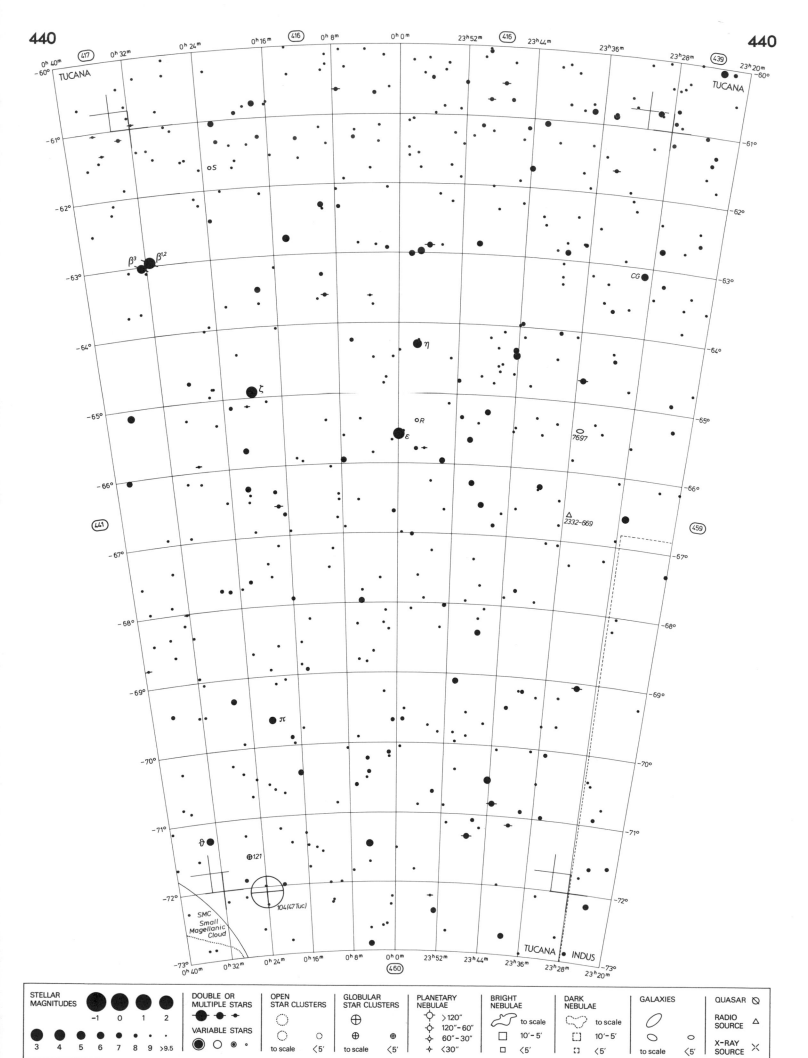

© 1988 WILLMANN-BELL, INC.

Barry Rappaport & Wil Tirion

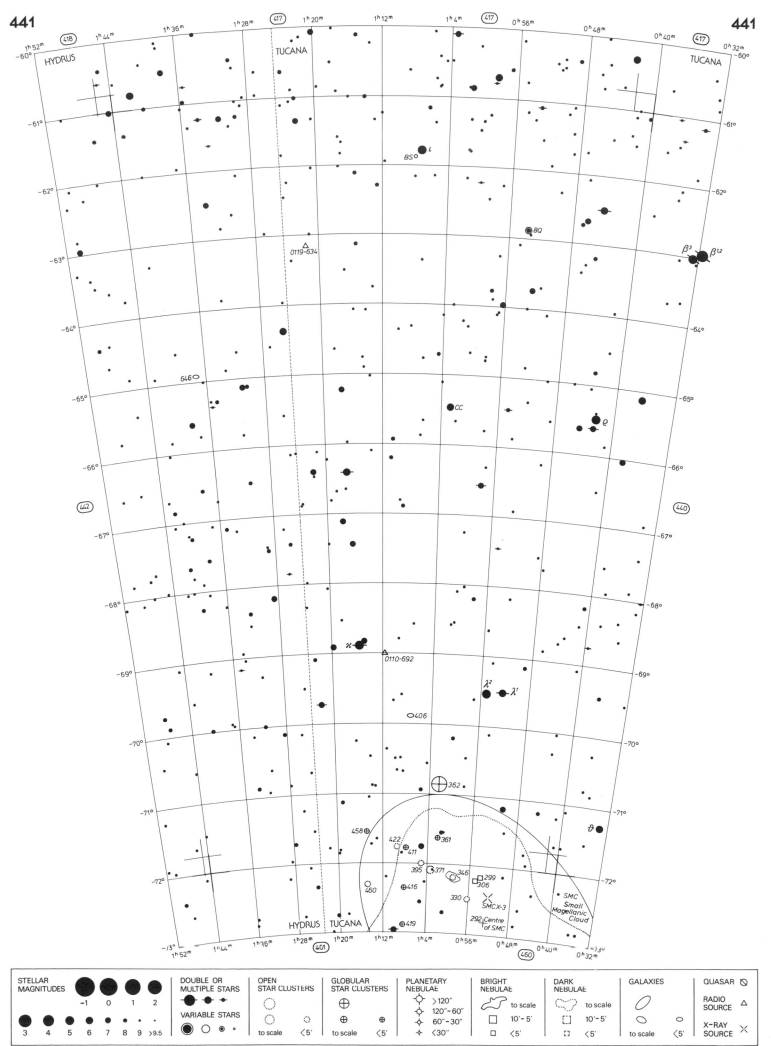

© 1988 WILLMANN-BELL, INC.

Barry Rappaport & Wil Tirion

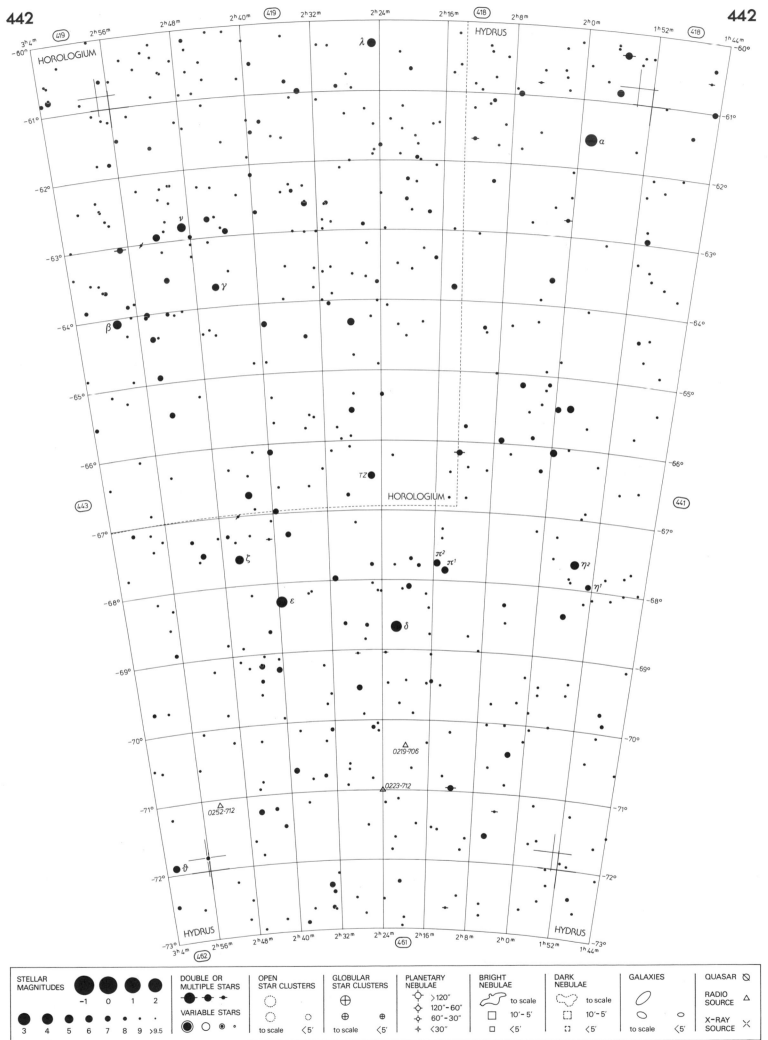

HOROLOGIUM

HYDRUS

HOROLOGIUM

HYDRUS

HYDRUS

STELLAR
MAGNITUDES

-1 0 1 2

3 4 5 6 7 8 9 >9.5

DOUBLE OR
MULTIPLE STARS

VARIABLE STARS

OPEN
STAR CLUSTERS

to scale   <5'

GLOBULAR
STAR CLUSTERS

to scale   <5'

PLANETARY
NEBULAE

>120"
120"-60"
60"-30"
<30"

BRIGHT
NEBULAE

to scale

10'-5'

<5'

DARK
NEBULAE

to scale

10'-5'

<5'

GALAXIES

to scale   <5'

QUASAR

RADIO
SOURCE

X-RAY
SOURCE

© 1988 WILLMANN-BELL, INC.

Barry Rappaport & Wil Tirion

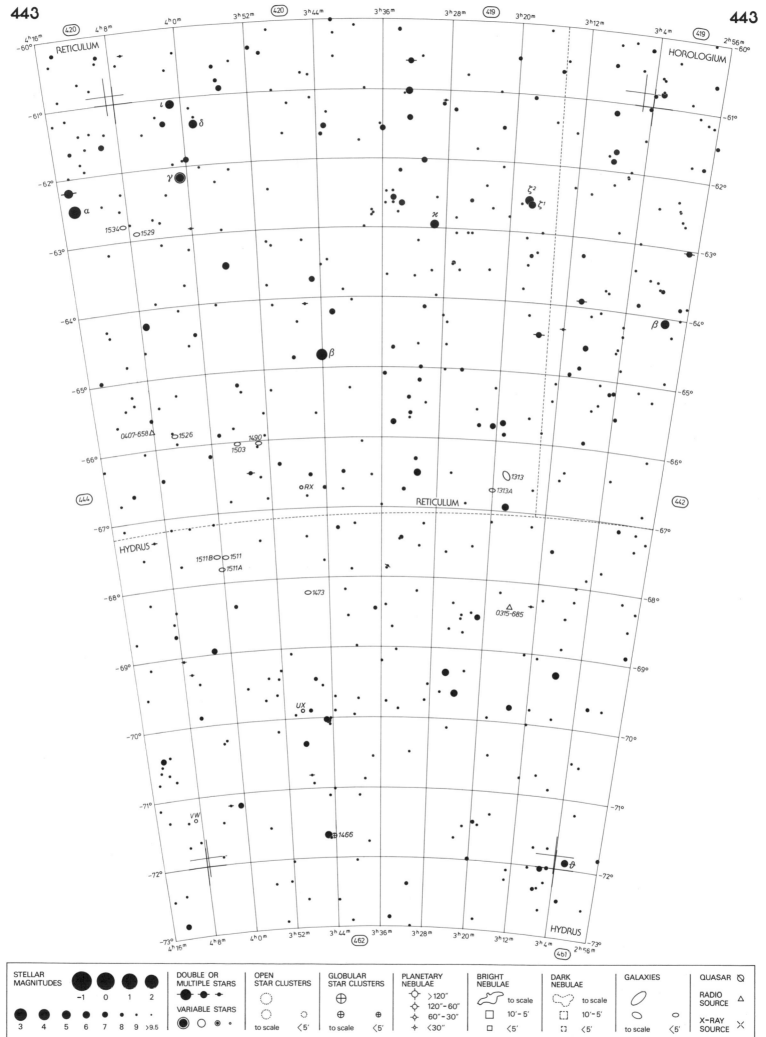

STELLAR MAGNITUDES

-1 0 1 2

3 4 5 6 7 8 9 >9.5

DOUBLE OR MULTIPLE STARS

VARIABLE STARS

OPEN STAR CLUSTERS

to scale <5'

GLOBULAR STAR CLUSTERS

to scale <5'

PLANETARY NEBULAE

>120"
120"-60"
60"-30"
<30"

BRIGHT NEBULAE

to scale

10'-5'

<5'

DARK NEBULAE

to scale

10'-5'

<5'

GALAXIES

to scale <5'

QUASAR

RADIO SOURCE

X-RAY SOURCE

© 1988 WILLMANN-BELL, INC.

Barry Rappaport & Wil Tirion

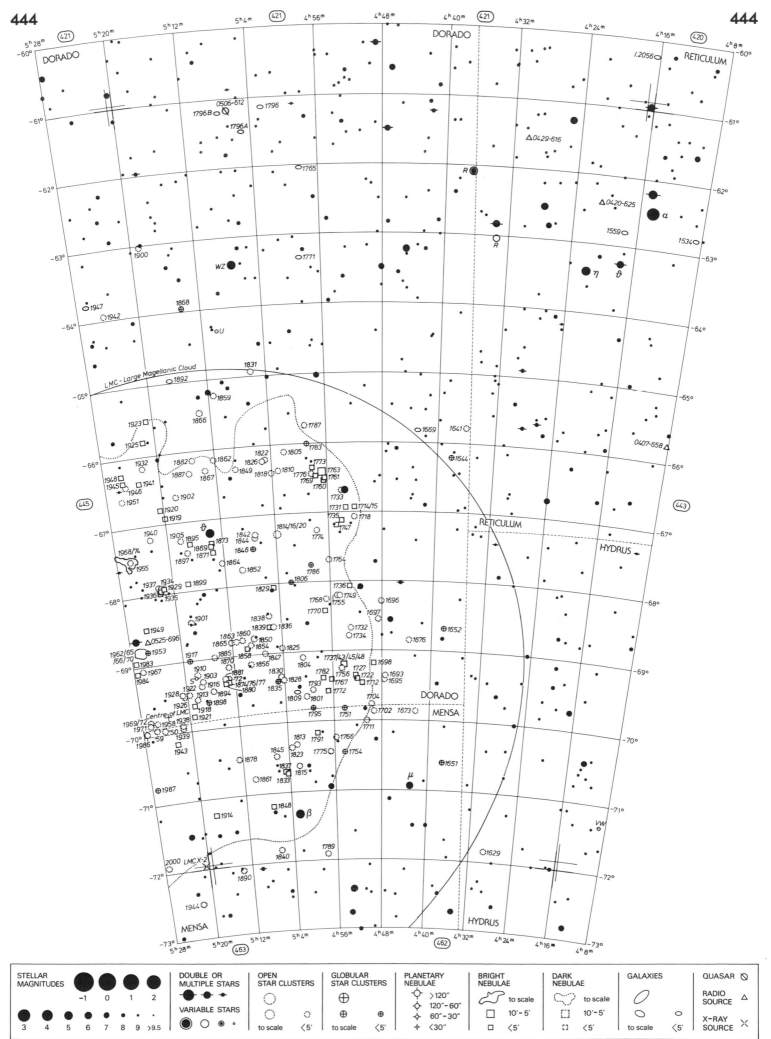

© 1988 WILLMANN-BELL, INC.

Barry Rappaport & Wil Tirion

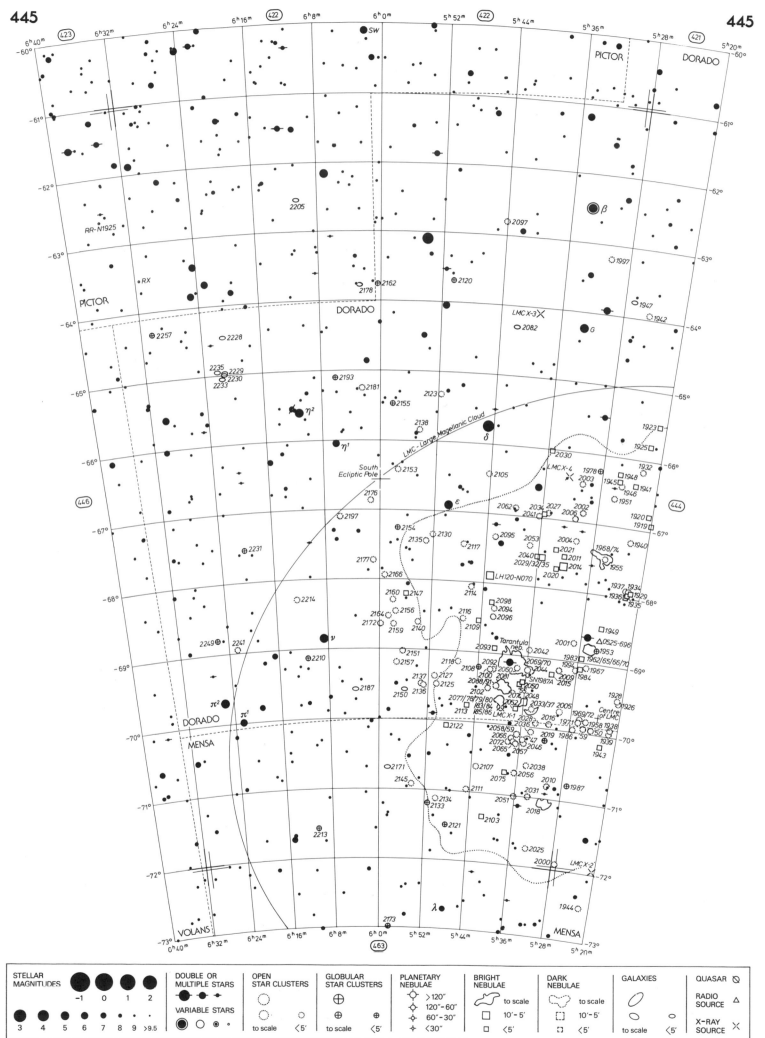

STELLAR MAGNITUDES

-1	0	1	2
3	4	5	6	7	8	9	>9.5

DOUBLE OR MULTIPLE STARS

VARIABLE STARS

OPEN STAR CLUSTERS
to scale   <5'

GLOBULAR STAR CLUSTERS
to scale   <5'

PLANETARY NEBULAE
>120"
120"-60"
60"-30"
<30"

BRIGHT NEBULAE
to scale
10'-5'
<5'

DARK NEBULAE
to scale
10'-5'
<5'

GALAXIES
to scale
<5'

QUASAR

RADIO SOURCE

X-RAY SOURCE

© 1988 WILLMANN-BELL, INC.

Barry Rappaport & Wil Tirion

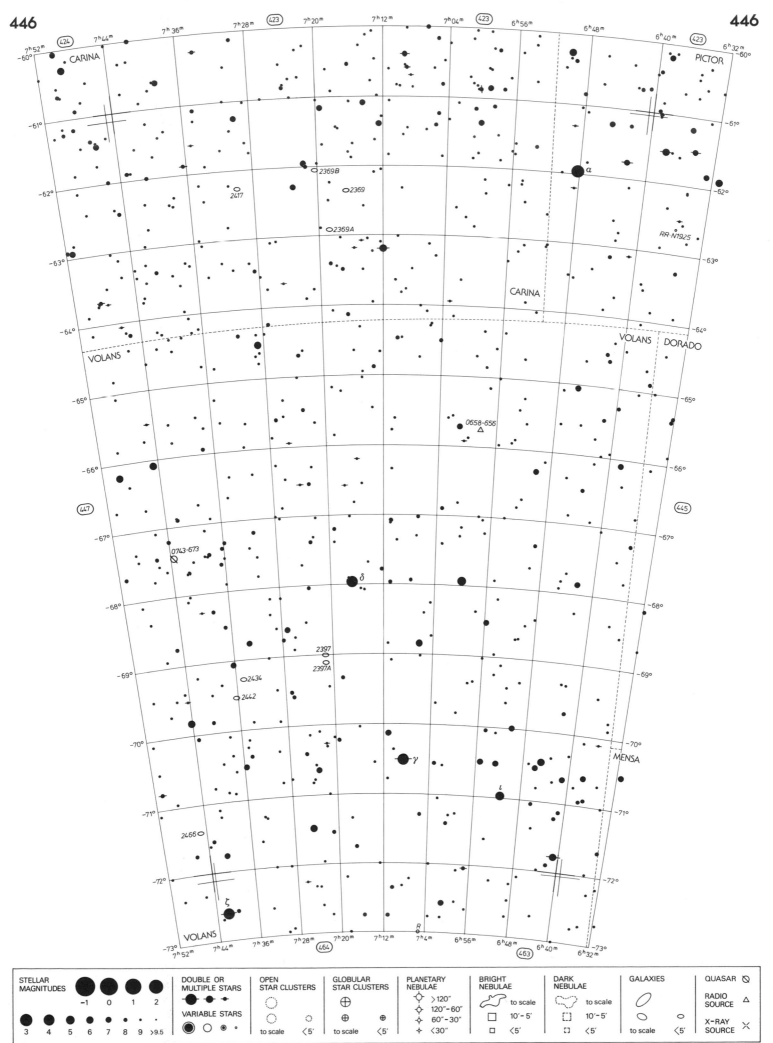

CARINA

PICTOR

2369B
2417
2369
2369A
RR·N1925

CARINA

VOLANS DORADO
VOLANS

0658-656

0743-673

δ

2397
2397A
2434
2442

γ

ι

MENSA

2466

ζ

VOLANS

R

© 1988 WILLMANN-BELL, INC.

Barry Rappaport & Wil Tirion

STELLAR MAGNITUDES	DOUBLE OR MULTIPLE STARS	OPEN STAR CLUSTERS	GLOBULAR STAR CLUSTERS	PLANETARY NEBULAE	BRIGHT NEBULAE	DARK NEBULAE	GALAXIES	QUASAR
-1 0 1 2	VARIABLE STARS	to scale <5'	to scale <5'	>120" 120"-60" 60"-30" <30"	to scale 10'-5' <5'	to scale 10'-5' <5'	to scale <5'	RADIO SOURCE X-RAY SOURCE
3 4 5 6 7 8 9 >9.5								

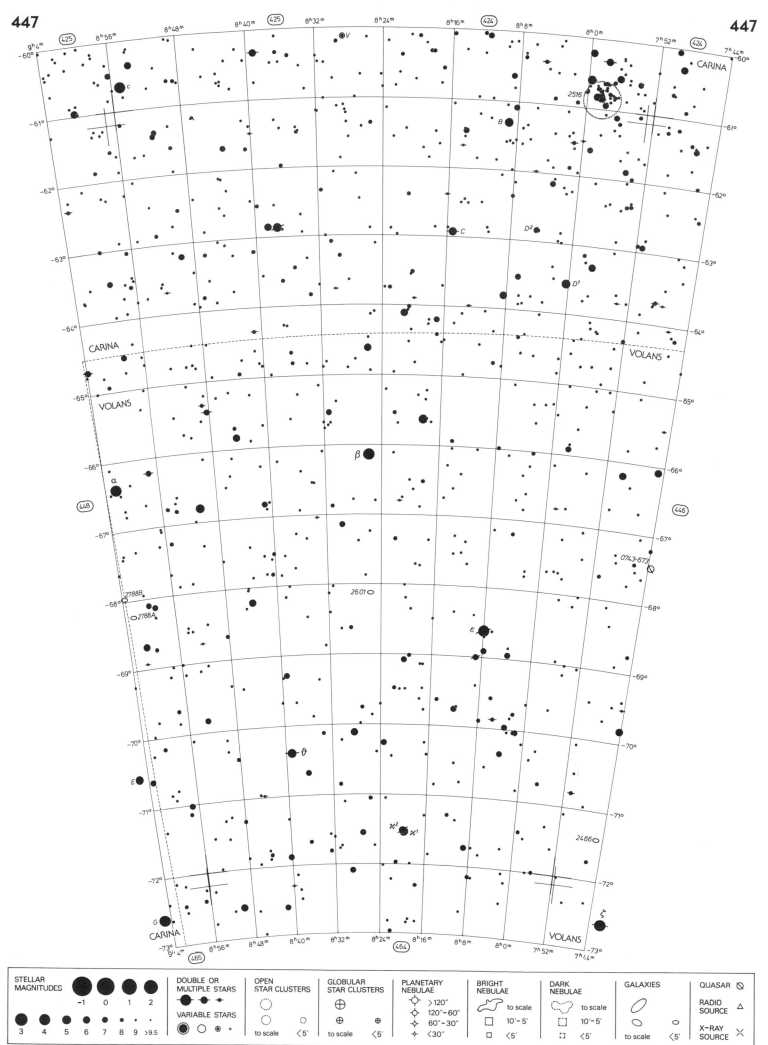

© 1988 WILLMANN-BELL, INC.

Barry Rappaport & Wil Tirion

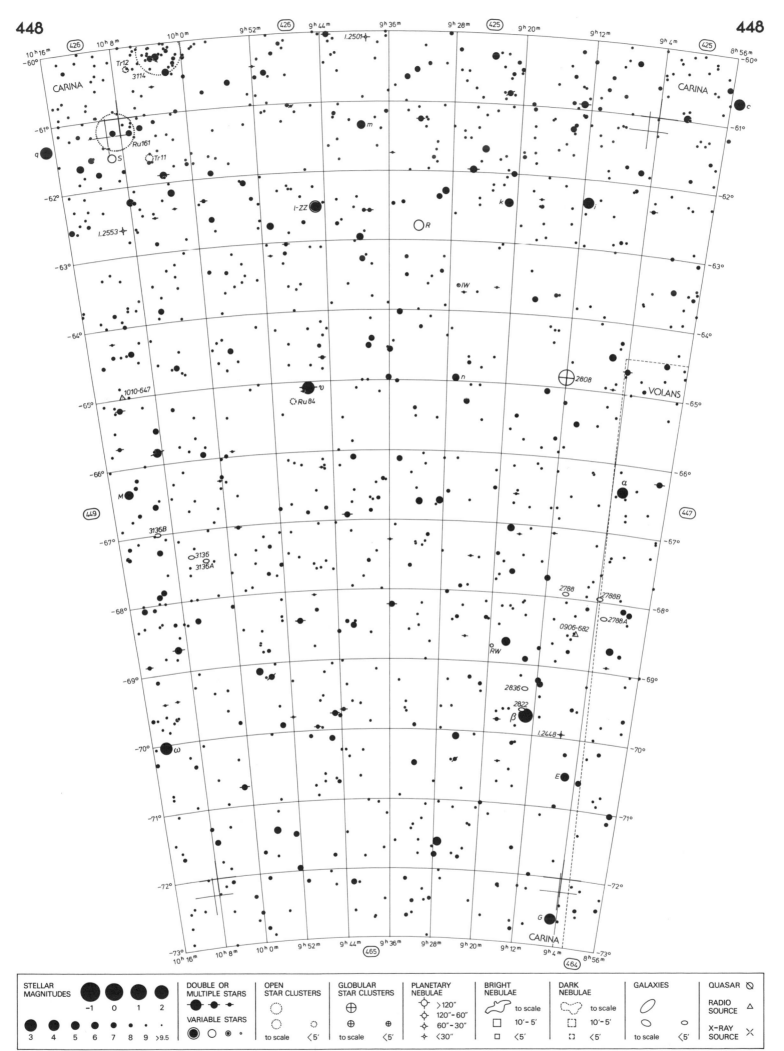

STELLAR MAGNITUDES

-1	0	1	2

3	4	5	6	7	8	9	>9.5

DOUBLE OR MULTIPLE STARS

VARIABLE STARS

OPEN STAR CLUSTERS

to scale   <5'

GLOBULAR STAR CLUSTERS

⊕   ⊕

to scale   <5'

PLANETARY NEBULAE

>120"
120"-60"
60"-30"
<30"

BRIGHT NEBULAE

to scale
10'-5'
<5'

DARK NEBULAE

to scale
10'-5'
<5'

GALAXIES

to scale   <5'

QUASAR

RADIO SOURCE

X-RAY SOURCE

© 1988 WILLMANN-BELL, INC.

Barry Rappaport & Wil Tirion

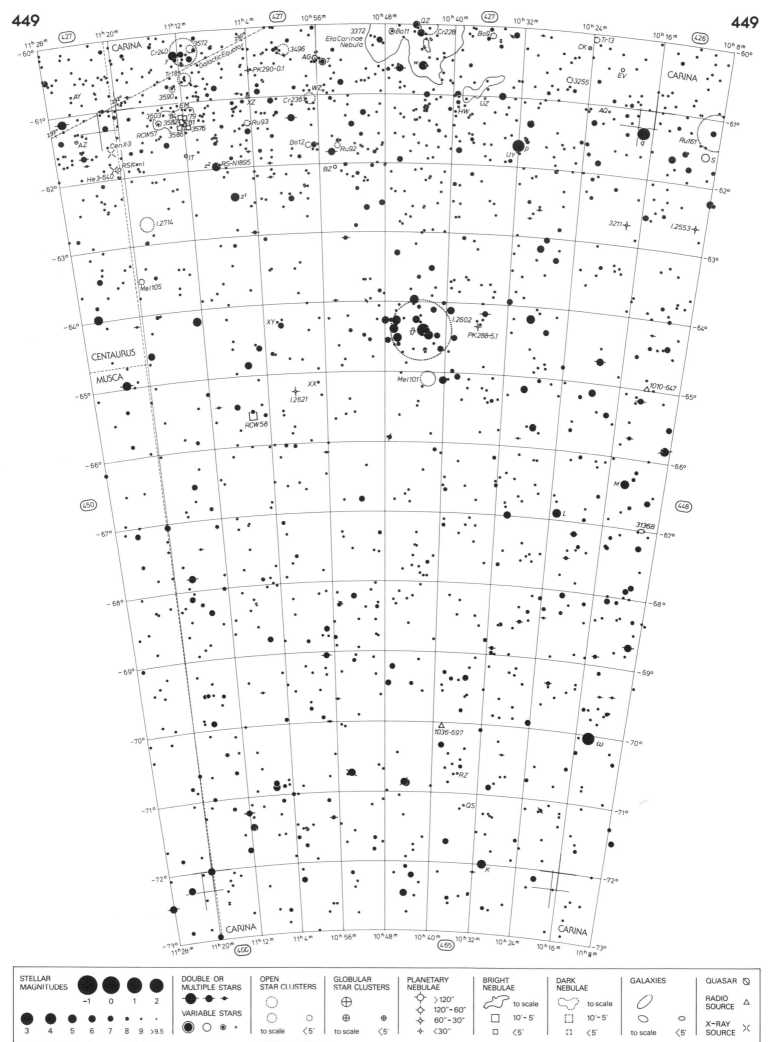

© 1988 WILLMANN-BELL, INC.

Barry Rappaport & Wil Tirion

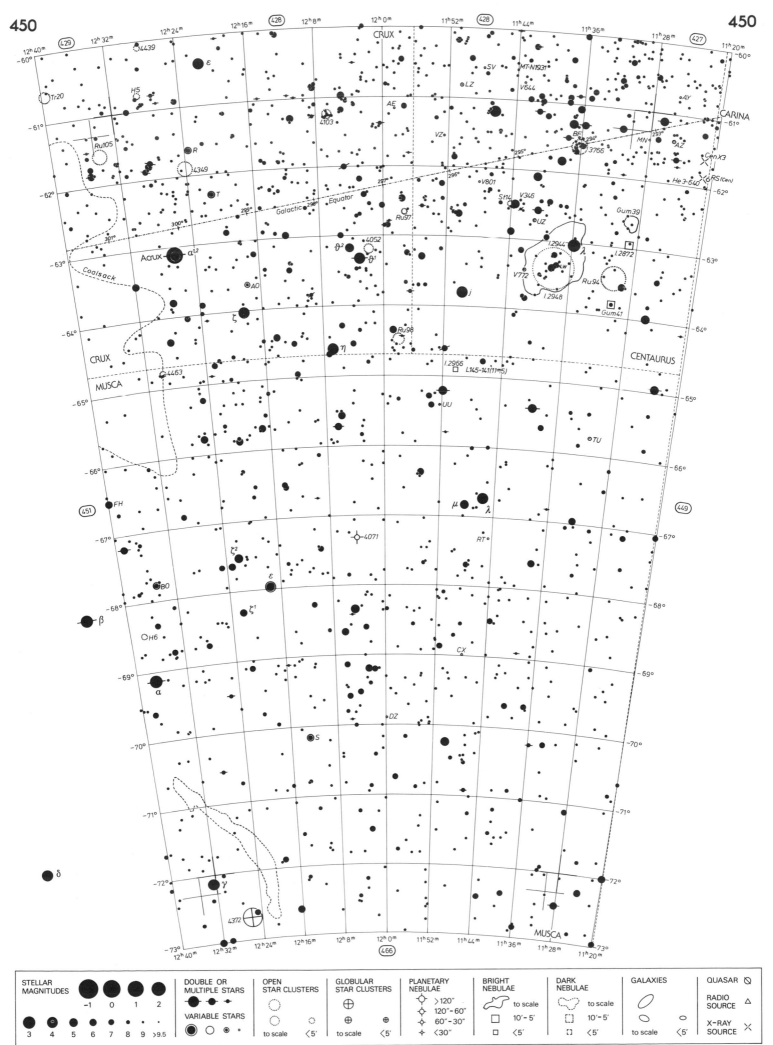

© 1988 WILLMANN-BELL, INC.

Barry Rappaport & Wil Tirion

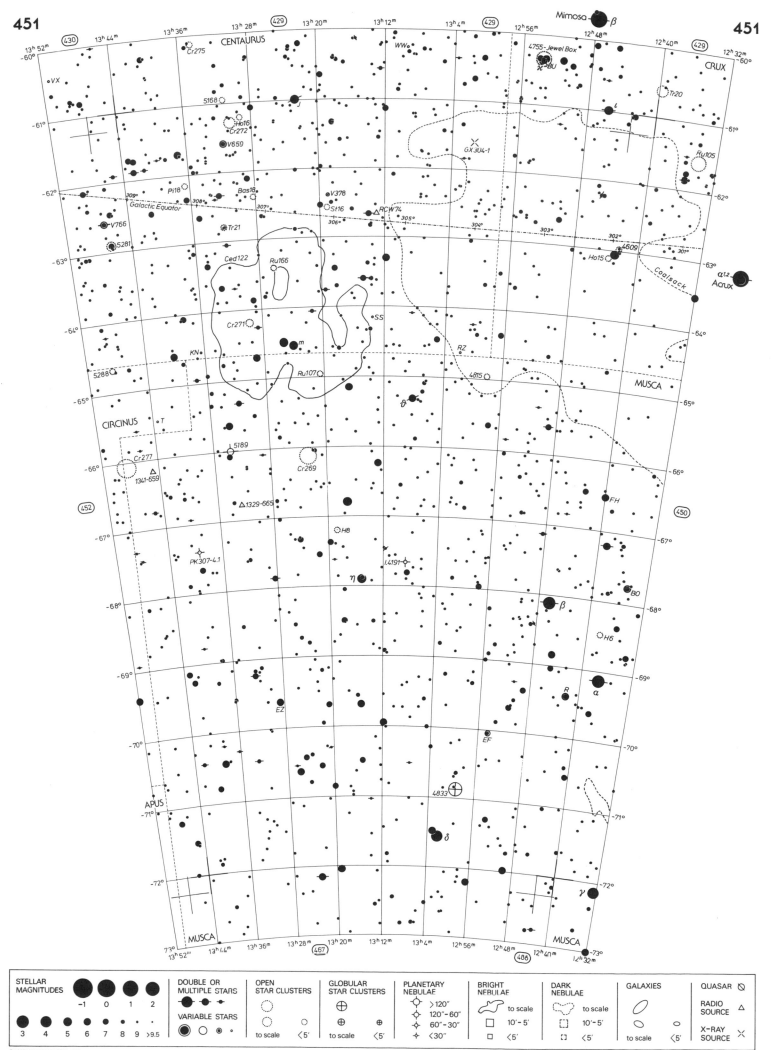

© 1988 WILLMANN-BELL, INC.

Barry Rappaport & Wil Tirion

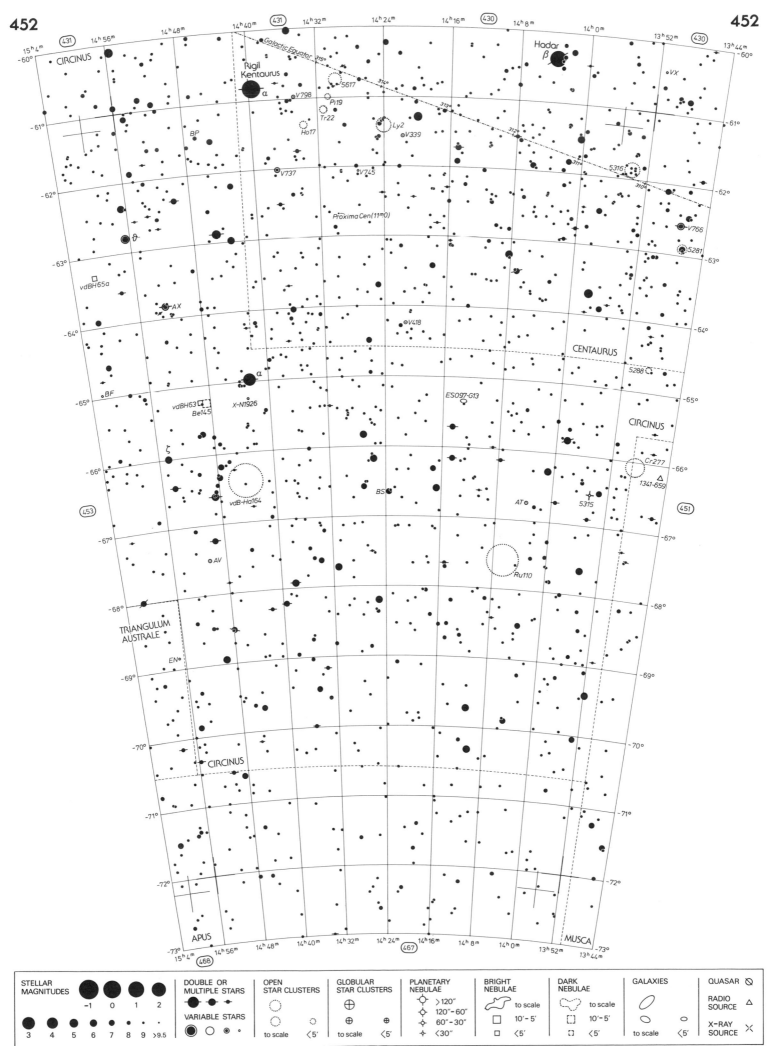

STELLAR MAGNITUDES							DOUBLE OR MULTIPLE STARS	OPEN STAR CLUSTERS	GLOBULAR STAR CLUSTERS	PLANETARY NEBULAE	BRIGHT NEBULAE	DARK NEBULAE	GALAXIES	QUASAR
-1	0	1	2				VARIABLE STARS	to scale	to scale	>120″	to scale	to scale	to scale	RADIO SOURCE
3	4	5	6	7	8	9 >9.5		<5′	<5′	120″-60″ 60″-30″ <30″	10′-5′ <5′	10′-5′ <5′	<5′	X-RAY SOURCE

© 1988 WILLMANN-BELL, INC.

Barry Rappaport & Wil Tirion

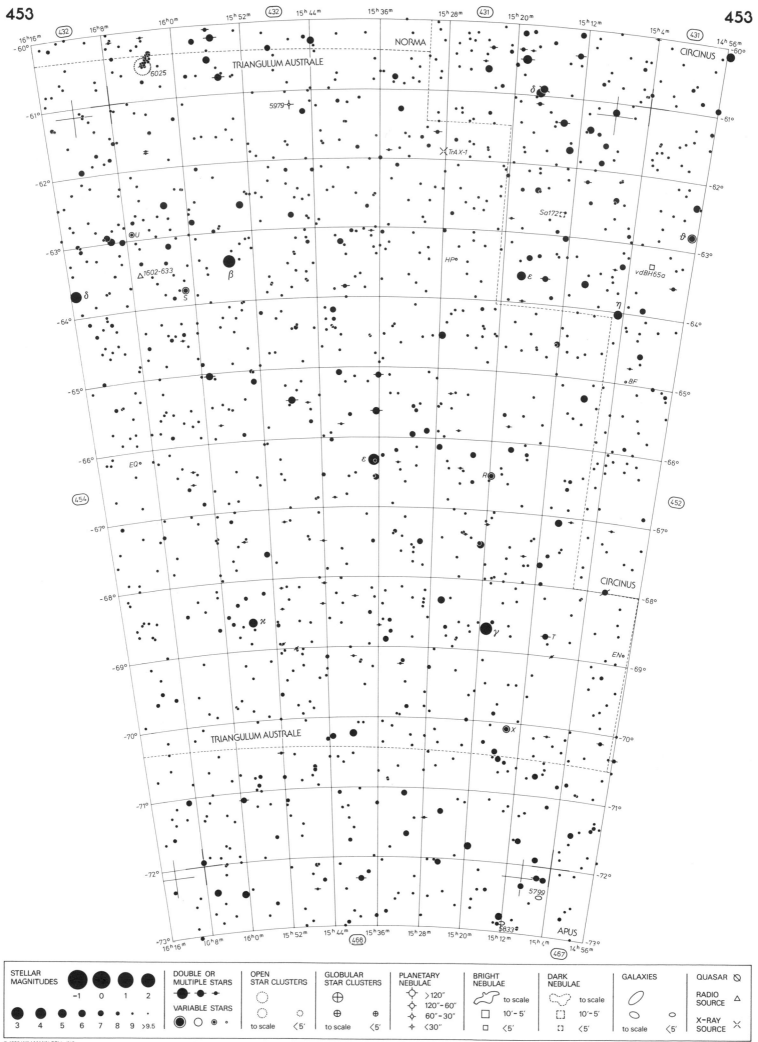

© 1988 WILLMANN-BELL, INC.

Barry Rappaport & Wil Tirion

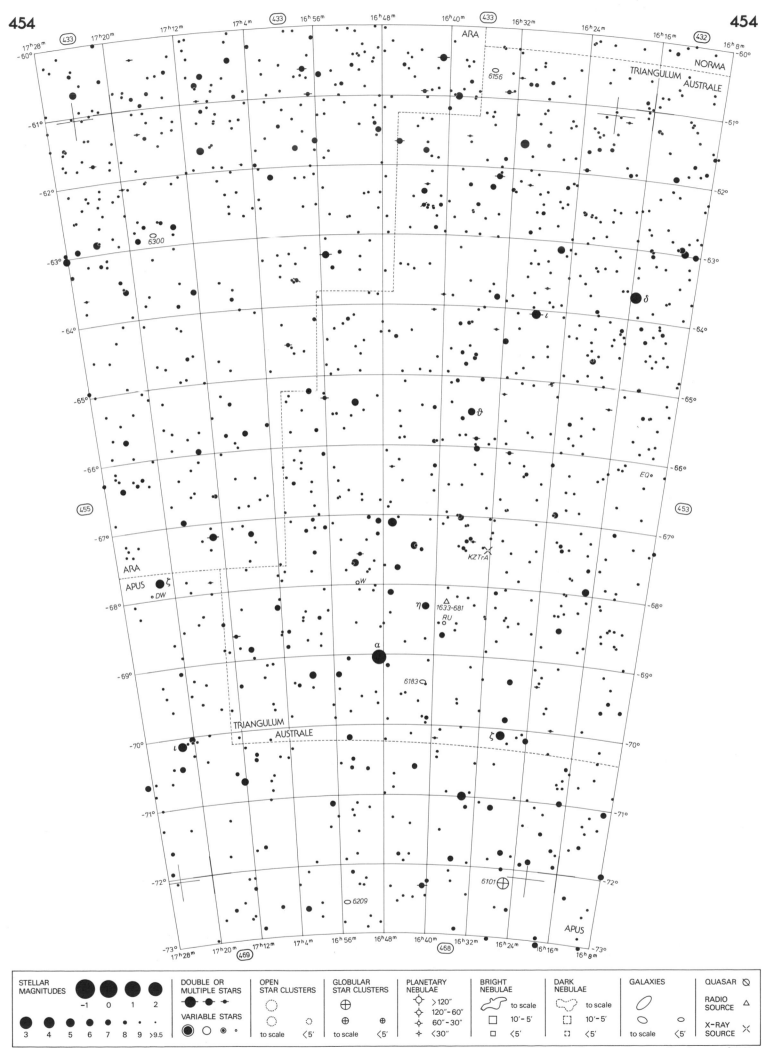

© 1988 WILLMANN-BELL, INC.

Barry Rappaport & Wil Tirion

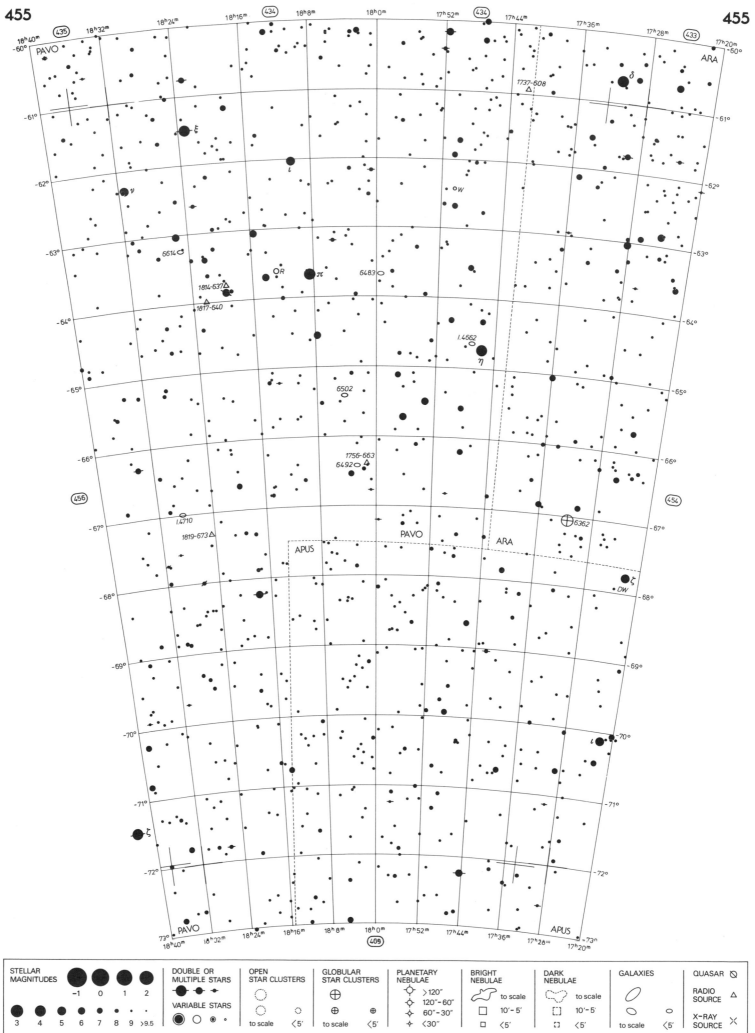

STELLAR MAGNITUDES

-1 0 1 2

3 4 5 6 7 8 9 >9.5

DOUBLE OR MULTIPLE STARS

VARIABLE STARS

OPEN STAR CLUSTERS

to scale   <5'

GLOBULAR STAR CLUSTERS

to scale   <5'

PLANETARY NEBULAE

>120"

120"-60"

60"-30"

<30"

BRIGHT NEBULAE

to scale

10'-5'

<5'

DARK NEBULAE

to scale

10'-5'

<5'

GALAXIES

to scale   <5'

QUASAR

RADIO SOURCE

X-RAY SOURCE

© 1988 WILLMANN-BELL, INC.

Barry Rappaport & Wil Tirion

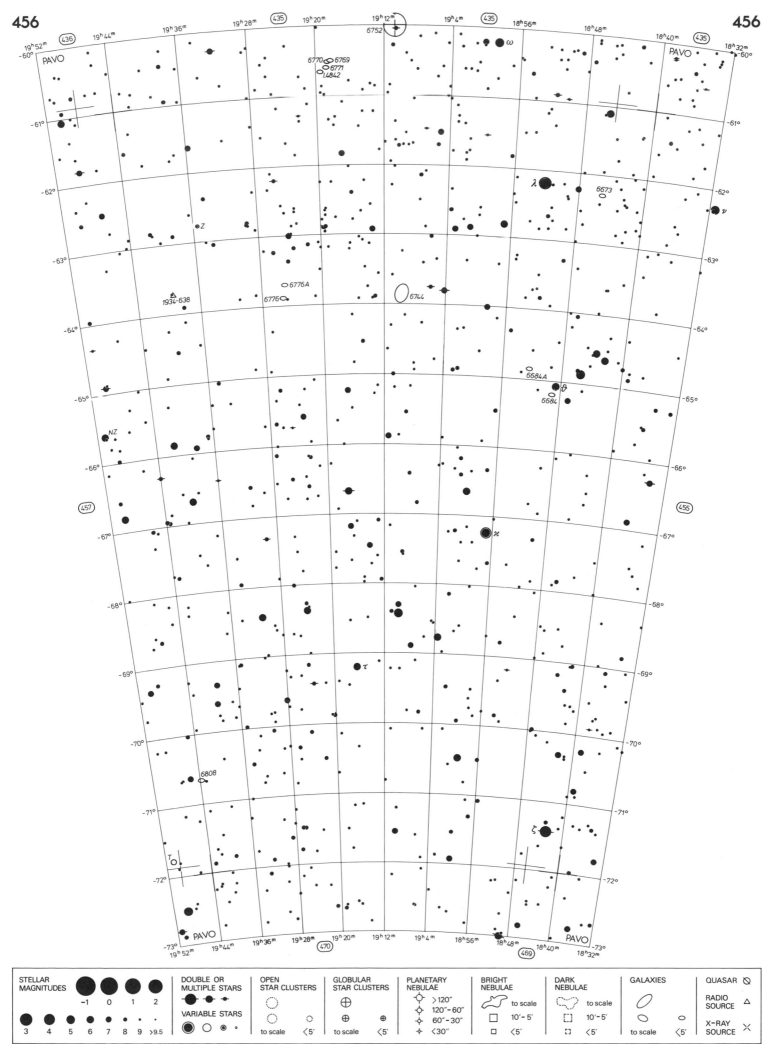

© 1988 WILLMANN-BELL, INC.

Barry Rappaport & Wil Tirion

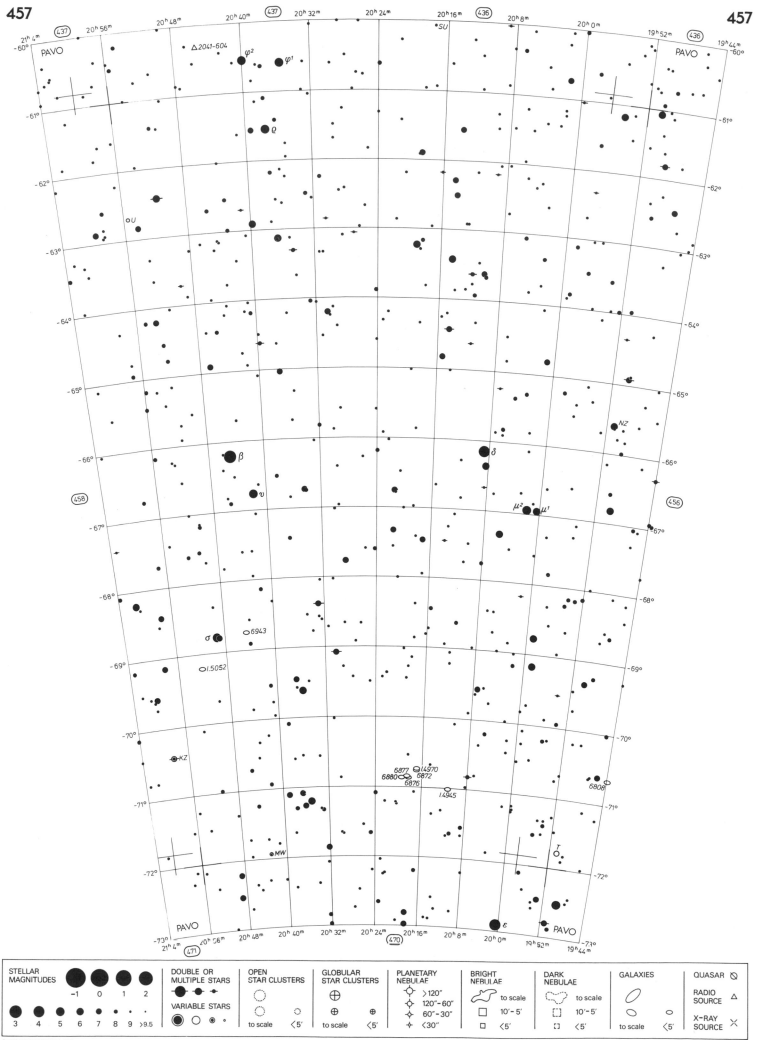

Barry Rappaport & Wil Tirion

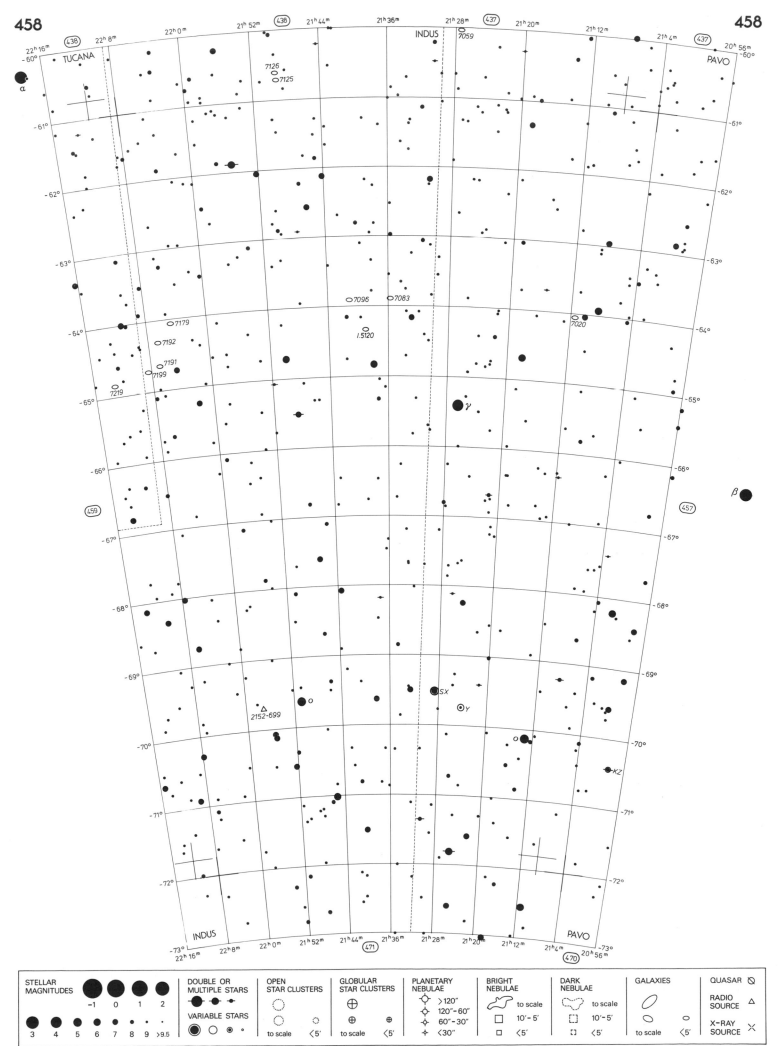

© 1988 WILLMANN-BELL, INC.

Barry Rappaport & Wil Tirion

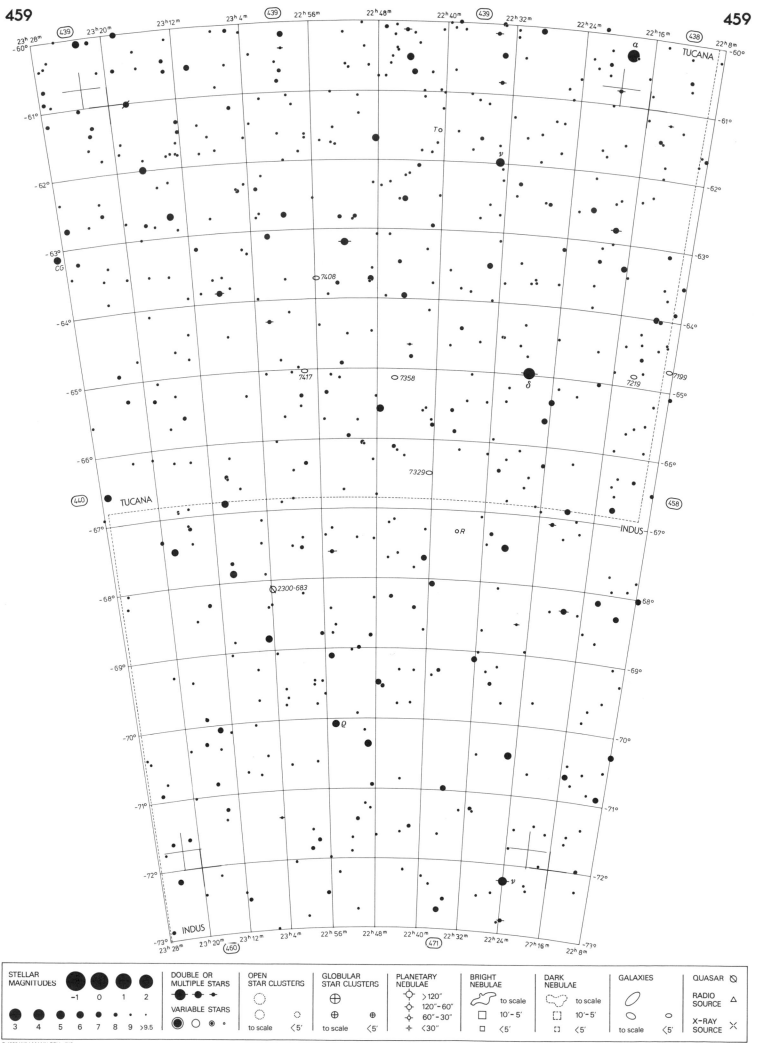

© 1988 WILLMANN-BELL, INC.

Barry Rappaport & Wil Tirion

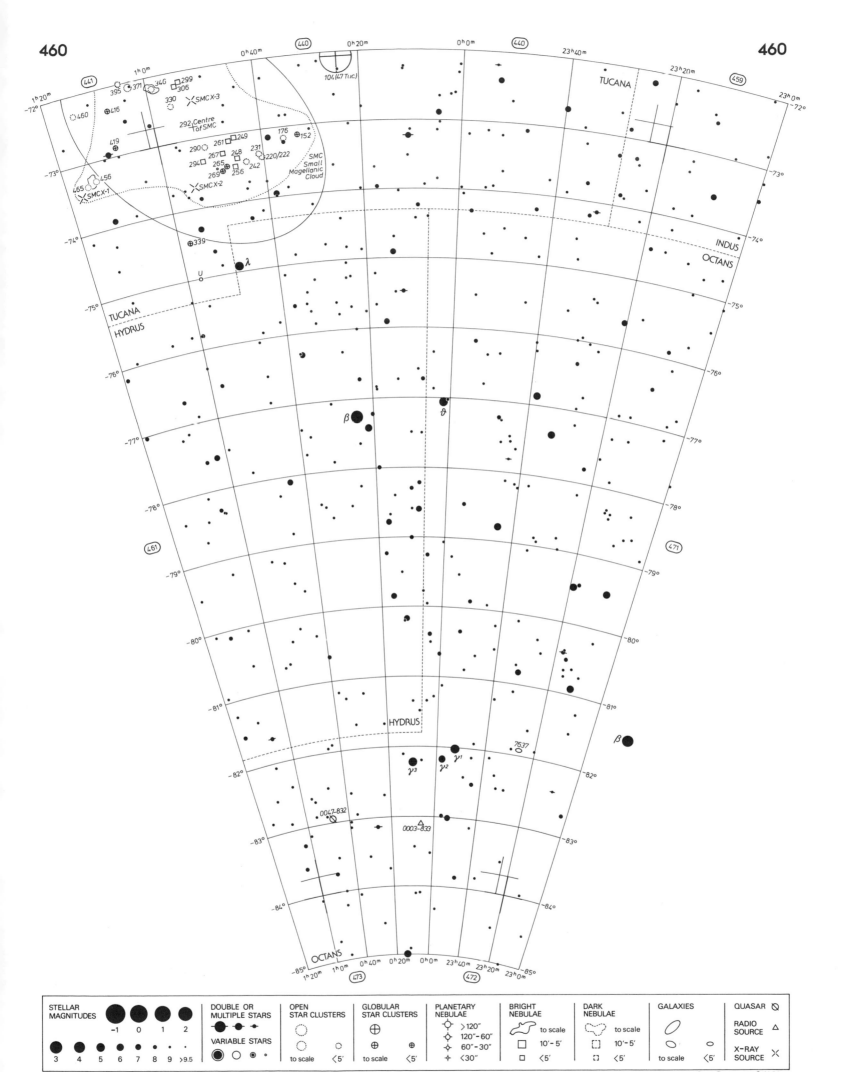

© 1988 WILLMANN-BELL, INC.

Barry Rappaport & Wil Tirion

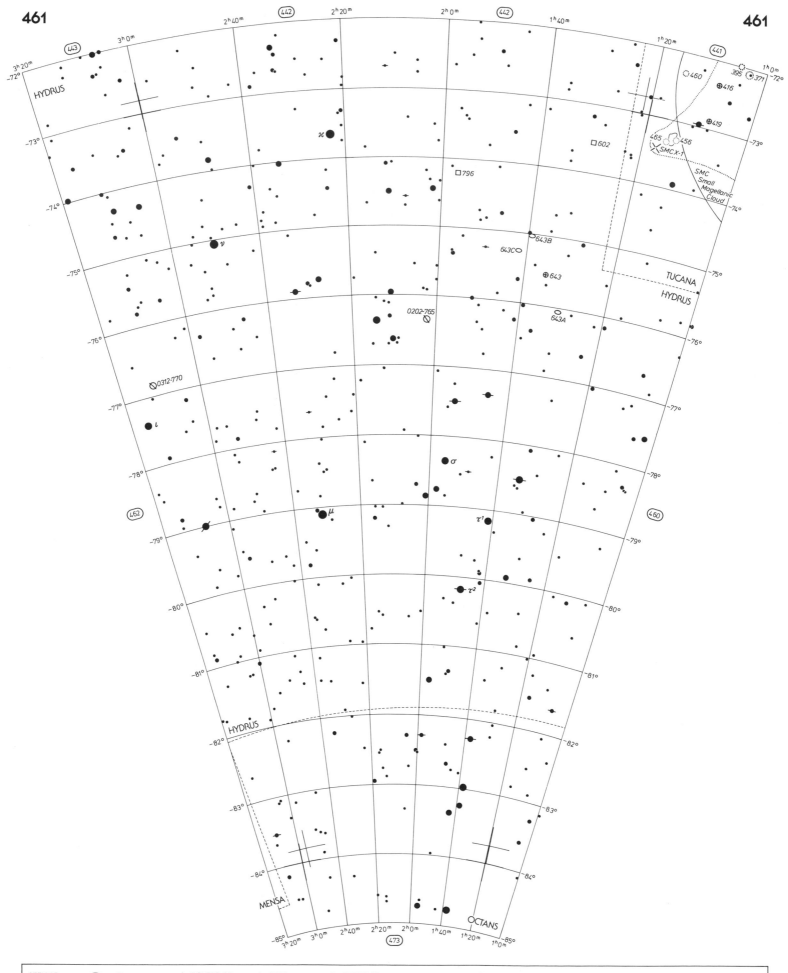

© 1988 WILLMANN-BELL, INC.

Barry Rappaport & Wil Tirion

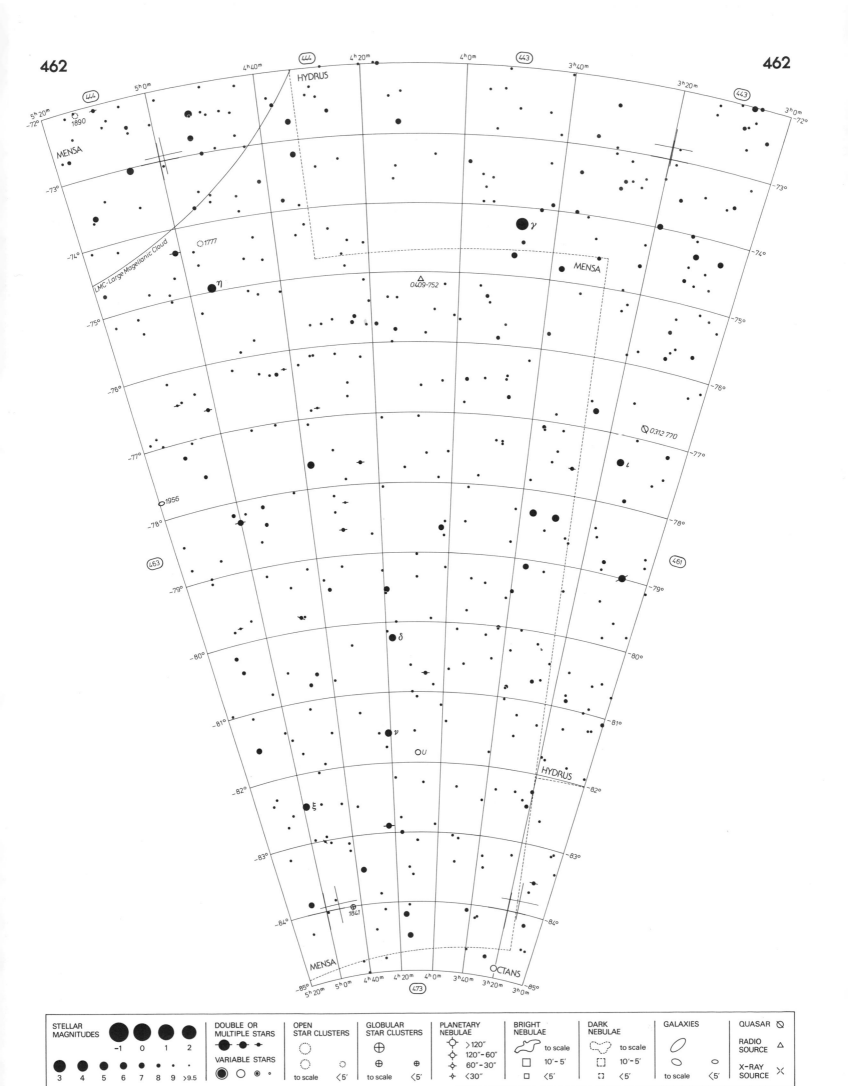

© 1988 WILLMANN-BELL, INC.

Barry Rappaport & Wil Tirion

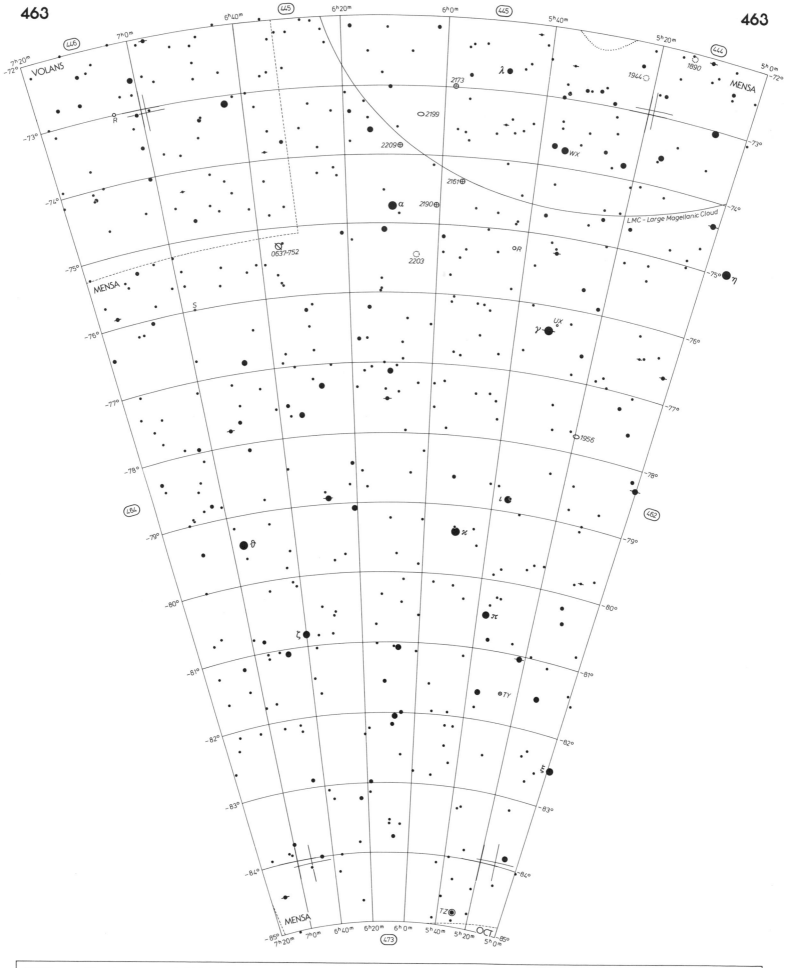

STELLAR MAGNITUDES	DOUBLE OR MULTIPLE STARS	OPEN STAR CLUSTERS	GLOBULAR STAR CLUSTERS	PLANETARY NEBULAE	BRIGHT NEBULAE	DARK NEBULAE	GALAXIES	QUASAR

© 1988 WILLMANN-BELL, INC.

Barry Rappaport & Wil Tirion

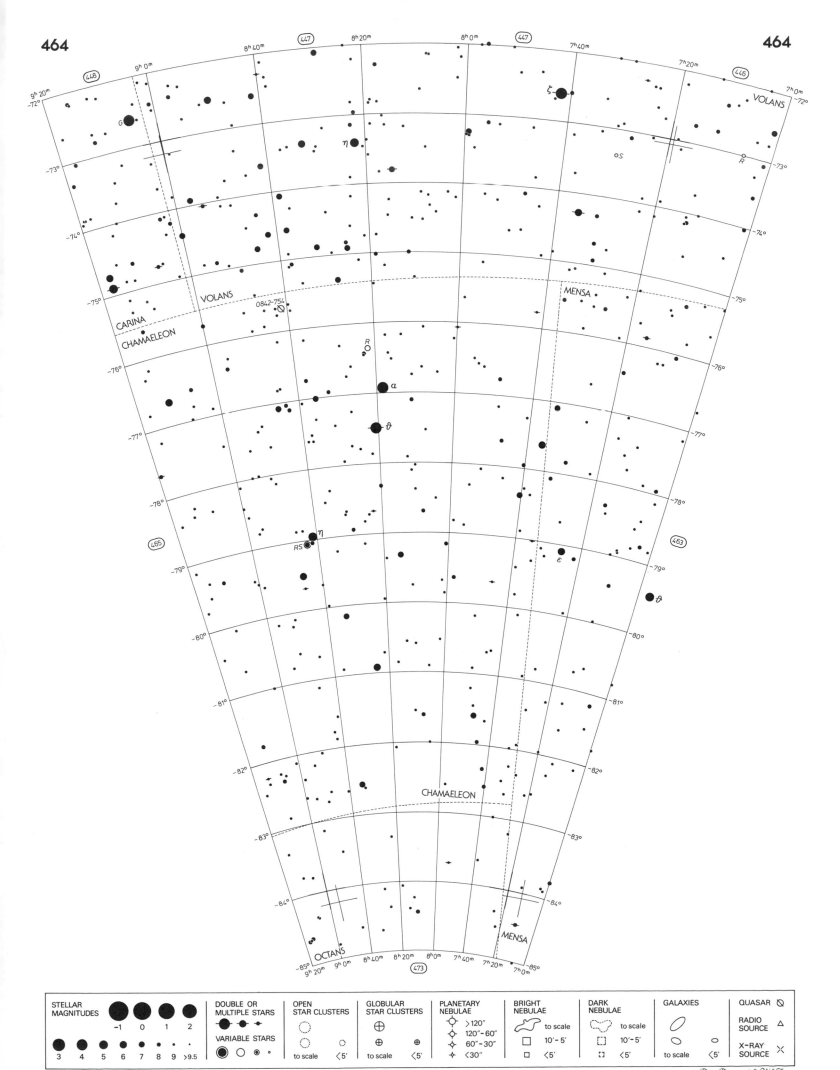

STELLAR MAGNITUDES	DOUBLE OR MULTIPLE STARS	OPEN STAR CLUSTERS	GLOBULAR STAR CLUSTERS	PLANETARY NEBULAE	BRIGHT NEBULAE	DARK NEBULAE	GALAXIES	QUASAR
							RADIO SOURCE
	VARIABLE STARS						X-RAY SOURCE

STELLAR MAGNITUDES
−1 0 1 2
3 4 5 6 7 8 9 >9.5

DOUBLE OR MULTIPLE STARS

VARIABLE STARS

OPEN STAR CLUSTERS
to scale   <5'

GLOBULAR STAR CLUSTERS
to scale   <5'

PLANETARY NEBULAE
>120"
120"−60"
60"−30"
<30"

BRIGHT NEBULAE
to scale
10'−5'
<5'

DARK NEBULAE
to scale
10'−5'
<5'

GALAXIES
to scale   <5'

QUASAR

RADIO SOURCE

X-RAY SOURCE

© 1988 WILLMANN-BELL, INC.

Barry Rappaport & Wil Tirion

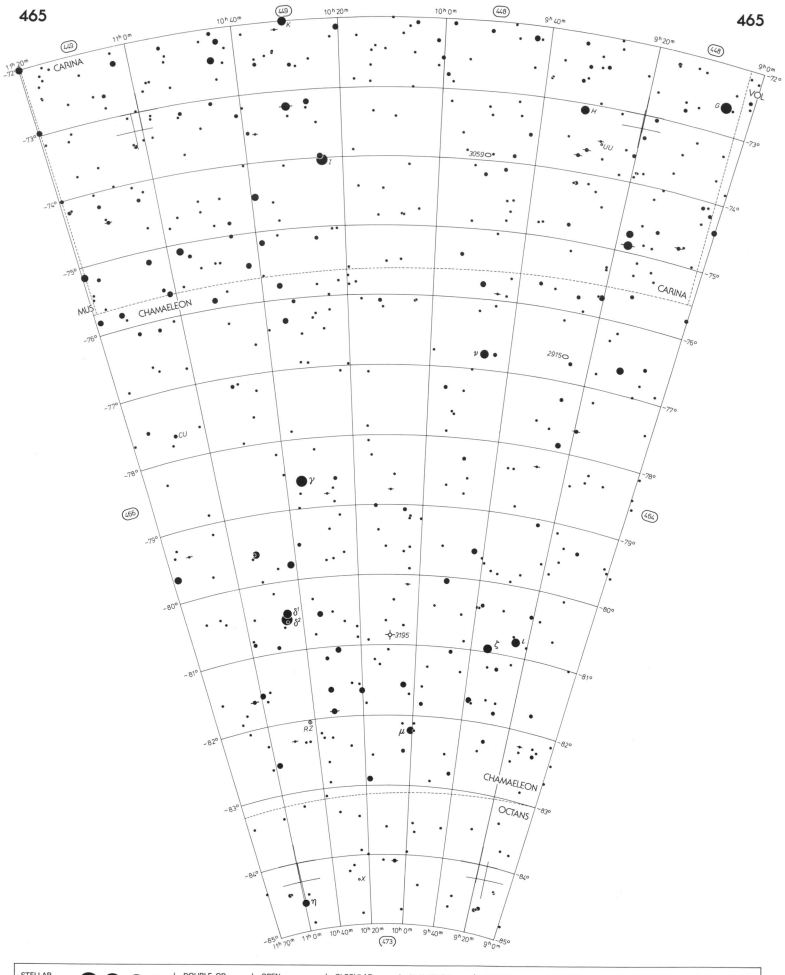

© 1988 WILLMANN-BELL, INC.

Barry Rappaport & Wil Tirion

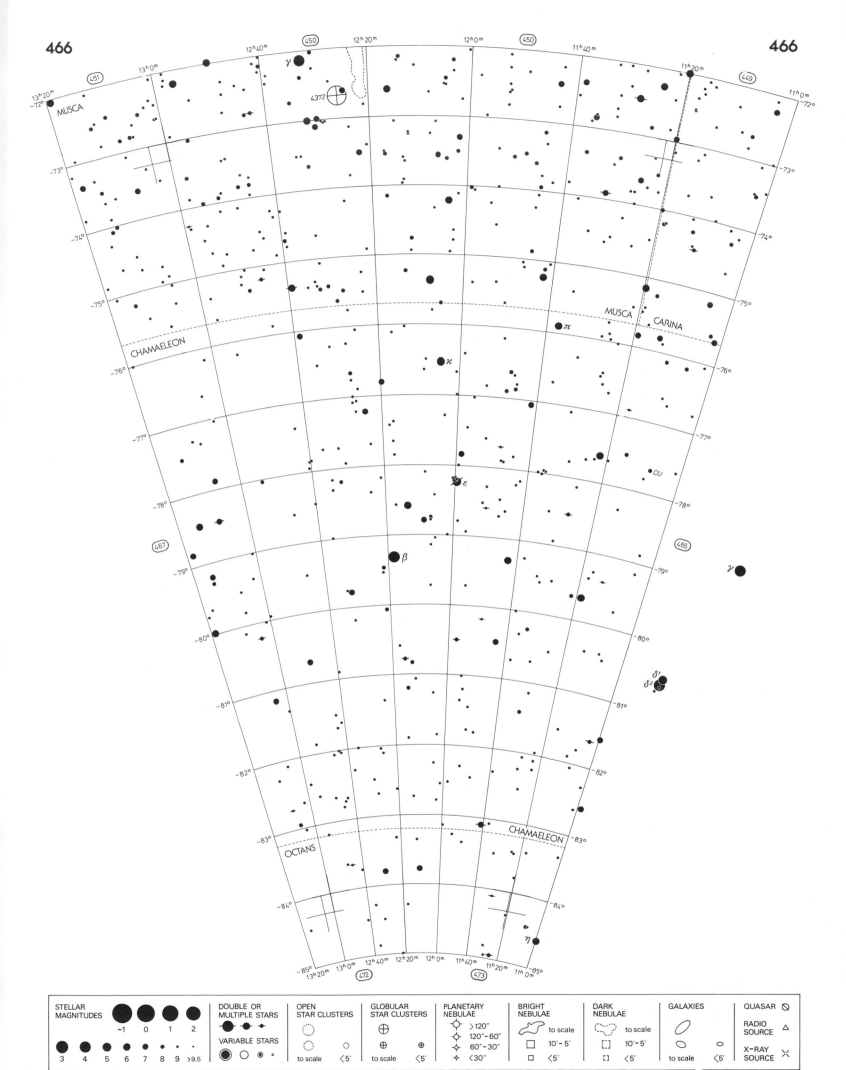

© 1988 WILLMANN-BELL, INC.

Barry Rappaport & Wil Tirion

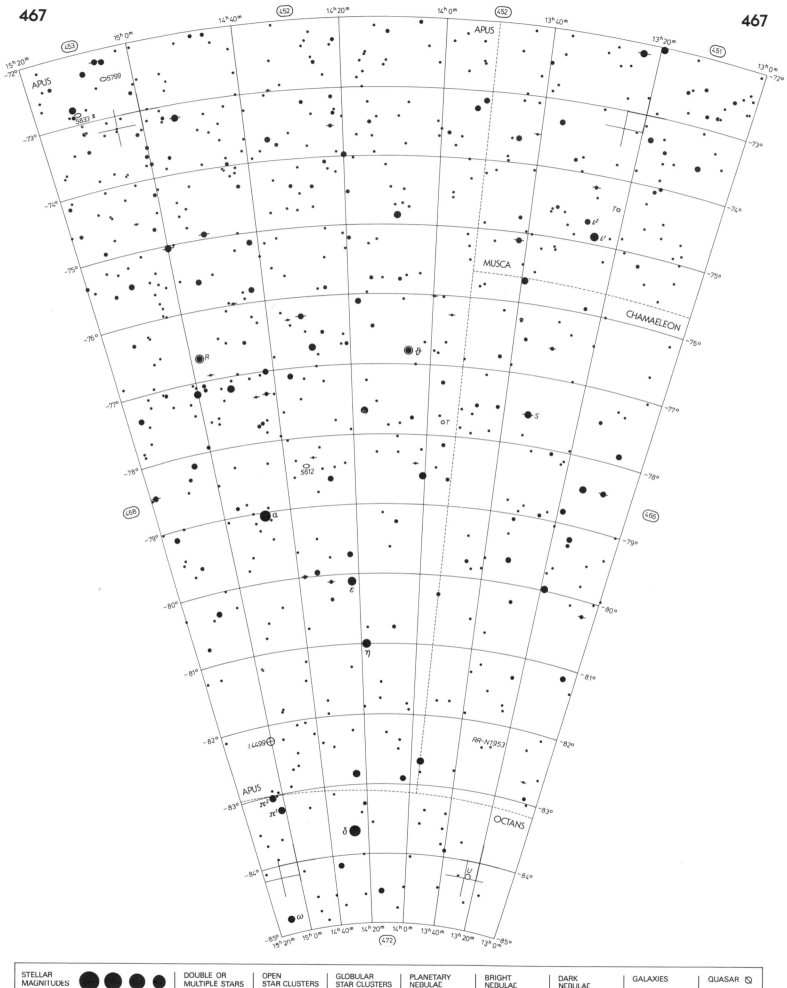

© 1988 WILLMANN-BELL, INC.

Barry Rappaport & Wil Tirion

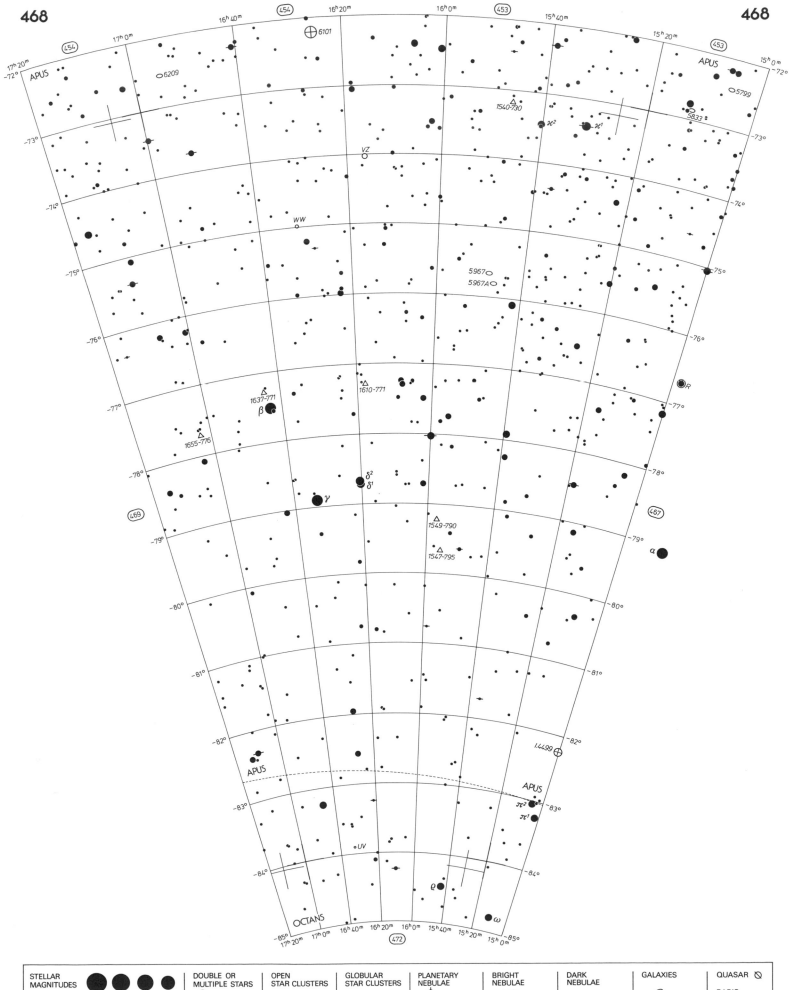

STELLAR MAGNITUDES
-1 0 1 2
3 4 5 6 7 8 9 >9.5

DOUBLE OR MULTIPLE STARS
VARIABLE STARS

OPEN STAR CLUSTERS
to scale   <5'

GLOBULAR STAR CLUSTERS
to scale   <5'

PLANETARY NEBULAE
>120"
120"-60"
60"-30"
<30"

BRIGHT NEBULAE
to scale
10'-5'
<5'

DARK NEBULAE
to scale
10'-5'
<5'

GALAXIES
to scale   <5'

QUASAR
RADIO SOURCE
X-RAY SOURCE

© 1988 WILLMANN-BELL, INC.

Barry Rappaport & Wil Tirion

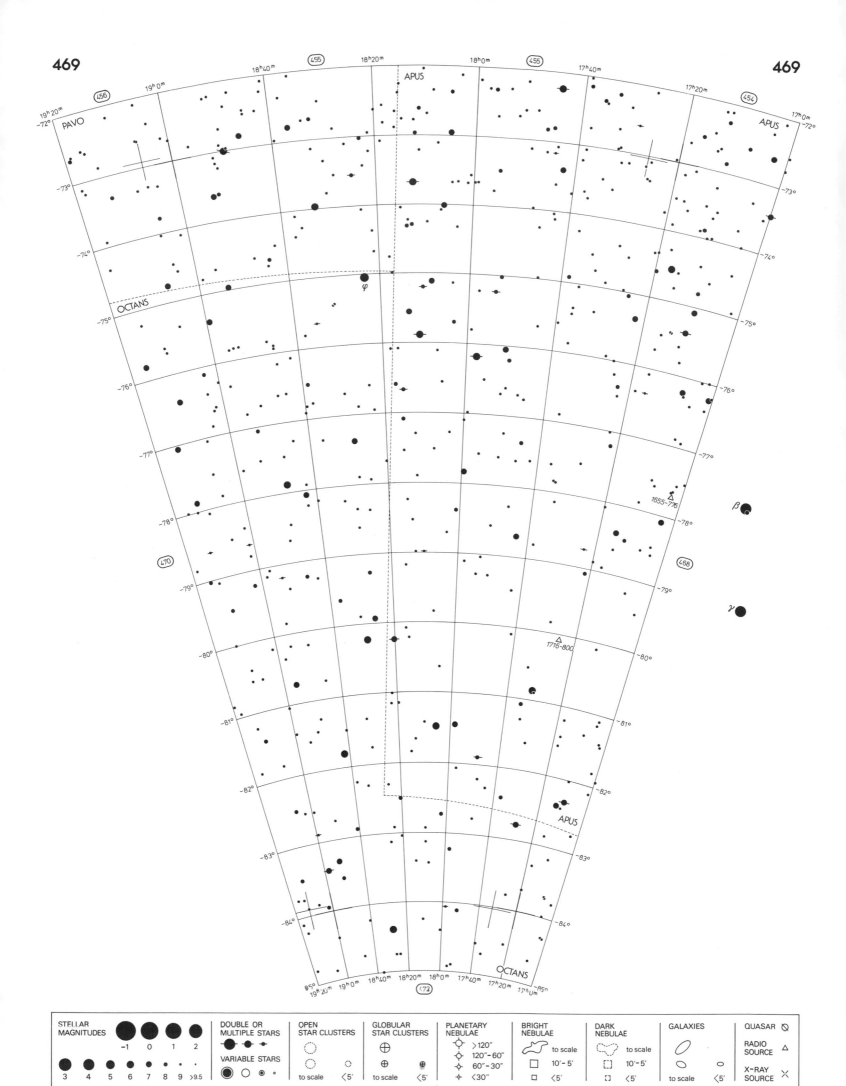

© 1988 WILLMANN-BELL, INC.

Barry Rappaport & Wil Tirion

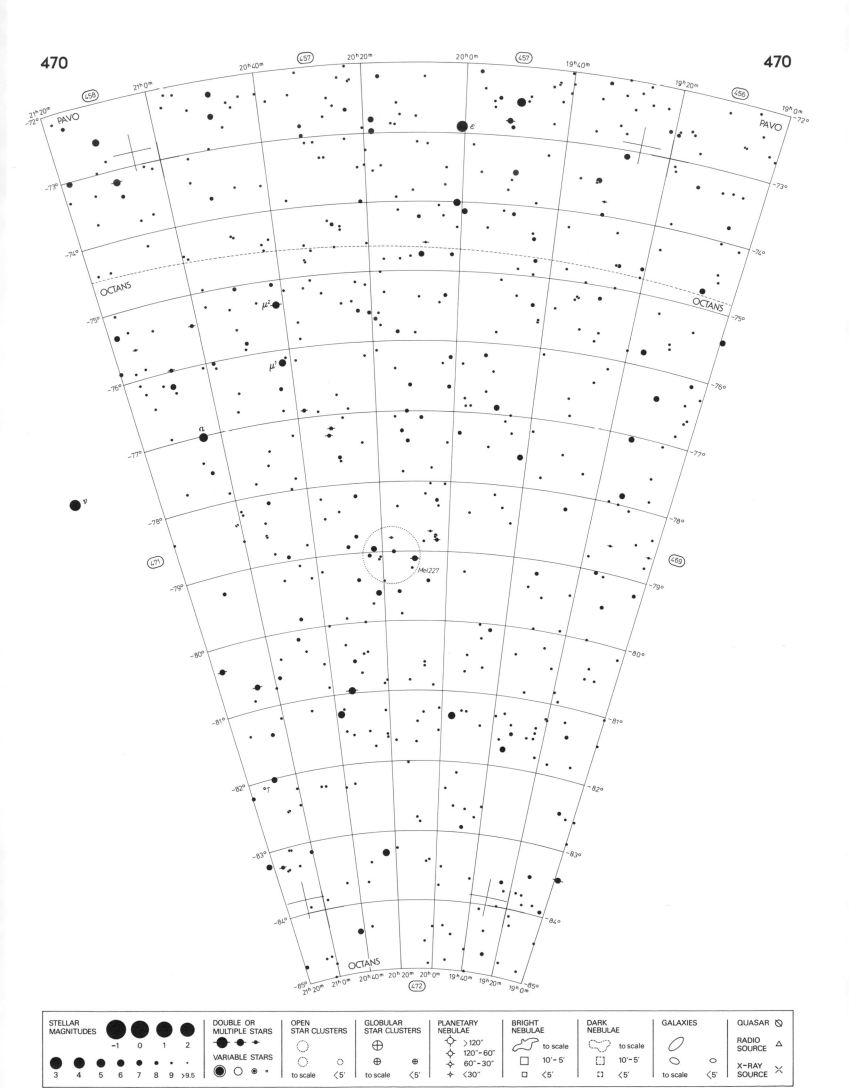

© 1988 WILLMANN-BELL, INC.

Barry Rappaport & Wil Tirion

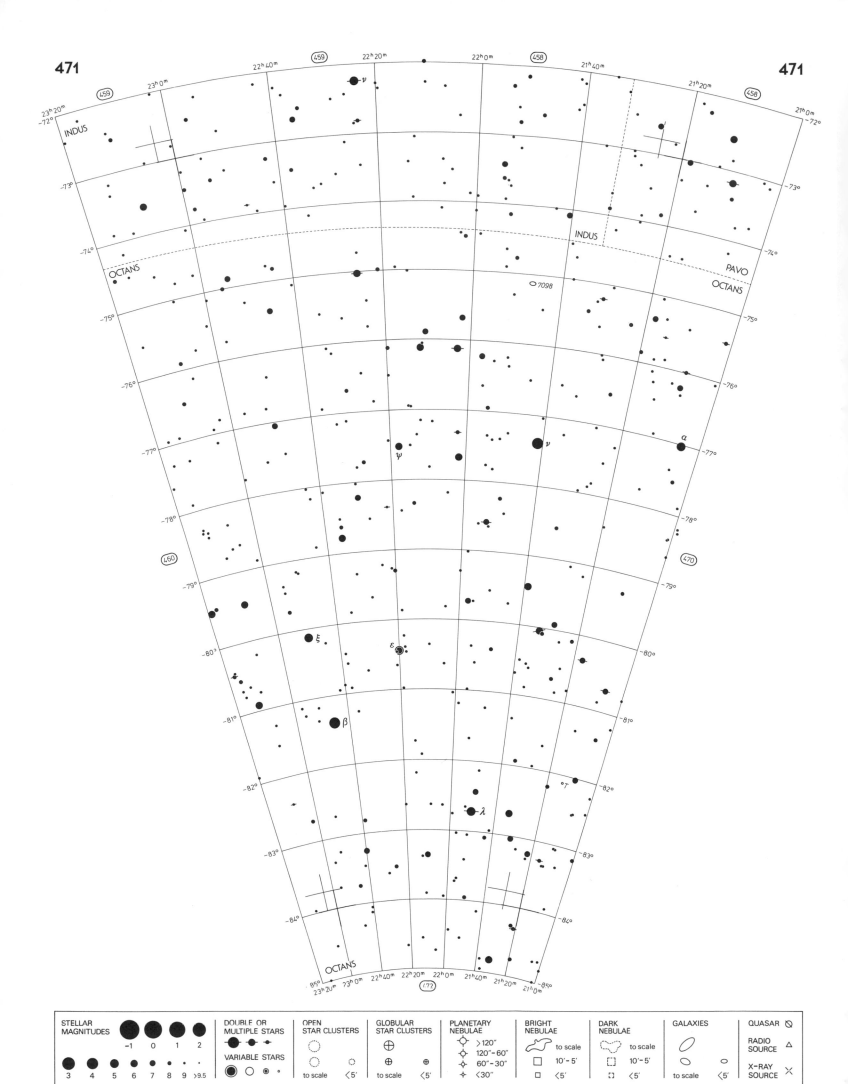

© 1988 WILLMANN-BELL, INC.

Barry Rappaport & Wil Tirion

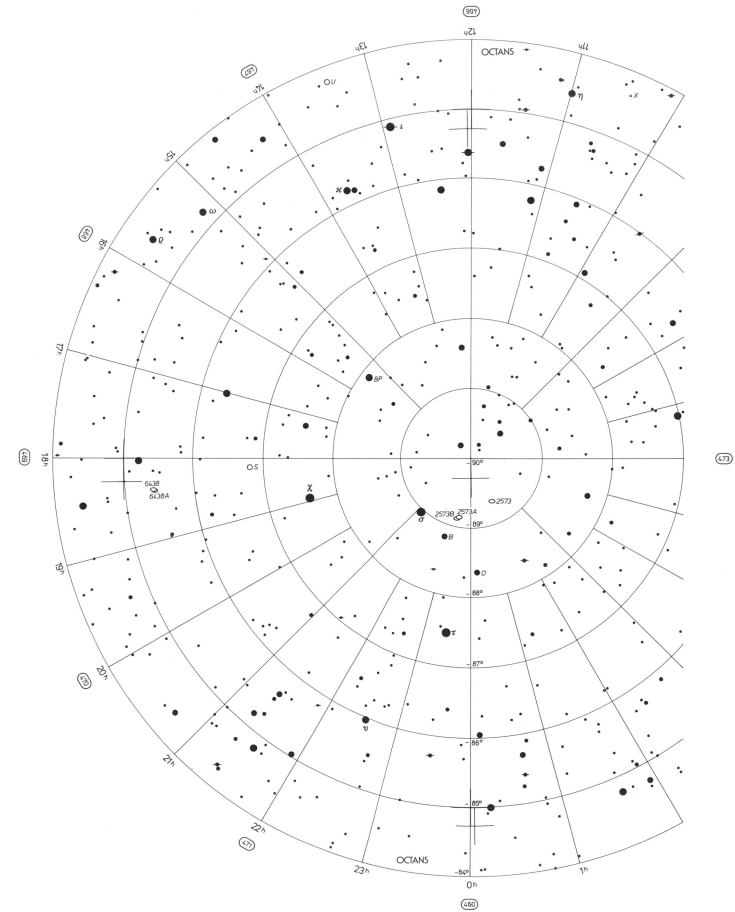

OCTANS

OCTANS

© 1988 WILLMANN-BELL, INC.

Barry Rappaport & Wil Tirion

STELLAR MAGNITUDES	DOUBLE OR MULTIPLE STARS	OPEN STAR CLUSTERS	GLOBULAR STAR CLUSTERS	PLANETARY NEBULAE	BRIGHT NEBULAE	DARK NEBULAE	GALAXIES	QUASAR
-1 0 1 2	VARIABLE STARS	to scale ⟨5'	to scale ⟨5'	⟩120" 120"-60" 60"-30" ⟨30"	to scale 10'-5' ⟨5'	to scale 10'-5' ⟨5'	to scale ⟨5'	RADIO SOURCE X-RAY SOURCE
3 4 5 6 7 8 9 ⟩9.5								

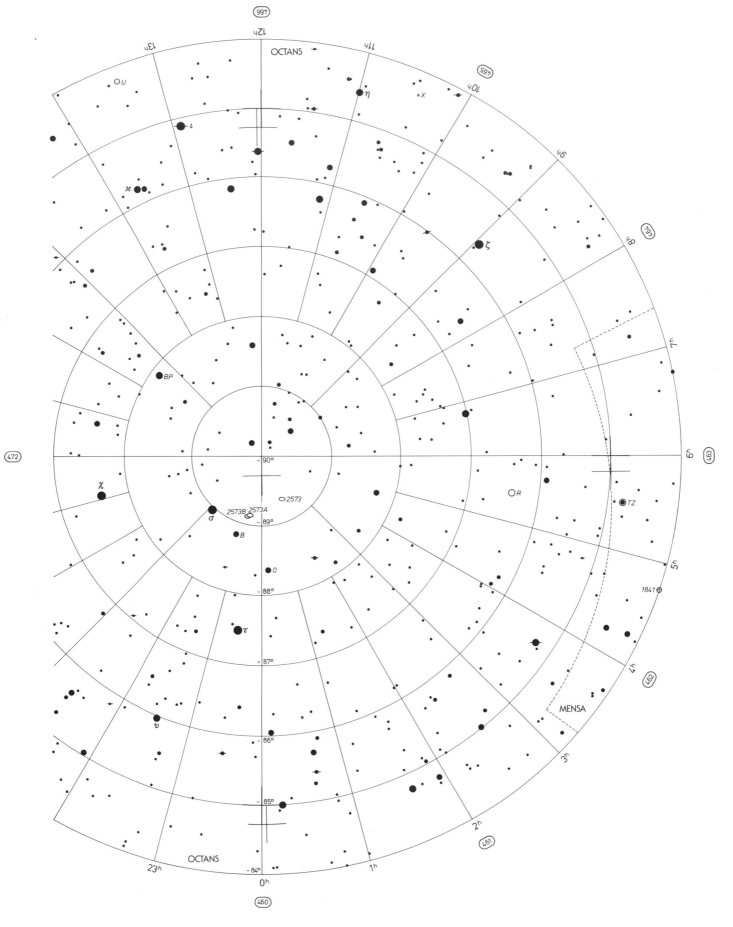

© 1988 WILLMANN-BELL, INC.

Barry Rappaport & Wil Tirion

URANOMETRIA 2000.0
Volume 2

The Southern Hemisphere to +6°

AZIMUTHAL EQUAL-AREA PROJECTION

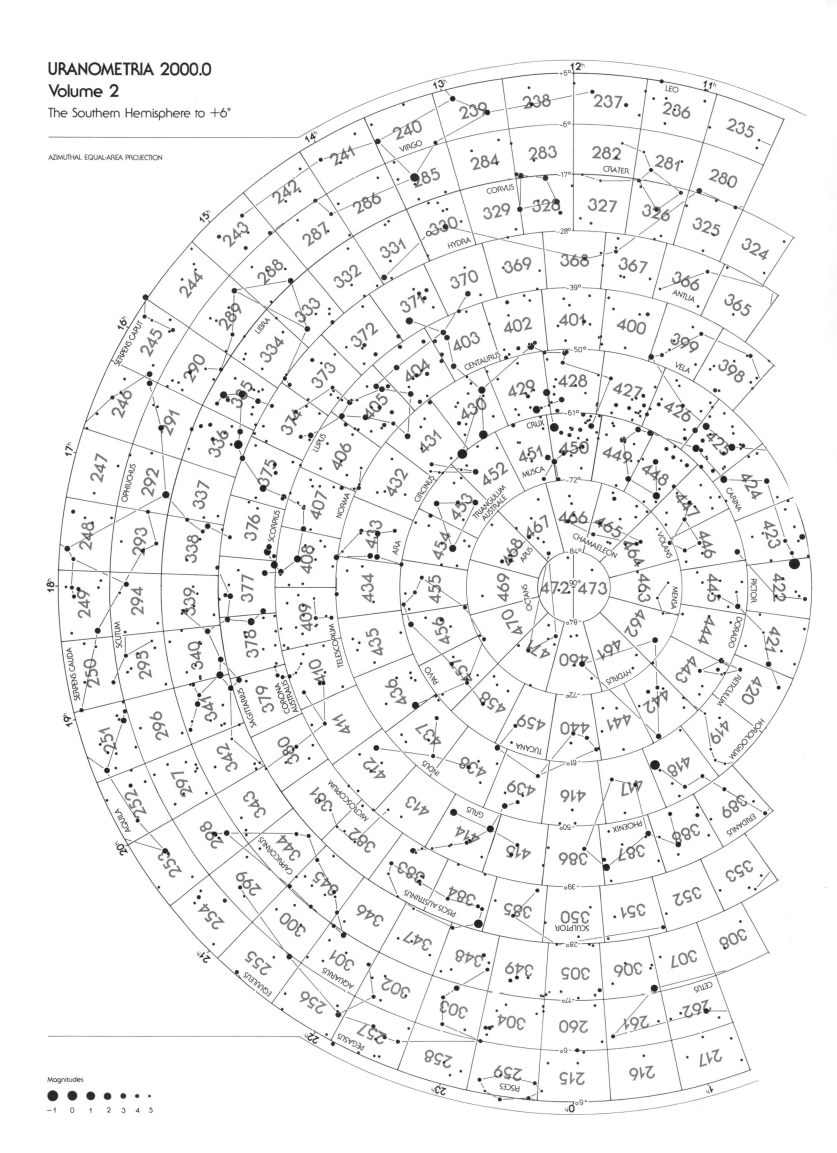

Magnitudes

-1 0 1 2 3 4 5

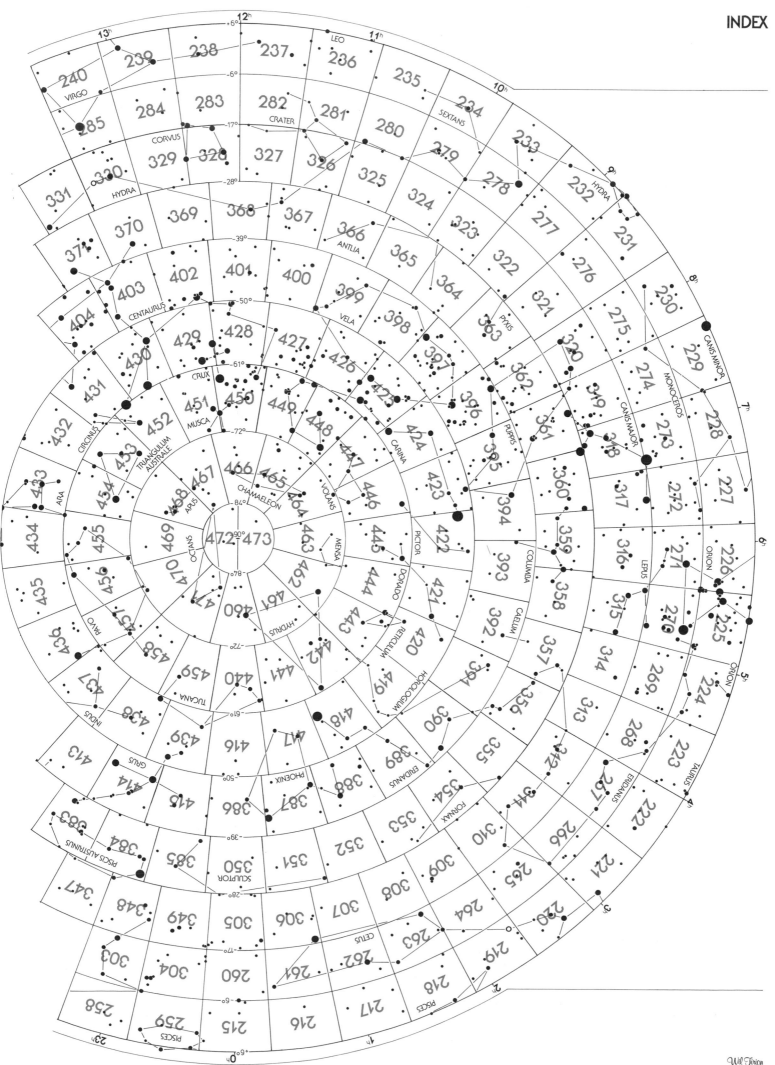

Wil Tirion

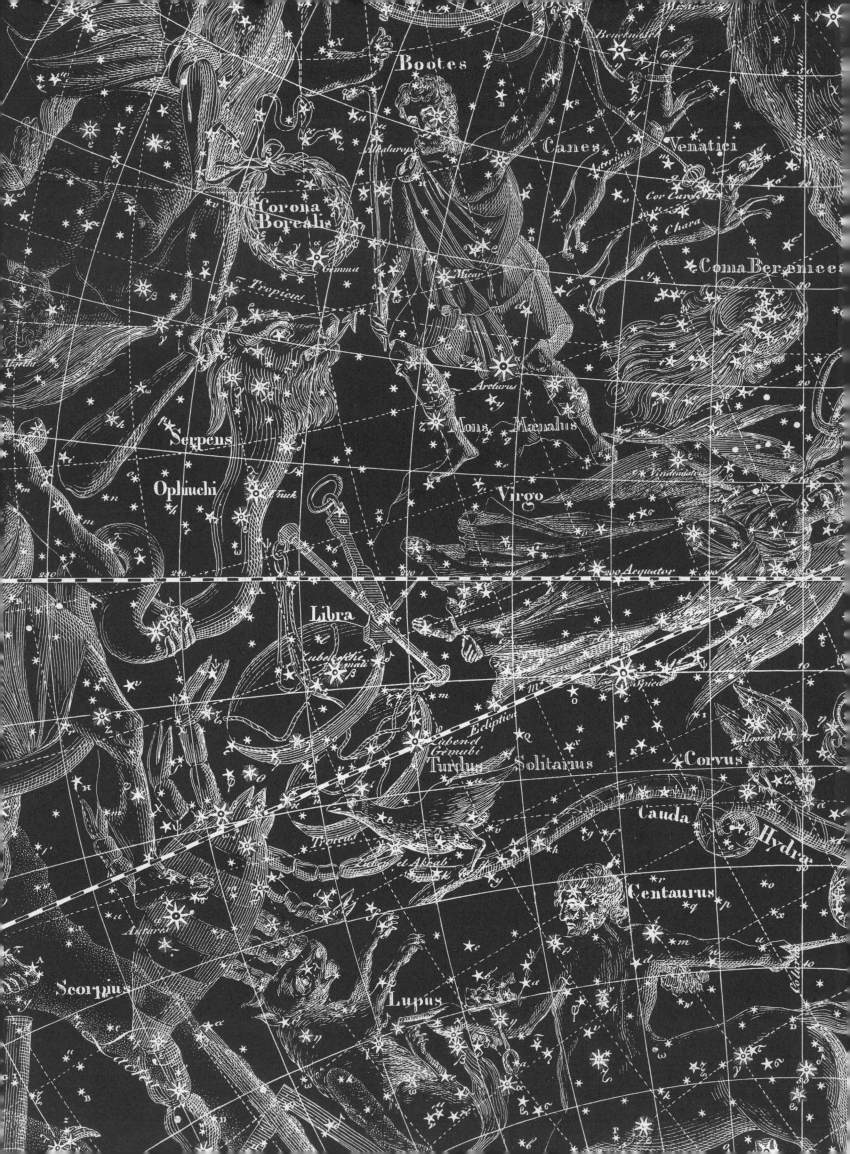